Becoming a Great Inclusive Educator

Disability Studies in Education

Susan L. Gabel and Scot Danforth
General Editors

Vol. 21

The Disability Studies in Education series
is part of the Peter Lang Education list.
Every volume is peer reviewed and meets
the highest quality standards for content and production.

PETER LANG
New York • Bern • Frankfurt • Berlin
Brussels • Vienna • Oxford • Warsaw

Becoming a Great Inclusive Educator

SECOND EDITION

Edited by Scot Danforth

PETER LANG
New York • Bern • Frankfurt • Berlin
Brussels • Vienna • Oxford • Warsaw

Library of Congress Cataloging-in-Publication Data
Names: Danforth, Scot, editor.
Title: Becoming a great inclusive educator / [edited by] Scot Danforth.
Description: Second edition. | New York: Peter Lang, 2017.
Series: Disability studies in education; vol. 21 | ISSN 1548-7210
Includes bibliographical references.
Identifiers: LCCN 2017010709 | ISBN 978-1-4331-3485-2 (paperback: alk. paper)
ISBN 978-1-4331-4344-1 (ebook pdf) | ISBN 978-1-4331-4345-8 (epub)
ISBN 978-1-4331-4346-5 (mobi)
Subjects: LCSH: Inclusive education—United States.
Children with disabilities—Education—United States. | Special education—
United States. | Mainstreaming in education—United States.
Classification: LCC LC1201 .B44 2017 | DDC 371.9/0460973—dc23
LC record available at https://lccn.loc.gov/2017010709
DOI 10.3726/b11150

Bibliographic information published by **Die Deutsche Nationalbibliothek**.
Die Deutsche Nationalbibliothek lists this publication in the "Deutsche
Nationalbibliografie"; detailed bibliographic data are available
on the Internet at http://dnb.d-nb.de/.

The paper in this book meets the guidelines for permanence and durability
of the Committee on Production Guidelines for Book Longevity
of the Council of Library Resources.

© 2017 Peter Lang Publishing, Inc., New York
29 Broadway, 18th floor, New York, NY 10006
www.peterlang.com

All rights reserved.
Reprint or reproduction, even partially, in all forms such as microfilm,
xerography, microfiche, microcard, and offset strictly prohibited.

Printed in the United States of America

This book is dedicated to the memory of Dr. Ellen Brantlinger.
Ellen was a great teacher, a brilliant scholar, and a strong advocate for social justice.
She was a supportive friend and mentor to many inclusive educators.
We miss her.

Contents

Chapter One: Transformation 1

Section One: Foundations of Successful Inclusion 23

Chapter Two: Knowing Disability 25
Chapter Three: Teaching for the Disability Rights Movement 45
Chapter Four: What Is Best in the American Dream 79

Section Two: The Living Tradition of Inclusive Education Practice 101

Chapter Five: Collaboration and Co-teaching 105
Chapter Six: Friendships in the Classroom 115
Chapter Seven: Partnerships with Parents and Families 127
Chapter Eight: Encouraging Positive Behavior 137
Chapter Nine: Differentiated Instruction 151
Chapter Ten: School Reform 165

Section Three: Narratives of Inclusive Education Struggle and Success 177

Chapter Eleven: A Journey into Inclusive Education 181
    Carrie D. Wysocki
Chapter Twelve: It Takes a Whole School 193
    Kimberly Millstead

Chapter Thirteen: Using "Numbers and Narrative" to Support Inclusive Schooling 203
   Meghan Cosier

Chapter Fourteen: "It's always about the kids, not us": Successful Elementary Co-teaching 217
   Zachary Rossetti

Chapter Fifteen: Spilt Milk Counts: Belonging and Moving on Down the Hall... 229
   Stacey Hodgins and S. Anthony Thompson

Chapter Sixteen: Inclusive Education: A Messy and Liberating Venture 239
   Emily Nusbaum

Chapter Seventeen: "I don't have a special world for her to live in: She has to adapt to this one": On Becoming a Renaissance Middle Schooler 251
   Alicia A. Broderick

Chapter Eighteen: Including Talia: A Mother's Tale 267
   Kathy Kotel

Chapter Nineteen: Respecting and Reaching All Learners in English Language Arts Classes: A Glimpse into a New York City High School 281
   Fran Bittman, Sarah Bickens, & David J. Connor

Chapter Twenty: What 20+ Years of Secondary Inclusion Has Taught Us 297
   Douglas Fisher and Nancy Frey

Chapter Twenty-One: "Now, I'm part of the family [...] well, almost!": Family Matters for Schooling Success 305
   John Colin and Srikala Naraian

Chapter Twenty-Two: On the Ethical Meaning of Human Differences: A Non-Disabled Child in Inclusive Schools 319
   Scot Danforth

Chapter Twenty-Three: A Sense of Belonging: Student Perspectives on Inclusive Education 329
   Rebecca Brooks

Chapter Twenty-Four: Including Students with Developmental Disabilities: Simple, Not Easy 341
   Michael F. Giangreco

Chapter Twenty-Five: Conclusion—Old Habits, New Thinking 353

CHAPTER ONE

Transformation

> **Guiding Questions**
> - What kind of personal and professional transformation is experienced by many of the best inclusive teachers?
> - How can you grow and develop into a great inclusive educator?

Neither society nor the public schools stand still. Social norms of attitude and action shift like enormous tectonic plates, often barely noticed in silent motion, sometimes smashing dramatically together to shake the ground beneath our feet. We are moved, as individuals and communities, and we begin to think, feel, and behave in new ways.

Inclusive education is a profound transformation of public schooling that has gained acceptance and widespread practice in the United States over the past two decades. Increasing numbers of students with disabilities are educated in general classrooms. The ground beneath concepts of disability and diversity in the schools has undoubtedly shifted in a positive direction, moving toward the acceptance of many forms of humanity into the common community.

But the public schools and general and special educators are often poorly prepared to be successful in the new configuration. Many teachers, veterans and rookies alike, are simply not ready to do inclusion well. In response to inclusion as the current challenge and opportunity for public school teachers, the most obvious question is also the most ambitious and hopeful: How can you be part of a positive transformation, both within yourself and within your school? How can you develop yourself into a great inclusive teacher?

THEN IT ALL CHANGED

"I spent thirty eight years working for the Company. It was a great place to work." The smile left Ida's face. She looked away and sighed at the window. "But then it all changed."

It was late August, 1983. I was on an Amtrak train traveling down the Atlantic Coast of the United States toward Virginia. I struck up a conversation with Ida, the elderly woman seated next to me. We had something in common. She had worked for many years for the Foxboro Company, a large manufacturer of industrial control systems located in my hometown in Massachusetts.

"What happened at the Company?" I hesitated to ask. It was evident that her emotions were still quite raw. But she seemed to want to talk about it.

"One Friday, I left the office just the way it was." Her face quivered as she spoke. "When I returned at my desk on Monday morning, they had taken my typewriter away. My IBM Selectric, a beautiful machine. They brought in computers [...] computer screens on every desk [...]." Her voice trailed off.

I waited for her to continue. But she was silent. Her story was over. The day her employer replaced the typewriters with a computer system, she retired. She had worked very happily in a pre-digital office environment for her entire adult life. The onset of advanced technology, from her perspective, ruined everything that she knew and loved about her job. It wasn't just an exchange of office tools, a desktop monitor replacing an electric typewriter, that flipped her world upside down. It wasn't just that old tasks would be carried out in a new way. It was a complete change in the very nature of the work. As far as Ida was concerned, her beloved job had ended.

From our historical vantage point, we can look at Ida's situation and realize that she was confronted by the dramatic cultural shift that has been called the Computer Revolution (Berkeley, 1962) or the Digital Revolution (Collins & Halverson, 2009). Scholars have described this massive social change as matching the significance and impact of the Industrial Revolution. It wasn't a matter of a single company buying some computers for their offices. The growth of computer technologies transformed all aspects of society, including communications, education, recreation, and commerce. Our way of life was effectively reprogrammed.

Ida didn't know how to change herself to fit the demands of the new computer world. She didn't know how to live this new way of life.

Increasingly, American teachers find themselves in Ida-like shoes, overwhelmed by the educational changes brought about by what Ben Mattlin (2012) has called the "disability rights revolution." Since the 1960s, the United States has gone through a dramatic social transformation, bringing disabled persons out of the shadows, offering them increasing measures of equality and dignity. Society is undergoing comprehensive redefinition. Our communities are inching toward a new normal whereby persons of many abilities and appearances share common spaces, activities, and interactions. The 1990 Americans with Disabilities Act, a broad anti-discrimination law guaranteeing disabled persons equality and access to all strands of community life, is just one indication of the profound social change that has occurred and is still occurring.

Changes have taken place in the status of disabled Americans, very gradually over many decades of hard-fought activism and advocacy. For citizens with disabilities, the revolution has been painfully slow. But many public school teachers have felt the cultural shift with the abruptness of Ida's return to work on Monday morning. Suddenly, they find that their classroom, their school, and their job have been altered by the presence of students with disabilities. Seemingly out of nowhere, inclusive education descended and turned traditional classrooms upside down and inside out. Although the movement in the United States espousing inclusion arguably began with a 1985 speech made by Madeleine Will, Assistant Secretary of the federal Office of Special Education and Rehabilitative Services, many teachers experience inclusion as a change that hit their classrooms overnight.

Over the past two decades, as I have worked with hundreds of general and special educators in many different cities and states, they have often told me an inclusive education version of Ida's tale. Some teachers related a similar story of lament and loss, of how schools took a wrong turn toward inclusion, how their work life was made difficult by the diversity of students in their classrooms. Other teachers told a story of excitement and opportunity, of schools finally fulfilling the promise of a democratic society, of working closely with colleagues to meet the needs of all students.

Virtually all these educators, regardless of how they viewed the initiation of inclusion in their classroom, have spoken of feeling unprepared for teaching successfully in the new inclusive classrooms and schools. Like it or not, pro-inclusion, anti-inclusion, or somewhere in-between, they have felt poorly prepared. "New times"—as inclusive education researcher Roger Slee (1998, p. 440) has neatly called them—are here. But most teachers are simply not ready. Weak preparation for inclusion takes on many faces.

A special education teacher told me about her principal calling her into his office on the first day of school to tell her that she was now the building's designated "inclusion teacher," responsible for a school-wide effort to move students with disabilities into mainstream classes. She walked out into the hallway and sat down on the floor. She wanted to do inclusion, but she didn't know where to begin.

A ninth grade teacher explained to me that her principal selected her "Introduction to Spanish" class as the ideal foreign language course for disabled students to take. She felt exhilarated at the chance to improve her teaching and get more kids involved in a second language. But she was hesitant to work with the special education teacher who was assigned to co-teach in her classroom. The special educator did not speak, read, or write Spanish.

Sometimes the lack of readiness is shared by a group of educators. A middle school teacher asked me to attend an end-of-school-year meeting with her seventh grade team and building principal. The principal told the group of general and special educators that they would start doing inclusive education in September. The mandate from the district central office proclaimed that students with disabilities would be educated in the general classrooms. My challenge was to explain to the principal and the team that doing inclusion well would require extensive preparation on their part. They would need to read articles and books, develop a new set of professional skills, examine their deepest ethical beliefs about ability and community, and find time for general and special educators to plan lessons and solve problems together. I offered my services as a free consultant to support their learning and growth. I explained that this was an important undertaking that would require substantial professional growth over years.

When I finished my little three-minute speech about the intensive work and preparation required to do inclusion well, the principal looked at her watch and said, "OK, then, Dr. Danforth. We have a very full agenda today. But you can have ten more minutes." I looked around at the faces of the seventh grade team. Some of the teachers had expressed excitement about changing to an inclusive model of instruction. Some had expressed reluctance and anxiety about doing something they really didn't understand very well. All of them had me for ten whole minutes of preparation. No wonder Ida retired.

INCLUSION RISING

American public schools are educating more and more students with disabilities in general education classrooms. Inclusive education has been gaining sheer quantitative ground for at least the last twenty years.

The United States Department of Education keeps tabs on where students with disabilities spend their school day by tallying the hours spent in general classrooms with nondisabled peers and the hours of segregated programming spent only with disabled classmates. They release annual data showing how many students with disabilities spend over eighty percent of their public school time in general education. I describe these students as *highly included*, for the most part receiving an inclusive education, learning the general curriculum side-by-side with nondisabled learners.

Over the past two decades, there has been a steady, unrelenting increase in the number of students with disabilities in the United States included in general education classrooms. In 1992, the first year of available federal data on inclusion, only thirty-nine percent of all students with disabilities were *highly included*. By 2014, almost sixty-three percent of all students with disabilities were highly included (see Figure 1). This gradual, stable trend constitutes an over fifty-seven percent increase in the participation of disabled students in general education (Individuals with Disabilities Education Act Data, 2016).

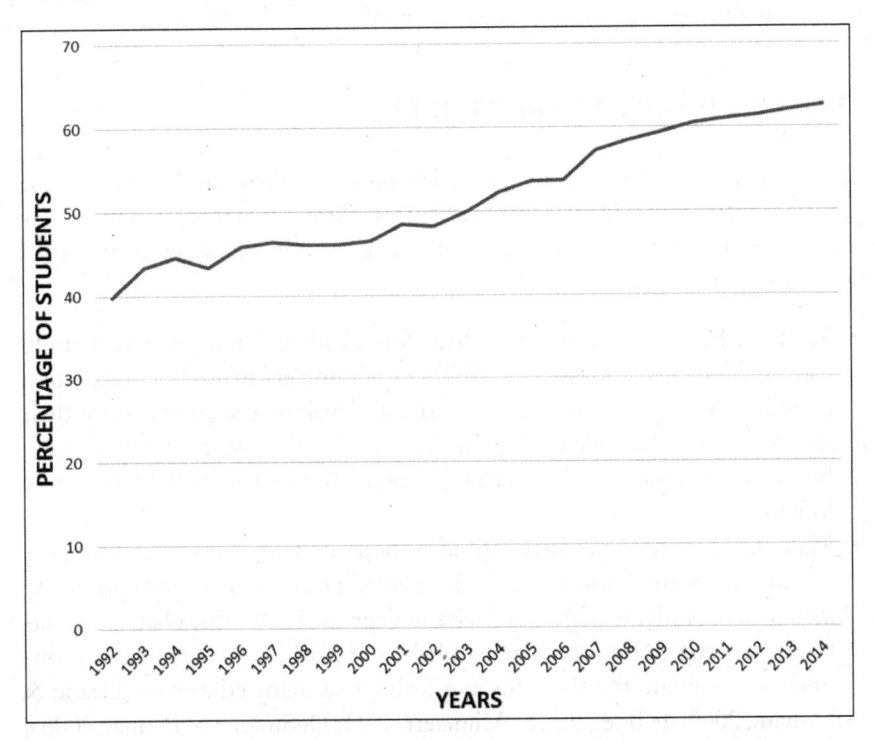

Figure 1.1. Percentage of all students with disabilities, ages six to twenty-one, who spent over eighty percent of time in general education classrooms, 1992–2014.

Think about it this way. The primary way that the American public schools provide *special education* is now through *general education*. The main (not sole!) responsibility for the education of most students with disabilities has shifted from special educators to general educators. Wayne Sailor and Blair Roger (2005, p. 506) succinctly explain that "all students are considered general education students" and "general education teachers are responsible for all students." The variability of students' abilities is no longer good reason to create segregated classrooms and schools. It is now a rationale for more creative and effective teaching in the general classroom.

The professional work of special education teachers and paraprofessionals has gone through a corresponding change. Rather than teaching small groups of students with disabilities in separate classrooms and schools, many special educators now work in support of inclusive education. They co-teach with general education teachers in mainstream classrooms and provide instructional and behavioral expertise in the form of consultation. They work closely with general educators on the modification and differentiation of lessons. In many instances, they have become experts on creating multiple forms of access to academic content knowledge for students with a variety of learning styles and needs.

A WHOLLY DIFFERENT EXPERTISE?

In the midst of all this dramatic change, a widespread problem exists. Although the public schools have marched steadily toward greater levels of inclusion, surprisingly few teachers—general or special—are ready to succeed in this new instructional configuration.

- Most teachers have received very little formal education to prepare them to teach in an inclusive classroom. Neither their university teacher preparation programs nor the continuing professional development provided by their school districts has been adequate (Avramidis, Bayliss, & Burden, 2000; Burke & Sutherland, 2004; Kamens, Loprete, & Slostad, 2000; Stanovich & Jordan, 2002).
- Many teachers hold negative attitudes about students with disabilities, experience emotional discomfort with disabled persons, or simply oppose the inclusion of students with disabilities in general classrooms. Damaging cultural stereotypes and old-fashioned habits of disability stigmatization continue to dominate the thoughts and feelings of many educators (Daane & Latham, 2000; de Boer, Pijl, & Minnaert, 2011; DeSimone & Parmar, 2006a; Kochhar, West, & Taymans, 2000; Lohrmann & Bambara, 2006; Orr, 2009).
- Many teachers, chiefly due to inexperience and poor professional preparation, lack confidence and skill in working with students with disabilities. They are confused, overwhelmed, and ill-prepared to work effectively in inclusive classrooms and schools (Embury & Kroeger, 2012; Janko, Schwartz, Sandall, Anderson, & Cottam, 1997; Janney, Snell, Beers, & Raynes, 1995; Jobling & Moni, 2004; McLeskey, Waldron, So, Swanson, & Loveland, 2001; Orr, 2009; Sadler, 2005; Sims, 2008).
- New teacher candidates, even when provided with coursework and a practicum devoted to inclusive education, do not necessarily feel more confident or comfortable teaching in inclusive classrooms. Initial teacher preparation is frequently insufficient to prepare new teachers to be competent and accepting inclusive educators (Gao & Mager, 2011; Mitchell & Hegde, 2007; Woodcock, Hemmings, & Kay, 2012).

After spending her first year as a high school English teacher co-teaching in inclusive classrooms, Emily Sims (2008, p. 58) stated bluntly, "I didn't know anything [...] I had no idea how co-teaching was supposed to work, and neither did my collaborating teachers." Inclusive education researchers DeSimone and Parmar (2006b, p. 338) aptly capture the situation by describing American teachers as "grossly under-prepared [...] for the realities of inclusion teaching."

When noted special education researcher Michael Gerber (2012, p. 71) analyzed the current state of inclusive education teacher preparation, he corroborated the findings of other researchers by writing that "there is little evidence that general education teachers, or special education teachers, for that matter, receive sufficient training in a number of critical teaching skills, e.g., systematic instruction, behavior management, and design and evaluation of instruction."

But Gerber's thinking on the subject traveled a half step further. He wondered if inclusion might, in some way, be *unlike* other best practices that university teacher education programs typically teach and public school teachers usually learn pretty well. Even when general and special education teachers gain the crucial inclusion research knowledge and practical skills at the university, they often do not employ the best inclusive practices in the classroom. Gerber concluded that "the observable divide between 'best' and 'actual' practices [...] can no longer be dismissed as a result only of inadequate professional preparation [...]. The skills needed to establish and maintain meaningful and productive inclusion of students with disabilities may represent *a wholly different kind of expertise* than has been presumed (Gerber, 2012, p. 71, italics added).

Learning to be an effective inclusive teacher, in this analysis, is somehow different than gaining other kinds of pedagogical knowledge and skills. It is different than learning the best methods to teach algebra. It is different than learning the most effective ways of teaching young children to read. It is different than learning how to encourage positive student behavior in the classroom.

What is this *wholly different kind of expertise* employed by the competent inclusive teacher? What is this acumen, this awesome professional capacity, this handful of magic beans, that turns an *ordinary* teacher into a successful *inclusive* teacher?

TEACHING AGAINST THE GRAIN

To understand what it means to become an effective inclusive educator, we first must examine *how* learning to truly do inclusion well is different than the experience of learning to teach an academic subject area or resolve classroom behavior problems. All of these are professional endeavors that involve the development of new knowledge and skills. What makes inclusive teaching dissimilar is the social and political climate surrounding the activity.

Let's imagine a high school mathematics teacher working conscientiously to expand her teaching repertoire by learning how to teach algebra. She takes a graduate course at the local university. She attends sessions on theory and practice at a mathematics teaching conference. Maybe she joins a professional working group of algebra teachers in her district. They get together to share lesson plans, technology tips, and insights culled from experience.

The blossoming algebra teacher undoubtedly enjoys the support and admiration of her colleagues. She is gaining knowledge and skills in a highly respected academic area. The other mathematics teachers view her professional growth as a positive development. Her school principal is pleased to see her take on a new challenge. She might be ready to take on some new class assignments.

Let's imagine the same high school teacher accepting the challenge of developing herself as an effective inclusive educator. She attends a conference on the research and practice of inclusion. She takes a graduate course on differentiated teaching for diverse students. Since the school district doesn't have a professional working group on inclusion, she and a friend who teaches at the local middle school start their own. They hold meetings at a little coffee shop, and the group members begin to share the successes and challenges of inclusive practice.

In many—perhaps most—cases, this high school teacher who is learning about inclusion would not receive wholehearted and unreserved support from other teachers in her building or her school principal. In fact, she might find her professional colleagues to be skeptical, dismissive, or openly critical of her efforts. They might fear that if her mathematics classes become highly inclusive, very soon all the general educators will be expected to teach more students with disabilities. She might gain a reputation as a rabble-rouser, miscreant, or troublemaker.

Unlike teaching algebra or reading, inclusive education is what educational researcher Roger Simon (1992, p. 140) calls "teaching against the grain," challenging the common configuration of beliefs and practices we have inherited from tradition in order to create new, more just modes of belief and practice. The phrase "against the grain" literally means moving in the direction opposite to the flow of the timber in a piece of wood. If a person tries to saw a wooden board against the grain, the lie of wood fibers asserts a powerful friction against the movement of the blade. Grab a hand saw and try. It is very hard to cut wood against the grain.

The grain that inclusive educators teach against consists of two entangled, powerful elements. First, inclusive teachers fight to change the old attitudes, beliefs, and social practices that devalue and discriminate against students with disabilities. Many principals and teachers still cling to the cruel belief that school communities are at their best when students with disabilities are not present, when they are segregated to isolated classrooms and schools. The common educational message, both silent and spoken, is that segregation is unobjectionable, even beneficial. This age-old discriminatory practice is a divisive scheme that splits school communities on the basis of concepts of ability and bodily functioning.

Scholars have called this prejudicial attitude *ableism*, a term that parallels to racism, sexism, or homophobia (Hehir, 2005). Rauscher and McClintock (1996, p. 198) define ableism as a "pervasive system of discrimination and exclusion that oppresses people who have mental, emotional, and physical disabilities." Phil Smith (2010, p. 7) has written that ableism is "the persecution and discrimination of people with so-called disabilities by the dominant, normate culture." Jan Valle and David Connor equate ableism with white privilege.

> A "luxury" of privilege is not having to think about one's status. Just as European-Americans rarely think about the benefits brought by their skin color, able-bodied people are privileged in not having to think about things that disable people must contemplate. For example, when planning a simple trip to a restaurant, an able bodied person does not have to think about accessible public transportation, accessible doorways and table seating, and an accessible restroom because the world is configured with able bodied people in mind. (Valle & Connor, 2010, p. 18)

The deep prejudice of ableism is painfully obvious to persons with disabilities while remaining obscured from the awareness of most nondisabled persons.

The second element of the cultural grain that inclusive educators struggle against is what educational historians David Tyack and Larry Cuban (1995, p. 85) have called "the basic grammar of schooling," the traditional structure of classrooms, of teacher's work, and the social role of students. For over a hundred years, schools have divided children by age into grades, placed thirty or so into a room with one teacher, and broken learning into subjects. Teachers have been expected to control students, deliver lessons on subject content, and monitor students as they complete assignments. These ways of organizing and conducting teaching and learning in the public schools have become essential to our cultural understanding of what a real school is. No matter what reforms public schools have undertaken, the basic grammar of schooling has endured.

When special education first developed in the early 1900s, one primary reason it was accepted as a reform by the public schools was because it did not conflict with the grammar of schooling. The public schools were already engaged in placing students of different ability levels into various academic tracks. Special education offered an additional system of tracks for students who lagged behind or who otherwise did not seem to fit into usual instructional procedures (Danforth, Ferguson, & Taff, 2005; Lazerson, 1983; Tyack & Cuban, 1995). One could even argue that special education helped the standard grammar of schooling remain intact by creating an efficient process for handling students who did not progress academically from grade to grade (Skrtic, 1991).

Segregated classrooms and schools for students with disabilities are central to the basic grammar of schooling. Segregated special education is a hundred-year-old practice that many teachers and school leaders simply assume is essential to the orderly operation of a public school. To the ears of many educators, proposals that schools teach students with and without disabilities in the same classrooms sound like a radical assault on the basic, trusted structures and conventions of public education.

Once we understand that inclusive education is teaching against the cultural grain, we quickly realize that learning the *wholly different kind of expertise* of inclusive teaching goes far beyond the acquisition of new professional knowledge and skills. This inclusion thing is a bigger, more ambitious, and gutsy undertaking.

But how do you become a great inclusive educator?

TRANSFORMATION

"While most teachers give the idea of inclusion their support, they experience the actual change toward inclusion as a radical disrupting of old and familiar values, attitudes, norms, and practices [...]. Transformation requires these teachers to draw on their transformative capacity and begin redefining themselves. This requires that they develop an alternative sense of themselves, not only as teachers but as individuals." (D'Amant, 2012, p. 54)

Professor Michael Giangreco and his colleagues at the University of Vermont conducted a study of the first-hand experiences of general education teachers who taught students with "severe" disabilities in their classrooms. They made a fascinating, profound discovery. Seventeen out of the nineteen teachers in the study experienced what the researchers called a "transformation," a dramatic change in their thoughts and feelings about disabled students accompanied by an accompanied increase in professional learning and skills. What was this personal and professional transformation? How did it happen?

The Vermont researchers interviewed nineteen general classroom teachers who "had a student who was identified as severely disabled in their general education classroom on a full-time basis" (Giangreco, Dennis, Cloninger, Edelman, & Schattman, 1993, p. 360). These were students with significant impairments, described as having a combination of "severe orthopedic disability," "profound retardation," and "intensive special education needs" (Giangreco, Dennis, Cloninger, Edelman, & Schattman, 1993, p. 360–1).

The teachers had very little background or training in inclusive education. Only two of the nineteen teachers reported receiving any professional education on inclusion or teaching students with disabilities in the prior three years.

The teachers began the experience with feelings of caution and reluctance. "They described their emotions with the terms 'reluctant,' 'scared,' 'nervous,' 'leery,' 'apprehensive,' 'unqualified,' 'angry,' and 'worried.'" They felt apprehension, and some "questioned the wisdom of such a placement" (Giangreco, Dennis, Cloninger, Edelman, & Schattman, 1993, p. 363).

Most of the teachers only agreed to allow the disabled students into their rooms under a series of provisions. The students had to be accompanied by paraprofessionals assigned to support them. Most only agreed to participate in inclusion "on a trial basis," under the understanding that the disabled student's placement was not permanent and could be changed if it did not go well (Giangreco, Dennis, Cloninger, Edelman, & Schattman, 1993, p. 363).

What happened next was surprising. Over the course of the school year, simply by having an experience working with the disabled student each day, seventeen of the nineteen teachers gradually yet radically changed.

> The cautious and negative comments used to discuss their initial reactions were replaced by descriptors such as "positive," "good," "successful," "interesting," "amazed," "pleased," "great," "wonderful," and "enjoyment." (Giangreco, Dennis, Cloninger, Edelman, & Schattman, 1993, p. 364)

The teachers found themselves taking responsibility for the learning of the students with disabilities. Further, the seventeen teachers who experienced the transformation overwhelmingly agreed that they would welcome students with disabilities in their classroom in the future.

When asked to explain how their attitudes, thoughts, and feelings changed, the teachers described going through a personal experience of emotional discomfort and cognitive dissonance, what one teacher described vaguely but powerfully as a "nagging feeling I'm not doing enough" (Giangreco, Dennis, Cloninger, Edelman, & Schattman, 1993, p. 365). What they experienced in their daily work with the disabled students did not match their fearful, negative expectations. Learning in this unsettled, uncomfortable space, they developed "an emerging recognition that their initial expectations regarding the student with disabilities were based on unsubstantiated assumptions" (Giangreco, Dennis, Cloninger, Edelman, & Schattman, 1993, p. 365). They started the inclusion experience with a series of previously unquestioned beliefs about disability that they discovered to be inaccurate.

The way these teachers came to this realization is important. Giangreco and his team report that teachers proceeded from an initial recognition or awareness that their beliefs and values were distorted toward a revised interpretation of disability through a process of reflection. Their experiences with the disabled students prompted them "to reflect and reconsider previously assumed positions" about the social and educational meaning of disability (Giangreco, Dennis, Cloninger, Edelman, & Schattman, 1993, p. 365).

Similarly, O'Donoghue and Chalmers (2000, p. 895) describe inclusive teachers moving through a challenging personal experience of "values clarifying," a process of self-examination by which teachers sort out how inclusion fits with their current system of values. Having students with significant disabilities in their general classrooms disrupts their usual ways of thinking, providing opportunities for ethical reflection and growth.

Adult education scholar Jack Mezirow coined the term "critical reflection" to describe a deep, profound process of self-examination engaged in by teachers and other adults who question the very structure and content of their systems of belief. Critical reflection means "challenging the validity of presuppositions in prior learning" (Mezirow, 1990, p. 12), interrogating what one assumes to be true, and then shifting one's perspective into a new space that is more useful, open, and flexible. It is a personal process involving both emotional and intellectual developments, leading to a new way of interpreting and acting in the world. What seems to be common sense is upended, pulled apart, and reconfigured into a more effective and rational way of understanding and taking action (Mezirow, 1990; 1991; 1995; 2000).

Teachers and other professionals are very familiar with thoughtful processes of problem-solving that involve examining all available data about a situation, considering multiple possible choices of action, and then selecting the option that has the greatest, rationale chance of yielding positive results. But critical reflection goes far beyond these standard modes of competent problem-solving to question the beliefs, values, and assumptions implicit in the way that the problem itself is framed.

Giangreco and his research team discovered seventeen general classroom teachers who utilized their experiences teaching students with disabilities as an opportunity to ask themselves sharp-edged questions about typically uncontested interpretations of disability and schooling.

- Do students with disabilities rightly or naturally belong in separate classrooms with special educators?
- Are students with disabilities lesser or incomplete humans who require our fear, anxiety, and rejection?
- Can general educators learn to accept and teach students with disabilities?
- What is my ethical stance on the value and meaning of human diversity? What does this stance mean for who I am, both as a professional and as a human being?

Through a process of critical reflection, these seventeen general classroom teachers arrived at a set of new understandings and beliefs about both the students with disabilities and themselves as teachers. These new assumptions came hand in hand with a novel series of actions. First, they learned to view the student with a disability "as a person rather than a disability," as a human being of equal value with all other humans (Giangreco, Dennis, Cloninger, Edelman, & Schattman, 1993, p. 365). Second, they built "a personal relationship with the student" (Giangreco,

Dennis, Cloninger, Edelman, & Schattman, 1993, p. 365). The walls of misunderstanding and distortion that maintain negative stereotypes crumbled through the creation of meaningful interpersonal relationships with the disabled students. Third, the teachers came to the realization that they could be successful in the inclusive arrangement. It often required the development of new instructional skills, but the teachers found that they were up to the challenge. As one teacher said, "You don't know until you're actually in the trenches doing it; I just never found it to be difficult" (Giangreco, Dennis, Cloninger, Edelman, & Schattman, 1993, p. 365).

International inclusive educator Antoinette D'Amant found a similar phenomenon in her study of twenty teachers and principals practicing inclusive education in rural schools of South Africa. The cultural tradition of schooling was deeply entrenched in stigmatizing practices of social exclusion, on the basis of race, social class, and disability. When the teachers first tried to teach in an inclusive way, they were attempting a challenge that was nearly unthinkable by local norms. As one teacher described,

> It was initially very difficult to accept or implement inclusion with our general lack of tolerance and interest in accepting difference. Before, if you were disabled, or you had a learning barrier, you were useless, there is nothing that you can do; you don't think as others do, you don't have any skills, you can't work. There is nothing that I can do to help you […]. If you get a child who is disabled, even the parent of that child says the child is a curse. This stigma from the community is something that goes a long way back. (D'Amant, 2012, p. 56)

D'Amant tracked how, beginning in a culture of disability shame and pity arguably deeper and more foreboding than in the United States (Du Toit & Forlin, 2009), some of the teachers engaged in an internal, ethical struggle. They experienced a transformation that shook them from top to bottom, challenging and ultimately reforming their sense of ethical identity. The inclusive educators described their personal change process in these words.

> I see inclusion in here (pointing to her heart) not anymore out there […]. I didn't think about these things before. Now I have learned to care about these learners who have barriers to learning. I've learned to treat every learner, and all people, equally and give support where it is needed. I feel different as a person now […]. (D'Amant, 2012, p. 58)

For some—certainly not all—teachers, the experience of teaching in inclusive classrooms opened a profound door to new personal growth, to hopeful attitudes and practices of acceptance and compassion. The path through that doorway was not simple or easy, not straight and predictable. The experience was filled with "numerous tensions, contradictions, and constraints" (D'Amant, 2012, p. 59) that made for rocky, uncertain travel. But it was a path of rare personal learning. One of inclusive South African teachers noted,

> For me it has become a never-ending journey. There are challenges all the time. The more you see, the more you solve and address things, the new things come up all the time and you wonder if we'll ever achieve this dream of an inclusive society. There are challenges, but I think they are good challenges because they make us think. (D'Amant, 2012, p. 58)

BECOMING A SUCCESSFUL INCLUSIVE EDUCATOR

This book is informed by my own troubled and hopeful thinking over the past two decades as I have worked with general and special educators teaching in inclusive classrooms and schools. From my experiences learning side-by-side with teachers, paraprofessionals, and school administrators, I now understand that becoming a great inclusive teacher requires an out-and-out, through-and-through, soul-shaking, scalp-to-toenails, personal and professional transformation of the nature and degree described by researchers Giangreco and D'Amant. It requires a powerful process of personal change and growth, a metamorphosis from one state of being to another. In the process of becoming a great inclusive teacher, we quite literally grow to be a very different—and I would say *better*—person.

The purpose of this book is to provide support, guidance, and resources for educators who are attempting to transform into successful inclusive teachers. It would be foolish for me to promise that reading this book will magically produce this transformation. Human intellectual and emotional growth is more complex than that. Adult transformative learning is not guaranteed by decoding all the pages of any text. What this book *can do* is supply educators working in inclusive classrooms with a useful path of personal change and the necessary conceptual and practical provisions for the journey. This book is offered as a worthy guide, a faithful companion, a friend for teachers working and struggling to become inclusive educators. I invite you to tuck it into the outer pocket of your backpack where you can grab it quickly and refer to it often.

In this book, I frame the process of transformation in terms of four specific, very personal challenges that educators must successfully confront in order to become excellent practitioners of inclusive education. These four challenges provide a framework for guiding personal and professional growth. Although they are presented in a sequence, they are not intended as an ordered series of steps. The four challenges present themselves to educators simultaneously and repeatedly. They offer us life lessons that we can learn over and over again, often gaining greater degrees of depth and meaning with each cycle. It is likely that no educator can fully graduate from or completely eclipse these challenges. Throughout an inclusive teacher's career, they continue to reappear in different forms, each iteration providing more opportunity for growth and improvement.

1. **Beginning with Deep Humility**: The vast majority of nondisabled persons are held back by brain-loads of misleading, erroneous, and prejudicial ideas about disability and persons with disabilities. We must honestly confront and interrogate the biased beliefs that so many of us hold.
2. **Understanding the Purpose of Inclusion**: Most educators do not know that inclusive education is intentional ethical action within the on-going Disability Rights Movement. We must place our daily work in the public schools into historical context of the movement of disabled citizens seeking equality and dignity.
3. **Cultivating the Ethical Commitments of Inclusion**: The efforts of the best inclusive teachers are fortified by a deep exploration of their ethical commitments, fueled by beliefs about the value of human diversity, seeking the best ways for diverse communities to live and learn together. We must undertake a thoughtful, flexible, continuous examination of our ethical beliefs.
4. **Steeping Yourself in the Tradition of Inclusive Practice**: For over twenty years, teachers, school leader, parents, and researchers have worked to figure out the best practices of inclusion. This pedagogical craft is both richly developed and ever-yearning for further advancement. We must immerse ourselves in the thriving tradition of teaching practice.

BEGINNING WITH DEEP HUMILITY

For the first challenge, we attend to the obvious. The great majority of teachers and school leaders *do not have disabilities.* This is a phenomenon that has gained strikingly little attention from educational researchers and practitioners. This is an issue that would matter deeply under any circumstances. But the fact that it is routinely overlooked makes it all the more deserving of our attention.

The bulk of public school educational professionals, the people who make important decisions about what it means to have a disability and how to educate students with disabilities in the public schools, know very little about how life looks and feels to a person with a disability. They have little real grasp of what living with a disability means to people who have disabilities.

This prevalent lack of lived experience having a disability among educators leads to profound misunderstandings about what the experience of disability means in the lives of individuals, families, and communities. We are not surprised that white people often do not fathom the thoughts and feelings of African-Americans. We are not amazed that men often fail to appreciate the experiential perspectives of women. We are not shocked that lifelong citizens of our country frequently miscalculate the motivations, priorities, and needs of new immigrants. We need to wake up to the fact that nondisabled persons tend to be sorely confused about how persons with disabilities view their impairments, their lives, and their futures.

Nondisabled educators like me need to become aware of just how little we really know about living with a disability. Educators who do not have disabilities often believe that what people with disabilities really wish for and need is to quite miraculously overcome or be cured of their impairments. This self-centered and self-serving assumption celebrates one's own "normality" as a physical and social achievement while simultaneously ignoring the actual life experiences, perspectives, and goals of people with disabilities.

Speaking from first-hand experience, I can tell you that admitting this can be very difficult, especially for a person like me who was fully trained in the research and theory of the field of special education. Armed with two graduate degrees, I spent many years as a nondisabled expert on disability. That means that I was just as mistaken as any other nondisabled person about how people with disabilities thought and felt about their lives. But I was doubly dangerous due to my view of myself as a well-educated and knowledgeable expert.

The disability community has adopted the saying, "Nothing About Us Without Us" to speak to the need to include disabled persons at the table when important decisions about the lives of persons with disabilities are made (Charlton, 2000). The idea is that only persons who have lived with a disability can speak truthfully from a perspective that is informed by that very distinct life experience, from the position of one who *knows* in a very personal way. This honors the fact that there are forms of understanding derived from the human experience of disability that are simply unavailable to persons without disabilities.

Certainly, a person who does not have a disability might learn much about disabilities. This learning may come through reading books and conducting research. A nondisabled person can earn a graduate degree in rehabilitation, special education, or disability studies. Or better yet, one can gain a particularly useful awareness from having a close personal relationship with a person with a disability, growing within the heightened learning space that only friendship and intimacy can provide.

In my own experience, my road out of the uninformed arrogance of being a nondisabled expert on disability toward a more humble and realistic understanding of what it can mean to live with a disability has been built of personal relationships with disabled friends. Only through creating and sharing friendships with multiple persons with disabilities did I become aware of how little I actually understood. From there, through relationship and dialogue, I began to learn.

The process was painfully slow, most likely because my expertise covered my neural receptors with egotistical Teflon, allowing potential learning experiences to slide off without making much impact on my hardened beliefs. Only through years of working, talking, laughing, and living side-by-side with disabled friends and colleagues did I truly learn to *know that I did not know*. In Chapter 2, we examine what we nondisabled educators (do not) know about disability.

UNDERSTANDING THE PURPOSE OF INCLUSION

The second challenge for the teacher who wants to become a successful inclusive educator is to understand the larger ethical purpose of creating classrooms and schools where students with and without disabilities learn together. This ethical purpose is best addressed not only by studying the writings of educational researchers or school-based practitioners. For the actions of the inclusive teacher are truly well-played notes in a larger cultural symphony, the Disability Rights Movement whereby disabled persons have sought their civil rights in the United States. This human purpose is best understood by studying the history of the Disability Rights Movement, the collective effort to achieve the full participation of disabled persons in all the valued aspects of community life.

The well-known story of civil rights in the United States is the narrative of African-Americans, led by Martin Luther King, seeking integration, equality, and acceptance. A lesser-known but greatly parallel civil rights story involves persons with many disabilities uniting as a disability community to stand up to customary practices of exclusion and marginalization. We examine this historical narrative in Chapter 3. Learning about this crucial story helps educators working in inclusive classrooms view the rejection and discrimination that their students often face as specific instances of a larger cultural landscape of cruelty and prejudice. They can begin to understand their daily work in inclusive classrooms as the very best of what a democratic people hopes to be, optimistically pursuing enduring values of justice, equality, and dignity for all persons.

CULTIVATING THE ETHICAL COMMITMENTS OF INCLUSION

The third challenge for the developing inclusive teacher is the thoughtful, considered examination of the ethical beliefs and commitments that inform her practice. The word "commitments" is crucial in this context because it emphasizes the lived and practical nature of this exploration. The continuous cultivation of a series of ethical beliefs about what matters most in the world and how to bring something of value to students, families, and communities is not merely an academic exercise. It is not a task involving multisyllabic words and high-minded phrases reverberating around in dusty old libraries far from the real action of life. To hold a commitment is to be personally and fully devoted to a cause, to set one's heart, mind, and body in a direction of action because it is likely to improve the lives and well-being of children, families, and communities. In this sense, our highest purposes and ideals are activated in our daily interactions and professional work. Undoubtedly, we must be thoughtful and intentional in crafting these ideals.

Frequently, I speak with experienced teachers who feel a yawning gap between what they believe and what they actually do, a disconnection between what they hope to achieve as an educator and what they think their work with students truly means. This rift is often born of the many moral compromises that educators make as they, over time, become more deeply entangled in the standard social practices of their schools and the complex human struggles of their daily pattern of human interaction. Many teachers have told me that they feel stuck, or they feel a lack of flexibility in their school to live and behave in a more intentional and ethical way. There is often a temptation to leave our greatest ideals on a high and distant shelf, label them naïve and unrealistic, and then plod forward with mediocre habits of action.

Successful inclusive educators do not ignore the gap between their ethical beliefs and their daily work in schools. They intentionally toil in the gap. They enter into that uncomfortable space, explore their commitments and behavior, and figure out how to better enact their most cherished ideals. This kind of work is filled with emotion, challenging to the mind and heart, and troubled by ambiguity and uncertainty. But it is crucial to the journey of becoming a great inclusive teacher. We take up this challenge in Chapter 4.

STEEPING YOURSELF IN THE TRADITION OF INCLUSIVE PRACTICE

The fourth challenge addresses difficulties that teachers have in gaining meaningful access to the very full and rewarding tradition of inclusive educational practices. Many inclusive educators trace the history of inclusive schooling back to a 1985 speech made by Madeleine Will at the Wingspread Conference in Racine, Wisconsin. Will (1986) called for special education and general education to share the responsibility for the education of students with disabilities. By any reading, her proposal constituted the mildest endorsement for inclusive education. It was not the forcefulness of her argument but the timing that mattered. Federally mandated special education programs across the country had been in place for less than a decade, but many educators and parents were already growing concerned with the new system of segregated classrooms and schools that comprised American special education. An eager audience was very ready to pick up Will's polite words and fulfill them with passionate, purposeful action.

Over the past quarter century, the social practice of teaching students with and without disabilities together in integrated classrooms has developed in public schools across the United States. Researchers, theorists, school-based practitioners, and parents have advanced our practical understanding of how to do inclusion well. This movement in the United States is matched by parallel developments in many other countries, including Canada, the United Kingdom, Australia, and across Europe. There is now a rich and complex inclusive tradition that interlaces concepts, practices, and purposes.

Any newcomer to inclusive education deserves and needs a head-to-toe plunge in the enriching, inspiring waters of this evergrowing tradition of professional knowledge, classroom practice, and social justice mission. But too many teachers who try to become more inclusive in their daily classroom work find themselves sitting high and dry, seemingly without ready access to the rich font of intellectual, ethical, and practical resources that have been fashioned by inclusive educators over the past quarter century.

Imagine that you are a musician who decides to learn how to play blues guitar. In order to grasp the emotional, intellectual, and spiritual nuances of this art form, in order to enrich yourself as a practitioner of this way of experiencing the world and expressing a range of human emotions, you would be well advised to fully immerse yourself in the cultural heritage of blues music in America. Many musicians have gone before you to build this complex and deep musical genre. You may drink of their music and their lives by studying the history of blues music in America. You may experience the tradition first-hand by seeking out local and national practitioners of this art, learning at their side through conversation and, of course, playing music together.

How can you do the same for inclusive education practice? How can you tap into the best of this living tradition of teaching? If you can land a job at a great inclusive school, you have the glorious luxury of learning the tradition from your colleagues through observation and conversation. That situation, unfortunately, is quite rare. For the millions of teachers who work in public schools where mediocre or poorly informed versions of inclusion are carried out every day, I offer this volume as assistance.

Section One of this book, comprised of Chapters 2–4, invites educators into a thoughtful exploration of the first three challenges. I call Section One the "Foundations" because, like the foundation of a house or building, it provides the essential grounding and stability for everything that rests on top of it. In this case, it explores the conceptual and ethical challenges of becoming an inclusive educator.

Sections Two and Three focus on what the best inclusive educators *actually do*. The chapters of Section Two examine the pedagogical craft, the professional practices that make up the always growing tradition of inclusive teaching. These are the classroom and school practices, derived from decades of intensive work by researchers and school-based practitioners, that create and sustain effective inclusive classrooms.

Section Three provides a series of true, first-person narratives written by teachers, researchers, and parents, detailing the struggles and successes of inclusive education in American public schools. This narrative gathering of wise friends represents my best attempt at bringing many artisans of the living tradition of inclusive practice to your classroom door to offer guidance, examples, and support. These stories offer readers an initial dip into the deep and full waters of the inclusive teaching tradition.

To some extent, the stories in Section Three offer illustrations of the best inclusive practices described in Section Two. But they do much more. First, they demonstrate that any attempt to enact best instructional practices, when applied in a lived context with real children and adults, takes on a messy life of its own. Real classrooms and schools are untidy places that defy the rationalized formulas and neat recipes of the instructional design experts. Further, the stories stretch our thinking far beyond the recommended best practices to engage the complex ethical, human, practical decisions that educators and parents make every day. The stories allow us insight into the uncertain, shifting terrain of public schooling and the difficult dilemmas that confront professionals and parents.

My invitation to you, at this point, throughout the book, and long after you have set these pages down, is be bold, daring, and hopeful. Leap into these new waters, hold the hands of your colleagues and students, and swim as if someone's life depends on it. It does.

REFERENCES

Avramidis, E., Bayliss, P., & Burden, R. (2000). A survey into mainstream teachers' attitudes towards the inclusion of children with special educational needs in the ordinary school in one local education authority. *Educational Psychology, 20, 2,* 191–211.

Berkeley, E. C. (1962). *The Computer revolution.* New York: Doubleday & Co.

Burke, K., & Sutherland, C. (2004). Attitudes toward inclusion: Knowledge vs. experience. *Education, 125, 2,* 163–172.

Charlton, J. I. (2000). *Nothing about us without us: Disability oppression and empowerment.* Berkeley: University of California Press.

Collins, A., & Halverson, R. (2009). *Rethinking education in the age of technology: The digital revolution and the schools.* New York: Teachers College Press.

Daane, C. J., & Latham, D. (2000). Administrators' and teachers' perceptions of the collaborative efforts of inclusion in the elementary grades. *Education, 121, 2,* 331–338.

Danforth, S., Ferguson, P., & Taff, S. (2005). Place, profession and program in the history of special education curriculum. In E. Brantlinger (Ed.), *Who benefits from special education? Remediating (fixing) other people's children* (pp. 1–25). Mahwah, NJ: Lawrence Erlbaum.

D'Amant, A. (2012). Within and between the old and the new: Teachers becoming inclusive practitioners. *Perspectives in Education, 30, 1,* 53–60.

de Boer, A., Pijl, S. J., Minnaert, A. (2011). Regular primary schoolteachers' attitudes towards inclusive education: A review of the literature. *International Journal of Inclusive Education, 15, 3*, 331–353.

DeSimone, J. R., & Parmar, R. S. (2006a). Middle school mathematics teachers' beliefs about inclusion of students with learning disabilities. *Learning Disabilities Research and Practice, 21*, 98–110.

DeSimone, J. R., & Parmar, R. S. (2006b). Issues and challenges for middle school mathematics teachers in inclusion classrooms. *School Science and Mathematics, 106*, 338–348.

Du Toit, P., & Forlin, C. (2009). Cultural transformation for inclusion, What is needed?: A South African perspective. *School Psychology International, 30, 6*, 644–666.

Embury, D. C., & Kroeger, S. D. (2012). Let's ask the kids: Consumer constructions of co-teaching. *International Journal of Special Education, 2*, 102–112.

Gao, W., & Mager, G. (2011). Enhancing preservice teachers' sense of efficacy and attitudes toward school diversity through preparation: A case of one U.S. inclusive teacher education program. *International Journal of Special Education, 26*(2), 92–107.

Gerber, M. M. (2012). Emerging issues in teacher education for inclusion in the United States. In C. Forlin (Ed.), *Future directions for inclusive teacher education: An international perspective* (pp. 71–80). New York: Routledge.

Giangreco, M. F., St. Denis, R., Cloninger, C., Edelman, S., & Schattman, R. (1993). "I've counted Jon": Transformational experiences of teachers educating students with disabilities. *Exceptional Children, 59, 4*, 359–372.

Hehir, T. (2005). *New directions in special education: Eliminating ableism in policy and practice.* Cambridge, MA: Harvard Education Press.

Individuals with Disabilities Education Act Data, United States Department of Education. http://www.ideadata.org/PartBData.asp. Retrieved December 27, 2016.

Janko, S., Schwartz, I., Sandall, S., Anderson, K., & Cottam, C. (1997) Beyond microsystems: Unanticipated lessons about the meaning of inclusion. *Topics in Early Childhood Special Education, 17*, 286–306.

Janney, R. E., Snell, M. E., Beers, M. K., & Raynes, M. (1995). Integrating students with moderate and severe disabilities: Classroom teachers' beliefs and attitudes about implementing an educational change. *Educational Administration Quarterly, 31*, 86–114.

Jobling, A., & Moni, K. B. (2004). "I never imagined I'd have to teach these children": Providing authentic learning experiences for secondary pre-service teachers in teaching students with special needs. *Asia-Pacific Journal of Teacher Education, 32, 1*, 5–22.

Kamens, M. W., Loprete, S. J., & Slostad, F. A. (2000). Classroom teachers' perceptions about inclusion and preservice teacher education. *Teaching Education, 11, 2*, 147–158.

Kochhar, C. A., West, L.L., & Taymans, J. M. (2000). *Successful inclusion: Practical strategies for a shared responsibility.* Upper Saddle River, NJ: Prentice Hall.

Lazerson, M. (1983). Origins of special education. In J. G. Chambers & W. T. Hartman (Eds.), *Special education policies: Their history, implementation, and finance* (pp. 15–44). Philadelphia: Temple University Press.

Lohrmann, S., & Bambara, L. (2006). Elementary education teachers' beliefs about essential supports needed to successfully include students with developmental disabilities who engage in challenging behaviors. *Research & Practice for Persons with Severe Disabilities, 31, 2*, 157–173.

Mattlin, B. (2012) *Miracle boy grows up: How the disability rights revolution saved my sanity.* New York: Skyhorse Publishing.

McLeskey, J., Waldron, N. L., So, T. H., Swanson, K., & Loveland, T. (2001). Perspectives of teachers toward inclusive school programs. *Teacher Education and Special Education, 24*, 108–115.

Mezirow, J. (1990). *Fostering critical reflection in adulthood: A guide to transformative and emancipatory learning*. San Francisco, CA: Jossey-Bass.

Mezirow, J. (1991). *Transformative dimensions of adult learning*. San Francisco, CA: Jossey-Bass.

Mezirow, J. (1995). Transformation theory of adult learning. In M. R. Welton (Ed.), *In defense of the lifeworld: Critical perspectives on adult learning* (pp. 39–70). Albany, NY: SUNY Press.

Mezirow, J. (2000). *Learning as transformation: Critical perspectives on a theory in progress*. San Francisco, CA: Jossey-Bass.

Mitchell, L. C., & Hegde, A. V. (2007). Beliefs and practices of in-service preschool teachers in inclusive settings: Implications for personnel preparation. *Journal of Early Childhood Teacher Education, 28, 4*, 353–366.

Orr, A. C. (2009). New special educators reflect about inclusion: Preparation and K–12 current practice. *Journal of Ethnographic & Qualitative Research, 3(4)*, 228–239.

Rauscher, L., & McClintock, J. (1996). Ableism and curriculum design. In M. Adams, L. A. Bell, & P. Griffen (Eds.), *Teaching for diversity and social justice* (pp. 198–231). New York: Routledge.

Sadler, J. (2005). Knowledge, attitudes and beliefs of the mainstream teachers of children with a preschool diagnosis of speech/language impairment. *Child Language Teaching and Therapy, 21, 2*, 147–163.

Sailor, W., & Roger, B. (2005). Rethinking inclusion: Schoolwide applications. *Phi Delta Kappan, 86, 7*, 503–509.

Simon, R. I. (1992). *Teaching against the grain: Texts for a pedagogy of possibility*. Westport, CT: Praeger.

Sims, E. (2008). Sharing command of the co-teaching ship: How to play nicely with others. *English Journal, 97, 5*, 58–63.

Skrtic, T. M. (1991). *Behind special education: A critical analysis of professional culture and school organization*. Denver, CO: Love.

Slee, R. (1998) Inclusive education? This must signify 'New Times' in educational research. *British Journal of Educational Studies, 46, 4*, 440–454.

Smith, P. (2010). *Whatever happened to inclusion? The place of students with intellectual disabilities in education*. New York: Peter Lang.

Stanovich, P. J., & Jordan, A. (2002). Preparing general educators to teach in inclusive classrooms: Some food for thought. *Teacher Educator, 37, 3*, 173–183.

Tyack, D. B., & Cuban, L. (1995). *Tinkering toward utopia: A century of public school reform*. Cambridge, MA: Harvard University Press.

Valle, J., & Connor, D. (2010). *Rethinking disability: A disability studies approach to inclusive practices*. Boston, MA: McGraw Hill.

Will, M. C. (1986). Educating children with learning problems: A shared responsibility. *Exceptional Children, 53*, 411–415.

Woodcock, S., Hemmings, B., & Kay, R. (2012). Does study of an inclusive education subject influence pre-service teachers' concerns and self-efficacy about inclusion? *Australian Journal of Teacher Education, 37(6)*, 1–11.

SECTION ONE

Foundations of Successful Inclusion

In this section, we explore the first three challenges, asking troubling yet hopeful questions about our own knowledge of disability, the historical positioning of inclusive education, and our deepest ethical beliefs and values.

1. Beginning with Deep Humility: The vast majority of educators, whether they realize it or not, are encapsulated in a set of ideological beliefs about disability and disabled persons that limits their effectiveness as inclusive teachers. We must begin with a raw, honest examination of prejudice and bias.
2. Understanding the Purpose of Inclusion: Inclusion is a fairly limited proposition if we view it as merely the next incarnation of traditional special education research and practice. Inclusion has a greater and clearer ethical purpose if we understand it as one aspect of the on-going Disability Rights Movement.
3. Cultivating the Ethical Commitments of Inclusion: Unfortunately, *diversity* has become a cheap buzzword that fills every educational book and policy document. Sometimes we educators all chant *diversity*! together without seriously challenging our ethical commitments. The best inclusive teachers undergo a serious and continuous exploration of their ethical commitments about humanity and community.

These three challenges run deeper—more personal—than the usual array of professional learning and knowledge. These are as much about *who you are as a person* as they are about what you do as an educator.

SECTION ONE

Foundations of Successful Inclusion

CHAPTER TWO

Knowing Disability

> **Guiding Questions**
> - Why do many talented and dedicated educators fail to include students with disabilities in their thinking about social justice in the schools?
> - What is the ideology of ability? How does it impact the attitudes and behavior of principals and teachers?
> - How can inclusive educators begin to confront and move beyond the limitations of the ideology of ability?

It is often best to begin learning with an appraisal of what we already know about a subject and then move optimistically forward from there. For most American educators, especially the majority who do not have disabilities, this starting place is confusion and contradiction, a batch of misguided ideas about disability and persons with disabilities that serves as a powerful obstacle to inclusion. In this chapter, I explore the misconceptions and gaps that frequently muddle my own mind and the minds of some very talented educators. The path to becoming a successful inclusive teacher necessarily encounters and re-encounters the persistent problem of what we nondisabled educators believe and know (or [...] don't know) about disability. Necessarily, we are knocked back on our heels, lowered to a place of deep humility. From there, stripped of arrogance, ready to learn, we can begin again.

A CUP OF COFFEE

> "Discrimination is not something that mean people do, it's something that is carried out by good people under the influence of much bigger social and cultural norms." (Davis, 2015, pp. 249–250)

I was excited about talking through some ideas that I had for writing a book about inclusive education. I had spent many years working with inclusive schools in different parts of the United States. I had taught university courses on inclusion and collaborated on research on the topic. I had written and edited articles and books in the field of disability studies. All this experience culminated in an idea for a book filled with stories written by teachers, parents, and researchers about successful experiences with inclusion in the public schools. It would be offer support and guidance about how to become an inclusive educator.

But I wanted to run my ideas by Theo, a graduate student in Education and Disability Studies. His sharp mind as well as his life experiences as a man with a physical disability made him an ideal sounding board and critic for my still emerging thoughts.

I asked Theo to join me for a conversation at a nearby coffee shop. We chatted amicably as we traveled down the busy sidewalk of the urban campus. It was a warm day, and we enjoyed trading ideas back and forth.

When we reached the coffee shop, Theo rolled to a stop. I looked down at the three-inch chunk of concrete between the sidewalk and the bottom of the door. I had come to this cafe a hundred times before. I wrote much of my last book in that wonderful little restaurant. But I had never noticed that entering the shop required a three-inch step up from the sidewalk below. Theo's wheelchair could never make it.

"Oh, God, Theo," I shook my head in embarrassment. "I'm sorry. I should have known. I can't believe I didn't know."

Theo chuckled. "This is fine. We can go elsewhere." His words floated with the buoyant lilt of a Kenyan accent. His face lit up brightly with a wide smile.

I still couldn't believe it. I stared at the pavement and shook my head in frustration.

As I stared at the sidewalk, my face flushed red with humiliation.

THE POLITICS OF ACCESS

In early 1960, four students at North Carolina A & T College walked into a F. W. Woolworth Store in Greensboro, North Carolina. They sat down at the lunch counter and ordered coffee. The lunch counter staff refused to serve the young men, and the store manager told them to leave.

At that time, across the South, it was not uncommon to see a "We Serve Whites Only" placard in the window of a restaurant or store. The actions of the four African-

American college students on that February day in Greensboro quickly expanded into a large, sit-in protest involving hundreds of activists. Similar protests and store boycotts followed in numerous cities in North Carolina and other Southern states.

About four months later, the Woolworth's lunch counter in Greensboro began serving African-American customers. Some ordered coffee (National Museum of American History, 2012).

Almost four decades later, in 2008, a man named George Lane arrived at the Polk County, Tennessee, courthouse for his court hearing. The building did not have an elevator, so he climbed out of his wheelchair and crawled up two flights of stairs in order to reach the court room. He later reported that court employees and the presiding judge stood at the top of the steps and laughed at him. After his case was not heard in the morning, he crawled back down the two flights to get lunch. When he did not crawl back up again for the afternoon session, he was held in contempt of court and jailed.

George Lane filed a lawsuit against the State of Tennessee, claiming that the State's failure to make the court accessible was a violation of the Americans with Disabilities Act (ADA). The ADA requires, among other things, that government buildings be fully accessible to persons with disabilities.

In 2004, the United States Supreme Court, in a five to four vote, ruled in favor of Mr. Lane, affirming that the State of Tennessee has a legal obligation to make the Polk County Courthouse accessible to persons with disabilities (Cohen, 2004; Lane, 2004).

A SIGN IN THE WINDOW

I was staring at the sidewalk wondering how four Supreme Court Justices could think that a disabled man should crawl up steps to get into a government building when I heard Theo politely clearing his throat. I looked up from my historical thoughts to see my friend grinning at me.

"So I'm a man without a coffee shop," he jested, reminding me of our present situation. He thought it was funny, but I was red-faced and ashamed. There I was, the Coordinator of my university's Disability Studies Program, and I didn't even know that the entrance to my favorite campus coffee shop did not accommodate a wheelchair.

But, of course, I have to admit. I'm a guy who does not have a disability. I have devoted much of my adult life to serving as an ally to the disability community in the Disability Rights Movement, supporting their efforts to seek civil rights and access to opportunities. No matter how long I study disability issues, teach courses, and spend time with disabled friends, I am still a nondisabled guy. My experiences inevitably only allow me a very limited understanding of what it means to live with a disability.

So I didn't notice the coffee shop doorway.

"Come on," Theo waved to me as he zoomed his electric wheels down the sidewalk. "We'll go down here."

We went to a national chain coffee shop with full wheelchair accessibility in the entrance and the restrooms. We drank our coffee and talked about my ideas for a great book on public schools that provide students with disabilities full access to general classrooms and offer nondisabled young persons the incredible opportunity to learn with disabled friends.

Two weeks later, I ventured back to my favorite coffee shop. This time, my taste buds had a lingering, nasty attitude, and the double vanilla latte tasted like warm turpentine. I tapped away on my laptop, writing an introductory chapter for my inclusion book. But I had a hard time concentrating on the work. After a while, I look up at the young woman behind the counter. I imagined her carrying a large cardboard sign up to the front of shop. She fastened it to front window.

WE SERVE ABLE-BODIED PEOPLE ONLY.

I had spent enough time in that coffee shop, and I had chatted casually with the young woman working the counter many times. She seemed nice enough. I doubted that she would ever post such a cruel sign on the front of the shop.

But I knew that the sign was there. Maybe no one intended for it to be there. But it was surely there. Theo and I saw it.

Maybe the real error here was an act of omission rather than commission, a problem not so much of what someone did as *what someone didn't do*. Apparently, no one working for the coffee shop thought to make the entrance accessible.

Bear in mind that this is no ordinary coffee shop. This is one of those fair trade and freedom of thought coffee houses you often see near university campuses. From the indie rock music to the intentionally shabby décor and culturally diverse clientele, the whole scene has a hip, eclectic vibe. Standing in the long line waiting to order were: three undergraduate sorority girls wearing Ugg boots and Pink sweatpants; a rough-skinned homeless man who typically enjoys free coffee; a twenty-something couple covered in colorful art who work at the tattoo and piercing parlor two doors down; a group of graduate students from China, India, and the United States discussing the polysyllabic nuances of the latest technical conundrum; and an African-American woman with a small hair-braided girl joyfully picking out a frosted muffin from the glass display case.

In this edgy and seemingly pluralistic cafe, where the apparent ethos is "Be Who You Are, Whoever You Are," no one thought about how important it was to allow people who use wheelchairs into the store.

As I walked to Men's Room at the back of the shop, I thought to myself, *But why? Why didn't they even think of it?*

Disability studies scholars have written about the social invisibility of people with disabilities. When they are not present in the workplace, the classroom, the house of worship, or halls of government, nondisabled people tend to not notice the absence. People who do not have disabilities are frequently unaware that people with disabilities are excluded. Their bodies and civil rights are both out of sight and out of mind (Brueggemann, White, Dunn, Heifferon, & Cheu, 2001; Siebers, 2008).

I opened the Men's Room door to find an enormous bathroom with a small sink and down-tilted mirror. A handrail had been installed next to the toilet. I couldn't believe my eyes.

Later that evening, I saw Theo in class at the university.

"Hey, Theo, you know our favorite, inaccessible coffee shop?" I asked.

"Yes, thank you for reminding me of that highly inclusive establishment," he quipped.

"Well, I went into their Men's Room the other day. And guess what?"

"What?" Theo looked at me with open, expectant eyes.

"Their Men's Room is completely accessible for people using wheelchairs. Wide doorway, big open room, hand rails, sink height, down-tilted mirror, everything."

Theo exploded in ironic laughter. He knew far better than I that living with a disability involves daily experiences with the contradictory and the ridiculous.

It struck me that there was something more than "out of sight, out of mind" going on here. Certainly nondisabled people were failing to be aware of the presence or absence of disabled persons. But there was something strange happening even when nondisabled people *do* recognize and think more fully about disability.

The social and architectural world filled with ridiculous contradictions has been fashioned primarily by people like me, people who don't have disabilities. We have been the dominant group in making decisions about who has access, who gets to participate, and what access and participation consist of. Given that fact, it would not be an unreasonable stretch to say that the many social and physical environments that disrespect and exclude disabled people are reflections of the flawed and prejudicial thinking of nondisabled people.

Perhaps nondisabled people have a cognitive gap, a mental breach, that allows us to simply not notice people with disabilities and therefore fail to take into account their lives and needs. Often we aren't even aware that people with disabilities are present in our social world. And even when we nondisabled people actually do apply our attention and thinking to disability, our cognitions are erroneous and irrational. We simply don't make much sense.

But what does all this mean for the American public schools? The public schools, like the coffee shops of America, have been developed and managed as social institutions by nondisabled people. Our public schools that educate millions of children and youth with disabilities are run by adults who do not have disabilities. Are those adults any better equipped to understand disability than a Disability Studies faculty member or the manager of his favorite coffee house? Are principals and teachers intentionally creating access to the many "coffee shops" that the public schools have to offer? Or are they placing cruel, discriminatory signs in the windows? Let's take a brief look at three outstanding public schools and the dynamic, nondisabled principals who lead them.

A MAGNIFICENT URBAN SCHOOL

As I drove down the bustling main street, I observed small shops and restaurants selling hot bowls of phở with beef or carne asada-filled tacos. Side streets featured tight rows of neatly kept, concrete and stucco homes. The neighborhood surrounding two elementary schools, Skyview and East, was home to thousands of families living in economic poverty. There was a large immigrant population from Viet Nam. There were also many Mexican-American families where Spanish is the prima lingua of the household.

As I walked up to the front of Skyview Elementary School, Principal Delaney greeted me with a big handshake. She had invited me to visit her school.

We proceeded to tour the campus, ducking in to observe teaching in classrooms at every grade level. I observed in many classes and spoke to instructors. Some of the classrooms had two teachers, a general educator and a special educator. I watched with keen interest in these co-teaching arrangements. Co-teaching is one of the main ways that inclusive schools provide instruction and social support to classes comprised of students with and without disabilities (Cook & Friend, 1995; Friend, 2008; Mastropieri, Scruggs, Graetz, Norland, Gardizi, & McDuffie, 2005).

Ms. Delaney casually commented that all of the special educators spent their day co-teaching in general classrooms. I was immediately impressed because co-teaching is common practice in a school-wide approach to inclusion. This wasn't just one or two ambitious teachers trying to do inclusion. This was a whole school effort.

But I also noticed the flat tone of the principal's voice. She was not overly self-impressed with this. It was simply another day at Skyview, and this was how they did their jobs. I made a mental note to ask her about this later.

When we wrapped up the tour, Ms. Delaney walked me back to her office for a few minutes of conversation. She plopped down in her principal's chair with a sigh.

"My big plan right now is to figure out how to set up a health clinic on our campus. Not just for our students. For the families, too. Have you been to East?"

"No, not yet," I replied. She was referring to nearby East Elementary School. "I'm going there next."

"Be sure to ask them about their health clinic. They even provide dental care. Can you believe that? It is really a model for what we want to create here."

"I will. Thanks." I paused for a moment, wondering how long I would have her attention. In my experience, getting quality time with a school principal is almost impossible. "I was impressed with the co-teaching I saw this morning. The teachers seem to work very well together. Do you educate all of your students with disabilities in the general classrooms?"

"Yes, we do. All inclusion for all the kids. And it works." She grabbed some papers from a folder and set a series of test score graphs in front of me. She proceeded to explain the data. "Look at these standardized test scores by grade level. The red line is kids with disabilities. The blue is all the other students."

I examined the graphs. She pointed dramatically at each page.

"Up, up, and here [...] up!"

Over the past three years, the red lines and the blues lines climbed steadily in Reading and Math for every grade level. It was the kind of test score data that inclusive education researchers rarely gather and publish.

"Wow," I exclaimed. "How do you explain the improvement for kids with and without disabilities?"

"I'm sure there are lots of factors. We've been pushing hard on reading and math, on improving our teaching. But a big part of it is the co-teaching. It reduces the teacher to student ratio in those classrooms, giving extra help not only to the kids with disabilities but to other kids, too. English language learners, struggling readers, everyone."

"Can I ask you how Skyview became an inclusive school? I'm always interested in how an inclusive school initially got started on that path."

Ms. Delaney smiled. "At first, I was afraid, I have to admit. Or hesitant. I would say, hesitant. I came here three years ago, and in my first week, all of the special education teachers showed up in my office. The whole bunch crammed in this little office. They wanted to do inclusion across the whole school. Right away."

"What did you think?"

"I listened to them. They were gung-ho. They said that the special classes weren't working. And the isolation discriminated against the disabled kids, stigmatized them. They wanted to start inclusion with co-teaching."

"Did you start right away?"

"Yes, but we needed help. We didn't know enough about it. And maybe about half of the general classroom teachers supported the idea. So we brought in some consultants, flew them in from Syracuse, New York. They worked with us throughout that whole first year. Lots of readings and workshops."

"By the end of the first year, was everyone on board?"

"Not everyone. I still had about five general educators who didn't like the idea. They said they didn't sign up to teach kids with disabilities."

"So what did you do?"

"I steered around them as best I could. Avoided placing kids with disabilities in their rooms. And then three of them left the school at the end of that first year. They sort of saw the writing on the wall. This place really wasn't for them. We had a mission, a future set out in front of us. And they didn't want it."

"And now?"

"I can't say everything is perfect. Every school has problems, you know, challenges to work on. But we're educating all kids with disabilities in general classrooms. We co-teach at every grade level. Our special educators co-plan the lessons with their gen ed partners. We think we've got something pretty unique going on."

"And the parents? Do they like it?"

"They do. I have to say that I didn't ask them their opinion up front. I really didn't want to try to explain inclusion to parents who had no experience with it. I didn't want to scare them. Or get their hopes up too high. In case we failed. I thought to myself, if we can figure out how to do this very well, then everyone will be satisfied."

"Would you say that worked out?"

"Oh, yes, definitely. We persevered, pushed through, and learned how to do inclusion. We're pretty good at it now. Teachers, kids, and parents are happy with what we're doing." She pointed again to the stack of graphs on her desk. "The test scores prove it. These show the progress we are making, not just for kids with disabilities. For all kids."

I thanked Ms. Delaney for the school tour and the wonderful discussion of inclusive education at her school. I climbed in my car and drove two short miles down the busy main street to East Elementary School.

ANOTHER MAGNIFICENT URBAN SCHOOL

The principal of East Elementary, Ms. D'Agostino, beamed with pride as she walked me through her freshly painted campus. The concrete block buildings were over fifty years old, but the bright colors and large murals gave the entire school a fresh appeal.

"We think of this as a full service school," she explained as we walked briskly. I got the impression that she always moved fast. "We serve the meals [...] our kids are 100% free breakfast and lunch. We have donated clothing and shoes for kids who need them. We provide free dental and health."

The cell phone attached to Ms. D'Agostino hip buzzed. She snatched it quickly and turned away from me to answer. It was her assistant calling to tell her she had an important visitor.

"Excuse me," she turned back to speak to me, "I have a parent who needs to talk to me."

She hustled over to speak to man standing near the front office. He wore shorts and a tee shirt that was two sizes too small. He was barefoot, and his face was covered in a couple days of unshaven beard. Ms. D'Agostino shook his hand

and smiled. I couldn't hear their conversation. But I could sense the respect that Ms. D'Agostino communicated to the man.

After a few minutes, the principal returned to continue our tour.

"That was Mr. Florio. He is one of our strongest advocates, a very important parent. Last year, when the district threatened to raise our class size, he led a group of vocal parents who stood up for us at the School Board meeting."

"What happened?" I asked naively.

"The district was facing a budget crunch. They issued over five hundred pink slips to teachers. Despite the budget problems, we've been able to keep our K through three classrooms at twenty-one students or less. These kids need that kind of attention, especially in the early grades. Most of our kids learn English in school. If they are going to have any kind of a chance to succeed, they need small classes in the early grades."

I nodded in agreement. I thought to myself that the small class size she was championing as helpful for English Language Learners and the co-teaching often used in inclusive schools both took advantage of the same idea. Reducing the ratio of teachers to students is often a good way to provide strong social support and effective instruction (Bourke, 1986; Finn & Achilles, 1990; Robinson, 1990).

"That Mr. Florio," the principal continued, "he came to the Board meeting. There was a group of very passionate parents who testified on our behalf. But Mr. Florio spoke with such eloquence and such power. To this day, I believe that his words turned the tide. He shamed those School Board members into doing the right thing."

"That's amazing," I commented.

Ms. D'Agostino checked her watch. I knew she didn't have much time for me. I suddenly remembered Ms. Delaney's advice and asked about the health clinic. Ms. D'Agostino proudly walked me over to the square building at the edge of the school campus.

"The school nurse is on this side"—we entered through a steel door into a small office with a desk and some medical supplies—"and the full clinic is on the other side. All our students get free medical and dental. They come in to see the nurse. If it is something serious, she passes the child through the blue doors to doctors at the clinic on the other side. Plus, we have a free dentist two afternoons a week."

"So members of the community, even adults, can access the clinic from the other side?"

"Yes, that's how it works. For liability and security reasons. Students enter the clinic from the campus side, and members of the community enter from the street side."

"And medical and dental care are free for anyone in the community?"

"Anyone. We've partnered with two non-profit agencies. They supply the care—the staff and equipment—and we provide the building. Everyone wins."

Ms. D'Agostino then walked me across to the main office. On the wall were a series of graphs showing school standardized test scores for the past ten years. The trend line was flat, then it dipped down for two years. Then it rose gradually back up in the most recent four years.

"These two low years were right before I arrived here," Ms. D'Agostino explained as she traced the line with her fingers. "This place was a mess when I got here. It would take me all day to describe all the problems. The numbers started coming up in my second year. We started getting it together, and we've improved every year since."

"I'm impressed." I smiled. "Do you mind if I ask if the test scores for students with disabilities have risen in the same way?"

She pointed to another graph with a rising trend line. "I can say we've been pretty successful there. I think we've made some important improvements for all the students."

I knew that I wanted to ask her about inclusive education practices in her school, especially after what I observed at Skyview Elementary right up the road. I hesitated. I found this principal to be incredibly competent, a real powerhouse of ability and energy. I could see how her efforts were making a big difference in this inner city school. I feared that asking her about inclusion would be like searching for the one weakness in an otherwise impeccable work of art.

I pushed the words out of my mouth. "I visited Skyview this morning [...] and saw their inclusion program [...] ummm [...] are you doing co-teaching like they are?"

"No. We have four intervention classes. The intervention teachers are too busy in their classrooms. They don't have time to be in the general classrooms."

"Would you describe your school as inclusive?"

"We handle inclusion on a case-by-case basis. Some special ed kids can handle the general classroom, and some can't. We want to place each child in the class where he can succeed."

Her statement was one I had heard a million times before. Instead of viewing inclusion as a broad, social justice effort to create classrooms that respect and support all students, she described inclusion as an individual placement decision for a specific student. I would call that old-fashioned *mainstreaming*, not inclusion. The idea is not to create a general classroom setting that provides support and differentiated instruction to meet the needs of all students. The idea is to allow the general education classes to remain primarily inaccessible but smuggle in an occasional disabled student who has the capacity to adapt. This kind of mainstreaming puts the main responsibility for the accessibility of the classroom on the individual child.

In my experience, this kind of outdated and uninspired rationale for exclusion is still preached in some university Introduction to Special Education courses. If the kid can swim in deep water, he goes in the deep pool. If not, he goes in the shallow pool. Some kids in the shallow pool, with great effort and the right "interventions," might make it into the deep pool. If kids in the shallow pool are stigmatized in the eyes of teachers and children, that is unfortunate. But that is the way the system works.

A MAGNIFICENT BORDER TOWN SCHOOL

Two weeks later, I visited Eldridge Elementary School. After touring the school, I sat down with Principal Guiterrez. Eldridge is located in what Mr. Guiterrez described as a "border town," an area close to the Mexican border where most of the children are the sons and daughters of recent immigrants. The majority of the students come from low-income families where Spanish is the primary or only language. At school, they learn to speak and read and write English. But they do much more.

Four years earlier, Principal Guiterrez and the faculty at Eldridge switched to a dual language immersion model. Rather than gradually transitioning the students from learning in Spanish to learning in English, the students are learning to read and write and think in both English and Spanish. They study with one teacher in one language during the morning. After lunch, the students switch to a second teacher who instructs in the second language. This innovative dual language approach follows a substantial body of educational research that demonstrates that young children can benefit from mastering two languages simultaneously (Cobb, Vega, & Kronauge, 2006; Howard, Sugarman, & Christian, 2003).

Mr. Guiterrez beamed when he showed me bar graphs demonstrating the dramatic improvements in standardized test scores, in English and Spanish, in Reading and Math.

"The academic performance of our second graders," he boasted, "precisely match the level of performance in the elementary schools in the wealthiest neighborhoods in the state. We know these kids can achieve, and we know how to help them reach their potential."

I had to agree. Everything I had seen that morning was impressive.

As usual, I broached the topic of students with disabilities. I always have to ask.

"We have six or seven students now with autism. We have found that they can do very well in the dual language immersion model," Mr. Guiterrez explained. "And we have a number of students with Down Syndrome. Of course, we serve those students in their own special education classroom […]."

Mr. Guiterrez kept talking, but I stopped listening. I got stuck on the words *Of Course […] […] […] […] […] Of Course, those kids with Down Syndrome have a separate classroom […] Of Course.*

CONTRADICTIONS

Why do highly successful school principals and teachers with a very full commitment to cultural diversity fail to see how students with disabilities *should* fit within their progressive, multicultural vision? As the left hand pursues social justice, the right upholds ableist segregation. Why?

Over the years, I have experienced many schools in urban or low income areas where the lack of economic capital in the surround neighborhoods is matched by the lack of enthusiasm, love, and positive energy within the school building. The fact that students live in poverty, have dark skin, or speak a language other than English at home often serves as an excuse for bankrupt teaching and disrespectful professional behavior.

Skyview, East, and Eldridge are very much the opposite, tremendous examples of what very purposeful, high-energy schools serving a diverse student body can be. These schools are blessed with leaders and faculties who believe in the dignity and ability of their students and families.

But I still can't make sense of the stark contradiction. All three schools have highly effective principals and faculties who care deeply about their students. Why is only one of three an inclusive school? Why do the other two practice segregation on the basis of disability?

Then my mind returned to my friend Theo and the campus coffee shop. I chuckled bitterly as I recalled my own failure to realize that my favorite campus caffeine hangout would not allow Theo to enter. I was strangely capable of working for years on disability right issues while forgetting all about people with disabilities when it came to the entrance to that coffee house.

Was I really any different than the principals and teachers at Eldridge and East Elementary?

And the little café itself was a profound contradiction. The inaccessible front door would not allow anyone using a wheelchair to enter. But once inside, a person with a disability would be treated to a fully accessible Men's Room.

Is this what life in America is like for persons with disabilities, a strange funhouse where the mirrors distort, twist, and confuse?

KNOWING WHAT WE DON'T KNOW

Journalist Joseph Shapiro (1994, p. 3) has written, "Nondisabled Americans do not understand disabled ones." Without the lived experience of being disabled, of knowing exclusion and discrimination based on disability first hand, nondisabled people like me, Ms. D'Agostino, Mr. Guiterrez, and the coffee shop workers are subject to profound misunderstandings. When it comes to the lives and needs of disabled persons, our thoughts processes are weak and partial, odd minglings of inattention and focus, foolishness and reason.

Behind the befuddling coffee shop with the fully accessible Men's Room and the three-inch curb bump at the front entrance; behind my absurd capacity to work for disability rights while not noticing that my favorite java stop was not wheelchair accessible; behind the elementary school principals and teachers who combined a powerful devotion to social justice education with an oppressive approach to students with disabilities, lies the fact that non-disabled people often think and behave in strangely inconsistent and irrational ways when it comes to people with disabilities.

We nondisabled folks know very little about living with a disability, and what we do know is often a weird hodgepodge of unfounded notions and cruel prejudices. Our minds are log-jammed with pitiful phrases like *Of Course*, bad cultural habits left over from long ago that need critique and revision.

Noted disability studies scholar Irving Zola (1983, p. 56) once commented that the reason that disabled people need to come together in a social movement to take control of their own lives is not because nondisabled people don't care but because "they do not know." What he meant was people without disabilities simply get it wrong when it comes to understanding disability. But why? Why are nondisabled people, even highly successful and caring educators, so bewildered when it comes to disability?

IDEOLOGY OF ABILITY

Perhaps no one has answered this question as succinctly and yet profoundly as disability studies scholar Tobin Siebers. He has coined the phrase *ideology of ability* to capture a powerful, often unacknowledged mode of foundational belief that permeates our daily lives, from the laws, institutions, and economic system down to our thoughts and actions. At the very bottom of our everyday thinking and action, of our persistent cultural prejudice against disabled persons, is the ideology of ability.

In our shared, cultural thinking, we believe that *being human means being nondisabled*. Take a moment to let that sink in. It is an enormous, world-changing idea. When we think of life, of living, of being a person, we don't include disability as an option or alternative within our understanding. We simply assume that being alive means being able-bodied.

> The ideology of ability represents the able body as the baseline of humanness. Absence of ability or lesser ability, according to this ideology, makes a person less than human. (Siebers, 2008, p. 139)

Disabled persons are understood as either not fully human, or they are less valuable, imperfect versions of humanity.

The ideology of ability plays out in a number of more specific beliefs about ability and disability. Of the many specific beliefs that Siebers details, I will explain four in order to provide a useful sampling of the concept.

- "The ideology of ability simultaneously banishes disability and turns it into principle of exclusion." (Siebers, 2008, p. 10)

In the United States, there are currently residential institutions for people with visual impairments, hearing impairments, intellectual disabilities, autism, and psychiatric disabilities. According to the most recent federal data, over five percent of all children and adolescents with disabilities live in hospitals or institutions (Individuals with Disabilities Education Act Data, 2016). Almost one in five students considered to have emotional or behavior disorders are housed in locked hospitals or residential programs (Individuals with Disabilities Education Act Data, 2016).

The public schools in the United States have isolated classrooms and schools for children with autism, behavioral disorders, learning disabilities, intellectual disabilities, visual impairments, and hearing impairments. In 2010, over fourteen percent of all disabled students in the United States spent their entire school day in buildings fully isolated from nondisabled students (Individuals with Disabilities Education Act Data, 2016). Almost half of all students with intellectual disabilities have no opportunities to interact with or create friendships with nondisabled students because they attend segregated schools (Individuals with Disabilities Education Act Data, 2016).

A national survey of almost 6,000 nondisabled middle school students found that less than ten percent currently shared a classroom with a student with an intellectual disability. Not surprisingly, the systematic social separation left nondisabled students with a desire to avoid interaction with students with intellectual disabilities. The study authors sadly concluded that "little appears to have changed in the past thirty years regarding people's perception of ID." (Siperstein, Parker, Bardon, & Widaman, 2007, p. 451)

In the United States, disability and exclusion go together like inhalation and exhalation. Forcibly housing a disabled young person in a hospital or residential facility secluded from the general community, or providing schooling in a classroom or school that allows no contact with nondisabled young people seems completely reasonable.

- "Disability is always individual, a property of one body, not a feature common to all human beings, while ability defines a feature essential to the human species." (Siebers, 2008, p. 10)

In the American public schools, a disability is typically viewed as a flaw that belongs to one person. Students are thought to clearly fall into one of two groups, those with disabilities and those without.

What is lost in this simplified thinking is an appreciation for how human beings actually vary, for the thousands and thousands of physical, developmental, and cultural differences occurring across the population of students.

Even more, this oversimplification of humanity pretends that human ability and life itself are consistent and predictable. "As a living entity, the body is vital and chaotic," explains Siebers (2008, p. 26). It doesn't hold still in a state of safety and robotic regularity.

The human body and mind are frail, fragile, and unreliable. All persons are prone to illness, accidents, weakness, and inconsistency. Our minds forget or succumb to distraction. Our bodies become injured or sick, tired or uncomfortable. Much about an individual's ability to perform a given task fluctuates with changes in mood, concentration, strength, comfort, and environmental conditions. Consistency is an illusion. A task that a person completes easily one day or one moment is difficult or impossible the next. The greatest baseball player hits three home runs one day and then strikes out three times the next. All persons are simultaneously able and unable, competent and incompetent.

Even if we accept the dramatic oversimplification of life created by categorizing persons as either disabled or able-bodied, the public schools still consider disability to be purely individualized. Disability is a feature of an individual, not a social characteristic like race or gender that makes one part of a uniquely valuable community. Rarely do teachers and school leaders think about students with disabilities as cultural minority group that bring numerous positive contributions to a school.

Educational researcher Scott Thompson (2011) has contrasted the way that schools and professionals think about disabled students with how they think about lesbian, gay, bisexual, and transgender (LGBT) students. Increasingly, secondary schools have created student clubs called Gay/Straight Alliances for the purpose of uniting LGBT students, supporting LGBT identities, and gathering heterosexual allies into communities of peer support. These Alliances can be a powerful social force to increase the level of tolerance and acceptance in a school building. They are a great example of how public schools can truly celebrate human diversity while also strengthening community.

But Thompson observes that schools do not create similar student clubs to bring together disabled students and their nondisabled allies. Disability is not viewed in the public schools as a positive cultural identity to be celebrated. Disabled students are not thought to be part of a positive social group that makes a meaningful contribution to the learning, vitality, and social cohesion of the school community. There is no opportunity for pride and identity under the banner of Disability in the public schools.

- "Disabled people must try to be as able-bodied as possible all the time." (Siebers, 2008, p. 10)

Just as Pinocchio strives to become a real boy, so, too, a disabled person should seek full human status. It is expected that disabled persons will attempt to shed their disability through some kind of medical, rehabilitation, or educational intervention. If a cure or recovery is not possible, then a person with a disability should pursue standards of behavior and appearance that greatly imitate those of nondisabled persons.

For years, I taught in and consulted with segregated school programs for students with labels of emotional disturbance or behavioral disorder. Virtually every one of these school programs employs a behavioral system of points and levels to encourage improved student behavior (e.g., Knitzer, Steinberg, & Brahm, 1990). Individuals who comply with the rules and expectations of the school earn points and gradually work their way up the chart of levels. At the top of the level chart is the ultimate reward, the greatest incentive for good behavior. Students who reach the top level and maintain compliant behavior are considered for a possible change in school placement to a mainstream school. That is, one of the great motivators that these schools employ is the opportunity for students to earn their way out of segregation, earn admission to the school for nondisabled students. That is where they have a chance to become, or at least seem like, a nondisabled student (Danforth & Smith, 2005).

The underlying premise is that students with disabilities should want to become nondisabled. In fact, they should work to earn that prize. Ablebodiedness (or ablemindedness) is a valued goal, a state of humanity that students with disabilities should seek. There is no way for a disabled student to be proud of himself as a disabled person. He must try to modify himself to become fully human.

- "Overcoming disability is an event to be celebrated. It is an ability in itself to be able to overcome disability." (Siebers, 2008, p. 10)

A staple of modern journalism, of newspapers, magazines, and television news, is the stock story about a heroic person who is overcoming her disability. The story is intended to be inspirational, moving, a positive account of a person with a disability. The person is described as a role model, as someone for nondisabled persons to respect and disabled persons to emulate.

For example, a dramatic story about a very impressive high school graduate aired recently on the popular morning television show *Good Morning America*. On the ABC website, the video is accompanied by a short, written story.

Paralyzed California Teen Fulfills Vow to Walk at High School Graduation

A California teen paralyzed nearly all his life lived up to his big promise this week and walked on stage to accept his high school diploma.

For the last three years, seventeen-year-old Patrick Ivison of San Diego has been going through intensive training for Tuesday's ceremony, enduring six hours per day of physical therapy, according to KGTV in San Diego.

He vowed to everyone he knew that he was going to walk on stage during commencement.

"There's always that like, oh, I've got, you know, all of America expecting me to get through this," Ivison told KGTV. (Paralyzed California Teen, 2012)

Good Morning America host George Stephanopoulos introduces the video clip with a line straight from the ideology of ability: "Of all the great moments at all the graduations this year, this one may be the most inspiring." The video clip shows Patrick sitting in his wheelchair at his high school graduation. He is called to the stage to receive his diploma. A large man standing in front of him pushes a mechanical walker up to his chest. Patrick, wearing his flowing graduation gown, is hoisted to a standing position by a crank mechanism. He then leans on the walker for balance. Legs wobbling, crowd on their feet cheering, the muscular assistant backing up with two hands on the walker, the high school graduate slowly walks to center stage. Triumphantly, he receives his diploma and then sits back in his wheelchair.

There are two stories here, one that makes it to the television screen, and one that does not. There is a story about a young man paralyzed in a car accident who earned a perfect 4.0 GPA in his high school studies. He is an outstanding student who will attend the University of Southern California. Expectations and possibilities for paralyzed young men and women have changed greatly since the days when Ed Roberts first attended the University of California at Berkeley in the early 1960s. High schools and universities are now far more accessible and supportive for students with disabilities. This talented young man has done well in high school, and he has a bright future ahead of him.

Notice that this story of Patrick's academic success and hopeful future does not engage the ideology of ability. It is wonderful story about individual achievement and social change. But it also is not the story that appears on *Good Morning America*. It is a rather ordinary narrative that might be told among friends at a backyard barbeque, but it that lacks heavy duty inspiration and tearfulness for big-time TV.

A more heroic and formulaic story of overcoming disability is the one that actually plays on the national morning television show. This one fully engages the ideology of ability by featuring Patrick's extraordinary achievement: He busted his rear end for three years in order to appear as nondisabled as possible for four minutes in front of a large audience. For about twenty-six steps, on that grand stage, with assistance from a rolling walker and a strong assistant, he walked [...] almost like other graduates. In this story, his great achievement is not his straight A average and acceptance to a top university. It is his four very public minutes of almost walking, of imitating the bodily motion of a person who does not have a physical disability.

As Patrick received his diploma, television announcer Stephanopoulos says, "The entire arena stood, too, shoulder to shoulder with Patrick." If Patrick acts nondisabled, if he strives unbelievably hard to overcome his disability, if only temporarily and with both human and mechanical assistance, then the crowd of nondisabled persons rally to his side. They are with him. If he can, through determination and hard work, try to lose his disability, then he has a many great supporters.

The message from *Good Morning America* is a standard, oft-repeated version of the ideology of ability. What Patrick and others like him should do is struggle and toil endless hours to approximate the life and activity of a person without a disability. But living a highly successful life as a man with a disability [...] that is not a story worth telling.

DISABILITY LESSONS

What does Tobin Siebers' ideology of ability teach us about my experiences with the coffee shop and the three magnificent schools? For now, let's begin with one enormous but simple lesson.

The main problem that people with disabilities confront each day is not located within the workings of their bodies and minds. The main problem resides in the social and physical world that the dominant group of non-disabled persons has constructed, a world that fails to provide access, support, and dignity to persons with disabilities.

If we want to make our communities more compassionate and livable for everyone, we need to view the fact that Theo cannot enter the coffee shop as a shared, political problem involving barriers to participation, not as a personal problem consisting of a failed or ineffective body. If we frame this issue as a political problem, then it is the responsibility of all community members to do the moral work of removing all kinds of barriers—architectural, attitudinal, institutional—that exclude and insult people with disabilities. This allows people with and without disabilities to work together toward creating a community where a diverse citizenry can participate and prosper.

This way of viewing the situation is far more pragmatic and hopeful than framing this as Theo's personal problem. If we view this as his problem, then our message to Theo is that his body is broken and in need of repair. He should go to a hospital or a rehabilitation center to get himself fixed. Once his body is appropriately adjusted, made normal or functional, then he'll be able to enter the coffee shop.

The great social justice educator Paulo Freire (1970, p. 122) described the inherent cruelty that takes place when we adopt what he calls "a focalized view of problems." Too often, we blame a complex social issue on a specific person or group, typically the person or group most harmed by the issue. During the early 1970s, I can recall my parents making this mistake by framing the many public protests and court battles of African-American civil rights movement as "the Negro Problem." This obviously oppressive misunderstanding of the complexity and breadth of the social problems not only lacks compassion. It also sidesteps the opportunity to understand the real causes of The Problem.

When we settle for pinning a cheap target on the back of the persons most in need of our support and compassion, we are doing what William Ryan (1971) called "blaming the victim." We are inaccurately identifying the persons who suffer beneath a host of social misfortunes and brutalities as the cause of their own abuse. In this cruel scheme, rape victims entice their abusers into action, poor people create economic systems that distribute wealth disproportionately, and disabled persons are the reason for their own systematic exclusion.

One powerful way to avoid falling into a focalized view and blaming victims is to engage in a process of personal education and growth, opening up our critical awareness and our consciousness to the wider social conditions that perpetuate the physical and social obstacles to participation and success that disabled persons experience. We need to learn about how and why people with disabilities are routinely excluded and disrespected in our society. When we begin to understand that Theo and other persons with disabilities confront countless variations of the blocked coffee shop doorway across the many dimensions of their lives—school, employment, transportation, recreation, relationships, to name a few—then we stop blaming Theo for the hateful signs displayed in restaurant windows. When we open our minds to how cruelty operates under the guise of seemingly unobjectionable social practices, we can begin to become part of the solution to social injustice.

REFERENCES

Bourke, S. (1986). How smaller is better: Some relationships between class size, teaching practices and student achievement. *American Educational Research Journal, 23*, 558–571.

Brueggemann, B. J., White, L. F., Dunn, P. A., Heifferon, B. A., & Cheu, J. (2001). Becoming visible: Lessons in disability. *College Composition and Communication, 52*, 3, 368–398.

Cobb, B., Vega, D., & Kronauge, C. (2006). Effects of an elementary dual language immersion program on junior high school achievement. *Middle Grades Research Journal, 1*, 1, 27–47.

Cohen, A. (January 11, 2004). Can disabled people be forced to crawl up the courthouse steps? *New York Times.* Retrieved from http://www.nytimes.com/2004/01/11/opinion/editorial-observer-can-disabled-people-be-forced-crawl-up-courthouse-steps.html?pagewanted=all&src=pm.

Cook, L., & Friend, M. (1995). Co-teaching: Guidelines for creating effective practices. *Focus on Exceptional Children, 28*, 3, 1–16.

Danforth, S., & Smith, T. J. (2005). *Engaging troubling students: A constructivist approach.* Thousand Oaks, CA: Corwin Press.

Davis, L. J. (2015). *Enabling acts: The hidden story of how the Americans with Disabilities Act gave the largest US minority its rights.* Boston, MA: Beacon.

Finn, J. D., & Achilles, C. M. (1990). Answers and questions about class size: A statewide experiment. *American Educational Research Journal, 27*, 557–577.

Freire, P. (1970). *Pedagogy of the oppressed.* (Myra Bergman Ramos, Trans.). New York: Herder & Herder.

Friend, M. (2008). Co-teaching: A simple solution that isn't simple after all. *Journal of Curriculum and Instruction, 2*, 9–19.

Howard, E. R., Sugarman, J., & Christian, D. (August 2003). *Trends in two-way immersion education: A review of the research.* Baltimore, MD: Center for Research on the Education of Students Placed At Risk, Johns Hopkins University.

Individuals with Disabilities Education Act Data, United States Department of Education. http://www.ideadata.org/PartBData.asp. Retrieved December 27, 2016.

Knitzer, J., Steinberg, Z., & Brahm, F. (1990). *At the school house door: An examination of programs and policies for children with behavioral and emotional problems.* New York: Bank Street College of Education.

Lane, C. (May 18, 2004). Disabled win right to sue states over court access. *Washington Post*, p. A01.

Mastropieri, M. A., Scruggs, T. E., Graetz, J., Norland, J., Gardizi, W., & McDuffie, K. (2005). Case studies in co-teaching in the content areas: Successes, failures, and challenges. *Intervention in School and Clinic, 40*, 5, 260–270.

National Museum of American History (2012). Greensboro Lunch Counter. Retrieved from http://americanhistory.si.edu/news/factsheet.cfm?key=30&newskey=53.

Paralyzed California Teen Fulfills Vow to Walk at High School Graduation (2014). Retrieved from http://abcnews.go.com/US/paralyzed-teen-fulfills-vow-walk-high-school-graduation/story?id=16557742.

Robinson, G. E. (1990). Synthesis of research on effects of class size. *Educational Leadership, 47*, 7, 80–90.

Ryan, W. (1971). *Blaming the victim.* New York: Pantheon.

Shapiro, J. P. (1994). *No pity: people with disabilities forging a new civil rights movement.* New York: Times Books.

Siebers, T. (2008). *Disability theory.* Ann Arbor, MI: University of Michigan Press.

Siperstein, G. N., Parker, R. C., Bardon, J. N., & Widaman, K. F. (2007). A national study of youth attitudes toward the inclusion of students with intellectual disabilities, *Exceptional Children, 73*, 4, 435–455.

Thompson, S. A. (2011). A queer circle of friends, indeed! The school social as intervention or as movement. *International Journal of Inclusive Education, 16*, 10, 1–16.

Zola, I. K. (1983). Developing new self-images and interdependence. In N. M. Crewe & I. K. Zola (Eds.), *Independent living for physically disabled people* (pp. 49–59). San Francisco, CA: Jossey-Bass.

CHAPTER THREE

Teaching for the Disability Rights Movement

> **Guiding Questions**
> - What are the ethical goals of the Disability Rights Movement?
> - How is the Disability Rights Movement like or unlike other civil rights movements (e.g., African-Americans, women, Latinos, LGBT community)?
> - How can knowledge of the Disability Rights Movement inform the actions of inclusive educators today?

Disability studies scholars David T. Mitchell and Sharon L. Snyder (2000, p. 3) have observed, "One might think of disability as the master trope of disqualification." Having a disability places an individual in unending jeopardy of social exclusion. Students with disabilities receiving instruction in general education classrooms might be viewed as having trap doors beneath their desks. At any moment, the educators can pull the lever. The door flops open, and the student drops down a shaft leading to a segregated special education setting.

If inclusion is an overly optimistic classroom placement for an individual who is viewed as lacking qualities of normality, then this scenario makes sense. If inclusion is a reluctant social experiment, then retreating when challenges arise is understandable.

But when educators understand inclusive education as intentional ethical action within the on-going Disability Rights Movement, everything changes. The efforts of teachers and leaders in public schools are cast in the historical context of the movement of *disabled citizens seeking equality and dignity. Inclusion takes on important democratic dimensions, and the work gains new ethical meaning, not only in the lives of students and families, but in the lives of teachers who want to make a contribution to the social progress of society.*

TEACHING FOR A JUST SOCIETY

"Movements represent the principle of flux and change: they are the processes through which a society channels its energies for renewal and transformation." (Palmer, 1998, p. 164)

In the darkest midst of the Great Depression, Professor George S. Counts (1932) of Teachers College posed a provocative question, *Dare the school build a new social order?* In an era of widespread unemployment, human suffering, and economic uncertainty, Counts wondered what role teachers should play in the intentional improvement of society. How can teaching contribute in a positive way to re-envisioning and reforming the larger community? How can teachers help communities become more ethical and equitable?

Counts saw teachers as political actors deeply engaged in the most troubling and exciting social issues of the day. Undoubtedly, the next generation, the children of today's schools who will grow up to lead American businesses, government, and cultural institutions, will not merely replicate the society of their youth. The many terrains of economic, technological, and cultural life evolve over time. Schools must provide young people with an education that prepares them to thoughtfully meet a variety of complex social and ethical challenges in a changing world. Counts believed that teachers should be purposeful and ethical professionals seeking the improvement of society both today and tomorrow.

In this chapter, I examine the purpose of inclusive education in light of the history of the Disability Rights Movement in the United States. I must note that many researchers and authors place inclusive education as an outgrowth of special education. They position inclusive teaching as one form of special education practice. I certainly acknowledge that special educators often play an important role in the success or failure of inclusion. But the fact is that inclusion happens in and profoundly changes general education classrooms. It opens up those general classrooms, those mainstream communities of learning and relationship, to students who have historically been rejected as unfit and unwanted. That concerted and purposeful effort to create access and social acceptance in the general education community for students with disabilities is nothing less the Disability Rights Movement occurring in the public schools.

The Disability Rights Movement, gathering steam in the late 1960s and continuing today, consists of a complex array of oppositional and hopeful actions—civil disobedience, law suits, legislative work, education—focused on dramatically changing American society. While the Movement has tackled a number of different issues, from accessible public buses to funding for personal care assistants that allow people to move from nursing homes to their own apartments and houses, the overall purpose has been to create a society that is accessible to disabled persons and that values their important contributions in everyday life (Fleischer & Zames, 2011; Pelka, 1997; Shapiro, 1994; Stroman, 2003).

The Disability Rights Movement seeking justice and inclusion is far from over. If we imagined, quite naively, that the 1990 passage of the Americans with Disabilities Act (ADA) was the victorious end of the civil rights road, we were wrong. At best, it stands as a monument to the important work of disability activists and what they have achieved so far. But it certainly is not the final, celebratory chapter of this narrative of social progress in the United States. If there ever will be such a chapter, it is in the future, and it will only occur after much more hard work.

For educators, this means that the continuing work of the Disability Rights Movement happens in inclusive classrooms and schools. These are the spaces of opportunity for teachers and school leaders, the spaces where we can contribute to the larger effort of the Movement.

CONTRIBUTING TO THE COLLECTIVE CONSCIOUSNESS

> "A significant social movement becomes possible when there is a revision in the manner in which a substantial group of people, looking at some misfortune, see it no longer as a misfortune warranting charitable consideration but as an injustice which is intolerable in society." (Turner, 1969, p. 321)

The Disability Rights Movement has been led primarily by disabled persons and powered by organizations of disabled persons. But there have been significant contributions by nondisabled persons and groups, especially parents of persons with disabilities and enlightened social service professionals. There are very real opportunities for persons without disabilities, including educators, to contribute to the Movement in a meaningful way. But those opportunities require that nondisabled educators understand what it is they are contributing to.

Sharon Barnartt and Richard Scotch (2000, p. 31) have used the word "collective consciousness" to describe the shared system of beliefs developed and utilized by disability activists. Disability rights activists have unified around a belief system, a more or less common way of understanding the problems disabled persons face in their lives and the best solutions to those issues. It is a way of thinking filled with

> ideas that transform perceptions and ultimately legitimate opposition to extant cultural beliefs or social structural arrangements. This opposition to cultural beliefs is necessary in order to motivate people to seek change, because cultural beliefs naturally seek to conserve

the social and political order. Some scholars have called a collective consciousness an 'oppositional consciousness' [...]. It is this oppositional consciousness that can cause people to engage in risky contentious political action. (Barnartt & Scotch (2000, p. 31)

This oppositional or critical consciousness has rejected the standard cultural beliefs about disabled persons that hold people back in order to imagine a more positive identity for disabled persons and a more equitable and just society for all.

Tobin Siebers (2008) teaches us that this development of a collective consciousness among disabled persons involves an intensive reexamination of what had traditionally been viewed as private or personal suffering. Among disabled and nondisabled persons alike, prior to the Disability Rights Movement, it was simply assumed that having a disability was synonymous with a life of personal suffering. Being blind, being deaf, or having an intellectual disability, was understood as tragic, a life of private emotional pain arising inevitably from the condition itself. The remarkable achievement of the early disability activists was the transformation of that concept of personal suffering into "an experience supportive of strong and positive political values" (Siebers, 2008, p. 190). People with disabilities created a shared allegiance with one another and a common identity. The source of suffering was redefined as the society's or community's response to the person with an impairment. The problem was not the variability of human bodies and minds but the unjust and cruel ways that communities responded to those human differences.

The solution devised by the Disability Rights movement did not involve altering bodies or fixing minds. Improving the lives of persons with disabilities required not a heroic cure of the individual's condition but purposeful social action to change society. The Movement refashions social norms of belief and behavior concerning human differences in order to respect and support all persons.

The best inclusive educators understand and participate in the "collective consciousness" of the Disability Rights Movement. They understand the story of the Movement and how their daily work in schools makes a very real contribution to expanding disability rights today. The purpose of this chapter is offer an overview of the history of the Disability Rights Movement in the United States. This history is understandably limited in scope, attending to only handful of crucial events in the civil rights march of disabled Americans. I hope this introduction to the history of the Movement spurs readers to run to libraries, bookstores, and websites to learn more. Fortified by a knowledge of the difficult road of social progress that has brought disabled citizens to where they are now, to where we all are now, inclusive educators can better understand and occupy their imperative role as disability rights activists in the public schools.

BEFORE THE DISABILITY RIGHTS MOVEMENT: THE LEAGUE OF THE PHYSICALLY HANDICAPPED

Finding a job in the United States during the Great Depression of the 1930s was a daunting task. For disabled workers, the problem of the lack of available jobs was only further compounded by discriminatory hiring and employment practices. Often disabled persons only secured part-time jobs, or they worked the same job as coworkers but received a lower rate of pay. It was not uncommon for employers to require job applicants to pass a physical examination, regardless of the physical demands of the position.

Historian Paul Longmore (1998; Longmore & Goldberger, 2000) recounts the experiences of disabled persons seeking jobs in New York City in the 1930s.

- Florence Haskell, a woman who used crutches, applied for a secretary job. "The man told me […] 'I'm afraid you'll have to take a physical.' […] I was really hit between the eyes. I never visualized that [my handicap] would be a reason for me not to get a job […]. He disqualified me […]. I was very hurt, upset, and mad" (Longmore, 1998, para. 4).
- Sylvia Flexer, a woman who used crutches and wore a leg brace, tried to get a job as a librarian or English teacher. Sylvia explained, "I found I couldn't get a job because I was handicapped." She decided to get more training in office and business practices. After graduating from a business school with training in stenography, typing, and adding machine operation, she again tried the job market. "[I]n my naivete, I figured, 'I'll graduate from the Drake Business School and they're all going to grab me.' […] Well, nobody grabbed me […]. Some people who graduated got jobs […] they didn't begin to be as good as I was" (Longmore, 1998, para. 4).

Corporations and private companies routinely viewed highly capable and eager disabled persons as incompetent workers, ineligible for paid employment.

Some disabled adults hoped that the Roosevelt Administration's New Deal work programs would be less discriminatory than the private sector. After all, the work relief programs provided by seemingly progressive federal agencies such as the Public Works Administration, the Works Progress Administration (WPA), and the Civilian Conservation Corps were specifically designed to create government-funded jobs for unemployed workers. Certainly, then as today, many persons with disabilities were out of work. But the New Deal programs routinely turned away disabled job applicants as "unemployable," worthy only of low levels of public or charitable relief (Longmore & Goldberger, 2000, p. 898). In fact, the Emergency Relief Bureau (ERB) of New York City, in compliance with official WPA policy, refused to hire persons with disabilities (Longmore, 1998; Longmore & Goldberger, 2000).

In May, 1935, Florence Haskell, Sylvia Flexer, Hyman Abramowitz and three other young adults with physical disabilities asked to meet with ERB Director Oswald W. Knauth in order to express their concerns over the biased hiring policies of the agency. They were told that the Director would meet with them the next week.

The determined young adults sat down and said they would not move until the Director met with them. This began a sit-in protest in the ERB office, perhaps the first organized disability rights protest in the United States. Flener Basoff, one of the protesters, later explained why the group refused to move.

> (T)he government was handing out jobs [...] everybody was getting jobs; newspaper people, actresses, actors, painters, and only handicapped people weren't worthy of jobs [...]. Those of us who [...] were militant just refused to accept the fact that we were the only people who were looked upon as not worthy, not capable of work. (Longmore & Goldberger, 2000, p. 899)

By the next day, hundreds of supporters had gathered outside in support of the sit-in. The local and national news media, including the *Daily News*, *New York Post*, *New York Herald Tribune*, and the *Washington Post*, picked up the story (Fleischer & Zames, 2011; Pelka, 1997; Longmore, 1998).

On the sixth day, Director Knauth agreed to meet with the protest group leaders. They demanded that Knauth hire fifty disabled workers immediately and add ten more each week. They must receive reasonable wages, and they must work side-by-side with nondisabled workers in integrated work settings. There would be no "special" workplaces just for the workers with disabilities.

ERB Director Knauth rejected the demands, claiming that that his agency was not a charity: "This is not an organization to give work to those who are permanently unemployable" (Longmore, 1998, para. 10).

On the ninth day of the protest, Director Knauth brought in the police to break up the protest. They arrested eleven persons.

Later that same day, over three hundred protesters gathered at the corner of 54th Street and Eighth Avenue. When the police rousted the bunch, the activists moved their protest to the WMCA radio station where Director Knauth was speaking on-air in celebration of the first anniversary of the ERB (Longmore & Goldberger, 2000).

The next day, after another unsuccessful meeting with Director Knauth, the protesters took their fight to the Mayor's office. Over fifty demonstrators, led by persons with disabilities, gathered in City Hall Plaza. Mayor LaGuardia refused to meet with the group (Fleischer & Zames, 2011; Pelka, 1997; Longmore, 1998; Longmore & Goldberger, 2000).

The League for the Physically Handicapped recruited more members. In November, 1935, they picketed in front of the offices of the New York City WPA. The League promoted their action with a flyer that read:

> The Handicapped still are discriminated against by Private Industry. It is because of this discrimination that we demand the government recognize its obligation to make adequate provisions for handicapped people in the Works Relief Program. (Longmore, 1998, para. 10)

During 1935 and 1936, a series of League protests in front of the New York City WPA resulted in the hiring of about 1,500 disabled workers.

But local victory was not enough. The leaders of the League knew that the main problem behind the New York office of the WPA was a national government policy that refused to consider persons with disabilities as employable. They decided to take their case to Washington. Through a campaign of letters and telegraphs, they arranged for a meeting with national leaders of the WPA.

In May, 1936, thirty five League members met with WPA Labor Relations Director Nels Anderson in Washington, DC. He told them they would not be allowed to speak with WPA head Harry Hopkins. To their disappointment, Anderson merely reiterated the current policy of hiring discrimination. He suggested that since they were unemployable, they should seek assistance from relief and charitable agencies in New York.

The delegates exploded. Sylvia Flexer, twenty-one years old and the League's president, announced: "We are going to stay here until Mr. Hopkins does see us. Until then nothing can make us leave." The next day she said that League members were "sick of the humiliation of poor jobs at best [and] often no work at all." They wanted "not sympathy—but a concrete plan to end discrimination [...] on W.P.A. projects" (Longmore, 1998, para. 12).

The League members refused to leave the WPA offices. On Monday, after two days of protest, Harry Hopkins met with the group. Hopkins maintained that the WPA did not discriminate against job applicants with disabilities. He demanded that the League provide proof of biased employment practices in the WPA. Incongruously, the leader of an enormous federal jobs relief agency that faithfully adhered to a policy of not hiring disabled persons did not believe that discrimination against disabled person in the public and private sector employment existed. He asked for proof (Longmore, 1998; Longmore & Goldberger, 2000).

In this meeting with a Roosevelt New Deal administrator, and in further meetings in 1937, the League was unable to make any progress. They submitted Hopkins written proof, a report titled "Thesis on the Conditions of the Physically Handicapped," offering factual documentation of widespread prejudicial employment practices. Hopkins was not swayed by the facts (Fleischer & Zames, 2011; Pelka, 1997; Longmore, 1998; Longmore & Goldberger, 2000).

During the Spring of 1937, as the WPA began laying off workers across the country, many of the gains won by the League in New York evaporated. Over 600 disabled WPA workers in New York City were fired (Longmore, 1998).

By 1938, the League of the Physically Handicapped had disbanded. This battle was over.

These first acts of civil disobedience of the activist group that called itself the League for the Physically Handicapped did not succeed in changing the prejudicial hiring policy of the New Deal work program. But they did create a new kind of political association that defined disability in a very new way, creating "a precursor of disability pride" (Pelka, 1997, p. 191).

Historian Richard Scotch (2001) has described the passage of Section 504 of the Rehabilitation Act of 1973 as emblematic of a dramatic cultural shift in the United States, altering our understanding of persons with disabilities from persons needing charity to persons seeking their civil rights. Disabled persons were not defined as tragic figures requiring charitable donations. They were viewed as a cultural minority, victimized by of a variety of political oppressions but also a social source of unity, identity, and pride. Some four decades before that landmark federal legislation changed the political landscape, before the various civil rights movements seeking justice for African-Americans and women, the League for the Physically Handicapped in New York City invented that forward-thinking idea.

Despite the short lifespan and limited practical accomplishments of the League, the group broke new ground in two specific ways. First, the members came together as coalition of persons with disabilities with an explicit political purpose, to shift the thinking of citizens and leaders away from disability as an individual failing and toward disability as the result of unjust policies and social practices. They "fought job discrimination and contested the ideology of disability that dominated early-twentieth-century public policies, professional practices, and societal arrangements" (Longmore & Goldberger, 2000, p. 888).

The League attempted to redefine the meaning of disability in relationship to employment and economic sustenance. They pressed government leaders to jettison their conventional image of persons with disabilities as objects of charity, as persons who receive some level of financial support because they are incapacitated. In its place, the League promulgated a new, progressive concept of disabled persons as active and able citizens. They portrayed themselves as workers, as talented employees capable of making a substantial contribution. Simultaneously, with every strategic move they made, they represented themselves as highly intelligent participants in the democratic political process.

Second, they invented a new kind of political group, a bold association of disabled persons demanding respect and inclusion in American society.

Their audacity is surprising given that era's attitudes toward cripples. To resist society's prejudice, they had to engage in public acts of defiance at a time when the president of the United States found it necessary to keep his disability largely hidden. (Longmore & Goldberger, 2000, p. 904)

Bonded by common life experiences as the objects of discrimination, they provided one another with support and friendship, and they elevated one another as valued human beings while working to teach the dominant, nondisabled society to do likewise.

Prior to the research of Paul Longmore (1998; Longmore & Goldberger, 2000), the work of the League was forgotten. Activists of the modern Disability Rights Movement in the 1970s did not profit from the League's groundbreaking thinking and action. Much of the Movement's strategic playbook enacted by disability activists since the 1970s was actually pre-written decades earlier by the pioneers of the League of the Physically Handicapped. The League's Depression Era concept of disabled persons as a minority group seeking dignity and justice foreshadowed the beliefs and efforts of disability rights activists in years to come (Fleischer & Zames, 2011; Longmore & Goldberger, 2000).

DEINSTITUTIONALIZATION OF PERSONS WITH INTELLECTUAL DISABILITIES[1]

"Before the civil rights movement, Black people had to go to the back of the bus to find seating. Many people with disabilities could not even get on the bus. In the 1970s the civil rights movement opened the way for disabled people to integrate into society, to gain control over their lives, to move out of institutions." (Roberts, 1989, p. 231)

After World War II, Americans were convinced that the best place for a person with mental retardation to live was not in his or her own home, not in the community with family, friends, and other citizens. In the two decades after the War, the number of persons with "mental retardation" (now called "intellectual disability") living in large state institutions in the United States rose by sixty-five percent, almost double the increase of the general population of Americans. In 1946, 116,828 persons with mental retardation were incarcerated in institutions. By 1967, the number of persons with mental retardation housed in institutions had grown to 193,188 (Trent, 1994).

In the late 1960s and early 1970s, the opinion of the mental retardation professionals, political leaders, and general public turned against institutional care. Between 1967 and 1988, the number of persons with mental retardation living in large state institutions dropped by more than half. Historian James W. Trent (1994) reported that forty-four large state institutions had completely closed between 1970 and 1994.

Deinstitutionalization was the social movement to close public institutions and training schools that housed thousands of persons with intellectual disabilities, thereby shifting those persons into more integrated, community-based residences. It began with dozens of passionate exposes, muckraking journalistic accounts in newspapers, magazines, books, and later, on television. Starting during World War II and extending into the 1970s, the exposés illuminated the inhumane and often brutal conditions of public institutions, displaying the raw cruelty to the public in shocking words and photos.

Disability studies scholar Steven J. Taylor (2009) has documented the early advocacy work of the cadre of World War II religious objectors who performed alternative national service in large state mental hospitals and training schools. About three thousand men—pacifists largely from "peace churches" such as Mennonites, Quakers, and Brethren—worked in public institutions in the United States as part of the Civilian Public Service (CPS), a government-approved alternative to military service for conscientious objectors (COs).

The institutional conditions these earnest men of faith found were deeply troubling. The wards were overcrowded and understaffed. Often one staff member was responsible for supervising over one hundred disabled persons. The buildings where patients resided were often filthy and run-down. The patients received virtually no treatment, training, or educational services. The care provided to patients was minimal. They frequently lacked the most basic necessities; clothing, decent food, hygiene, safety, privacy, health care, and recreational activities. Staff members controlled the large patient populations with violence, coercion, and physical restraints. Brutality—including killings—was committed by both paid staff members and by so-called "high grade" patients who were often used to monitor, control, and care for the other residents (Taylor, 2009; Trent, 1994).

Led by a group of four men who worked at the Philadelphia State Hospital, the COs worked to reform the institutions. They kept detailed diaries of their experiences, compiling over one thousand accounts from across the country in a single database documenting the atrocious living conditions and mistreatment of patients. They observed that the established professional organizations—the National Committee for Mental Hygiene and the American Psychiatric Association—did not work in an assertive and dedicated way on institution reform. So they founded a new organization called the National Mental Health Foundation devoted to promoting the improvement of the institutions (Taylor, 2009; Trent, 1994).

The writings and activism of the CPS men contributed directly to local newspaper exposes illuminating the intolerable conditions at Eastern State Hospital in Virginia, Mount Pleasant State Hospital in Ohio, Hudson River State Hospital in New York, and many others. Newspapers such as the *Chicago Daily News*, Tulsa's

Daily Oklahoman, and the *San Francisco News*, carried scathing, often heart-wrenching accounts of what it was like to live in filthy, crowded, and brutal institutions.

Journalists Albert Deutsch and Albert Q. Maisel worked closely with the COs, drawing extensively from their massive compilation of diaries. In April, 1946, Deutsch published exposes of the Philadelphia State Hospital and Cleveland State Hospital in New York's *PM* newspaper. He quickly followed this with a larger account in his widely read 1948 book *Shame of the States*. Maisel wrote a May, 1946, article for *Life* magazine that brought the issue in vivid style to a national audience.

The same year CPS men themselves published *Out of Sight, Out of Mind*, a provocative study based on their diaries of working in the institutions during the War. This book prompted coverage by *Time*, *Newsweek*, and local newspapers across the United States (Taylor, 2009; Trent, 1994).

The many vivid exposes and intensive work of the COs did not lead to national reform of state institutions. It resulted in some changes at the local level, the firing of a few hospital and training school superintendents, the improved staffing and conditions at a handful of institutions. Unfortunately, the National Mental Health Foundation was a short-lived, underfunded organization that had little lasting impact. The problem of dehumanizing institutional care continued.

During the 1950s, parents began organizing themselves to work as advocates for the improved treatment of their disabled children. Famous parents of persons with mental retardation wrote high profile books about their experiences, going public with what had traditionally been hidden in the shameful shadows. Books such as acclaimed novelist Pearl Buck's *The Child Who Never Grew* and Dale Evans Rogers's *Angel Unaware* reduced parental stigma and promoted a national dialogue about how to best care for and educate persons with mental retardation. Parents formed the National Association of Parents and Friends of Mentally Retarded Children, the powerful advocacy group now known as The Arc of the United States.

In the 1960s, President John F. Kennedy and his sister Eunice Kennedy Shriver played important roles in the national drive for institutional reform and the improvement of special education. President Kennedy revealed that he had a sister with mental retardation living in a private institution. In 1961, he formed the President's Panel on Mental Retardation. Two years later, he made a speech to Congress in support of legislation to increase funding and improve facilities in state institutions across the country.

> State institutions for the mental retarded are badly underfinanced, understaffed, and overcrowded. The standard of care is in most cases so grossly deficient as to shock the conscience of all who see them. (Taylor, 2009, p. 368)

Almost two decades later, the President's words echoed the writings of the World War II COs and the muckraking journalists.

In 1965, New York Senator Robert Kennedy made unannounced visits to the Willowbrook and Rome State Schools. He immediately made public statements denouncing the inhumane conditions at the two institutions.

> When I visited the institutions for the mentally retarded, and I think, particularly at Willowbrook, that we have a situation that borders on a snake pit. That the children live in filth. That many of our fellow citizens are suffering tremendously because of a lack of attention, lack of imagination, lack of adequate manpower. There's very little future for the children or for those who are in these institutions […] […]. I think all of us are at fault. I think it's long overdue that something be done about it. (Primo & Rivera, 1972)

Although Senator Kennedy called for the entire institution system to be reformed, the condition at the large state institutions did not change.

But two men were inspired by Senator Kennedy's actions: a Boston University professor of special education named Burton Blatt and a young, little-known New York City television reporter named Geraldo Rivera. Both were aware that when public officials visited state institutions, the medical directors often arranged for a deceptively pleasant experience. Wards were cleaned, and residents were washed and clothed. Institution visitors often witnessed an artificial dog-and-pony show that concealed the usual daily misery and mistreatment. So Blatt and Rivera each knew that the only way to capture the truth was through an investigation involving deception.

Burton Blatt hatched a dramatic plan to shine a bright, public light on institutional atrocities. Teaming up with photographer Fred Kaplan, who attached a hidden camera to his belt, Blatt visited the hidden "back wards" of four large state institutions. The secretly filmed photos depicted the deplorable neglect and abuse: countless rows of unattended infants in a room filled with cribs, crowds of naked training school residents standing around with nothing to do, and feces-smeared walls and urine-covered floors. They also took photos at the newer, cleaner Seaside Regional Center. Their book *Christmas in Purgatory* (1966) provided visceral evidence of the profound difference between the common mistreatment and neglect taking place in most institutions and the more positive alternative demonstrated by Seaside.

On his experience visiting the back wards, Blatt commented in unrelenting, distraught honesty,

> Our "Christmas in Purgatory" brought us to the depths of despair. We now have a deep sorrow, one that will not abate until the American people are aware of—and do something about—the treatment of the severely mentally retarded in our state institutions. We have again been caused to realize that "Man's inhumanity to man makes countless thousands mourn." (Blatt & Kaplan, 1966, p. vi)

If only, Blatt hoped aloud, politicians and citizens would care to end the cruelty. If only people cared enough to make the institutions clean, decent, humane places where persons with disabilities could live with some degree of dignity and comfort.

Geraldo Rivera was contacted by a whistleblower, a physician at Willowbrook State School in Staten Island, NY. The doctor had been fired because he encouraged parents to organize to push the institution to improve the conditions and care of their sons and daughters who resided there. Unannounced and without permission, Rivera entered Ward 6 at Willowbrook with a camera crew. He had heard full descriptions of what he would see there.

> The doctor warned me that it would be bad. It was horrible. There was one attendant for perhaps fifty severely and profoundly retarded children. Lying on the floor, naked and smeared with their own feces, they were making a pitiful sound, the kind of mournful wail that is impossible for me to forget. (Primo & Rivera, 1972)

But Rivera was still emotionally overwhelmed. There was no way to be prepared for what he witnessed. As the video camera captured disturbing images, Rivera struggled to describe the depressing power of the experience to his television audience.

> This is what it looked like. This is what it sounded like. But how can I tell about the way it smelled. It smelled of filth. It smelled of disease. And it smelled of death. (Primo & Rivera, 1972)

For perhaps the first time, after many decades of newspaper and magazine exposes providing verbal descriptions and photographs of similar atrocities, Rivera captured institutional wretchedness on video. His 28 minute documentary was aired initially to a large New York City audience, and it was later broadcast nationally. Although viewers could not fully experience the odor that Rivera described, they could witness in a viscerally compelling way the systematic cruelty that institutions were inflicting on persons with mental retardation.

Blatt and Rivera both employed the same strategy in their exposes. First, they showed the horrible conditions in the worst institutions. Then they offered depictions of better, cleaner, more humane institutions. This strategy offered a none-too-subtle moral lesson: Institutions could be reformed, and they could provide ethical and competent care for persons with mental retardation.

But could the institutions really be reformed? Or did the act of segregating a stigmatized population almost inevitably lead to inhumane conditions and treatment?

By the mid-1970s, many institutional reformers were depressed by the lack of change. Burton Blatt no longer believed his own moral lesson. He gave up on reforming institutions. It was a lost cause. Many professionals in the field of mental retardation likewise concluded that institutions, by their very nature, were irredeemable segregated environments of social control and systematic degradation. The public at large and many politicians were also convinced that institutions should either close altogether or should house far fewer persons. The new goal was to close the institutions and move the residents into more "normal" living arrangements in the community (Taylor, 2009).

The advocacy community rallied around a series of powerful and timely ideas articulated by Wolfensberger (1972), a faculty member at Syracuse University, in his book *The Principle of Normalization in Human Services*. Wolfensberger was an ardent crusader who by 1970 "had begun an apostolic campaign to denounce state schools and establish the community as the sole locus of services for retarded citizens" (Trent, 1994, p. 262). Drawing from the work of Danish and Swedish scholars, he preached that persons with mental retardation should be fully integrated into community life. His thinking emphasized the way that institutions cast persons with disabilities into devalued, socially deviant roles in society, thereby perpetuating labeling and dehumanization. He pushed for social service agencies to teach persons with mental retardation how to behave and function in the community while simultaneously creating social roles of dignity and value for them in society.

The practical result of the deinstitutionalization movement was striking. In 1967, state institutions in the United States housed 193, 188 persons with intellectual disabilities. Twenty-one years later, in 1988, only 91, 440 institution residents remained. Forty-four large state institutions closed doors during those years. According to a 2005 study, only 41,214 persons continued to be housed in large state institutions. Nine states no longer operated any large-scale institutions (Nelis & Rizzolo, 2005). The residents were shifted into community-based residential arrangements such as group homes and supported living.

But the movement was not a complete success. Emptying out the giant state institutions did not always translate immediately or easily in community integration and full acceptance. In many states, large state institutions were replaced by smaller ones with over sixteen residents (Trent, 1994). Local communities often fought against the creation of group homes or supported living arrangements, rejecting the presence of disabled citizens in their neighborhoods.

WINNING THE GREATEST LAW: SECTION 504

> Section 504 of the Rehabilitation Act of 1973 has been hailed as the first major civil rights legislation for disabled people. In contrast to earlier legislation that provides or extends benefits to disabled persons, it establishes full social participation as a civil right and represents a transformation of federal disability policy. (Scotch, 2001, p. 3)

To a member of the House of Representatives or the United States Senate, the Rehabilitation Act of 1973 probably seemed to be an uncontroversial piece of legislative business. The bill provided federal funding for the continuation and expansion of a variety of vocational programs for persons with disabilities. Essentially, federal benefits for disabled Americans were funded and carried forward with slight modification.

But there is more to this story. Much more. A very brief passage in the bill, a single sentence called Section 504, was not only completely new. Varela (1983, p. 41) observed that "'504' would become the rallying cry as important to disabled activists as the phrase 'black power' had been to civil rights activists a decade earlier." Section 504 was revolutionary.

In brief, almost cryptic wording, Section 504 said:

> No otherwise handicapped individual in the United States, as defined in section 7, shall, solely by reason of his handicap, be excluded from participation in, be denied the benefits of, or be subjected to discrimination under any program or activity receiving Federal financial assistance. (Scotch, 2001, p. 4)

Neither the federal government nor any organization receiving federal funds—including state and local governments, state universities, and the public schools—could engage in acts of discrimination against persons based on their disabilities. For the first time ever, the federal government took decisive action to stop discrimination against person with disabilities in the many organizations and agencies using federal money.

One might imagine that a 180 degree turn in federal disability policy could only occur after intense lobbying, passionate arguments, and a dramatic moment when a majority of national lawmakers suddenly saw the light. After many late nights of floor debate, illuminating social analyses, and powerful personal testimony explaining how people with disabilities in America suffer widespread discrimination, the normally unyielding lawmakers had an epiphany. We can even imagine a Jimmy Stewart character (from *Mr. Smith Goes to Washington*) making a barnburner of a speech, his voice raspy, and his sweaty hair flopping over his strained forehead. Suddenly the Senators understood, and they took the right action.

But that is not what happened at all. It was very much the opposite.

Section 504 was not discussed or introduced in any of the many committee meetings and hearing leading up to passage of the 1973 Rehabilitation Act. It was not debated on the floor of the House or the Senate. Not a single member of Congress or the Senate provided any reaction, pro or con, to this new policy. It also escaped the notice of the accountants and financial analysts who examine federal legislation for possible budgetary implications of policy changes. Prior to passage of the legislation, neither the House nor the Senate estimated any additional cost to the government for implementation of Section 504 (Scotch, 2001).

The lack of attention received by Section 504 stood in striking contrast to its importance. Section 504 would completely change the tone and direction of federal disability policy in the United States. For the first time ever, the national government offered not just programs of education and training or financial benefits for disabled persons who were out of work. Certainly, these kinds of programs were useful. But they fell short of addressing the central problem that persons with disabilities faced every day, the pervasive discrimination and prejudice that excluded disabled Americans from full participation in all avenues of society. For the first time ever, the government identified unfairness and bias as widespread political problems that harmed disabled citizens. And it offered a civil rights policy, an anti-discrimination law, as a solution (Fleischer & Zames, 2011; Scotch, 2001; Shapiro, 1994; Stroman, 2003).

John Nagle, chief of the Washington office of the National Federation of the Blind, a highly active lobbying group in support of passage of the Act, described Section 504 as a game-changer for disabled Americans.

> It establishes that because a man is blind or deaf or without legs, he is not less a citizen, that his rights of citizenship are not revoked or diminished because he is disabled. Most important of all [...] (it) creates a legal remedy when a disabled man is denied his rightful citizenship rights because of his disability. It gives him a legal basis for recourse to the courts that he may seek to remove needless barriers, unnecessary obstacles and unjustified barricades that impede or prevent him from functioning fully and in full equality with all others. (Scotch, 2001, p. 55)

This first national disability anti-discrimination law would later serve as the basis for the broader 1990 ADA.

How did Section 504—this quiet revolution—sneak its way into the Rehabilitation Act of 1973?

In 1972, Senator Hubert Humphrey and Congressman Charles Vanik proposed an amendment to the Civil Rights Act of 1964 that would expand the protection from discrimination based on race, color, and national origin to also include physical and mental disabilities. The Civil Rights Act of 1964 was a triumphant victory of the African-American civil rights movement. The Act prohibited racial or ethnic discrimination in employment and public accommodations. Title VI of the Act outlawed discrimination in any programs receiving federal dollars (Scotch, 2001).

The Humphrey-Vanik bill of 1972 made no headway in Washington. It was never brought up for a vote in the Senate or Congress. But the idea of a disability rights law derived greatly from Title VI of the Civil Rights Act was picked up by congressional staffers who worked on revising the 1973 Rehabilitation Act. Late in the process, after most of the committee hearings about the Rehabilitation Act had already passed, congressional staff members added the single line to the bill.

At a meeting of congressional staff members working on a mark-up of the bill, a concern was expressed: what happens to disabled persons after they receive vocational rehabilitation services? Even if the system worked perfectly, the most job-ready disabled person still had to face the prejudicial hiring practices and stigmatizing attitudes prevalent in American workplaces. Roy Millenson, a staff member for Senator Jacob Javits, ran to his office and returned with Title VI of the Civil Rights Act. It would serve as their guide. The group crafted language based on that provision and inserted it into Rehabilitation Act (Scotch, 2001).

While the story of the passage of Section 504 lacks Hollywood style drama and action, the story of what happened between the law's passage and enactment is filled with explosive conflict and political strategy. Strangely, in the case of Section 504, the real fight took place over the enactment of the law after it was signed by the President.

When a federal bill is passed, it is then given to a government agency for the development of the regulations that guide the implementation of the law. Section 504 was unlike any other element of the Rehabilitation Act. Rather than sending it to the Rehabilitation Services Agency, the administrative body that managed the delivery of vocational services and benefits, 504 was handed to the Office of Civil Rights (OCR) in the Department of Health, Education, and Welfare (HEW). The OCR lawyers and staff members had the challenging task of writing the policies and rules for the enforcement of Section 504. Once the regulations were written and approved, standard procedure called for publication followed by a brief period of public comment. After revisions and approval by the HEW Secretary, the regulations would be finalized through publication in the Federal Register (Scotch, 2001).

The process of writing and approving the Section 504 regulations stretched out over three and a half years. The original bill was signed by President Richard Nixon in September, 1973. The final regulations detailing how the law would be put into practice by the HEW under the Carter Administration were published in the Federal Register in May, 1977. The tortuous path from passage to enactment involved a long series of delaying tactics by the HEW heads—Secretary David Mathews and Secretary Joseph Califano—of two presidential administrations. A coalition of staff members in the Office of Civil Rights of the HEW and leaders of a number of disability advocacy groups conscientiously pushed the stalled regulation approval process forward. In the end, it took dramatic, forceful action by disability activists to get the landmark law enacted (Fleischer & Zames, 2011; Scotch, 2001; Shapiro, 1994; Stroman, 2003).

In June 1975, after repeated delays in enacting Section 504, a Howard University law student named James Cherry and the Action League for Physically Handicapped Adults teamed up with Georgetown University Law Professor Victor Kramer and his students to begin legal action against the HEW Secretary David Mathews. They filed a lawsuit in federal court in February, 1976, seeking to force Mathews to release the final regulations immediately. In defense of the slow timeline, HEW claimed that they were not required by law to issue any regulations. Judge John Smith of the U. S. District Court ordered Secretary Mathews to produce the necessary regulations. Despite the court order, the Secretary took no action (Fleischer & Zames, 2011; Scotch, 2001).

As the many months of delay dragged on, disability activists were in close communication with both one another and with OCR staff members and congressional aides, constantly strategizing about how to move the regulations forward. Advocacy groups for the blind, the deaf, and persons with physical disabilities came together in a cross-disability alliance, working for a common cause.

For many years, the President's Committee on the Employment of the Handicapped (PCEH) had been a relatively apolitical group that held an annual conference in Washington to discuss federal rehabilitation programs. In the early 1970s, the PCEH became a crucible for the growth of a national, cross-disability group alliance and the radicalization of disability advocates. Led by activists such as Eunice Fiorito and Judy Heumann of Disabled in Action (DIA) of New York City, the meetings became an opportunity to organize, educate, and strategize for a national disability agenda on behalf of all persons with disabilities.

After President Nixon vetoed an early version of the Rehabilitation Act in 1972, the DIA organized a demonstration on the Lincoln Memorial, a symbolic act that equated the freeing of the slaves with the independence and access sought by disabled citizens. They collaborated with a disabled Viet Nam veteran's group to occupy Nixon's New York campaign headquarters. The 1973 PCEH conference spawned another protest in support of the Rehabilitation Act. Hundreds of disabled and nondisabled protesters marched down Connecticut Avenue demanding passage of the law.

When the PCEH held their annual meeting in Washington, DC in 1974, Heumann and Fiorito organized workshop sessions in the lobby of the Washington Hilton. Away from the political mildness of the official meetings, this unauthorized, side conference involved over 150 participants in frank discussions of the social issues that disabled persons confronted every day. People with a variety of different disabilities, historically divided by organizations and interests, found themselves sharing perspectives and uniting over common concerns (Fleischer & Zames, 2011; Scotch, 2001).

The result was the formation of a powerful, cross-disability organization called the American Coalition of Citizens with Disabilities (ACCD). The ACCD would prove to be an important political force in the battle over Section 504 of the Rehabilitation Act of 1973 (Fleischer & Zames, 2011).

In late 1975, Judy Heumann went to work for the Berkeley (CA) Center for Independent Living (CIL). There she collaborated with Berkeley CIL founder Ed Roberts and Ann Rosewater of the Children's Defense Fund, spreading the word through the ACCD and other networks of people with disabilities about the battle for the enactment of Section 504. Berkeley became a hothouse of political strategy in the movement to pressure the HEW to issue the 504 regulations.

When President Jimmy Carter took office in early 1977, the sluggish approval process was handed over to a new administration. Rather than approving the regulations, new HEW Secretary Joseph Califano ordered yet another round of legal reviews, again setting back the clock for enactment of the law. Disability activists viewed his actions as just another in a long line of excessive postponements. In March, the ACCD board of directors voted to issue a public demand to Secretary Califano that he issue the regulations as written by April 4. If Califano did not issue the regulations, the ACCD threatened to stage nonviolent protests at multiple HEW offices, including those in Washington, DC and San Francisco (Fleischer & Zames, 2011; Pelka, 1997; Scotch, 2001; Shapiro, 1994; Stroman, 2003).

When Califano took over as HEW Secretary, disability activists thought that the long road of the 504 regulations would soon come to an end. President Carter had made strong statements in favor of Section 504 during the presidential campaign. He even criticized the Ford administration for moving too slowly in issuing the regulations. After weeks of meetings with the Secretary Califano, disability advocates were disappointed that the Secretary wanted to pause in order to further study the proposed regulations (Fleischer & Zames, 2011; Scotch, 2001).

A group of disability community leaders met with Califano on April 4 in a last minute effort to change his mind. Television crews filled the room. The Secretary held his ground. He said that he would not sign the regulations, citing the need for additional reviews. Under the public eye of television cameras, the disabled advocates stormed out of the meeting in protest (Scotch, 2001).

On April 5, 1977, disability rights protests took place at nine HEW offices around the country. Disability rights leader Ed Roberts (1989, p. 235) noted the significance of the fact that these demonstrators included "(p)eople with many kinds of disabilities—deafness, blindness, cerebral pals, spinal cord injuries, mental retardation, mental illness, and multiple disabilities" in a unified cross-disability alliance. Perhaps unlike any time prior, disabled citizens from many categories of impairment and corners of the country came together for a common cause.

A group of about 120 disability activists led by Judy Heumann took over the San Francisco HEW building. A smaller group of approximately forty demonstrators occupied the agency's offices in Washington, DC. The protestors demanded that the Carter administration issue the necessary regulations to enact Section 504 of the Rehabilitation Act of 1973 (Fleischer & Zames, 2011; Scotch, 2001).

In the Washington HEW office, Secretary Califano shut down the telephones and ordered that no food be allowed into the protesters. The activists ended their brief protest after twenty-eight hours (Fleischer & Zames, 2011; Shapiro, 1994).

The San Francisco sit-in became the main stage of the action, the final stand in the battle for the anti-discrimination law. As journalist Joseph Shapiro has documented fully in his book *No Pity*, many of the disabled protesters with complex medical needs risked their bodies and safety for the cause.

> Some of the most severely disabled protesters were literally putting their lives on the line, since they risked their health to be without catheters, back-up ventilators, and attendants who would move them every few hours to prevent bed sores, or who, with their hands would cleans impacted bowels every few days. None of these deprivations, however, deterred the demonstrators. Instead, they backfired. The protesters' success, in the face of forceful opposition, only bolstered their euphoria and determination. (Shapiro, 1994, p. 66)

The inconveniences and dangers only seemed to further unify and embolden the demonstrators.

These were the seasoned disability activists of the Berkeley CIL, a highly organized group of strategic political actors with close ties to liberal organizations and politicians in the Bay area. A host of community groups and local leaders rallied to their support, supplying food, mattresses, medical care, and showers. Contributors represented the widest possible variety of American cultural and political institutions, including McDonald's restaurants, the California Department of Health Services, the Delancy House drug treatment program, United Cerebral Palsy, local gay activists, Easter Seals, Safeway supermarkets, and the Black Panthers.

Labor unions, churches, and synagogues rallied behind the protesters, preparing meals from the donated food. They treated the protesters to a festive Easter dinner of meatloaf, green beans, and mashed potatoes.

Local politicians pitched in. Congressman Philip Burton arranged for the installation of pay phones for the protesters to use. California Director of Rehabilitation Ed Roberts, the same man who founded the Berkeley CIL, made a rousing speech to the crowd from his wheelchair. Television and newspaper coverage portrayed the disability protesters and their cause in a positive light (Fleischer & Zames, 2011; Shapiro, 1994).

After twelve days, Gene Eidelberg, an official for the HEW, testified in a congressional hearing that Secretary Califano was working on a number of changes to the Section 504 regulations that would substantially weaken the law. Among these planned modifications was the removal of the requirement that public schools make buildings and classrooms accessible to students with disabilities. When this news circulated among the San Francisco protesters, their resolve to see the sit-in through to the finish was further strengthened (Shapiro, 1994).

On April 28, 1977, Secretary Joseph Califano of the Carter Administration bowed to the overwhelming public pressure. He signed the regulations for Section 504, thereby enacting the law passed in 1973. The Secretary also signed the regulations to implement the 1975 Education for All Handicapped Children Act, the beginning of federally mandated public education for all students with disabilities. Judy Heumann and the group of stalwart activists had staged the most successful disability rights protest in American history. Almost half of the initial group of 120 protesters remained in the HEW offices for twenty-five straight days, the longest sit-in ever in a federal building (Fleischer & Zames, 2011; Shapiro, 1994).

When asked why the protest was successful, ACCD leader Frank Bowe quoted the words of an advisor to Martin Luther King: "People think that revolutions begin with injustices. They don't. A revolution begins with hope." Bowe concluded, "(T)he reason disabled people came together and demonstrated as they did in the Spring of that year was because *they had hope*" (Fleischer & Zames, 2011, p. 55, italics original).

"CHARTING A NEW WAY OF LIFE": INDEPENDENT LIVING MOVEMENT

Ed Roberts contracted polio at age fourteen. During his high school years, he spent eighteen hours per day lying on his back in an enormous iron lung that pressured his lungs to inhale and exhale oxygen. When he first attempted to enroll at the University of California, Berkeley, the California Department of Rehabilitation turned him down, saying that his impairment was too severe. He was deemed not worthy of their financial investment. But he convinced Rehab to pay for his education, and he arranged for the reluctant University administration to house him on campus in Cowell Hospital. He enrolled in 1962.

A year later, Roberts was joined in Cowell Hospital by John Hessler, a man with quadriplegia. By 1967, when Roberts was a graduate student in political science, Cowell housed twelve students with physical disabilities. They called themselves the Rolling Quads, and they made history.

Before the experiment housing disabled students in the infirmary at Berkeley, the most notable prior effort by a university to provide housing and support to disabled students had occurred at the University of Illinois. After World War II, Illinois created a program to enroll war veterans with disabilities. By 1962, the program had grown to include 163 students, 101 using wheelchairs. The campus featured ramps and curb-cuts. The disabled students had their own fraternity, annual magazine, and wheelchair sports leagues. But the program was run by the University. Although it created greater access to higher education, it was not a program operated by disabled persons for disabled persons.

Living and studying in the Berkeley hotbed of political activity, yet simultaneously experiencing numerous obstacles to their own freedom, Roberts, Hessler, and their University of California comrades came up with a new idea.

> In late night bull sessions on the hospital floor, Roberts and his friends, in their wheelchairs and iron lungs, would strategize constantly about breaking down the barriers they faced—from classrooms they could not get into to their lack of transportation around town—and dissect the protests for self-determination of minority students. (Shapiro, 1994, p. 47–48)

They learned from observing the strategy and philosophy of the campus civil rights protesters. They fashioned a new way of thinking about disability and the kinds of lives that disabled persons could live. They united as members of a cultural minority group to take control of their lives.

In 1969, the Rolling Quads received a federal grant for $81,000 and University funding for $2,000 to start the Physically Disabled Students Program (PDSP). The PDSP was an anti-dropout program dedicated to keeping minority students—in this case, disabled students—in school. But it did so in a unique way that combined the strategies of a self-help group with community organizing. The PDSP was managed and staffed by disabled students for disabled students. The services they provided matched the expressed needs of the students. The PDSP

- helped students find accessible off campus housing
- organized a pool of attendants to provide personal care
- created a wheelchair repair workshop
- modified cars and vans for wheelchair access
- provided advocacy and support for dealing with the many service bureaucracies, including the University and state and federal agencies
- offered peer counseling and financial advice
- supplied readers for the blind

In contrast to the usual model of rehabilitation, the orientation of the program was not to seek improvements in an individual's physical or psychological abilities but to provide the kinds of practical support that improved participation and access. As journalist Joseph Shapiro (1994, p. 51) observes, "Independence was measured not by the tasks one could perform without assistance but by the quality of one's life with help."

The program often provided services to disabled people in the community, regardless of whether they were enrolled in the University or not. Over time, Ed Roberts and the leaders of the PDSP soon saw a need to develop a new program that had a larger impact on the Berkeley community beyond the campus. Roberts (1989, p. 236) later explained that "a grave problem remained: Once graduated, where could these disabled people live—or work? How could they effectively move about their communities?"

In 1972, Roberts and his colleagues founded the Center for Independent Living (CIL), the first independent living center in the United States. They took the PDSP philosophy and practices into the community of Berkeley. The goal of the CIL was to facilitate

> active participation in society—working, having a home, raising a family, and generally sharing in the joys and responsibilities of community life. Independent living meant freedom from isolation and institutionalization; it meant the ability to choose where to live, how to

> live, and how to carry out the activities of daily living that most able-bodied people take for granted. It meant taking responsibility for political action and charting a new way of life. (Roberts, 1989, p. 237)

Similar independent living centers, each creating this new way of life whereby disabled persons took greater control of their own destinies, sprouted up around the country. Max Starkloff founded Paraquad in St. Louis in 1970 (Brown, 2000). Former patients of the Texas Institute for Rehabilitation and Research started a center in Houston in 1972. The Boston Center for Independent Living began in 1974 (Varela, 1983). Founded in 1982, the National Coalition of Independent Living Centers became the national organization unifying the hundreds of centers across the country.

The Independent Living Movement was an organized, multi-dimensional effort by disabled persons to take control of the variety of available services and supports in order to reach their goal of living and working in the community. It was a direct response to a number of features of the rehabilitation system in post-World War II United States as created and managed by non-disabled, medical professionals. The rehabilitation system often placed disabled persons in segregated residential facilities such as nursing homes, hospitals, and institutions. It also operated under the misguided assumption that disabled persons could only live in the community, go to school, and hold gainful employment if they gained many of the functional skills of non-disabled persons. This resulted in pervasive low expectations for what disabled persons could achieve and the quality of life they could experience (Berkowitz, 1987; Dejong, 1983; Roberts, 1989; Shapiro, 1994).

Ed Roberts (1989) has written that the success of independent living centers is due to their strong, clear focus on four specific goals. First and foremost is *the principle of self-determination*. "Disabled people must be involved in the development of services to meet their needs" (Roberts, 1989, p. 238). Disabled persons must be at the center of the management, governance, and staffing of the centers. Nondisabled allies serve primarily in support roles.

Secondly, all centers must hold to the highest expectations for the lives of persons with disabilities. They must publically express and enact an unbending belief in the "potential of people with even the most severe disabilities to live independent, productive lives with dignity and respect" (Roberts, 1989, p. 239). This is the counter-cultural focus of independent living centers, pushing back against the regressive tendency to assume that disability demands a less active or less fulfilling life.

Third is the role of centers in political engagement in the issues of the day. They serve as the leading advocacy organizations in the daily fight for the rights of disabled persons. Centers do more than organize and provide services. They must combat discrimination in its many forms and seek equality of opportunity for disabled persons.

Finally, independent living centers serve and support all persons with all disabilities, regardless of age, type of disability, or other social characteristics. The centers are the place where all disabled people may unite in order to support and nurture one another.

Irving Zola, a disabled scholar who is often viewed as the founder of the field of disability studies in the United States, once told a story that provided great insight into why the Independent Living Movement happened and why it was an important strand of the larger Disability Rights Movement. He entered the shop of a non-disabled prosthetist, a man who spent over fifty years designing and fitting prosthetics for persons with disabilities. The prosthetist noticed that Zola used a cane to walk due to having polio earlier in his life. He handed Zola a cane and asked him to try it out.

"It seems solid enough," Zola replied.

"Now watch this," said the prosthetist. He took the cane and pushed a little button on the handle. A twelve inch blade popped out of the cane.

Enthusiastically, the prosthetist brandished another cane, "This one is even handier. Look!" Again, he pushed a small button. The cane quickly transformed into an impressive iron black jack, a club weapon. "You know," the man explained, "in times like these, with so much crime in the streets, this self-defense cane should come in pretty handy."

"Yes," Zola replied sarcastically, "particularly if the thief lets me lean on him for support while I dismantle my cane" (Zola, 1983, p. 55).

What the experienced prosthetist, a non-disabled professional who had worked with people with artificial limbs for most of his lifetime, missed was the fact that Zola needed his cane for balance. If he raised his cane from the floor to push a button or to swing it at a street criminal, he would fall down.

Zola told this story to illustrate the fact that even highly knowledgeable and experienced disability service professionals—physicians, occupational therapists, rehabilitation therapists—who work closely with disabled persons have a very limited understanding of what people with disabilities actually need in order to live their lives. Moreover, the persons who most fully and intimately understand those needs are persons who have disabilities.

People with disabilities knew best. They needed to unite, work together, and forge their own future together. That is what Independent Living Centers were and continue to be all about (Berkowitz, 1987; Zola, 1983).

WINNING THE GREATEST LAW, PART 2: THE AMERICANS WITH DISABILITIES ACT

> "The time has come for the Senate to send a loud, clear message across this country: Individuals with disabilities, no less than all other Americans, are entitled to an equal opportunity to participate in the American dream. It is time for that dream to become a reality." Senator Orrin G. Hatch, as quoted by Young. (2010, p. 3)

At 10:00 AM, on July 26, 1990, a crowd of about three thousand dignitaries and disability advocates gathered on the White House south lawn to celebrate the signing of the ADA. As President George H. W. Bush signed the legislation into law, he called out, "Let the shameful wall of exclusion finally come tumbling down" (Young, 2010, p. 147).

The ADA of 1990 is a comprehensive anti-bias law prohibiting discrimination on the basis of disability in four far-reaching areas of community life; employment, public services, public accommodations, and telecommunications. It effectively took Section 504 of the Rehabilitation Act of 1973 to the next level, encompassing not only facilities and organizations receiving federal funding but private entities. It is the greatest achievement to date for the Disability Rights Movement, a public admission from the federal government that disabled citizens have suffered political oppression for generations and a sweeping civil rights law intended to decrease that oppression with the legal requirements of equal and fair treatment for disabled citizens (Colker, 2005; Fleischer & Zames, 2011; Weicker, 1991).

The "first victory" in the fight for the ADA, according to historian Jonathan M. Young (2010), was the defeat of President Ronald Reagan's attempt to limit the federal government's power to enforce regulations in three important areas of disability policy: Section 504, Public Law 94–142 guaranteeing an education to all students with disabilities, and the Architectural and Transportation Barriers Compliance Board (ATBCB). Reagan initiated the Task Force of Regulatory Relief in 1981 in an effort to reign in the welfare state, put a damper on the reach of governmental agencies, and reduce social program spending. Among the over 150 different pieces of government regulatory activity target by the Task Force were Section 504, ATBCB, and the federal special education law. Disability advocates understandably feared that the conservative administration would diminish these three government mechanisms that assured equal access for disabled persons.

C. Boyden Gray, chief counsel to Vice President George H. W. Bush, was selected to run the Task Force. Gray had no experience with disability policy. But he had spent over a decade as bridge partner with his close friend Evan Kemp, Jr., a lawyer who ran the Disability Rights Center, an organization focusing primarily on issues of employment discrimination. The Center also served an educational function by providing stories and photos to news organizations about activities and events in the disability rights movement. Kemp had been a strong critic of the Jerry Lewis Muscular Dystrophy Association Telethon, arguing that it portrayed disabled persons as stereotyped objects of pity.

In March, 1982, a crucial recommendation of the Task Force was leaked to the disability rights community. The Task Force was planning on allowing recipients of federal grants to calibrate the financial cost of a Section 504 accommodation in relationship to the perceived social value of the disabled person involved. If the person had a severe disability or an impairment with greater social stigma, then the accommodation could be avoided due to the lack of social value of the individual. A number of national disability advocacy organizations—including the National Council on Independent Living (NCIL) and Disability Rights and Education Fund (DREDF) led by Robert Funk and Pat Wright—worked closely with Kemp to fashion a strategy for opposition.

Disability rights leaders organized a letter-writing campaign. A deluge of over 40,000 letters from parents and advocates opposing the proposed modifications in policy drowned the White House. Justin Dart, called the father of the ADA by many in the disability community, traveled the country, holding public hearings on the recommendations. Thousands of disabled persons and parents of people with disabilities testified against the Task Force proposals. Dart, the pied piper of disability rights, cultivated a groundswell of grassroots energy in communities across the nation (Fay & Pelka, 2002).

Ultimately, it was the relationship between card partners Kemp and Gray that made the difference. Kemp convinced Gray to oppose the Task Force recommendations. Based on Gray's position and the public opposition, the Reagan administration dropped the proposed regulatory changes. The disability community had risen up to defeat a conservative White House.

Further, that early victory created alliances between the disability community and the Reagan administration that would be important in the days to come. Gray and Vice President Bush became highly interested and knowledgeable students of disability rights issues. When Bush spoke to disability groups, he tapped Kemp to help him write his speeches. Later, as President, Bush would become a crucial supporter of the ADA.

The beginning of the piece of legislation that ultimately became the ADA was a pair of reports written by the National Council on the Handicapped (later renamed the National Council on Disability, the NCD). The NCD was founded in 1984 by Congress with an initial charge of reviewing all federal programs related to disability. The goal of this new committee, working under the conservative ideology of the Reagan administration, was to propose ways for the federal government to shift disabled citizens off dependence on costly government programs toward employment and social independence. Republican Congressman Steve Bartlett of Texas told the Council, "You are to advise Congress in a whole new approach, a whole new concept on how to decrease dependence and increase independence" (Young, 2010, p. 43).

In 1986, the NCD issued a groundbreaking report titled *Toward Independence* that included a bold recommendation for a new civil rights law safeguarding persons with disabilities. Council leader Justin Dart once again criss-crossed America, holding consumer forums in every state, gathering personal accounts from disabled persons about their experiences of prejudice. Arlene Mayerson (1991, p. 4) of DREDF observed, "Throughout the states, individuals with disabilities repeatedly cited discrimination as the main obstacle to full participation in the community." The NCD's analysis was filled with and driven by the experiences of everyday people and the work of activists seeking change in their local communities. The NCD further developed a grassroots network of local disability advocates around the nation to serve as advisors and political foot-soldiers in the upcoming push for passage of the ADA.

The 1986 Council report carefully combined an equity rationale that would appeal to liberals with the conservative priorities of decreasing government expenditures and fostering individual responsibility. The overall goal of such a new law would be to "reduce barriers to opportunity and independence for people with disabilities, allowing more people with disabilities to remove themselves from Federal aid programs by achieving self-sufficiency and independence" (NCD, 1986, p. 24). Brilliantly, the Council report wrapped a civil rights solution in conservative themes of self-reliance and independence (Bagenstos, 2003).

The NCD's 1988 report *On the Threshold of Independence* again made the case for a comprehensive, federal civil rights law. But this second publication added supportive data from the U.S. Census and two Louis Harris and Company polls to dramatically illustrate the impact of widespread discrimination and exclusion on the lives of disabled Americans. The census and Harris data offered an alarming picture:

- Half of all persons with disabilities had an annual income of $15,000 or less. Among non-disabled persons, only one fourth had incomes in that low category.
- Forty percent of disabled adults did not graduate from high school. This was three times the rate for non-disabled adults.
- Two-thirds of working age adults with disabilities was unemployed. This stunning level of unemployment was contradicted by other data indicating that "(o)verwhelming majorities of managers" gave "disabled employees a good or excellent rating on their overall job performance" (NCD, 1988, p. 34). Moreover, seventy-five percent of workplace hiring managers said that the costs of employing a disabled worker were about the same as employing non-disabled workers.

- Disabled persons were three times more likely than non-disabled persons to never eat out at a restaurant. Almost two thirds of disabled persons had not gone to the movies in the last year.

The Harris poll concluded that "Americans with disabilities are uniquely underprivileged and disadvantaged. They are much poorer, much less well educated, and have less social life, have fewer amenities, and have a lower level of satisfaction than other Americans" (Mayerson, 1991, p. 4).

The final poll question asked disabled persons concerned whether legal protections should be extended to halt discrimination against them. "Three out of every four (seventy-five percent) disabled persons believe that civil rights laws that protect minorities against discrimination should also protect them" (NCD, 1988, p. 37). The poll data demonstrated that the consequences of social barriers to participation were significant, and a growing consensus about the appropriate remedy was emerging among disabled Americans.

Drawing from basic framework of *On the Threshold of Independence*, Senator Lowell Weicker (R-CT) and Congressman Tony Coelho (D-CA) introduced the first ADA in the United States House and Senate in April, 1988. As is often the case with politicians devoted to supporting the disability community, both Weicker and Coelho had personal experiences with disability. Weicker had a son with Down Syndrome. Coelho had been rejected in his application to become a Roman Catholic priest due to his epilepsy. Both played important roles in shepherding the legislation through the maze of congressional committees and partisan conflicts (Colker, 2005; Davis; 2015; Young, 2010).

No action was taken by Congress on initial version of the ADA. But the National Council on Disability, the disability community, and congressional sponsors used the introduction of the bill as an opportunity to educate representatives and galvanize community support. When Weicker lost his Senate seat in the 1988 elections, Iowa freshman Senator Tom Harkin leaped in enthusiastically to carry the baton as Senate sponsor.

National disability organizations, such as the Spina Bifida Association, United Cerebral Palsy, the National Easter Seal Society, and many others lobbied the Senate and Congress, informing elected representatives and their staffs about disability issues and the legislation. Although these organizations had traditionally been rivals in competing for funding, they worked together on this common effort.

On the home front, Justin Dart and Mary Golden of the Disability Rights Education and Defense Fund were the captains of the bottom-up effort, mobilizing the disability community in large cities and small towns from coast to coast (Fay & Pelka, 2002; Young, 2010).

> Between 1988 and 1990 Justin Dart chaired a total of 63 forums in all fifty states, Guam, and Puerto Rico, with over 7,000 people in attendance overall [...]. While traveling throughout the country, Dart collected upwards of 5,000 documents and tape recordings detailing discrimination, offering proposals, and urging passage of the ADA. (Young, 2010, p. 64)

Dart and Golden delivered boxes of testimonials to Congress, often presenting naïve representatives with the first evidence of disability discrimination they had ever known.

The election of President George H. W. Bush in 1988 was pivotal in the campaign for ADA. Two days before his inauguration, Bush vowed to support the passage of the legislation.

> I said during the campaign that disabled people have been excluded for far too long from the mainstream of American life [...]. One step that I have discussed will be action on the Americans with Disabilities Act in order, in simple fairness, to provide the disabled with the same rights afforded other, afforded other minorities. (Young, 2010, p. 77)

President Bush's advocacy for the ADA sent a strong message to Republicans in the House and Senate. Senators Harkin and Ted Kennedy (D-MA), working with Tony Coelho, led the way for the Democrats. The White House's endorsement was augmented by the support of Senators Orrin Hatch (R-Utah) and Robert Dole (R-Kansas) on the Republican side (Colker, 2005; Young, 2010).

Davis (2015) describes the intense and complex internal struggle between the White House, members of Congress and the Senate, congressional staff members, and disability rights advocates. Republicans were pressured by the business community to soften the requirements for accommodations and employment under the fear that bus lines, restaurants, and movie theaters would have to spend large sums of money on architectural modifications. Democrats were pushed by the disability community to hold firm to the anti-discrimination intent of the law while refusing to allow any single disability group (Deaf, Blind, etc.) to be short-changed. Ultimately, in a way rarely seen in current times, the Democrats and Republicans compromised to pass the legislation.

The final law, as signed by President Bush in July, 1990, contained a series of primary provisions designed to shift disabled persons from segregation, stigma, and second-class citizenship into the mainstream of American life (Davis, 2015; Mayerson, 1991; Colker, 2005):

- Employers, both public and private, are not allowed to discriminate against a person with a disability "in regard to job application procedures, the hiring, advancement, or discharge of employees, employee compensation, job training, and other terms, conditions and privileges of employment" (Colker, 2005, p. 19).

- Any public program or service may not discriminate on the basis of disability. Access to and participation in public programs and activities (including transportation such as railroads, busses, and planes) may not be denied to persons with disabilities. This expanded the reach of Section 504 to include branches of government not receiving federal dollars.
- All public accommodations—including restaurants, hotels, stores, and places of recreation—must provide for the "full and equal enjoyment" of their facilities, services, and activities. Any business or organization open to the public must not discriminate against disabled persons. Auxiliary aids or services must be provided as long as they do not "fundamentally alter the nature of the program or cause an undue financial burden" (Mayerson, 1991, p. 7).
- For existing buildings, architectural barriers must be removed as long the action is "easily accomplishable without much difficulty or expense" (Mayerson, 1991, p. 8). New construction, with some exceptions for smaller buildings, must be fully accessible.

Taken together, the various sub-sections of the ADA constitute a comprehensive law protecting persons with disabilities from unfair treatment and exclusion.

In 2008, the Americans with Disabilities Amendments Act was passed. The original ADA was often misunderstood by the courts. In many cases, judges were confused by the three-part definition of disability, thereby leading to poor enforcement of the law. The Amendments Act simplified and clarified the definition of disability so that judges would not get tangled up in technical questions about what constitutes a disability (Davis, 2015).

WORK TO BE DONE

Ideally, this chapter would end on a resounding note of triumph due to the passage of the ADA. But that would be less than honest.

Although the ADA stands as a powerful political statement about the inclusive and just intent of the American government and people, many scholars have lamented the biased and incompetent implementation of the law by federal judges. A number of studies of trial data have concluded that plaintiffs in ADA cases lose over ninety percent of the time, an incredibly low success rate by comparison to antidiscrimination suits filed under other civil rights statutes (Colker, 1999, 2005; Krieger, 2003; Mezey, 2005; O'Brien, 2001).

Trial judges and court of appeals judges have generally interpreted the law through the same stigma-burdened *ideology of ability* (Siebers, 2008) that fuels segregated classrooms and half-hearted efforts at inclusion in the public schools. Repeatedly, federal judges have issued summary judgments—typically a very rare move by a justice—halting trials before jury deliberations, ruling that plaintiffs do not even qualify as having a disability. Although the ADA has a broad and flexible definition of disability designed to include the wide variety of persons with impairments or serious health conditions, the courts have framed disability very narrowly, habitually preventing plaintiffs from receiving the benefits of the law (Locke, 1997; Colker, 2005).

For Americans with disabilities, the heightened expectations created by passage of the law were later dashed by the realities of the misguided application by federal judges.

> "[...] many members of the disability community have grown disappointed in the judicial implementation of the law. They believe that, largely as a result of the interpretation of the statute by federal court judges—in contradiction of Congress's intent—the ADA has failed to achieve the goals they envisioned. (Mezey, 2005, p. 166)

Sadly and ironically, disabled persons have often been excluded from the legal protections of the magnificent law passed in their name.

We can only conclude that the remarkable, hard-won gains of the Disability Rights Movement have not resulted in a final victory. There is no glorious moment when advocates and activists can simply rest, knowing that the game is won and the final destination has been successfully reached. As disability rights activist Arlene Mayerson (1991, p. 8) has encouraged, "We must all come together to make the vision of ADA a reality." There is still much work to be done to realize that vision in our communities and in our schools.

It may seem like teaching young people takes place far from the halls of Washington power and beneath the elevated plane of historical progress. The actions of disability rights leaders like Eunice Fiorito, Judy Heumann, Ed Roberts, and Justin Dart remind us that pursuing goals of equality and justice involves concrete actions by ordinary folks in everyday life. The Disability Rights Movement does not exist on some distant, exalted stage where larger than life, courageous heroes live up to our highest ideals while the rest of us watch in awe. The Movement lives every day, right now, in the decisions and actions of thousands of unheralded, uncelebrated persons across the country, in local communities where questions of access, participation, and dignity are posed and answered. These questions and opportunities for us to answer are alive and present every day in the actions of educational professionals who create inclusion or exclusion for young people in our schools.

As George Counts challenged educators many decades ago, dare we build a new order? Dare we create a just and caring community for young people where differences of ability and physical appearance are accepted, cherished, and celebrated?

Dare we?

REFERENCES

Bagenstos, S. R. (2003). The Americans with Disabilities Act as welfare reform. *William and Mary Law Review, 44, 3,* 923–1027.

Barnartt, S., & Scotch, R. (2000). *Disability protests: Contentious politics 1970–1999.* Washington, DC: Gallaudet University Press.

Berkowitz, E. D. (1987). *Disabled policy.* New York: Cambridge University Press.

Blatt, B., & Kaplan, F. (1966). *Christmas in purgatory: A photographic essay on mental retardation.* Boston, MA: Allyn and Bacon.

Brown, S. E. (2000). *Freedom of movement: Independent living history and philosophy.* Houston, TX: ILRU.

Colker, R. (1999). The Americans with Disabilities Act: A windfall for defendants, *Harvard Civil Rights-Civil Liberties Law Review, 34,* 99.

Colker, R. (2005). *The disability pendulum: The first decade of the Americans with Disabilities Act.* New York: New York University Press.

Counts, G. S. (1932). *Dare the school build a new social order?* New York: John Day Company.

Davis, L. J. (2015). *Enabling acts: The hidden story of how the Americans with Disabilities Act gave the largest US minority its rights.* Boston, MA: Beacon.

DeJong, G. (1983). Defining and implementing the independent living concept. In N. M. Crewe & I. K. Zola (Eds.), *Independent living for physically disabled people* (pp. 4–27). London: Jossey-Bass.

Fay, F., & Pelka, F. (2002). Justin Dart—An obituary. http://www.disabilityhistory.org/people_dart.html.

Fleischer, D. Z., & Zames, F. (2011). *The disability rights movement: From charity to confrontation* (updated ed.). Philadelphia, PA: Temple University Press.

Krieger, L. H. (2003). *Backlash against the ADA: Reinterpreting disability rights.* Ann Arbor: University of Michigan Press.

Locke, S. S. (1997). Incredible shrinking protected class: Redefining the scope of disability under the Americans with Disabilities Act. *University of Colorado Law Review, 107,* 124–125.

Longmore, P. K. (1998). Disability policy and politics, considering consumer influences. Paper presented to 1999 Switzer Seminar. Retrieved August 13, 2012 from http://www.mswitzer.org/sem99/papers/longmore.html.

Longmore, P. K., & Goldberger, D. (2000). The League of the Physically Handicapped and the Great Depression: A case study and the new disability history. *Journal of American History, 87,* 3, 888–922.

Mayerson, I (1991). The Americans with Disabilities Act—An historical overview. *Labor Lawyer, 7,* 1, 1–9.

Mezey, S. G. (2005). *Disabling interpretations: The Americans with Disabilities Act in federal court.* Pittsburg, PA: University of Pittsburg Press.

Mitchell, D. T., & Snyder, S. L. (2000). *Narrative prosthesis: Disability and the dependencies of discourse.* Ann Arbor, MI: University of Michigan Press.

National Council on Disability. (1986). *Toward independence: An assessment of federal laws and programs affecting persons with disabilities—with legislative recommendation.* Washington, DC: United States Government Printing Office.

National Council on Disability. (1988). *On the threshold of independence: Progress on the legislative recommendations from "Toward Independence."* Washington, DC: United States Government Printing Office.

Nelis, T., & Rizzolo, M. C. (2005). Use of state institutions for people with intellectual disabilities in the United States. Boulder, CO: Coleman Institute for Cognitive Disabilities.

O'Brien, R. A. (2001). *Crippled justice: The history of modern disability policy in the workplace.* Chicago, IL: University of Chicago Press.

Palmer, P. (1998). *The courage to teach: Exploring the inner landscape of the teacher's life.* San Francisco, CA: Jossey-Bass.

Pelka, F. (1997). *The ABC-CLIO companion to the disability rights movement.* Santa Barbara, CA: ABC-CLIO.

Primo, A. T., & Rivera, G. (1972). *Willowbrook: The last great disgrace.* New York: Sproutflix.

Roberts, E. V. (1989). A history of the Independent Living Movement: A founder's perspective. In B. W. Heller, L. M. Flohr, & L. S. Zegans (Eds.), *Psychosocial interventions with physically disabled persons* (pp. 231–244). New Brunswick, NJ: Rutgers University Press.

Scotch, R. K. (2001). *From good will to civil rights: Transforming federal disability policy.* Philadelphia, PA: Temple University Press.

Shapiro, J. P. (1994). *No pity: People with disabilities forging a new civil rights movement.* New York: Times Books.

Siebers, T. (2008). *Disability theory.* Ann Arbor, MI: University of Michigan Press.

Stroman, D. (2003). *The disability rights movement: From deinstitutionalization to self-determination.* Lanham, MD: University Press of America.

Taylor, S. J. (2009). *Acts of conscience: World War II, mental institutions, and religious objectors.* Syracuse, NY: Syracuse University Press.

Trent, J. W. (1994). *Inventing the feeble mind: A history of mental retardation in the United States.* Berkeley: University of California Press.

Turner, R. (1969). The theme of contemporary social movements. *British Journal of Sociology, 20,* 390–405.

Varela, R. A. (1983). Changing social attitudes and legislation regarding disability. In N. M. Crewe & I. K. Zola (Eds.), *Independent living for physically disabled people.* San Francisco, CA: Jossey-Bass.

Weicker, L. (1991). Historical background of the Americans with Disabilities Act. *Temple Law Review, 64,* 387–392.

Wolfensberger, W. (1972). *The principle of normalization in human services.* Toronto: National Institute on Mental Retardation.

Young, J. (2010). *Equality of opportunity: The making of the Americans with Disabilities Act.* Washington, DC: National Council on Disability.

Zola, I. K. (1983). Developing new self-images and interdependence. In N. M. Crewe & I. K. Zola (Eds.), *Independent living for physically disabled people.* San Francisco, CA: Jossey-Bass.

NOTE

1. The term "deinstitutionalization" is also used to describe the parallel but quite different closing of public psychiatric hospitals and the development of community mental health centers. Since deinstitutionalization of persons with psychiatric disabilities involved a distinct set of issues, this section of the chapter focuses on the movement to close institutions for persons with mental retardation or intellectual disabilities.

CHAPTER FOUR

What Is Best in the American Dream

> **Guiding Questions**
> - How do John Dewey's *vision of a democratic community* and his concept of *moral equality* help you understand what inclusive classrooms and school can be?
> - How does the *social model of disability* inform you about the relationship between social inequality and disability in society and schools?
> - What does Nel Nodding's *ethic of caring* add to your orientation to teaching in inclusive schools?
> - What other intellectual and ethical resources do you find helpful in your work as an inclusive educator?

Anyone who becomes a teacher has embraced a life of ethical purpose, engaging in a continuing struggle to contribute to the well-being of children, families, and the larger society. In the United States, we acknowledge that a high quality public education furthers what we call the American Dream, a shared set of democratic ideals initiated by the authors of the Constitution and the Declaration of Independence and continued by our beliefs and actions today. We are dedicated to the challenge of providing ways for all citizens to have equal access to "life, liberty, and the pursuit of happiness."

The work of teachers creating equal access for all is troubled by traditional practices of American public education that exclude, segregate, and disrespect people with disabilities. Conventional, often unquestioned ways of thinking and acting in the public schools actively work against the democratic goal of equal access. When teachers face up to this fact and accept moral responsibility for their own beliefs and actions, they confront the contradictions and weaknesses of their personal systems of ethical understanding and commitment. Inclusive teachers take this intellectual and practical work very seriously, devoting themselves to the on-going task of ethical growth and development.

AGAINST THE GRAIN OF INEQUALITY

> "None of the changes need to achieve integration is rooted in technique [...]. Rather, these changes originate in a vision and a knowledge of people with disabilities as equals of other people." (Biklen, 1992, p. 188)

Martin Luther King, Jr., was imprisoned in April, 1963, for leading a march in protest of racial segregation and discrimination in Birmingham, Alabama. A group of eight local clergy published a letter in the *Birmingham News* condemning the timing and tactics of King's civil disobedience. Writing in the margins of the newspaper from his jail cell, King composed a response to the clergy. In one passage of his letter, he criticized the ministers for praising the work of the police on that day. The police used biting dogs and powerful water-cannons to subdue the nonviolent protesters.

King then asked the clergy why they didn't acclaim the protesters for taking positive action against the unjust laws and social order of racial oppression. It seemed to King that the clergy had overlooked the most hopeful part of the day's events, the organized actions of ordinary citizens seeking social justice. King described the protesters as "heroes," the highest examples of the American democratic tradition.

> One day the South will know that when these disinherited children of God sat down at lunch counters, they were in reality standing up for what is best in the American dream and for the most sacred values in our Judaeo-Christian heritage, thereby bringing our nation back to those great wells of democracy which were dug deep by the founding fathers in their formulation of the Constitution and the Declaration of Independence. (King, 1963, paragraph 36)

For Martin Luther King, the people who took peaceful action to oppose social injustice and seek a more caring and fair community were enacting the greatest principles of the democratic way of life.

In this chapter, I challenge educators who work in the public schools to reflect deeply on their own their own ethical commitments in light of the reality of the on-going oppression of persons with disabilities in the United States. I challenge teachers and school leaders to actively pursue *what is best in the American dream*. As King eloquently exclaimed, ideals such as human equality and freedom are the most cherished values in the democratic tradition. But they only gain relevant and purposeful meaning when people put these elements of the democratic faith into action, when critical thought on current circumstances is matched with practical actions taken in the world.

The great Brazilian educator Paulo Freire (1970) used the word *praxis* to represent the unity of reflective thought and action, the coupling of informed, judicious consideration and goal-oriented human activity. In order to take action to create social change, persons and groups must reflect deeply on the reality of the situation, looking beyond the fog of conventional, superficial understandings in order to understand the causes of social injustice and human suffering. Purposeful action to bring about dramatic progress must be guided by an authentic, critical engagement with the underlying social causes of injustice.

For our purposes, we can understand Freire as advising us that knowing *how to* set up and maintain an inclusive classroom or school where students with and without disabilities learn well together is insufficient if educators do not have deep, thoughtful understandings of *why* one would pursue inclusion in the first place. If teachers do not hold a strong commitment to the Disability Rights Movement, then the pedagogical practices of inclusion are merely a palette and brushes in search of an artist. The practical *how-to* and the reflective *why* are inseparable aspects of inclusive teaching. Doing and thinking, taking action and reflecting deeply, operate in unison.

The goal of this chapter is to supply educators with intellectual resources to begin the hard work of deep reflection, of serious ethical examination, of exploring sharp-edged questions and creating livable answers. To those important ends, I offer intellectual resources that many inclusive educators find helpful when thinking about the widespread oppression of disabled persons and the most hopeful pathways to dramatic social change in our communities and schools. Obviously, there is no way to provide all the resources that inclusive educators have employed in their ethical and political development. Inclusive educators draw from a wide variety of intellectual and spiritual resources, ranging from Mahatma Gandhi to Henry David Thoreau to bell hooks, from Liberation Theology to Multicultural Education to Disability Studies. This chapter provides an invitation to think about our ethical commitments and our purposes as educators. I introduce readers to a selection of important ideas that many inclusive educators use to clarify and fortify their own ethical commitments concerning social justice, equality, and democracy in schools.

First, we examine two ideas espoused by John Dewey, his *vision of a democratic community* and his concept of *moral equality*. The great American philosopher and educator John Dewey wrote and taught long before inclusive education was even imagined. His understanding of a democracy as a way of living together where all persons are embraced as equally valuable is still vital to the work of inclusive educators today.

Next, after grasping Dewey's vision of how democratic our communities can be, it is essential that we critically examine how our society and our schools fall short.

We need to understand the harsh reality of oppression in order to seek practical remedies and a hopeful road forward. The field of Disability Studies, an interdisciplinary tradition of social analysis looking at the experiences of disabled persons in many cultural contexts, helps us understand how social inequality is created and maintained. This profound protest literature created primarily by persons with disabilities to critique and overturn disability oppression in the world has resulted in what is often called the *social model of disability*, a way of thinking about disability that is tailor-made for democratic social change.

Fortified with Dewey's vision of what an egalitarian and diverse community can be, and armed with a critical consciousness of how people with disabilities are oppressed in society and schools, we pursue disability rights within the schools. Seeking social justice in the public schools is unlike other civil rights activity. It does not typically involve organizing public protests or filing class action lawsuits in district court. The work of teachers is a complex art of ethical interaction, a way of relating to children and teaching them to relate to one another. The work of educational philosopher Nel Noddings on the centrality of caring relationships provides profound, powerful guidance to the daily work of inclusive educators.

JOHN DEWEY'S VISION OF A DEMOCRATIC COMMUNITY

> (T)he task of democracy is forever that of creation of a freer and more humane experience in which all contribute. (Dewey, 1981a, p. 225)

Central to the aim of public schooling in the United States is the goal of very intentionally bringing young people into the daily attitudes and practices of the American democracy. Certainly, this means social studies lessons about the history of democracy and the structure of our federal and state governments. John Dewey reminds us that it means much more. Students need to understand democracy as a way of life, as an ethical approach to relating to other persons and creating communities. The best way to truly learn about this way of life is to experience it each day in school.

Dewey's vision of democracy involves an understanding of the mutual relationship between the individual and the community. The well-being of the community and the full development of individuals operate in reciprocal tandem. The goal of the democratic society is to create communities of equality and social support so that the free expression and full development of the individuality of each citizen is a paramount concern. The task of the individual person in the democracy is to contribute his or her unique talents and effort to the daily interactions and activities that support the community of freedom and equality.

Dewey's understanding of democratic community is a very down to earth, over-the-side-fence approach to living together. Equality is not just some grandiose word chiseled into inscriptions beneath marble statues of Presidents and civil rights leaders. It is made real, literally created, in the face-to-face conversations and interactions of common people. Two neighbors lean against the fence that divides their properties. Each stands at the edge of her own individuality. Each leans against what they have in common. The neighbors talk about interests and concerns that are inevitably shared by persons who live side by side. In these everyday social exchanges that take place in side yards, shopping centers, houses of worship, and schools, the equality of persons can be made and remade (Martin, 2002; Ryan, 1997; Westbrook, 1993).

A great example of what Dewey's concept of democratic community means at the level of interpersonal interactions and relationships is provided by Doug Biklen and Jamie Burke's (2006, p. 166) notion of "presuming competence." To presume competence in interaction with a disabled person is to avoid ascribing deficit and defect ideas to the humanity of the person. Instead, one interprets a body or actions that may seem unusual, that may perform in surprising ways, as completely reasonable, as ordinary and making good sense within the experience of the disabled person.

A teacher who presumes competence adopts an orientation of deep respect for the individuality and life experience of the disabled person. The teacher's

> obligation is not to project an ableist interpretation on something another person does, but rather to presume there must be a rationale or sympathetic explanation for what someone does and then try to discover it, always from another person's own perspective. (Biklen & Burke, 2006, p. 168)

Appreciating the humanity of the person with a disability, honoring him or her as an equal, requires an attitude of understanding and discovery. The educator moves past common, stereotyped interpretations of why a person speaks, moves, or behaves in a certain way in order to understand how those words or actions are examples of how this unique individual operates in the world.

For example, Jamie Burke, a young man with autism, typically types to communicate his ideas. He struggles to form his thoughts and expressions into vocalized speech. He learned to type with the support of a facilitator who provides support by holding his arm or hand. In a classroom discussion, his typed production of language is slow by comparison to the rapid oral articulations of his classmates. And the adult facilitator can be an awkward presence in the conversation. Not many teens have an adult at their side assisting with communication.

Presuming competence, in this instance, means eclipsing stigmatized concepts of autism and the unusual aspects of Jamie's way of communication in order to adopt an open and accepting orientation toward Jamie and what he has to say. We listen with intent and respect in order to value his words and access the distinct personality and perspective behind the words. We avoid the ableist trap of assuming that slow language production is a sign of lesser intelligence or linguistic pathology.

We hear Jamie, listen to Jamie, and appreciate what he has to contribute to the class discussion.

JOHN DEWEY'S CONCEPT OF MORAL EQUALITY

> The democratic faith in human equality is belief that every human being, independent of the quantity or range of his personal endowment, has the right to equal opportunity with every other person for development of whatever gifts he has. (Dewey, 1981a, 227–278)

During World War I, the United States military gathered leading psychologists from universities across the country to develop intelligence tests for use in deciding the rank and job placement of enlisted soldiers. After the War, many of these psychologists consulted with public schools in devising intelligence tests for the purposes of predicting student achievement and placing students into a number of different instructional tracks such as college preparatory, vocational, or special education. The goal was to sort students more efficiently based on their "true" intellectual capacity (Chapman, 1990; Zenderland, 2001).

The effort to sort students into different tracks based on intelligence often divided students on the basis of race, immigration status, heritage language, and social class. Students in the lower tracks and special education programs of the early 1900s were frequently boys from immigrant, low income families (Danforth & Smith, 2005; Lazerson, 1983).

In a pair of articles published in the *New Republic* in 1922, John Dewey (1976a, 1976b) critiqued the use of intelligence measures as a way of thinking about the learning and growth. He was concerned with the often unquestioned assumption that persons who succeed—in education, career, or gathering wealth—are intellectually superior while persons who experience less of these forms of success must have inferior mental capacities.

> We accept standards of judging individuals which are based on the qualities of mind and character which win under existing social conditions conspicuous success. The "inferior" is the one who isn't calculated to "get on" in a society such as now exists. (Dewey, 1976a, p. 295)

He found this conventional thinking about inferiority to be "lopsided and disordered" (Dewey, 1976a, p. 295), severely misunderstanding why people really succeed or fail.

When examining the performance of different persons, Dewey taught, we can understand an individual's talent only in relationship to a specific activity or goal. One person might be able to jump higher than most. Another is an efficient and speedy typist. A third is a very skilled vegetable gardener. But the conventional idea that some people have a higher level of some general capacity that applies to many different tasks, a mental ability or intellectual talent that allows for success in many different situations is simply foolishness. Dewey (1976a, p. 296) wrote, "(T)he idea of abstract, universal superiority and inferiority is an absurdity."

Teachers should not be led astray by orthodox notions about some students having "higher IQ's" or other students being "low functioning." These vague, crude descriptions of student learning or achievement can sadly convince us not to notice what so-called "low achieving" students are doing well. For example, over many years of ethnographic research observing in classrooms, Chris Kliewer (2008) found that teachers often assume that children with Down Syndrome can't possibly learn to read. So they aren't even aware when those students exhibit obvious literacy skills right before their eyes. The tragedy is that teachers frequently fail to provide the necessary instruction to support the student's literacy growth.

Dewey counseled teachers to pay very close attention to how individuals perform on each task, noting both how well they do, when they struggle, when they succeed, and the student's strategy for completing the task. In-depth understanding of how students succeed or fail in specific tasks and conditions are far more useful to teachers than IQ scores and standardized measures.

Beyond the fact that intelligence tests made little practical sense for educators, Dewey was concerned with how the idea that each individual has a level of general intelligence harms our democratic way of life. This notion seemed to him as simply a convenient way for people who had more power, status, or money to pat themselves on the back, to claim that they were deserving of privilege due to their innate intellectual preeminence.

> The current loose use of these conceptions (i.e., superior and inferior intelligence) suggests overcompensation on the part of those who assume that they belong to a superior class. It appears like an attempt to escape from the limitations and incapacities which we all know, subconsciously at least, that we possess. (Dewey, 1976a, p. 296)

Rather than honestly admitting that all persons have multiple strengths and weaknesses, that all achieve varying degrees of competence and incompetence in numerous activities throughout the day, the wealthy and powerful declare that their elevated bank balance or social standing is evidence of their high IQ. They maintain that social inequality is not created by human activity, what people actually do together in our communities, but is an inevitable outcome of differential levels of inborn intelligence. The truly talented people simply and rightly win.

Dewey was worried that standardized testing and concepts like intelligence quotient, seeming to arise from a psychological science, would be used in undemocratic ways to perpetuate the existence of an aristocratic class. His lifetime of scholarship attests to his devotion to democracy in the United States as a way for people of many talents, interests, and values to live together on an equal political footing (Martin, 2002; Ryan, 1997; Westbrook, 1993). In his second *New Republic* essay, he turned to early American democratic founders Thomas Jefferson and John

Adams to make his point. Both "agreed that equality is moral, a matter of justice socially secured, not of physical or psychological endowment" (Dewey, 1976a, p. 299). To put it more simply, equality—a belief that all persons are of equal value to the community regardless of their talents or wealth—only exists when people come together to make it happen. Equality, in this light, is a moral goal that thoughtful people achieve together for everyone.

He coined the important concept called "moral equality" (Dewey, 1976a, p. 299) to capture a democratic way of thinking about how students differ from one another. The fact that all students are unalike, that they differ in a million different ways—physical size, appearance, interests, personality, needs, strengths, weaknesses—is obvious. But what shall we make of these differences? Dewey encourages us not to think about differences in terms of hierarchies of superior and inferior, higher and lower, better and worse. Instead, he teaches us to view student differences through a lens of incomparability.

"Moral equality means incommensurability, the inapplicability of common and quantitative standards" (Dewey, 1976a, p. 299). We should avoid concocting a grand standard or overarching concept that we should use to compare students to one another. For example, the common language of "grade level performance" and our many descriptions of students as performing above, below, or at grade level are a distraction from the real work of teaching. Truly understanding students as learners requires that we set aside the practice of ranking students.

Acting on the basis of moral equality begins with rejecting the misguided goal of comparing one student to the rest of the class or to a statistical average. We then open ourselves to appreciating each student in and of herself, carefully observing and recognizing the distinct qualities found in each unique individual.

As educators working in an era in which high stakes testing has seemingly forced us to use hierarchical comparisons, evaluations of higher and lower, it may be difficult for some to grasp Dewey's idea. Our political leaders repeatedly tell us that all students in a certain grade should advance to the same level of learning. These leaders foolishly pretend that (1) all students grow at the same pace and (2) all students grow in the same ways (e.g., talents, interests). Dewey reminds us to set aside this penchant for ranking children so that we can appreciate and support the growth and development of each student.

To help us understand his concept of moral equality, Dewey offered art as an area of human activity that is analogous to the unique learning and behavior of each individual.

Imagine spending an afternoon in a marvelous art museum, viewing all the paintings and sculptures. Now think of what it would be like to go through the gallery with a standardized evaluation rubric. Your job is to rate each piece of art by comparison to the other works. The goal is to create an aesthetic ranking, a hierarchy from best to worse. As you imagine yourself doing this, think of how this way of viewing the art distracts you from truly appreciating each work. Think of how the actual enjoyment of viewing the many works of art is lost by this hollow orientation to what should be a wonderful day at the museum.

Thankfully, most of us do not behave this way. When we enter an art gallery, our concern is not whether a specific piece is ranked sixty-fourth out of 353 sculptures. Instead, we soak in what each work of art has to give. Our approach is one of understanding and appreciating each work, simply embracing it on its own terms. If we make comparisons across pieces, the purpose is not ranking but noticing how different artists use color, light, or contrast, how different paintings communicate and expose something real and true about the subject. We may wonder about the artist's purposes or her emotional state at the time. We may think about the social and historical context of the artist's work, the political and cultural world that surrounded the artist and influenced her. Our entire focus delves into the work itself, attempting to know it as a significant piece of expression and meaning.

Following John Dewey's advice, we can view an individual child as a matchless work of art. Our goal with each student is to simultaneously accept that individual's uniqueness while providing a supportive context where that young person can grow, develop, gain knowledge and skill.

Dewey also used an arboreal metaphor to teach this same concept. We might imagine that each child is like a distinctive plant. We are called to nurture each to grow in its own ways, rising to its own height, wrapped in its own bark, spreading its own branches, sprouting its own idiosyncratic leaves and flowers. But we don't expect an oak to become a violet, or vice versa.

> (A) violet and an oak tree are equal when one has the same opportunity to develop to the full as a violet which the other has as an oak. (Dewey, 1981b, p. 346)

We should not misread this as a commitment to reduce children to "types" or "categories." He is speaking to the countless variations of individuality. Dewey wants us to understand that an oak tree and a violet tree can each grow fully and beautifully without ever becoming identical trees. A gardener tending to the well-being of the two trees would provide water, soil, and care to help each tree become are fuller and greater version of itself.

Renowned inclusion researcher Roger Slee (2011, p. 14) has written, "Inclusive education [...] offers an audacious challenge to the attachment of ascending and descending values to different people." In our democratic eyes, all students are of equal value. Our challenge as educators tending to the growth of many unique children is to provide instruction and social support so that each can grow and learn, so that each can become a more capable version of herself. As we look across the classroom, we see Alberto and Sally and Phil and Maya, and we know that each can blossom fully in this classroom. If we supply the right kind of learning and social environment, each can mature and magnify, becoming a more Awesome Alberto, Stupendous Sally, Fantastic Phil, and Magnificent Maya.

THE SOCIAL MODEL OF DISABILITY

In 1975, a group of disabled persons in England calling themselves The Union of the Physically Impaired Against Segregation (UPIAS) built a new idea with profound consequences.

> In our view, it is society which disables physically impaired people. Disability is something imposed on top of our impairments, by the way we are unnecessarily isolated and excluded from full participation in society. Disabled people are therefore an oppressed group in society [...]. For us as disabled people it is absolutely vital that we get this question of the cause of disability quite straight, because on the answer depends the crucial matter of where we direct our main energies in the struggle for change. We shall clearly get nowhere if our efforts are chiefly directed not at the cause of our oppression, but instead at one of the symptoms.
> (Union of Physically Impaired Against Segregation, 1975, p. 3–4)

This revolutionary statement is the basis for the *social model of disability* that has been further developed by an interdisciplinary field of academic scholarship called Disability Studies (e.g., Albrecht, Seelman, & Bury, 2001; Barnes, Oliver, & Barton, 2002; Davis, 1997, 2002; Gabel, 2005; Linton, 1998; Oliver, 1990). What began as a new concept of physical disability has been extended over the years into our thinking about all disabilities, including intellectual disabilities (Bogdan & Taylor, 1994; Kliewer, 1998), autism (Savarese & Savarese, 2010), and learning disabilities (Connor & Ferri, 2010).

Let's take note of the striking features of this revolutionary way of framing disability. First, unlike virtually all other models or theories of disability used in professions like special education, medicine, and psychology, this concept is crafted by people who have disabilities. This idea comes not out of the prejudices and fears and misunderstandings of nondisabled persons but from the lived experiences of persons who have disabilities.

How does that matter? Imagine I send you across the university campus to an academic department that specializes in understanding the lives and experiences of women. In this unique department, brilliant researchers and scholars work tirelessly to comprehend everything they can about women in our society. When you arrive at this academic department, you walk the hallways. Some office doors are open. You peak in to find that, in every instance, the professor inside is a man! Then you read the names on the closed office doors. Those names are all male names!

How could this be? How could an entire academic department devoted to research, scholarship, and teaching about women's lives be filled with [...] men?

We may laugh at that silly example. But it displays our point. We don't expect men to lead the way in helping us understand the lives of women. We should not expect nondisabled persons to lead the way in understanding the lives and experiences of disabled persons.

Second, the UPIAS used the words *impairment* and *disability* in a very specific way that became foundational to disability studies scholars. Impairment directs our attention to individual variations in the biology of the physical body or mind. A person may have weak legs due to childhood polio. Another person may have an extra chromosome, such as with Down Syndrome. A third person may have a condition that affects the functioning of the optic nerve, blurring her vision.

The original intent of the UPIAS was to define impairment as a bodily anomaly that limits functioning or activity. But our current thinking is even broader. Now we recognize not only the fact that some persons have specific bodily or mental conditions that play out in reduced functioning or performance. We also acknowledge, quite simply, that bodies and minds vary in countless ways that matter in terms of what people can do and how they actually live. People have bodies that are tall, short, wide, thin, strong, weak, fast, slow, and so on. In this sense, the word *impairment* helps us focus on bodily and mental variations that matter in people's lives.

The UPIAS defined d*isability* as a political addition to the bodily impairment. On top of the impairment is how society—people in communities, government, media, organizations, families, and schools—interpret, feel about, think about, and respond to human differences. That cultural layer of response to impairment is oppression. That is the disability, the cost exacted from people with impairments because of the prejudice, exclusion, and institutionalized bias. Over the decades, the field of disability studies has continued to build on this initial articulation.

Disability studies scholars generally distinguish between two main theories of disability that are prominent in the United States, the *medical model of disability* and the *social model of disability*. The medical model is the dominant orientation in American society, including the public schools. The medical model was developed by non-disabled persons, including professionals in fields like medicine, rehabilitation, psychology, and special education. It posits the following:

- Disability is an individual phenomenon, something that exists within a person's body and/or brain. It is a biological or psychological flaw that a person has.
- The difficulties that a person with a disability confronts on a daily basis in the world are primarily due to that person's functional limitations, what her body or brain is unable to do.
- Disability is a "personal misfortune" (Siebers, 2008, p. 45), a tragedy that renders an individual less than normal.

- The people who understand disabilities the best are nondisabled, scientific experts working in fields like medicine, rehabilitation, psychology, special education, etc.
- What a person with a disability needs most is a medical, rehabilitation, or educational program that makes him less impaired and more normal.
- After a person with a disability has been successfully cured, treated, or rehabilitated, then that person may be prepared for reintegration or inclusion in the general community.

The medical model is implicit in standard public school practices of diagnosis, labeling, and intervention. A common goal of school practices based in the medical model is to diagnose learning, behavior, and sensory deficits in children and then provide isolated classrooms or schools where students can receive interventions offering therapy for those areas of deficit. The basic idea is that if the child with the disability "functions" at a higher level—more normal—then she is ready for the mainstream classroom.

The social model, following in the tradition founded by the UPIAS, defines disability as the series of systemic and pervasive barriers to inclusion, participation, success, and happiness that isolate and oppress persons whose bodies and minds do not conform to social conventions of appearance and functioning. Society attaches stigma to many physical and psychological variations of humanity, thereby rendering those persons as lesser citizens. The politics of disability are harsh and widespread, including exclusion from meaningful participation in employment, education, recreation, housing, and social relationships.

The social model holds the following beliefs:

- Disability is a social and political fact consisting of the community's prejudiced response to human bodily and mental differences.
- A person with a disability confronts on a daily basis a variety of barriers to participation and success. These barriers are attitudinal (prejudice), architectural (inaccessible built environment), and institutional (discriminatory and exclusive organizations and social systems).
- Disabled persons are part of a political minority group that seeks its civil rights in a fashion much like African-Americans, women, the LGBT community, etc.
- The people who understand disabilities the best are the persons who have the disabilities.
- What a person with a disability needs most is respect, acceptance, and access to all aspects of the community; including education, employment, recreation, housing, transportation.

- Inclusion happens when communities and organizations acknowledge their history of oppressive practices and make an intentional, concerted effort to remove barriers to participation.

In the social model, people with disabilities are understood as a cultural minority group seeking their civil rights, attempting to be included in all avenues of community life. The social model of disability views human differences as a legitimate and disability as a valued cultural identity. Through actively resisting the social and political forces of exclusion and oppression, disability can become a source of identity and pride (Gabel & Peters, 2004).

I can recall the day when I first realized this. I was walking through the hallways of my university, and I saw my friend Karen Hagrup riding through the hallways on her wheelchair. Karen was also a faculty member. She had worked for many years for independent living centers. She was the first person who introduced me to disability studies ideas. Blending the social model of disability with feminist ideas, she was a powerful advocate for women with disabilities.

As Karen zipped down the hallway with a giant smile on her face, it suddenly dawned on me. I called out, "Hey Karen, I just realized something!"

"Oh yeah," she grinned at me, "What is that?"

"I realized [...]" I hesitated. My ideas were still forming in my mind. Then the words came together just right, "I realized that you are proud to be a disabled woman."

It was an odd statement. There was nothing in the thousands of pages of special education research that I had to read over decades that even remotely suggested this idea.

Karen was already smiling fully before I started to speak, but I swear that her smile actually grew even larger, even wider, in that moment.

"Yes! I am!" she called out as she whirled around and rolled triumphantly away. "I am very proud!"

Despite all the cultural messages that tell women with disabilities not to view themselves as capable, attractive, smart, and valuable (Thomson, 1997), Karen had developed a very positive sense of herself as a disabled woman. That empowering fact is vital to the social model of disability and to disability studies.

Further, in the social model, disability is often described as a social construction. This does not mean that disability is not real. What it means is social and cultural activity such as language and thought are used to interpret the meanings of variations of the human body and mind. Through that complex cultural activity, meaning is granted to the variety of bodily or psychological configurations and to the persons who embody them. In this sense, what Down Syndrome or deafness or a learning disability actually mean is determined by people through interactions and communications, through social thought and language. It can change over time, and it can vary greatly depending on the social group or context.

For example, parents of students with disabilities and public school educators do not always share the same understanding of what disability means. This rift can lead to misunderstandings and conflicts between families and schools (Michelson, 2000; Valle, 2009). Similarly, inclusive educators often find themselves disagreeing with more traditional educators about what disability means in the public schools.

In my own historical research on the scientific construct "learning disability," I learned about how that disability was socially constructed over time in the United States. I discovered that the notion itself came together as a practically useful but scientifically loose concept among a small number of psychologists and physicians after World War II. The early idea of a "brain injury" grew out of the concept of mental retardation as researchers identified a sub-group among persons they believed were quite unlike others with that diagnosis.

For decades, brain injury researchers labored greatly in anonymity, working in small clinics and institutional settings around the United States, often conducting case studies based on their clinical work. They communicated with one another both informally and through standard scientific venues such as conferences, meetings, and academic journals. They used a variety of different terms and definitions for what they saw as a complex condition of learning difficulty. Only when pressured in the 1960s by a growing parent advocacy movement did the many different concepts and terms get quickly squeezed into one learning disability concept with a single identifiable definition. The political fervor created by parents pushed the researchers to bundle their variety of concepts and definitions under one heading, the learning disability much as we know it today (Danforth, 2009, 2011a, 2011b; Danforth, Slocum, & Dunkle, 2010).

Social constructionism teaches us that the practical and political meanings of disabilities vary depending on the beliefs and actions of all of us. They change over time because of what real people think and say and write and do. Human action can bring about change, sometimes turning on a dime, but more often by way of a frustrating, zig-zag path. With much effort and patience, we can change disability from a personal tragedy to a positive social identity.

The work of disability studies scholars has been dedicated to creating opportunities for people with disabilities to be understood in a more positive light and accepted as valued community members. Central to that work is the creation of new, more hopeful and respectful ways of thinking about disability and people with disabilities.

NEL NODDINGS' ETHIC OF CARING

> The main aim of education should be to produce competent, caring, loving, and lovable people. (Noddings, 1995, p. 368)

There I was, a quivering ball of anxiety, sitting in my car in the parking lot of my daughter's kindergarten. I had just walked her into the school and left her at her classroom door. Suddenly, I understood what educational philosopher Nel Noddings had written about the need for schools to make caring, interpersonal relationships a high priority.

As I walked away from my daughter's classroom that morning, I found myself making a simple wish. I wished that the adults and children in her classroom and school were very ethical people who would treat my daughter with love and kindness. Most obviously, I wanted this because I love my daughter deeply and I don't want her to suffer mistreatment or cruelty. But I also wished this for my daughter because I know that she will thrive as a developing young person in a social environment where people care deeply about one another and treat one another fairly. This kind of caring classroom is not only crucial to her happiness. It is vital for her growth as a moral being. She will become a person who of compassion, respect, and love if she grows up in a community where those values live and breathe every day (Berkowitz & Bier, 2005; Watson, 2003).

I am not alone in wishing this for my child. I know from conversations that I have had with scores of parents over the years that this wish for a caring community for our children is universal. While I and other parents undoubtedly want our children to learn the academic skills that are needed to succeed in further education and employment, we all share a single, most important wish; that our child be loved and cared for at school.

Not only do we want the adults and other children to treat our child in a caring and respectful way. We want the culture of compassion and caring in the school to be so pervasive and strong that our child learns to become part of that way of life, that she learns to be a person who develops loving and nurturing relationships with others.

Philosopher Nel Noddings (1984, 1992, 1995) has written very thoughtfully and fully about this universal parental wish. Noddings critiques the public schools for losing their balance, for tipping so far in the direction of standardized test scores that the highest priority of promoting "the growth of students as healthy, competent moral people" (Noddings, 1992, p. 10) has been largely abdicated. Teaching young people academic content and skills without caring for them deeply and without teaching them how to create caring relationships with one another is an empty educational mission.

> (M)any otherwise reasonable people seem to believe that our educational problems consist largely of low scores on achievement tests. My contention is, first, that we should want more from our educational efforts than adequate academic achievement and, second, that we will not achieve even that meager success unless our children believe that they themselves are cared for and learn to care for others. (Noddings, 1995, pp. 675–6)

A number of researchers argue that nurturing the development of empathy, social concern, and responsibility among children does not conflict with goals of academic development. In fact, in most cases, schools that focus intentionally and wholeheartedly on ethical behavior and caring interpersonal relationships also do very well in academic subject area learning (Benninga, Berkowitz, Kuehn, & Smith, 2003; Elliot, 1998).

Noddings teaches us that we develop into moral persons by participating in relations of care, connections that bind us to one another and nurture us each as individuals. Morality is learned in social interactions and lasting connections that mutually support the participants. The process of developing and maintaining caring relations between individuals is central to the development of moral character.

In schools and classrooms, this means both the relationships between teachers and students and between students and their peers. Noddings challenges teachers to not only feel a sense of caring or believe that caring about students is a priority. She challenges us to live an ethic of caring in our daily interactions with young people and to help our students learn how to enact an ethic of caring in their own lives.

What is an ethic of caring in the schools? "Caring gives priority to relationships (Noblit, Rogers, & McCadden, 1995, p. 681). A caring relation is an interpersonal connection between two human beings—an educator who provides care and a child or adolescent who receives care. It is a relationship in which the educator accepts the student for who she is while holding her best interests as the highest priority. This connection may be brief or lasting. But an enduring relation that gains depth and survives struggles over time is the most impactful and meaningful in the lives of children.

Keep in mind that acts of caring take place in the midst of the usual, daily activities of teaching. An ethic of caring is not an add-on, an extra, a luxury that teachers provide to students if they have a little time after all the usual educational responsibilities have been handled. An ethic of caring is an overall orientation to interacting with students that is central to everything that teachers and schools do.

Noddings (1984, 1992) offers two specific relational concepts to help guide the work of teachers in classrooms, *engrossment* and *motivational displacement*. These two concepts help educators to understand how to live an ethic of caring in our relationships with students.

Engrossment is the experience of offering ourselves completely and without qualification to the needs of another person. Often this involves listening and providing emotional support. But this can also take place when are being playful or joking around with a student. It can happen when we are asking probing questions, leading a discussion, or offering a word of encouragement. The key is that we are fully receptive to another human being, taking in the words and perspective of another, receiving that individual completely and without judgment.

Literally, the word engrossment means "written in large handwriting." Engrossment is a bodily, emotional, and mental act of perceiving another person in large letters written across the sky. When we embody engrossment in our work with a child or adolescent, the student is larger than life in our perception and attention. At the moment, whether we are providing assistance with a mathematics problem or emotional support in a moment of distress, our thoughts and feelings are filled with this one individual. The student written in the sky encompasses the totality of our focus. We are fully there, present, ready, attending to that individual's life and well-being.

Motivational displacement describes the way that the purposes and needs of the student become the complete goal of the teacher. At the moment of interaction, the experience involves great intensity and concentration. Whatever motivations, concerns, or goals the teacher may have are, in the moment, pushed aside by the eminent priority of the well-being of the student. All attention and effort is devoted to the singular goal of fulfilling the best interests of that person.

But what does an ethic of caring actually look like in the classroom? Ethnographers George Noblit and Dwight Rogers have spent many hours in classrooms studying how teachers enact an ethic of caring. They found that caring relationships are vital to the life of the learning community (Noblit, 1993; Noblit, Rogers, & McCadden, 1995; Rogers, 1994).

> (Caring) is the glue that binds teachers and students together and makes life in the classroom meaningful […]. It is through concerned and responsive teachers' attempts to recognize, understand, and respect their student that trust is established and caring relationships are built in the classroom. These caring relationships between teachers and students create possibilities—opportunities for academic as well as interpersonal learning to occur. (Noblit, Rogers, & McCadden, 1995, p. 681)

Relationships are the very heart and soul of the classroom as a human community. When teachers and student create caring relationships based on trust and respect, then the community can flourish as a space of learning.

In many instances, the relational challenge for teachers comes when they are teaching students whom they experience as unlike themselves. Simply put, teachers often find it easier to understand and communicate with students who are members of their own cultural group. That group may be defined in a variety of ways, including race, social class, religion, sexual orientation, nationality, and disability. Students who share the teacher's social identity and participate in his own cultural values and practices are often easier to understand, relate to, and connect with.

Communication and interaction with students from other cultural groups often takes effort and practice. For example, if a white teacher has little life experience forming relationships with African-Americans, then teaching African-American children requires an attitude of openness and acceptance. The teacher must learn about the cultural styles of speech, behavior, language, and attitude in order to fully appreciate his students' talents and abilities.

Multicultural educator Valerie Ooka Pang (2005) has explored the importance of caring relationships in bridging the cultural gaps between teachers and students who come from different social groups in society. Many students belong to racial and language minority groups that the dominant, white, middle class culture stereotypes as lazy and incompetent. Unfortunately, it is often too easy for teachers from the dominant cultural group to interpret the social behavior, interpersonal style, and academic performance of minority students as indications of their intellectual or moral inferiority. Pang emphasizes the need for teachers to "develop strong cross-cultural communications" and learn "cultural awareness" in order to fully understand and support their students (Pang, Rivera, & Mora, 1999, pp. 27–28). Strong, trusting relationships promote the development of "healthy cultural identities and high academic self-concepts," thereby creating a comfortable and productive social setting where students grow and learn (Pang, Rivera, & Mora, 1999, pp. 27–28). Caring relationships can be a way for teachers and students to span cultural differences and overcome limiting stereotypes.

Professor Pang's work is relevant to inclusive educators for two specific reasons. First, for many decades, segregated special education classrooms have been disproportionately filled with students of color. African-American males, and to a lesser extent, Latino males, are overrepresented in the special education system (Harry & Anderson, 1994; Harry, Klingner, Sturgis, & Moore, 2002; Harry & Klingner, 2006; Losen & Orfield, 2002). Once identified as having a disability, students of color are placed in segregated special education classrooms significantly more often than their white peers (Fierros & Conroy, 2002). One cannot work effectively with students with disabilities in the American public schools without addressing the fact that many of these students are from cultural minority groups and live in economic poverty (Brantlinger, 1994, 2001; Danforth & Smith, 2004).

Second, multicultural educators, who have spent many years helping teachers work across the lines of culture and language to improve relationships, understanding, and trust, are now beginning to acknowledge that disability and disability identity is part of their important work. Persons with disabilities are now understood by multicultural scholars as an oppressed minority group that has similar experiences of discrimination and exclusion of other minority groups (Ayres, Quinn, & Stovall, 2009; Chapman & Hobbel, 2010; Steinberg, 2009).

Just as dominant culture, white, middle class teachers often experience students from minority cultural groups as distinctly different from themselves, so too dominant culture, non-disabled teachers frequently experience disabled students as foreign, inexplicable, and peculiar. Nondisabled teachers who do not have a strong foundation of life experiences in relationships with disabled persons may feel uncomfortable, anxious, or fearful around students with disabilities (Danforth & Navarro, 1998; Giangreco, St. Denis, Cloninger, Edelman, & Schattman, 1993). The need to build caring relationships as a bridge between races and social classes is parallel to the need to create relationships of trust and acceptance that foster understanding between nondisabled teachers and disabled students (Bogdan & Taylor, 1987).

LET THE PRUNES SING

Anyone familiar with wonderful, paradoxical stories from the ancient tradition of Zen Buddhism knows that many of them go something like this. A person seeking wisdom or enlightenment or truth goes on a long journey to learn at the bare feet of a great holy man. The hope is that the holy man will offer words of prophetic advice that will help the traveler achieve a higher form of knowledge or consciousness. Inevitably, the holy man makes an enigmatic, confounding statement like "Catch Sunshine in Your Ear" or "Let the Prunes Sing." The wisdom-seeker is left with the challenge of figuring out what this puzzling tidbit of wisdom actually means.

What I love about these stories is the way they end before the truly important part of the narrative occurs. The enlightened sage has offered a teaspoon of metaphorical guidance meaning who-knows-what. Just a few enigmatic, seemingly precious words. After the story ends, the seeker must figure it all out without the assistance of the sage. All alone, climbing back down the mountain, the seeker is challenged to figure how to apply the advice to the practicalities of her daily life. That is the fascinating part. After the sage gives the advice, the knowledge seeker is left alone, thrown back on her own resources. She must draw from her own reservoir of ideas, beliefs, and values to make sense of the advice and make her way through a complicated, often not very receptive or loving world.

This chapter has provided what I consider to be sage advice from some brilliant minds. I hope this brief introduction encourages you to read books and articles written by John Dewey, Ned Noddings, Tobin Siebers, and many others. Just like the Zen story seeker, your journey continues long after you take in these morsels of advice. Sorting out ethical commitments in a complex world is a challenge that does not end. It is exhausting, sometimes frustrating work. But there is no task more important for teachers than exploring current social and political issues and considering deeply the ethical impact of our actions. These thoughtful deliberations are not just empty encounters in armchair philosophy that do not matter. These reflections are not about counting angels on the head of a pin. These ethical explorations concern the real lives of children, families, and communities. What teachers believe makes a difference every day to real kids. Go forth and let the prunes sing.

REFERENCES

Albrecht, G. L., Seelman, K. D., & Bury, M. (2001). *Handbook of disability studies*. Thousand Oaks, CA: Sage.

Ayres, W., Quinn, T., & Stovall, D. (2009). *Handbook of social justice in education*. New York: Routledge.

Barnes, C., Oliver, M., & Barton, L. (2002). *Disability studies today*. Cambridge, UK: Polity Press.

Benninga, J. S., Berkowitz, M. W., Kuehn, P., & Smith, K. (2003). The relationship of character education implementation and academic achievement in elementary schools. *Journal of Research in Character Education*, 1, 1, 19–32.

Berkowitz, M. W., & Bier, M. (2005). The interpersonal roots of character education. In D. K. Lapsley & F. C. Power (Eds.), *Character psychology and character education* (pp. 268–285). Notre Dame, IN: University of Notre Dame Press.

Biklen, D. (1992). *Schools without labels: Parents, educators, and inclusive education*. Philadelphia, PA: Temple University Press.

Biklen, D., & Burke, J. (2006). Presuming competence. *Equity & Excellence in Education*, 39, 2, 166–175.

Bogdan, R., & Taylor, S. J. (1994). *The social meaning of mental retardation: Two life stories*. New York: Teachers College Press.

Bogdan, R., & Taylor, S. (1987). Toward a sociology of acceptance: The other side of the study of deviance. *Social Policy*, 18, 2, 34–39.

Brantlinger, E. (1994). High and low income adolescents' views of special education. *Journal of Adolescent Research*, 9, 3, 384–407.

Brantlinger, E. (2001). Poverty, class, and disability: A historical, social, and political perspective. *Focus on Exceptional Children*, 33, 7, 1–19.

Chapman, P. D. (1990). *Schools As sorters: Lewis M. Terman, applied psychology, and the intelligence testing movement, 1890–1930*. New York: New York University Press.

Chapman, T., & Hobbel, N. (2010). *Social justice pedagogy across the curriculum*. Mahwah, NJ: Lawrence Erlbaum.

Connor, D. J. & Ferri. B. A. (2010). Learning Disabilities (special issue). *Disability Studies Quarterly* 30, 2. Retrieved on June 20, 2012 from http://dsq-sds.org/issue/view/46.

Danforth, S. (2009). *The Incomplete child: An intellectual history of learning disabilities*. New York: Peter Lang Publishing.

Danforth, S. (2011a). The actuarial turn in the science of learning disabilities. *Learning Disability Quarterly*, 34, 2, 123–136.

Danforth, S. (2011b). Romantic agrarianism and movement education in the United States: Examining the discursive politics of learning disability science. *Educational Philosophy and Theory*, 43, 6, 636–651.

Danforth, S., & Smith, T. J. (2005). *Engaging troubling students: A constructivist approach*. Thousand Oaks, CA: Corwin Press.

Danforth, S., & Navarro, V. (1998). Speech acts: Sampling the social construction of mental retardation. *Mental Retardation*, 36, 1, 31–43.

Danforth, S., Slocum, L., & Dunkle, J. (2010). Turning the educability narrative: Samuel A. Kirk at the intersection of learning disability and mental retardation. *Intellectual and Developmental Disabilities, 48*, 180–194.

Davis, L. J. (Ed.). (1997). *The disability studies reader.* New York and London: Routledge.

Davis, L. J. (2002). *Bending over backwards: Disability, dismodernism & other difficult positions.* New York: New York University Press.

Dewey, J. (1981a). Creative democracy—The task before us. In J. A. Boydston (Ed.), *John Dewey: The later works, 1925–1953, Volume 14* (pp. 227–228). Carbondale, IL: Southern Illinois University Press.

Dewey, J. (1981b). Ethics. In J. A. Boydston (Ed.), *John Dewey: The later works, 1925–1953, Volume 14.* Carbondale, IL: Southern Illinois University Press.

Dewey, J. (1976a). Individuality, equality, and superiority. In J. A. Boydston (Ed.). *John Dewey: The middle works, 1899–1924, Volume 13* (pp. 295–300). Carbondale, IL: Southern Illinois University Press.

Fierros, E. G., & Conroy, J. W. (2002). Double jeopardy: An exploration of restrictiveness and race in special education. In D. Losen. & G. Orfield (Eds.), *Racial inequity in special education* (pp. 39–70). Cambridge, MA: The Civil Rights Project at Harvard University and the Harvard Education Press.

Freire, P. (1970). *Pedagogy of the oppressed.* (Myra Bergman Ramos, Trans.). New York: Herder & Herder.

Gabel, S. (2005). *Disability studies in education: Readings in theory and method.* New York: Peter Lang.

Gabel, S., & Peters, S. (2004). Presage of a paradigm shift? Beyond the social model of disability toward resistance theories of disability. *Disability & Society, 19*, 6, 585–600.

Harry, B., & Anderson, M. G. (1994). The disproportionate placement of African American males in special education programs: A critique of the process. *The Journal of Negro Education, 63*, 4, 602–619.

Harry, B., Klingner, J. K., Sturges, K. M., & Moore, R. F. (2002). Of rocks and soft places: Using qualitative methods to investigate disproportionality. In D. Losen & G. Orfield (Eds.), *Racial inequity in special education* (pp. 71–92). Cambridge, MA: The Civil Rights Project at Harvard University and the Harvard Education Press.

Harry, B., & Klingner, J. K. (2006). *Why are so many minority students in special education? Understanding race and disability in schools.* New York: Teachers College Press.

King, M. L. (1963). Letter from a Birmingham jail, paragraph 36. Retrieved on June 25, 2012 from http://www.africa.upenn.edu/Articles_Gen/Letter_Birmingham.html.

Kliewer, C. (1998). *Schooling children with Down Syndrome: Toward an understanding of possibility.* New York: Teachers College Press.

Kliewer, C. (2008). *Seeing all kids as readers: A new vision for literacy in the inclusive early education classroom.* Baltimore, MD: Paul H. Brookes.

Lazerson, M. (1983). Origins of special education. In J. G. Chambers & W. T. Hartman (Eds.), *Special education policies: Their history, implementation, and finance* (pp. 15–44). Philadelphia, PA: Temple University Press.

Linton, S. (1998). *Claiming disability: Knowledge and identity.* New York: New York University Press.

Losen, D. J., & Orfield, G. (2002). *Racial inequity in special education.* Boston, MA: Harvard University Press.

Oliver, M. (1990). *The politics of disablement.* London: MacMillan.

Martin, J. (2002). *The education of John Dewey: A biography.* New York: Columbia University Press.

Michelson, J. R. (2000). *Our sons were labeled behavior disordered: Here are the stories of our lives.* Troy, NY: Educator's International Press.

Noblit, G. W. (1993). Power and caring. *American Educational Research Journal, 30,* 23–38.

Noblit, G. W., Rogers, D. L., & McCadden, B. M. (1995). In the meantime: The possibilities of caring. *The Phi Delta Kappan, 76,* 9, 680–685.

Noddings, N. (1992). *The challenge to care in schools: An alternative approach to education.* New York: Teachers College Press.

Noddings, N. (1995). A morally defensible mission for schools in the 21st century. *The Phi Delta Kappan, 76,* 5, 365–368.

Pang, V. O., Rivera, J., & Mora, J. K. (2000). The ethic of caring: Clarifying the foundation of multicultural education. *The Educational Forum, 64,* 1, 25–32.

Ryan, A. (1997). *John Dewey and the high tide of American liberalism.* New York: W. W. Norton.

Savarese, E. T., & Savarese, R. J. (2010). Autism and the concept of neurodiversity (special issue). *Disability Studies Quarterly, 30,* 1. Retrieved on June 20, 2012 from http://dsq-sds.org/issue/view/43.

Siebers, T. (2008). *Disability theory.* Ann Arbor, MI: University of Michigan Press.

Slee, R. (2011). *The irregular school: Exclusion, schooling, and inclusive education.* New York: Routledge.

Thomson, R. G. (1997). *Extraordinary bodies: Figuring physical disability in American culture and literature.* New York: Columbia University Press.

Union of Physically Impaired Against Segregation. (1975). Fundamental principles of disability. Retrieved June 18, 2012, from http://www.leeds.ac.uk/disability-studies/archiveuk/UPIAS/fundamental%20principles.pdf.

Valle, J. (2009). *What mothers say about special education: From the 1960s to the present.* New York: Palgrave MacMillan.

Westbrook, R. F. (1993). *John Dewey and American democracy.* Ithaca, NY: Cornell University Press.

Zenderland, L. (2001). *Measuring minds: Henry Herbert Goddard and the origins of American intelligence testing.* New York: Cambridge University Press.

SECTION TWO

The Living Tradition of Inclusive Education Practice

In Section Two, we begin an exploration of the fourth challenge.

> Steeping Yourself in the Tradition of Inclusive Practice: Through practical experimentation and research analysis, working for over two decades, educators and parents have developed a growing repertoire of promising inclusive education practices. Joining this tradition of pedagogy involves learning what this tradition has created [...] so far.

> "Teaching is hard. Teaching well is fiercely so." (Tomlinson, 2000, p. 11)

> "Good instruction is good instruction: the goals and procedures are clearly articulated; the instruction is relevant, accessible, and responsive; and the tasks are interesting and challenging, but reachable with effort. Disabled students benefit from good instruction, just as all students do." (Broderick, Mehta-Parek, & Reid, 2005, p. 200)

Imagine that you are hired to teach in a school where doing inclusion well is as ordinary and everyday as breathing oxygen. The question of whether or not to embrace inclusion as a crucial social goal was long ago eclipsed by the daily task of working together to develop and refine the classroom and school practices that make inclusion successful. Over many years of concerted effort, cooperation between professionals and families, and intensive adult learning, a tradition of knowledge and practice has grown. To a new teacher, the culture of knowledge is thick, deep, powerful, and practical, providing guidance and sustenance at every step. As a newcomer, you find yourself surrounded by supportive colleagues who gently and patiently pass on their wisdom, helping you find your way as an inclusive educator. You step into this wonderful environment and immediately begin to soak it up like a happy sponge.

It is likely that the wisdom of the inclusive tradition would be passed on to you in two specific ways. First, the veteran teachers and the students' families would tell you stories. They would share the narratives of struggle and success that they have experienced as they have built the inclusive teaching craft. Drawn from the depths of their own experiences, these stories would express how inclusion came about in this place, how it grew and grew up, and how it is practiced in the present day. These tales would provide exemplars of thought and practice for your emulation, serving as an open invitation to bring yourself and your talents into the living narrative of that unique school. And the stories would also open up complex issues and challenging questions for conversations, allowing you to enter into uncertain spaces where the answers refuse to fall off the trees into your apron pockets.

Second, sometimes linked to the stories but also standing alone, you would receive advice. The families who have sent a string of siblings to the school and the veteran teachers would tell you and show you how they do what they do. They would share the lessons that they have learned. They would prod, nudge, and encourage you toward more inclusive and accepting pedagogical practices. Think about this. Here is something for you to consider.

The purpose of Section Two is to provide you with an opportunity to steep yourself in the rich tradition of inclusive instructional practices that have been developed by general classroom teachers, special educators, parents, students, and researchers over the past twenty-five years. The chapters of Section Two offer an overview of the professional practices that most successful inclusive educators employ in their daily work. Quite purposefully, the knowledge presented in this practice is delivered in the form of morsels of advice, suggestions for the development of your teaching practice.

This overview of inclusive practice is by no means comprehensive. There is no realistic way to capture every innovative and fascinating practice devised by the creative, limitless minds of inclusive teachers. Furthermore, these chapters not meant to imply that every educator utilizes every practice described. The practices offered here are best viewed as a brief summary of the multiple dimensions of the inclusive teaching tradition.

The craft of inclusive teaching has been derived from empirical investigation and trial-and-error, culled from the best creativity of practicing teachers, school leaders, loving parents, and dedicated inclusive educational researchers. It offers a glimpse of the current state of the art of inclusion, the limited but best that we currently know about being successful at inclusive education. If you accepted a teaching job at a highly inclusive school, a place where the tradition of inclusion had been alive, cultivated carefully by caring, thoughtful practitioners for many years, these are the main practices that you would be encouraged to learn, embrace, and further enhance.

The living tradition of inclusive education has deep roots in the past, growing upward from the experiences of educators who invented new ways of teaching. Those innovations began as half-baked, original, untried ideas about what teachers and students might do together in the classroom. At first, bold teachers experimented with these novel ideas, testing them in the classroom. Through both systematic empirical study and the thoughtful reflections of wise teachers, these raw creations were refined and improved.

The growing, developing tradition was passed on to other teachers, by word of mouth and publication, through workshop, conference presentation, and teacher's blog. Over many years, as the craft of inclusive education was developed, as the practices were sharpened and polished, the circle of educators in the United States, Canada, Australia, Europe, and elsewhere widened. The conversation about how to do inclusive education best went worldwide.

Built on the lessons of the past, drawn from the aggregated experiences and wisdom of courageous educators over decades, the tradition of inclusive teaching lives in the present and looks to the future. As inclusion is put into practice today in schools around the world, teachers, researchers and parents continue to not only implement a series of effective practices. As they enact the best of what we know about teaching in inclusive classrooms and schools, they also continue to innovate and refine, improving and trying out new ways of teaching students of all abilities. They know that the tradition of inclusive teaching only lives and breathes if the current practice is more than a derivative repetition of what has been done before. In this sense, inclusive education remains fresh and alive only if today's practitioners continue to experiment and boldly develop new versions of the old craft.

THE HEART OF SUCCESSFUL INCLUSIVE TEACHING

Inclusive education researchers Lani Florian and Kristine Black-Hawkins (2011, 2012) have articulated three central principles that drive effective inclusive pedagogy practice. Successful inclusive teachers:

1. *Create a classroom community that supports the learning of all students.* This approach shifts the "focus from one that is concerned with only those individuals who have been identified as having 'additional needs' to the learning of all children in the community of the classroom." Rather than having a general educator teach the so-called nondisabled students while the special educator attends to those with special needs, the general education classroom is fashioned as an accepting space with "learning opportunities that are suffi-

ciently made available for *everyone*, so that all learners are able to participate in classroom life" (Florian & Black-Hawkins, 2011, p. 818).
2. *Believe that all students are learners.* Students certainly vary greatly in how they learn best, how fast they learn, and what subjects or topics capture their interest. But they all learn, grow, develop, and progress. This belief rejects antiquated and limiting "beliefs about ability as being fixed and the associated idea that the presence of some will hold back the progress of others." Teachers actively enact the belief "that *all* children will make progress, learn and achieve" by "using a variety of grouping strategies to support everyone's learning rather than relying on ability grouping to separate ('able' from 'less able' students)" (Florian & Black-Hawkins, 2011, p. 818).
3. *Frame challenges not as student's problems but as invitations for teachers to work together to improve their teaching.* Teachers view "difficulties in learning as professional challenges for teachers, rather than deficits in learners." Teachers collaborate to develop "new ways of working to support the learning of all children." The recognized path to improved teaching is a strong commitment to "continuing professional development as a way of developing more inclusive practices" (Florian & Black-Hawkins, 2011, p. 819; Florian, 2006).

Instead of asking, *what is wrong with this child?* inclusive educators ask, *how can we teach better?* What can we do to be more effective for this student? What can we do to be more effective for all students? (Black-Hawkins & Florian, 2012; Florian, 2006; Florian & Black-Hawkins, 2011).

The practical advice and suggestions offered in the chapters of Section Two all begin and end with this important distinction. The goal is not to figure out what is "wrong" with students but to concoct, cook up, and create better ways to teach.

REFERENCES

Black-Hawkins, K. & Florian, L. (2012). Classroom teachers' craft knowledge of their inclusive practice. *Teachers and Teaching, 18,* 5, 567–584.

Broderick, A., Mehta-Parek, H., & Reid, D. K. (2005). Differentiating instruction for disabled students in inclusive classrooms. *Theory into Practice, 44,* 3, 194–202.

Florian, L., & Black-Hawkins, K. (2011). Exploring inclusive pedagogy. *British Educational Research Journal, 37,* 5, 813–828.

Florian, L. (2006). Teaching strategies: For some or all? *Kairaranga, 7,* 24–27.

Tomlinson, C. A. (2000). Reconcilable differences? Standards-based teaching and differentiation. *Educational Leadership, 58,* 1, 6–11.

CHAPTER FIVE

Collaboration and Co-teaching

> **Guiding Question**
> - How can you collaborate and co-teach with general/special education colleagues?

"(I)nclusion must view teaching as a finely crafted *group* enterprise and no longer the classical one-teacher-per-class model." (Gerber, 2012, p. 77, italics original)

In 1996, First Lady of the United States Hillary Rodham Clinton wrote a book called *It Takes a Village*. Expanding on the well-known proverb "It takes a village to raise a child," Clinton articulated a vision of childhood involving more than just the conventional two parents or the less traditional single parent providing the guidance and love to the growing child. In order to grow up safe, healthy, and learned, a child needs teaching, nurturance, and support from many people in the family and community.

Similarly, inclusive education frames teaching as more than a single teacher standing at a chalkboard in front of a class of students. Waldron & Van Zandt Allen (1999, p. 19) proclaim, "The days of the lonely teacher are over." The traditional picture of a solitary teacher who directs a classroom of students through a learning activity identical in content and process for all is replaced by a more social and complex vision of teaching and learning. In inclusive schools, the individual student is viewed as learning social and academic lessons from multiple adults as well as from classmates. Simply put, the adults (teachers, teacher's aides, other professionals) must be able to collaborate as an effective team, and often the students must do the same.

The most common form of collaboration among educational professionals in inclusive classrooms is co-teaching. Gately and Gately (2001, p. 41, italics original) define co-teaching as

> *the collaboration between general and special education teachers for all of the teaching responsibilities of all students assigned to a classroom.* In a co-taught classroom, two teachers, general and special educators, work together to develop a differentiated curriculum that meets the needs of a diverse population of students. In a co-taught classroom, teachers share the planning, presentation, evaluation, and classroom management in an effort to enhance the learning environment for all students.

Co-teaching means providing two teachers—most typically a general educator and special educator—for the entire class. Both teachers are responsible for all of the students (Scruggs, Mastropieri, & McDuffie, 2007; Smith & Leonard, 2005). This effectively cuts the teacher-to-student ratio in half, offering teachers an opportunity to provide more instruction, support, and guidance to each student.

The basic structures of co-teaching, the six most common models used by teachers, have been articulated by Marilyn Cook and Lynn Friend (2013). These should be viewed as a basic starting place, an initial vocabulary, not as the final word on what two creative teachers might create in the classroom.

ONE TEACH, ONE OBSERVE

One teacher takes the primary role, leading the instructional lesson, as the second teacher collects observational data. The purpose of the observing teacher is to collect data on a specific learning or behavior issue in the classroom. The data is gathered in an attempt to understand or solve a specific question. The data may be quantitative (e.g., behavior counts) or qualitative (e.g., descriptions of what students do and say). Both teachers should know why the data collection is happening, and the data should be analyzed together by the pair.

ONE TEACH, ONE DRIFT

One teacher is the main instructional leader in the lesson and the second teacher circulates among the students to provide specific forms of assistance. The "drifting" teacher operates as a flexible helper who supplies on-the-spot support and guidance to students in need. This may take the form of answering questions, scaffolding learning, or providing prompts and redirection to guide off task or misbehaving students.

PARALLEL TEACHING

The students are divided into two large, relatively equal groups. Each teacher is responsible for providing instruction to one group. Two simultaneous lessons are carried out.

The purpose of this structure is twofold. First, this format instantly takes advantage of the reduced teacher-student ratio. A classroom of thirty six eighth graders effectively becomes two side-by-side "classes" of eighteen students, each with its own teacher. Students have greater access to the teacher who is leading the lesson.

Second, while the two parallel lessons address the same academic content, they need not be identical. An element of differentiation may be employed. The same academic content may be taught in two different ways in order to better meet the needs of the students. Perhaps one group of students will benefit from a short Powerpoint presentation while the other group would learn better from engaging in small group activities. Maybe one group utilizes more complex and varied informational texts while the second group reads less advanced, less complicated materials.

STATION TEACHING

Stations or centers are learning activity hubs, kiosks or cubicles where the materials and opportunities for students to learn are packaged into a useful work space. Often stations or centers are locations in the classroom; a table in the corner, a carpeted area near the bookcases, a laboratory science bench, or a cluster of desks. Teachers load these sites with well-planned, neatly organized learning activities for individuals or small groups.

Often the goal is to organize sufficient information, guidance, and the necessary texts and other materials so that students can work with a minimal amount of adult supervision. In some cases, stations are deliberately designed to be supervised by a teacher or classroom aide who supplies specific support and assistance. Highly talented teachers often use their centers or stations repeatedly, re-loading them with new content and activities as the curricular timeline of the academic year progresses.

Operating a classroom filled with stations with two teachers is, not surprisingly, easier and more fun than going it alone. Imagine, for example, that the students are working in five stations scattered around the room. Perhaps one station is set up as a small group lesson center where new content is learned and four are designed as independent learning sites where students practice skills. One teacher might provide intensive, small group instruction at the new content station while the second teacher is freed up to assist and supervise students in the independent centers. This is just one example of how stations and teachers might be configured. The options are as endless as the imaginations of the two collaborating instructors.

ALTERNATIVE TEACHING

While parallel teaching typically refers to two teachers working with two student groups of equal size, alternative teaching describes situations when the majority of the class learns in one group and a smaller ("alternative") group participates in a different learning activity. The creation of a smaller, sidecar group is very strategic and may address a number of goals. For students with advanced levels of knowledge and skills, the small group can pursue extension activities that go beyond the scope of the standard curriculum. For students who struggle to learn the grade level curriculum, the small group may be an opportunity for either re-teaching or pre-teaching. Pre-teaching means providing foundational, preparatory instruction before the entire class begins a specific academic unit. Some students benefit greatly from learning vocabulary, concepts, or skills before participating in a whole class lesson. Re-teaching means remediation, breaking down what has already been taught in the class into segments and forms that are accessible to struggling learners.

TEAM TEACHING

For many educators, team teaching is what they envision when they think of co-teaching. The two teachers join together in a relatively seamless fashion as co-leaders or co-facilitators of a lesson. To an observer, the teachers seem to be in dialog with one another. They share in speaking to the class, giving instructions or explaining ideas, taking turns, finishing one another's sentences, bouncing questions and answers back and forth like two cooperating heads of the same teaching body. They might debate an issue, offering pros and cons. Or one instructor may talk while the other guides students through a visual demonstration, using physical objects or images on the screen. Many teachers attest that achieving this kind of unified, coherent interaction requires effective planning and a strong working relationship.

SUGGESTIONS AND ADVICE

Suggestion #1: Begin to create your co-teaching partnership by focusing on the interpersonal relationship. It is the very ground you both teach upon.

If the essence of co-teaching can be captured in a nutshell, it is this: the effectiveness of co-teaching directly reflects the quality of the working relationship between the two teachers. At best, a teaching team can soar to unforeseen heights. At worst, the duo can fail themselves and their students in profound ways.

If the two teachers collaborate well, the instructional power of the pair is magnified many times. The team promotes student growth and learning far more than what two independent teachers can do. But if the two teachers miscommunicate, conflict, and misunderstand one another, then the two teachers are less effective than having a single instructor teach the class (Cramer & Stivers, 2007; Gately & Gately, 2001; Scruggs, Mastropieri & McDuffie, 2007; Sims, 2008; van Hover, Hicks, & Sayeski, 2012).

Hold a meeting or a series of meetings before you begin to teach together. Get to know one another as unique individuals and as professional teachers (DeVore, Miolo, & Hader, 2011; NEA, 2013; Sims, 2008; Tannock, 2009). Of the *Six Steps of Successful Co-teaching* developed by the National Education Association, the first three focus on building a trustful, effective relationship prior to engaging in any shared teaching activities: "Begin by getting to know one another as persons, not as teachers [...]. Talk to one another as new acquaintances who could possibly become good friends" (NEA, 2013).

Second, after beginning to share who you are as persons, talk specifically about yourselves as teachers. Explain your teaching styles, "how you plan lessons, use texts, manipulative materials, and online resources, how you organize the students, how you utilize time, how you assess learning, and how you manage behavior" (NEA, 2013). Begin to examine how your styles might be complementary or might potentially clash. Rarely do two teachers simply leap into sweet harmony, twins separated at birth now reunited in seventh grade English class. Frequently, the merging of two teaching styles into a single team requires negotiation and compromise.

Notice that these steps require a very full and deep form of listening. Nowhere in your teacher education program were you taught how to create a relational foundation built of mutual respect. Nevertheless, this is exactly what developing a powerful co-teaching relationship requires. Listening with an open mind and heart, learning to hear the other person in a focused and supportive way, two teachers begin to create the quality of trust and communication to be an effective team in the classroom (NEA, 2013; Sims, 2008; Tannock, 2009; van Hover, Hicks, & Sayeski, 2012)

Follow this with a discussion of your strengths and weaknesses as a teacher. This step requires tremendous honesty. What do you do well? What do you like to do? What do you need to improve? What parts of teaching do you not like to do? This discussion allows the duo to begin to imagine how two teaching repertoires might join in a complementary fashion. Like two dancers now combined as partners, you each bring a variety of talents, preferences, and imperfections to the new alliance. If you do this right, the best steps, turns, and spins of each partner will not only be featured. They will compensate for the limitations of the other team member.

Suggestion #2: Take a long, patient view of the co-teaching partnership. This is a shared process of growth and learning that requires extensive effort and time.

High school teacher Emily Sims (2008, p. 62) advises: "Understand that it will take a while to get it right. Co-teaching, like any partnership, takes work. It is not going to be amazing from day one, and that is OK. Just be willing to do the work to make it happen."

Gately and Gately (2001, p. 42) have devised a three stage scheme that illustrates a general path of growth and improvement taken by co-teaching partners. This provides co-teachers with a rough roadmap for charting progress and understanding what is necessary to move ahead toward greater effectiveness as a team.

1. "Beginning Stage—Guarded, careful communication"—Initially, co-teaching partners often communicate in superficial and polite ways, being careful not to step on one another's toes. The two tend to operate at an emotional and practical distance from one another, perhaps in partial denial of the fact that they are sharing a classroom and a group of students. The duo operate more like the parallel play of toddlers, working side by side, each getting things done, but not cooperating substantially or combining in a mutual way. Communications are infrequent and partial, lacking a depth of meaning, demonstrating little sense of trust or unity. At this initial stage, the pair does not have a shared sense of mission. Sadly, some co-teaching partners do not progress beyond this level.
2. "Compromising Stage—Give and take communication, with a sense of having to 'give up' to 'get'"—In the second stage, each teacher understands that the effectiveness and emotional comfort of the shared classroom requires some degree of compromise by each person. The partners are beginning to develop a sense of trust. But they do not yet view themselves as contributing time, energy, and talent to a common enterprise, to a mutual team effort. They often feel like each is compromising to other person's needs, reluctantly giving up pieces of their own teaching style or educational values in order to make it work.
3. "Collaborating Stage—Open communication and interaction, mutual admiration"—At the most advanced level of co-teaching partnership, the communication is open, honest, comfortable, and effective. "The two teachers work together and complement each other. At this stage, it is often difficult for outsiders to discern which teacher is the special educator and which is the general educator" (Gately and Gately, 2001, p. 42). Interactions in the planning and teaching of lessons flow gracefully and easily. The teachers are each contributing halves of a cohesive instructional team.

At this advanced level of team performance, changes in one teacher's practices are not viewed as a personal loss or sacrifice. What may have seemed like compromises at earlier stages are now viewed as "steps you are willing to take to achieve your overall goal of working together" (Cramer & Stivers, 2007, p. 7). The typical focus on teaching practice as a personal, solitary craft comprised of a repertoire of your own choices and tastes is replaced by a shared goal of creating a harmonious and effective teaching team.

Suggestion #3: Pursue parity in the team teaching relationship. The roles and responsibilities of the two teachers for all of the students should be clear and equal in value.

All too often, when a general educator and special educator co-teach in the general teacher's classroom, the special educator is viewed as a lesser partner. The general educator is the leader, the captain of the academic content, the landlord of the classroom real estate. The special educator is a visitor who helps out, often focusing disproportionately on "her own" students, those with disabilities. The result is unfortunate. The special educator and the students with disabilities are unduly stigmatized, submerged to a second class citizenship within the class. Avoid this. Work hard, very hard, to avoid this distribution of effort and responsibilities.

If the co-teaching partnership is going to be truly effective, "the individuals in each pair should be on an equal footing" (Scruggs, Mastropieri, & McDuffie, 2007, p. 412). The team may begin with the general educator primarily taking the lead and the special educator serving as a classroom assistant. Especially in secondary classrooms with advanced academic content, this is not a surprising starting place. But the goal, as the teaching team grows and develops, is to become a partnership of two equal contributors who provide two real teachers for all students on an equal basis.

How? First, clearly plan who is going to do what (DeVore, Miolo, & Hader, 2011). Based on their extensive study of co-teaching in elementary and middle schools of Louisiana, Smith and Leonard (2005, p. 277) concluded that "the roles and responsibilities of general education and special education teachers (as well as those of other inclusion team members) need to be clarified." Role clarification is necessary in order for the two teachers to instruct and support all the students.

In their research in an inclusive preschool, Mogharreban and Bruns (2009, pp. 408–9) discovered that "(r)ole uncertainty became our most immediate and enduring challenge. The first hurdle was to figure out who should be doing what." They suggest that the teachers and other professionals involved in the classroom write out a detailed, clear list of the roles and responsibilities of each person. These lists can facilitate an in-depth discussion leading to clarification of jobs and assignments. Discuss what each person is doing for each unit of study or each lesson. Who is leading the presentation to the class? Who is monitoring and guiding students who struggle with attention or behavior issues? Who is helping the student cooperative groups understand the task expectations? Who is assessing the students' completed projects?

But this should not be a one-time occurrence. Numerous researchers emphasize the need for co-teaching partners to not only have an initial discussion about professional roles and responsibilities but to incorporate this conversation into regularly scheduled planning meetings. It is virtually impossible to succeed in co-teaching without planning together on a consistent basis (Mogharreban & Bruns, 2009; Scruggs, Mastropieri, & McDuffie, 2007; Smith & Leonard, 2005; Waldron & Van Zandt Allen, 1999).

This can be very difficult in schools where shared planning times are not worked into the weekly schedule. Sims (2008) implores co-teachers to find, make, or otherwise steal the time to plan together.

> If the school does not provide you with a common planning time, you have to find the time. Many teachers resent this and refuse to commit the extra time. Please do not adopt such an attitude. If you will not bend, your students will break. (Sims, 2008, p. 60)

Teaching together without planning together doesn't really qualify as teaching together.

Second, the special educator must become highly knowledgeable of the academic content in the class (Gately & Gately, 2001; Mastropieri, Scruggs, Graetz, Norland, Gardizi, & McDuffie, 2005). "Both teachers need to be familiar with all material being taught ever day" (Sims, 2008, p. 63).

This can be a significant challenge. But it is a challenge that special educators often meet. For example, it is not uncommon for a special educator in a high school to co-teach in three, four, or even five different content classes per day. This can mean having to master advanced mathematics, science, history, or a second language, often without the benefit of sufficient university coursework in the subject matter discipline. Many high school special educators view their first year co-teaching in an advanced content class as an opportunity to learn the course matter along with the students. Maybe it was fifteen years since you took geometry, but it all comes back. And it is often grasped more easily and fully the second time! Then the special educator is fully competent and ready for the course content by the second year of co-teaching.

Suggestion #4: Effective and productive co-teaching relationships rely on habits of action, repetitive activities that structure the partnership and create an opportunity for success. Be very intentional about adopting good team-making habits.

In recent years, teachers and teacher educators have been inundated with the notion of reflective practice, the idea that teachers should think in specific, observant ways about themselves and their practices in order to improve. A teacher can hardly eat lunch or park her car without some education expert demanding that she be more reflective! The deluge of writing and talk about reflection perhaps serves as a demonstration of the fact that what teachers do every day is primarily a matter of habit. If you want to know what a teacher will do on Tuesday, observe what he does on Monday. We all tend to do what we did the time before. We tend to take inhabit routines of action that give some sense of order and comfort to our work day.

Obviously, the demand that teachers become more reflective arises from the concern that too much teaching practice is mindless, a matter of empty habits, of behavior unexamined and unquestioned. But there is a positive side to our teaching habits. Rather than lament the way that humans tend to act in habitual ways, we can harness the power of habit by quite strategically choosing the best habits to adopt, the most effective behavior sets to incorporate into our daily routines. Co-teaching teams can become more successful by intentionally, by design, taking on habitual teaching behaviors that dramatically improve the cohesion and effectiveness of the teaching partners. Choose good habits and help one another institute them as standard operating procedure.

What are some good co-teaching habits? Researchers have recommended quite a few.

- Allocate a portion of each meeting to the task of reviewing student work. This helps both instructors focus on the learning progress as well as the difficulties and interests of each student (Tannock, 2009).
- Attend all meetings with parents and IEP conferences together. "You should both be present when speaking to parents or when being involved in any academic decisions about a student" (Sims, 2008, p. 63). The shared element of co-teaching knows no boundaries. Grading, communications, planning, presentations, classroom discipline […] there are two teachers with their hands in everything.
- Learn together. Nothing will boost the unity and power of the team more than working together on professional development and growth. Attend a workshop or conference together. Read and discuss professional articles and books. Thinking, learning, and talking to one another opens endless doors to new innovations and improvements (Cramer & Stivers, 2007).
- Both teachers work equally on differentiation of instruction, on modifications and accommodations to suit the needs of individual students. It may seem as if the special educator is the professional with expertise in modifying assignments and assessments to promote full access for students with disabilities. At first, this is likely to be true. But just as the special educator should make the effort to master the academic content of the class, so too should the general educator develop the skills of instructional differentiation and curricular adaptation (Smith & Leonard, 2005).

- Create shared assessment rubrics that help you calibrate and coordinate your grading practices. With two people handling grading, there is the danger that the whole activity becomes inconsistent and off-kilter. If you share grading rubrics that you develop together, you are more likely to be on the same page when evaluating student work and providing feedback to students (Smith & Leonard, 2005).

REFERENCES

Cook, L., & Friend, M. (2013). *Interactions: Collaboration skills for school professionals*. New York: Pearson.

Cramer, S., & Stivers, J. (2007). Don't give up! Practical strategies for challenging collaborations. *TEACHING Exceptional Children, 39*, 6, 6–11.

DeVore, S., Miolo, G., & Hader, J. (2011). Individualizing inclusion for preschool children using collaborative consultation. *Young Exceptional Children, 14*, 31–43.

Gately, S. E., & Gately, F. J. (2001). Understanding co-teaching components. *Teaching Exceptional Children, 33*, 4, 40–47.

Gerber, M. M. (2012). Emerging issues in teacher education for inclusion in the United States. In C. Forlin (Ed.), *Future directions for inclusive teacher education: An international perspective* (pp. 71–80). New York: Routledge.

Mastropieri, M. A., Scruggs, T. E., Graetz, J., Norland, J., Gardizi, W., & McDuffie, K. (2005). Case studies in co-teaching in the content areas: Successes, failures, and challenges. *Intervention in School and Clinic, 40*, 5, 260–270.

Mogharreban, C. C., & Bruns, D. (2009). Moving to inclusive pre-kindergarten classrooms: Lessons from the field. *Early Childhood Education Journal, 36*, 407–414.

National Education Association. (2013). *6 steps to successful co-teaching: Helping special and regular education teachers work together*. http://www.nea.org/tools/6-steps-to-successful-co-teaching.html.

Scruggs, T. E., Mastropieri, M. A., & McDuffie, K. A (2007). Co-teaching in inclusive classrooms: A metasynthesis of qualitative research. *Exceptional Children, 73*, 4, 392–416.

Sims, E. (2008). Sharing command of the co-teaching ship: How to play nicely with others. *English Journal, 97*, 5, 58–63.

Smith, R., & Leonard, P. (2005). Collaboration for inclusion: Practitioner perspectives. *Equity & Excellence in Education, 38*, 269–279.

Tannock, M. T. (2009). Tangible and intangible elements of collaborative teaching. *Intervention in School and Clinic, 44*, 3, 173–178.

van Hover, S., Hicks, D., & Sayeski, K. (2012). A case study of co-teaching in an inclusive secondary high-stakes world history I classroom. *Theory and research in social education, 40*, 3, 260–291.

Waldron, N., & Van Zandt Allen, L. (1999). Successful strategies for inclusion at the middle school level. *Middle School Journal, 30*, 4, 18–28.

CHAPTER SIX

Friendships in the Classroom

> **Guiding Question**
> - How can you promote the development of friendships among students with and without disabilities in the classroom?

Teachers and parents are aware that many nondisabled students have not been offered sufficient opportunities to develop friendships with disabled peers. Segregated programs separate nondisabled students from disabled classmates. Disabled young people miss out on the opportunities for fulfillment and learning available in the mainstream community of friends. Many students with disabilities experience loneliness and a lack of social connectedness in the public schools. In many cases, disabled students not only feel socially isolated. They are also the frequent target of acts of ridicule and teasing that deliver rejection with harshness and brutality.

But the harm cuts both ways. Nondisabled students often forego the joy and life-expanding experience of befriending a student with a disability. The possibility of connecting with and personally knowing a person with a disability has often been stolen away from the nondisabled child or adolescent who, due to the bodily absence of disabled classmates, doesn't even know what she is missing. Given a childhood bereft of significant relationships with disabled pals, it is not surprising when a nondisabled child grows into an adult who unthinkingly discriminates against persons with disabilities.

Educational researchers have applied a standard yet foolish logic to the problem of the lack of interpersonal relationships between disabled and nondisabled students. Stated bluntly, *persons with disabilities are to blame*. The problem is not that disabled youngsters, segregated away in special education classrooms and schools, lack access to opportunities to create relationships with nondisabled peers. The problem is not that the nondisabled peers often enact the ableist attitudes of the broader society by rejecting disabled children as unfit playmates and friends. The problem, in this line of thinking, is that young people with disabilities lack the communication and social skills necessary for effective interactions and relationship development. Central or corollary to their impairments is a social deficit that effectively blocks them off from performing the necessary behaviors to develop friendships (e.g., Cook, Gresham, Kern, Barreras, Thornton, & Crews, 2008; Gresham, 1997; Reichow & Volkmar, 2010).

Special educator H. N. F. Myers (2013, pp. 11–12) has summarized decades of research findings on the incredible assortment of social deficits said to afflict young persons with disabilities:

> Many students with disabilities have unique personal/social needs in addition to the academic issues related to their disability. Current research suggests a number of social difficulties that come with a diagnosis of a physical, emotional, or learning disability. Some of these include:
>
> - low self-esteem
> - higher levels of stress and anxiety
> - poor social skills
> - learned helplessness

Myers (2012, p. 12) goes on to declare that persons with disabilities often "demonstrate ineffective anger management" and have an increased risk of "suffering from depression, conduct disorders" and substance abuse problems.

If one were to believe this authoritative list of flaws compiled by special education researchers, the chances of a person with a disability finding a friend or having any sort of satisfactory relationship life are slim. They are too bogged down by their own overwhelming anxieties, explosive anger, self-defeating habits, and social incompetence to make a friend.

Prominent in this research tradition is the accompanying notion that children with disabilities are too unconventional in appearance and behavior to participate in meaningful friendships. A common truism recited in the research literature is that "children prefer peers with whom they have something in common. Children also prefer peers who are more like themselves in terms of dress, language, behavior, and ability" (Boutot, 2007, p. 156; DiSalvo & Oswald, 2002). That is, children like friends who look and act like they do. They want to look in the mirror when they look at a friend because there is psychological comfort in a high degree of social uniformity. It would seem that social homogeneity is the ideal climate for the development of interpersonal relationships.

Children without disabilities would choose disabled students for relationships if only those disabled students looked and acted more like nondisabled students.

Since the early 1980's, social skills development programs have been the standard remedy offered by researchers for disabled children whose behavior and communication seemed to lack the uniformity necessary for social success (Goldstein, 1980; Goldstein, 1988; McGinnis & Goldstein, 1984). The promise is that if disabled kids learn to interact in a way that more closely conforms to the normative social behaviors of nondisabled students, then they will fit in better socially. That act of social conformity, cast by researchers as improvements in social competence, will lead to more successful interactions and friendships with nondisabled peers (e.g., Boutot, 2007; Danko & Buysse, 2002; Grenier, Rogers, & Iarrusso, 2008; Hart & Whalon, 2011). As a result, many special educators recommend social skills intervention programs for students with many different impairments, including blindness (Zacks & Wolffe, 2006), deafness (Schloss & Smith, 1990), learning disabilities and ADHD (Giler, 2011), autism (Cumpata & Fell, 2010), intellectual disabilities (Antonello, 1996; Goldstein, Kaczmarek, & English, 2002), and emotional-behavioral disorders (Volz, Snyder, & Sterba, 2009).

Virtually everyone could benefit from some social skills training. That's not the question. The issue is the assumption that social uniformity is the basis for human relationships. Do we really believe that honest, supportive, and caring friendships among children in school happen best when students learn in a homogeneous environment? Does friendship work best when the friends are similar to one another?

Likewise, do we believe that young people who differ from one another—persons of different races, religions, social classes, or abilities—are unable to form strong friendships because they differ from one another? Is friendship thwarted by social diversity?

Historian Barry M. Franklin has traced the roots of the ideology of homogeneity to the response of American educators to the influx of immigrants and the growth of cities in the late nineteenth century. The agrarian model of community, based on rural, small town life, held that commonality made for safe and harmonious relationships. It was thought that a person naturally related in an orderly and stable fashion to like-minded, similar persons. Human diversity and cultural difference were assumed by many turn-of-the-century educators and leaders to be disruptions of the very moral fabric of community. Differences, as represented by unusual or even frightful newcomers from overseas, caused "the larger corruption of the nation's rural virtue" (Franklin, 1986, p. 7).

Drawing from progressive thought of the late twentieth and early twenty first century, inclusive education does not assume that uniformity of appearance, attitudes, and behavior are the moral foundation of community and human relationships. To the contrary, inclusion accepts the historical challenge and opportunity of the present moment, asking teachers, families, and young people to prosper in heterogeneous communities built of interpersonal relationships reaching across all lines of social difference (Sapon-Shevin, 1999, 2003). To inclusive educators, relationships filled with caring and fulfillment are not outgrowths of social uniformity but represent the flexibility and depth of the human spirit in action, the capacity of persons to be compassionate, understanding, and supportive to one another (Pang, 2005; Pang, Rivera, & Mora, 2000).

One can easily argue that social skills, thoughts and behaviors that actively take into account the feelings and perspectives of other persons, matter greatly in a complex, multicultural social environment. Making and maintaining a good friendship obviously requires some degree of social skill and effort by two persons. If we are specifically seeking a goal of improving friendships between students with disabilities and nondisabled peers, we acknowledge that both persons must make meaningful contributions to the relationship. The give and take, compromise and accommodation, of a friendship is a two way street, involving a pair of giving and devoted partners. The responsibility for the success of the relationship is shared equally by the two participating persons.

Social skills development programs undoubtedly have a role in helping young people to learn about how to be a good friend. This is true not because students with disabilities show up to the party lacking a set of magical friendship ingredients. This is true because many children and youth, regardless of whether they have a disability, have much to learn when it comes to the ethical and practical complexities of peaceful, cooperative, and fulfilling relationships.

The question for inclusive educators is not *how can we fix up the deficit-ridden disabled students so they can participate in relationships at school?* The vital question is *how can we create a school culture that supports the development of positive, support, nurturing interpersonal relationships across the many lines of human diversity? How can we and our students create a social environment where students who may be quite unalike learn to respect one another, love each other, and learn together?*

SUGGESTIONS AND ADVICE

Suggestion 1: Strive to build a classroom and school culture of acceptance. When the interconnected web of social relationships among the adults and the students is accepting and supportive of human and cultural differences, then you have the healthy, social foundation of an effective inclusive school.

The concept of acceptance as an ethical cornerstone to building relationships with persons with disabilities was first proposed by disability researchers Robert Bogdan and Steven Taylor (1989). Over years of sociological research, they noticed that, even in a society where people with significant disabilities are often rejected as outcasts, some nondisabled persons engaged in very deep, meaningful, caring relationships with disabled friends and family members. They decided to study these relationships to understand

> how nondisabled people who are in caring and accepting relationships with severely disabled others (people with severe and profound mental retardation or multiple disabilities) define them. Although the disabled people in these relationships sometimes drool, soil themselves, do not talk or walk-traits that most would consider highly undesirable-they are accepted by the nondisabled people as valued and loved human beings. (Bodgan & Taylor, 1989, p. 135)

They investigated these caring relationships involving over 100 persons with significant disabilities in order to understand the attitudes and thought processes that the nondisabled participants brought to these unique friendships.

Bogdan and Taylor discovered that the nondisabled participants in caring relationships with disabled loved ones enacted an accepting orientation to the humanity of the other person.

> An accepting relationship is one that is long-standing and characterized by closeness and affection. In our case, those involved are people with severe and obvious disabilities and ostensibly nondisabled others. In such relationships, the deviant attribute, the disability, does not bring stigma or discredit. The humanness of the person with a disability is maintained. The difference is not denied, but neither does it bring disgrace. (Bodgan & Taylor, 1989, p. 137)

Differences between persons were viewed as very real but not as reasons for rejection, detachment, or judgment. Central to the attitude of acceptance was a view of persons with a disability as "people, like us" (Bodgan & Taylor, 1989, p. 137). This ethical ethos espoused an understanding of a common, shared humanity enveloping persons with widely varying bodies and minds, abilities and appearances.

Bogdan and Taylor (1989) outlined four specific features of these accepting relationships. Each feature involves how the nondisabled persons, through beliefs, actions, and words, constructed the humanity of the disabled loved one. First, they attributed thinking and intelligence to the person with a significant disability. Even though many of the disabled persons spoke little or few words, the nondisabled relationship partner interpreted a variety of gestures and sounds as indications of intelligent thought and conscious purpose. Second, they viewed the person with a disability as a unique individual with a distinct personality, including interests, tastes, desires, and talents. Third, they were in touch with the many ways, often quite subtle and nuanced, that the disabled friend reciprocated affection in the relationship. Fourth, they incorporated the disabled loved one into a variety of relational networks, including family, church, and friendship groups. Taken together, these four features effectively normalized these relationships, allowing these connections to be strong and satisfying but also, in a sense, quite ordinary.

Developing this kind of acceptance as ethical orientation within classroom or a school requires two prongs of action. The first prong of action is the behavior and words of adults. De Schauwer, Van Hove, Mortier, and Loots (2009, p. 100) advise us that "Teachers and staff at school are important actors in the positive ethos of the school towards disabled children." The professionals must embrace and practice this ethic of acceptance, not only with students and adults with disabilities but with all persons who might be viewed as different or deviant. This accepting embrace of the shared humanity of all persons must include persons of many cultures, languages, religions, social classes, and races. The caring reach of active acceptance must extend to lesbian, gay and transgendered (LGBT) students, parents, and educators as well as members of all religious faiths. Inclusion is not just about disability and ability. It requires an ethical orientation of acceptance and respect across all human differences.

The second prong involves a very intentional, purposeful reaching out from adults to students, explaining the ethic of acceptance and showing students what it means in concrete interactions. The actions of accepting adults must be narrated and displayed to the students. If the adults are actively practicing acceptance in their own daily interactions with one another and with students, then the next step is to employ those public interactions and statements as educational illustrations, as models of how to treat one another and how to develop healthy interpersonal relationships. Educators can point to their own actions and the actions of other adults in the building as exemplars of ethical behavior and accepting relationships. They can also open up dialogues with students about the failures of the adults, the times when the educators are falling short of achieving an ethic of acceptance. This kind of ethical leadership by educators moves beyond merely asking students to comply with school rules or the directives of adult authority figures. The challenge to students each day is love one another within an understanding of a common, shared humanity (De Schauwer, Van Hove, Mortier, & Loots, 2009; McDougall, DeWit, King, Miller, & Killip, 2004; Walton, 2012).

Suggestion 2: Intentionally, very consciously work to "generate new meanings of disability" (Naraian, 2008, p. 117) among the students. Avoiding stereotyped or stigmatized ways of talking about and acting in relation to disability is necessary but insufficient. Educators should dialogue actively with students to develop new, more positive, embracing, and empowering ways of thinking about the meaning of disability and disabled persons.

Inclusion researcher Srikala Naraian (2008, 2011a, 2011b) has conducted multiple studies of how teachers, through their words and actions, actively construct and perpetuate both helpful and harmful meanings of disability. In this research, Naraian makes it clear that what a given student's disability means, or the variety of meanings that the disability takes on within the interactional space of the classroom, is created by teachers and students participating and making sense of things together. Not surprisingly, the adult in the room is very influential. Her words and actions carry tremendous weight in shaping the meaning of disability and the identity of the disabled child in the classroom.

In some cases, the behavior of students with disabilities appears unusual, unclear, or enigmatic. This is true in seemingly mundane instances of a student not paying attention in class and in more indefinite situations of students who do not communicate with oral speech. When the intent, purpose, or meaning of a student's behavior is ambiguous, the teacher is often the lead interpreter in the classroom. How can the teacher not only avoid the use of stereotypes and stigmatized understandings of disability but also help students explore more positive, possible explanations?

Naraian (2011a, p. 113) points out, "The role of the teacher in actively mediating student perceptions of each other is necessary for promoting more equitable relations in the classroom." The path to valuing and caring relations is through active dialogue with students, examining together the possible meanings of ambiguous student behavior or communications. The teacher should offer students opportunities to express multiple viewpoints and interpretations. This allows them to expand their thinking about who the student might be and what is actually possible.

Asking questions, making suggestions, opening room for students to offer different interpretations of what the student with disability is doing, thinking, or intending creates a space for the generation of novel meanings about identity and disability. The challenge for the instructor is in "actively scaffolding them to generate new meanings of disability. Such mediation might assist all students to exist in mutually empowering relations that could, in turn, transform the nature of the community in which they were embedded" (Naraian, 2008, p. 17). The underlying goal in such discussions is to create a culture among the students where a person with a disability is understood not in terms of deficit and isolation but is valued as an important member of the community. As disability studies scholar Claire Tregaskis (2004, p. 152) has encouraged, we need to cultivate a "valuing difference approach" whereby disabled persons and others may "acknowledge and celebrate their own difference from the norm."

Suggestion 3: Actively promote peer expectancies that frame persons with disabilities as valuable playmates and friends. Teach students to view disabled young people as attractive choices for play and friendship.

Carla A. DiSalvo and Donald P. Oswald (2002) conducted a thorough examination of all research about how the effort and actions of non-disabled students can increase the interactions and improve social behavior of students with autism. They reviewed scientific research on integrated play groups, peer tutoring, peer networks, and a variety of other planned intervention programs designed to utilize nondisabled students in fostering more social integration for disabled students in the schools. After concluding that many of these types of interventions are often effective, they point to what they found to be the key variable in this complex situation. They call it "peer expectancies" (DiSalvo & Oswald, 2002, p. 198).

What are *peer expectancies*? DiSalvo and Oswald (2002, p. 204) explain, "An individual's behavior is often affected by the expectations that his or her peers bring to the situation." If a disabled student enters a classroom where the peer group has an expectation of befriending the student, if they view the disabled student as a likely potential friend, someone they accept and believe they will enjoy, this expectation tends to influence the disabled student's behavior. He or she is far more likely to interact and communicate in friendly ways. Essentially, when the student with a disability is accepted and viewed in a positive light, that encourages relationship-building behavior from the disabled student. This increases the likelihood that friendships will initiate and develop.

To put it another way, DiSalvo and Oswald concluded that a social environment of acceptance, support, and caring is conducive to the development of friendships between disabled and nondisabled students. If students with and without disabilities are to be friends in the public schools, *what is needed is change in the attitude and behavior of the nondisabled students.* They need to view disabled students as potential friends and put forth genuine effort to create relationships with students who have disabilities.

De Schauwer, Van Hove, Mortier and Loots (2009, p. 101) warn that "friendships do not automatically follow from a mainstream school environment." Often, direction and intentional action on the part of the teacher is required. Teachers must be active leaders—through what they say and what they do—in setting the social norm of accepting students with disabilities and viewing them as valuable, attractive friends (Ruffina & Kuyini, 2012). The task for teachers is to directly teach nondisabled students to expect and seek friendships with disabled classmates. How?

- *Modeling*—Engage in caring, enjoyable relationships with disabled students. Make these relationships visible to students by interacting publically and speaking openly. Allow your own actions, words, and attitudes to stand as examples of what young people should do.
- *Interruption*—When students mistreat, reject, or otherwise behave in discriminatory ways toward students with disabilities, step in to interrupt the status quo (Chadsey & Han, 2005; Katz, Porath, Bendu, & Epp, 2012). Shine a bright light on the disrespectful behavior so that students can compare the actions to their own ethical standards. Encourage thoughtful examination

of the behavior (Sapon-Shevin, 2003). Use your authority to set limits, as needed.
- *Promotion*—Actively arrange for, encourage, and support interactions and friendships between students with and without disabilities. Nondisabled middle school students, when asked how to promote more friendships between students with and without disabilities suggested, "Create programs where both students with and without disabilities can hang out with each other. Don't always have us teach them; create programs that are fun for all of us" (Chadsey & Han, 2005, p. 53). Create afterschool clubs and activities that promote interaction between students of diverse abilities. During learning activities, set up study groups, work groups, and learning partnerships that integrate disabled and nondisabled students (Katz, Porath, Bendu, & Epp, 2012). Carter, Siseo, Brown, Brickham, and Al-Khabbaz (2008) advise that small group instruction is best for promoting the social valuing and integration of disabled young people. Danko and Buysse (2002) recommend watching students closely to see which pairs seem to click or share common interests. Then provide support and encouragement to pairs of possible friends when you see early signs of compatibility and interest.

Suggestion 4: Use paraprofessionals to provide assistance to the whole class, not just to the student with a disability. Avoid positioning the paraprofessional at the disabled student's shoulder. This causes social isolation and segregation within the inclusive classroom.

Many public schools employ special education paraprofessionals or teacher's aides as support personnel who work in inclusive classrooms. Paraprofessionals may bring tremendous experience and talent to the classroom. But they also tend to have a much lower level of professional preparation by comparison to fully certified teachers. Frequently, they are assigned to work as a one-to-one support person for the disabled student under the assumption that having an adult at the student's side at all times is useful and helpful.

A number of researchers have carefully examined what happens when paraprofessionals serve in this personal assistance role. Repeatedly, researchers have found that the presence of an adult helper in close proximity to an individual student creates a powerful barrier to interactions and friendships with classmates. This tends to foster increased dependence on the paraprofessional and decreased interactions with both the classroom teacher and other students. The well-meaning adult captures the student in an isolated bubble of abnormality, a stigmatized space that effectively blocks the social integration of the young person into the classroom setting. (Causton-Theoharis, 2009; Carter, Siseo, Brown, Brickham, & Al-Khabbaz, 2008; Carter, Siseo, Melekoglu, & Kurkowski, 2007; Chadsey & Han, 2005; Giangreco &

Broer, 2005; Giangreco, Edelman, Luiselli, & MacFarland, 1997; Katz, Porath, Bendu, & Epp, 2012; Ward, 2011).

How to avoid this? Sit down with the paraprofessional and thoughtfully create a plan to work together for the benefit of the whole class. A teacher and paraprofessional working together to instruct and support all students creates great opportunities, but it requires planning and discussion in order to create an effective teaching team. Where will the paraprofessional sit? Find a good desk and create a suitable workspace. During lessons, what will the paraprofessional do? Will you plan lessons together? What roles will the paraprofessional fill in the instruction, classroom management, and assessment? Make a written plan that you both understand and agree to (Devlin, 2008). Return to revise and improve the plan as needed.

Keep in mind that there may be specific times when the individual disabled student truly does need some assistance from another person. Carefully identify those moments when support is helpful. Ask the student when she needs support and what kinds of support work best for her. She is typically your best source of advice on this topic (Causton-Theoharis, 2009).

Create a plan for personal support that places multiple different people into the assistance role; students, paraprofessional, and teacher. In their research on providing support within inclusive high school classrooms, Carter, Siseo, Melekoglu, and Kurkowski (2007) found that peer support was much more effective than paraprofessional support. Utilize classmates as helpers whenever possible. Above all, devise a plan that works for the student, that delivers assistance that he finds both comfortable and effective.

REFERENCES

Antonello, S. J. (1996). *Social skills development: Practical strategies for adolescents and adults with developmental disabilities.* Boston, MA: Allyn and Bacon.

Bogdan, R., & Taylor, S. J. (1989). Relationships with severely disabled people: The social construction of humanness. *Social Problems, 36*, 2, 135–148.

Boutot, E. A., (2007). Fitting in: Tips for promoting acceptance and friendships for students with autism spectrum disorders in inclusive classrooms. *Intervention in School and Clinic, 42*, 3, 156–161.

Carter, E. W., Sisco, L. G., Brown, L., Brickham, D., & Al-Khabbaz, Z. A. (2008). Peer interactions and academic engagement of youth with developmental disabilities in inclusive middle and high school classrooms. *American Journal on Mental Retardation, 113*, 6, 479–494.

Carter, E. W., Siseo, L. G., Melekoglu, M. A., & Kurkowski, C. (2007). Peer supports as an alternative to individually assigned paraprofessionals in inclusive high school classrooms. *Research and Practice for Persons with Severe Disabilities, 32*, 4, 213–227.

Causton-Theoharis, J. N. (2009). The golden rule of providing support in inclusive classrooms: Support others as you would wish to be supported. *Teaching Exceptional Children, 42*, 2, 36–43.

Chadsey, J., & Han, K. G. (2005). Friendship facilitation strategies: What do students in middle school tell us? *Teaching Exceptional Children, 38*, 2, 52–57.

Cook, C. R., Gresham, F. M., Kern, L., Barreras, R. B., Thornton, S., & Crews, S. D. (2008). Social skills training for secondary students with emotional and/or behavioral disorders: A review and analysis of the meta-analytic literature. *Journal of Emotional and Behavioral Disorders, 16*, 3, 131–144.

Cumpata, J., & Fell. S. (2010). *A QUEST for social skills for students with autism or Asperger's.* Arlington, TX: Future Horizons.

Danko, C., & Buysse, V. (2002). Thank you for being a friend: Fostering friendships for children with autism spectrum disorder in inclusive environments. *Young Exceptional Children, 6*, 1, 2–9.

De Schauwer, E., Van Hove, G., Mortier, K., & Loots, G. (2009). 'I need help on Mondays, it's not my day. The other days, I'm OK.' Perspectives of disabled children on inclusive education. *Children & Society, 23*, 99–111.

Devlin, P. (2008). Create effective teacher-paraprofessional teams. *Intervention in School and Clinic, 44*, 1, 41–44.

DiSalvo, C. A., & Oswald, D. P. (2002). Peer-mediated interventions to increase the social interaction of children with autism: Consideration of peer expectancies. *Focus on Autism and Other Developmental Disabilities, 17*, 4, 198–207.

Franklin, B. M. (1986). *Building the American community: The school curriculum and the search for social control.* Philadelphia, PA: Falmer Press.

Giangreco, M. F., & Broer, S. M. (2005). Questionable utilization of paraprofessionals in inclusive schools: Are we addressing symptoms or causes? *Focus on Autism and Other Developmental Disabilities, 20*, 1, 10–26.

Giangreco, M. F., Edelman, S. W., Luiselli, T. E., & MacFarland, S. C. Z. (1997). Helping or hovering?: Effects of instructional assistant proximity on students with disabilities. *Exceptional Children, 64*, 1, 7–18.

Giler, J. Z. (2011). *Socially adept: Teaching social skills to children with ADHD, LD, and Asperger's.* San Francisco, CA: Jossey-Bass.

Goldstein, A. P. (1980). *Skill-streaming the adolescent: A structured learning approach to teaching prosocial skills.* Champaign, IL: Research Press Co.

Goldstein, A. P. (1988). *The prepare curriculum: Teaching prosocial competencies.* Champaign, IL: Research Press Co.

Goldstein, H., Kaczmarek, L. A., & English, K. M. (2002). *Promoting social communication: Children with developmental disabilities from birth to adolescence.* Baltimore, MD: Paul H. Brookes.

Grenier, M., Rogers, R., & Iarrusso, K. (2008). Including students with Down Syndrome in adventure programming. *Journal of Physical Education, Recreation & Dance, 79*, 1, 30–35.

Gresham, F. M. (1997). Social competence and students with behavior disorders: Where we've been, where we are, and where we should go. *Education and Treatment of Children, 20*, 3, 233–49.

Hart, J. E., & Whalon, K. J. (2011). Creating social opportunities for students with Autism Spectrum Disorder in inclusive settings. *Intervention in School and Clinic, 46*, 5, 273–279.

Katz, J., Porath, M., Bendu, C., & Epp, B. (2012). Diverse voices: Middle years students' insights into life in inclusive classrooms. *Exceptionality Education International, 22*, 1, 2–16.

McDougall, J., DeWit, D. J., King, G., Miller, L. T., & Killip, S. (2004). High school-aged youths' attitudes toward their peers with disabilities: The role of school and student interpersonal factors. *International Journal of Disability, Development and Education, 51*, 3, 287–313.

McGinnis, E., & Goldstein, A. P. (1984). *Skill streaming the elementary school child: A guide for teaching prosocial skills.* Champaign, IL: Research Press Co.

Myers, H. N. F. (2013). *Social skills deficits in students with disabilities: Successful strategies from the disabilities field.* Lanham, MD: Rowman & Littlefield.

Naraian, S. (2011a). Teacher discourse, peer relations, significant disability: Unraveling one friendship story. *International Journal of Qualitative Studies in Education, 24,* 1, 97–115.

Naraian, S. (2011b). Pedagogic voicing: The struggle for participation in an inclusive classroom. *Anthropology & Education Quarterly, 42,* 3, 245–262.

Naraian, S. (2008). "I didn't think I was going to like working with him, but now I really do!": Examining peer narratives of significant disability. *Intellectual and Developmental Disabilities, 46,* 2, 106–119.

Pang, V. O. (2005). *Multicultural education: A caring-centered, reflective approach.* Boston, MA: McGraw-Hill.

Reichow, B., & Volkmar, F. R. (2010). Social skills interventions for individuals with autism: Evaluation for evidence-based practices within a best evidence synthesis framework. *Journal of Autism and Developmental Disorders, 40,* 2, 149–166.

Ruffina, D., & Kuyini, A. B. (2012). Social inclusion: Teachers as facilitators in peer acceptance of students with disabilities in regular classroom in Tamil Nadu, India. *International Journal of Special Education, 27,* 2, 1–12.

Sapon-Shevin, M. (1999). *Because we can change the world: A practical guide to building cooperative, inclusive classroom communities.* Boston, MA: Allyn & Bacon.

Sapon-Shevin, M. (2003). Inclusion: A matter of social justice—How can we create schools that will help students thrive in a diverse society? *Education Leadership, 61,* 2, 25–28.

Schloss, P. J., & Smith, M. A. (1990). *Teaching social skills to hearing-impaired students.* Washington, DC: Alexander Graham Bell Association for the Deaf and Hard of Hearing.

Tregaskis, C. (2004). *Constructions of disability: Researching the interface between disabled and non-disabled people.* New York: Routledge.

Volz, J. R., Snyder, T., & Sterba, M. (2009). *Teaching social skills to youth with mental health disorders.* Boys Town, NE: Boys Town Press.

Walton, E. (2012). Using literature as a strategy to promote inclusivity in high school classrooms. *Intervention in School and Clinic, 47,* 4, 224–233.

Ward, A. (2011). Let's talk about teacher aides. *Kairaranga, 12,* 1, 43–50.

Zacks, S. Z., & Wolffe, K. E. (2006). *Teaching social skills to students with visual impairments.* New York: American Foundation for the Blind Press.

CHAPTER SEVEN

Partnerships with Parents and Families

> Guiding Question
> - How can you develop strong partnerships with parents and families?

Imagine you are the parent of a fifth-grade boy or girl. The academic year at Big Hill Elementary School begins in one week. You receive the following letter or email from the school principal.

Dear Big Hill parent:

Welcome to another exciting year at Big Hill School. We are excited that your child will be a Hilltopper!

We are pleased to partner with you in the education of your child. Research shows that when schools and families work together to support our students, they achieve higher academic standards, preparing them for success in college and career. When parents and families are fully involved, the children are the ones who win!

Because we believe so strongly in the power of our partnership with Big Hill parents and families, we encourage you to get involved from day one. We offer a variety of ways for parents to be involved:

- *Room Parents—Every classroom at Big Hill has two designated Room Parents who organize the families to provide necessary supplies and resources. All classrooms*

need a supply of writing paper, construction paper, pencils, markers or crayons, tissues, and miscellaneous other items. We count on our parents and families to provide these for the children.
- *Fall and Spring Parent-Teacher conferences*—For one week in both Fall and Spring, we go on a Modified Day Schedule so that teachers can meet with each student's parent(s). Regular, face-to-face meetings between teachers and parents are essential to good communication. These conferences help you and your teacher to stay on the same page as your child progresses.
- *Homework Club®*—Each classroom has a Homework Club® website where all of your child's homework assignments are stored. We ask that all parents assist with homework, checking your child's work and filling out the online assignment evaluation system. For technical assistance, please call the Homework Club ® Helpdesk at 1-800-HOMWORK.
- *Field Trip Monitors*—We are fortunate to have funds from the district so that each classroom can go on a small number of field trips each year. Trips to the zoo, the aquarium, and local museums provide important cultural learning experiences for our students. We count on parents to help us manage and care for the children. We ask that each child's parent(s) contribute one day per school year to help out on a field trip.

We look forward to wonderful year of learning!
Sincerely,
Principal Goodleader

If Big Hill Elementary School is located in a middle class or affluent neighborhood, the letter might also include:

- *The Hilltoppers Parents Foundation*—Last year this parent group raised funds to pay for a half-time art teacher, hardware and software for our Computer Lab, and resurfacing of the back parking lot. Events include the annual Jog-a-thon, the Pledge Drive, the Holiday Bazaar, and many other social events. Get active and have fun.

If Big Hill Elementary School is located in a poor or working class neighborhood, the letter might have elements like these:

- *Earn your GED!*—General Equivalency Development (GED) classes meet every Tuesday evening in the Library. These classes prepare you to take and pass the GED test.
- *English as a Second Language (ESL) classes*—If you want to learn to speak and write in English, or if you just want to improve on your English language skills, the ESL class meets on Saturday mornings in the Multi-Purpose Room.

At first glance, we notice that many public schools organize this kind of menu of parent involvement opportunities. Some schools send out letters or emails very much like this. Others post information listing parental activities on their websites. Others never gather together all the information about parent involvement in one location or distribute it in one communication, but they deliver the message clearly every day: These are the activities we prescribe for parents and families.

It seems difficult to disagree with Principal Goodleader's efforts. After decades of research, it is undeniable that the quantity of parent and family involvement in the education of a young person is closely connected to the degree of academic success experienced by that child or adolescent. These findings generally cut across all levels of education and all social and economic groups within American society. Henderson and Berla (2002, p. 72) summarize the research by stating definitively, "When families of all backgrounds are engaged in their children's learning, their children tend to do better in school, stay in school longer, and pursue higher education." Undoubtedly, parents need to be involved, and schools should work to promote and encourage that crucial involvement (Henderson, 1981; Henderson, 1987; Henderson & Berla, 1994, 2002).

But if we examine the Principal's letter more closely, we begin to see contradictions. The elementary school invites parents to become partners, sharing a mutual collaboration with the school professionals. The Principal is seeking a productive, working relationship between the educators and the parents of Big Hill because that relationship will benefit the students. Yet the structure and terms of the relationship are not created in a mutual fashion. The contributions of parents that will be recognized and valued in the relationship are determined by the educational professionals. These are clearly listed in the letter, as one party in the asymmetrical partnership is telling the other party what to do.

Many public schools assume that the terms and purposes of the teacher-parent relationship should be dictated by the priorities of the school and the professionals. While Principal Goodleader may optimistically seek a "partnership" featuring genuine collaboration and mutual good will between the school and the parents, the raw fact is that the school tends to dominate this relationship. Parents and principals, families and schools, are not equals in this partnership. Due to the formal, bureaucratic structure of the school, parents hold fewer and weaker cards in this interaction. In many cases, when this structural inequality between schools and parents or families is not critically examined by the school professionals, the forms of acceptable parental involvement are determined by the school personnel with little or no input from the parents. Family members have little say in the social practices that constitute their relationship with the school. The parents and families have little voice in deciding how they will contribute to the education of their children (Lareau & Muñoz, 2012).

Moreover, the letter only describes one side of the relationship, the time and energy that parents should supply to the partnership. What are the expectations for the educators? There is little mention of what the school professionals will contribute to the relationship, what the school will do for the children and the families.

Is this really a partnership? In a partnership, we would expect both parties to be equally involved in making decisions about what both participants will contribute to the relationship. The ideas of the school professionals and the thoughts of the parents would be combined, brought together into a shared plan through a respectful, open dialogue. Additionally, we would expect that the result of that dialogue would outline the expected behaviors for both educators and parents. Both would be expected to make worthwhile, substantial contributions to the partnership.

Many researchers have raised significant, critical questions about the structure and meaning of parental involvement in the education of their children. Often educators believe that parents are "involved" in their child's education if they attend parent-teacher conferences, help their child with homework, and volunteer to assist the class on field trips or fundraising efforts. A growing body of knowledge from research and practice directs us to view school relationships with parents and families in a much broader and deeper light, shifting our focus from how parents are fulfilling the short and narrow list of functions typically prescribed by schools to explorations of the seen and often unseen ways that parents and family members support the education of young students in the family.

> Although school staff believe "parental involvement" is defined as participating in organized activities at school, parents—particularly marginalized parents—view their contributions to school success in terms of informal activities such as providing nurturance, instilling cultural values, talking with their children, sending them to school clean and rested, checking homework, and a variety of other nontraditional activities. (López, Scribner, & Mahitivanichcha, 2001, p. 256)

This growing, critical research literature directs us to understand parents not in terms of "school-centered conceptions of parent roles" (Auerbach, 2007, p. 253), the behaviors and attitudes that schools often expect or even seek, but in relation to the many ways they enact their own cultural and familial values concerning their child's growth and learning.

Central to this critical body of research literature is the finding that traditional notions of parent involvement employed by many schools tend to privilege the cultural styles of behavior and communication of White, upper middle class families. Many culturally diverse parents and families experience marginalization and alienation when they interact with public school professionals. The diverse ways that parents of students of color, working class or poor parents, and families of students with disabilities support their children's learning and educational efforts are often overlooked and devalued by schools (Barton, Drake, Perez, St. Louis, & George, 2004; Ferguson, Hanreddy, & Ferguson, 2013; Horvat, Weininger, & Lareau, 2003; López, Scribner, & Mahitivanichcha, 2001; Shapiro, Monzo, Rueda, Gomez, & Blacher, 2004).

SUGGESTIONS AND ADVICE

Suggestion 1: Adopt a "posture of cultural reciprocity" (Harry, Rueda, & Kalyanpur, 1999, p. 125; Kalyanpur & Harry, 1997; Kalyanpur & Harry 1999), a practice of deeply respectful, valuing collaboration with parents and families.

A culturally responsive orientation starts with a critical awareness that the values and practices espoused by the school or school professionals are far from universal. They are culturally conditioned, partial, and not always very useful, especially when working with families who do not share these same belief systems. The bundle of ideas and assumptions about family life and education that you bring to the interaction with parents is an expression of your own cultural background and the ideological practices of your school. Gaining an awareness of the questionable, provisional nature of your own beliefs and practices opens you up to accept and appreciate the social norms of families of different cultures.

Integral to this awareness is understanding the political nature of the interactions between schools and families. Not all families have the same degree of social capital, of power in relationship to schools and other large, influential institutions. In most cases, White, upper middle class families have greater power in negotiating with schools and school systems than families of color and working class families (Horvat, Weininger, & Lareau, 2003). Given the highly bureaucratic and formal nature of special education systems in the United States, families of students with disabilities often experience school systems as complex, confusing, and alienating (Shapiro, Monzo, Rueda, Gomez, & Blacher, 2004). Phil Ferguson (2008) calls the relationship between families of disabled students and the schools "the doubting dance" (p. 48), "a troubled and troubling relationship, characterized by suspicion on both sides" (p. 57). Similarly, families of color are "less likely to have contact with schools, more likely to approach schools with wariness and mistrust, and more likely to encounter indifference and rebuff in their limited contact with educators" (Auerbach, 2007, p. 253–254).

Pay close attention to the many ways that parents and families who ostensibly have less power still work in strong support of their child's education. Notice how they love, care for, advocate for, and sustain their child. The ways that marginalized parents and families actively support their child's learning and growth are often unnoticed by teachers (Barton, Drake, Perez, St. Louis, & George, 2004). Parents who may not attend parent-teacher conferences or sign up to chaperone a field trip often provide numerous kinds of familial support and encouragement that do not show up on most teachers' radar (Auerbach, 2007; Ferguson, Hanreddy, & Ferguson, 2013; Horvat, Weininger, & Lareau, 2003). Make the effort to find out how these families love and care for their son or daughter.

Learn to respect ways of parenting and interacting with public schooling that diverge from the common formula promoted by most schools. By respecting their cultural practices, you empower yourself to work in support of their efforts, assisting them in raising and educating their child in the ways that make sense in light of their own worldview and values. You allow yourself to become a partner in a family's journey of bringing up a young person within the world as they know and experience it.

Suggestion 2: Actively seek the experiential stories told by parents and families members. If you hear these stories, truly taking them in, you will learn the suffering, hopes, joys, and needs of your student's family.

Truly valuing what the families of disabled students have to offer to their children and to schools "demands that we first seriously listen to families' accounts of their own experiences with both schools and disability" (Ferguson, Hanreddy, & Ferguson, 2013, p. 765). The deep trust that serves as the relational foundation of caring relationships with parents and families grows with "taking family voices seriously" (Ferguson, Hanreddy, & Ferguson, 2013, p. 765), with hearing and understanding their narratives of family life. Often this is best accomplished by visiting with families in their homes and in community locations where they feel comfortable (López, Scribner, & Mahitivanichcha, 2001). When professionals listen in a supportive and nonjudgmental way, this helps many families feel less threatened, less fearful, and less doubtful. They know that you are truly with them, on their side.

Central to this kind of deep listening is a valuing orientation that avoids the common deficit metaphor that drives many public school interactions with diverse parents and families. Frequently, educators believe that middle class parents are highly resourceful, talented, having much to contribute to the lives and education of their children. In contrast, lower class, immigrant, families of color, or families with disabled children are thought to be limited, deficient, lacking the human capacities to successfully raise their children and support their school learning.

Middle-class parents are seen as overflowing containers, whose involvement in schools is to be valued, but must be constrained in quantity. They are contrasted with low-income, urban parents who speak English as a second language and who are portrayed as empty containers, which need to be filled before they can give anything of value to the schools or to their own offspring (Lightfoot, 2004, p. 93). This "deficit model" (Barton, Drake, Perez, St. Louis, & George, 2004, p. 4) thinking often leads educators to casually and tragically conclude that "some parents just don't care" (Lightfoot, 2004, p. 91).

When you listen to the personal stories that parents and other family members tell, you reject pre-packaged, negative stereotypes in favor of a more realistic and sympathetic connection with family experiences and perspectives. You discover that parents are neither abundant vessels of overflowing ability nor empty repertoires of human deficiency. Just like teachers, they are fascinating human bundles of strength and vulnerability, talent and frailty. When expressed through personal stories, they become characters you can relate to, connect with, and care about. Storytelling and story listening become the interactional venue for caring/loving behaviors that allow school personnel to connect with families on a personal—rather than merely professional—level (Barton, Drake, Perez, St. Louis, & George, 2004, p. 266).

Suggestion 3: Collaborate with the outside agencies and organizations that provide support to the families. Building partnerships with the other sources of social support in the community multiplies your capacity to assist families.

Families of students with disabilities often work closely with a number of disability service providers, agencies, and professionals. Depending on nature of the impairment, a family may deal with half a dozen or more different care providers and support agencies. Similarly, families living in poverty frequently count on a series of community organizations that supply assistance with housing, medical care, and food. In order for school professionals to play a positive and effective role in helping families to meet their own needs, you must coordinate your efforts with other groups and persons who are involved in family assistance. This may mean collaborating with professionals from the local mental health center on providing behavioral and emotional support. It may take the shape of teaming up with a church, mosque, or synagogue in the community that offers after school care for the children of working parents. It will always mean getting out of the classroom and into the community where families actually live.

Keep in mind that effective cooperation between schools and community partners is depends on relationships, communication, and trust. It may seem like you can wait until a specific need arises to make contact and begin working together with a local agency. But the best practice is to make contact and create the relationship before a pressing problem arises. This requires that you know the important community organizations and service providers, the groups and individuals that families often count on. You have to learn who families rely on for support and assistance in a neighborhood. Contact those groups, meet with them, get to know those professional and community leaders. Build a foundation of trust and communication before you have to quickly spring into cooperative action.

Suggestion 4: Educate your students' parents and caregivers about inclusive education, what you are doing and why you are doing it. Many parents will not be familiar with what inclusion means, why we do inclusion, how it works, and the promise it holds for young people.

For many parents and families, inclusive education is strange and new. It is not the schooling that they experienced in their own childhood. So they need you to provide them with a basic introduction to inclusive education. What is inclusion? Why are you doing an inclusive model? Be prepared to explain to both parents of students with disabilities and parents of students without disabilities how an inclusive education provides academic and social benefits for their child (Dyson, 2007; Gibb, Young, Allred, Dyches, Egan, & Ingram, 1997; Peck, Staub, Gallucci, & Schwartz, 2004).

For the parent of a disabled student, explain that you and your professional colleagues are joining them in fighting against ableism and cruelty. For example, in their study of the experiences of families of students with autism, cerebral palsy, Down syndrome, and sickle cell disease, Neely-Barnes, Graff, Roberts, Hall, and Hankins (2010) found that parents use a wide variety of strategies to confront, fight against, and maneuver around ableism. They frequently confront and circumnavigate discriminatory attitudes and behavior that may harm their child. These parents

> had a keen awareness of and sensitivity to the ways in which their children experienced disability-related oppression, and they experienced it directly with their children. The parents had a stake in creating a more inclusive and tolerant community environment, as it would benefit both themselves and their children. (Neely-Barnes, Graff, Roberts, Hall, & Hankins, 2010, p. 256)

Inclusive educators should be allies of families of students with disabilities in fighting prejudice and creating communities of acceptance. Make it clear to your students' parents that you are working with them toward this goal.

Many parents want to be assured that their son or daughter's placement with general education classmates will not result in teasing and cruel treatment. They want to know that their child is not going to experience social rejection and isolation (Leyser & Kirk, 2004). Central to the inclusive mission of your classroom is the ethical education of all students on tolerance, acceptance, and even appreciation of human differences. Be prepared to explain how your inclusive classroom or school teaches young people how to be friends and provide support to one another, how relationships and community are valued.

Parents of nondisabled students may question whether the inclusive model means that their child gets less teacher attention or less instruction. This falls under the common folk theory that some students deplete the limited resources of the classroom, thereby harming the other students.

Peck, Staub, Gallucci, and Schwartz (2004) surveyed 389 parents of nondisabled elementary school children who shared inclusive classrooms with students with disabilities. Parents overwhelmingly found the inclusive classrooms to be beneficial for their child.

> Survey results generally indicated that parents felt that being in an inclusive classroom was good for their child, particularly in terms of their child's increased appreciation of the needs of other children and increased acceptance of differences in appearance and behavior among other children. (p. 141)

Eighty-seven percent said that the social experience of friendships with disabled classmates was positive. Only nine percent of parents said that they would not want to enroll their nondisabled child in an inclusive classroom again.

Still, many parents also expressed a belief that their child lost a portion of the teacher's time and attention by being the same classroom with disabled students. Twenty-two percent believed that their child forfeited instructional time from the teacher because of the presence of disabled classmates.

It is important for you to explain clearly to parents how your inclusive classroom operates, how you distribute your time and attention among the students, and how students work to support one another. If you are joined in the classroom by another teacher, a paraprofessional, or a speech and hearing specialist, be sure to explain these cooperative teaching arrangements to the parents. Many parents envision a classroom as a space with one adult. They need to know when and how professionals work together in the classroom in order to begin to understand how this arrangement benefits all of the students.

REFERENCES

Auerbach, S. (2007). From moral supporters to struggling advocates: Reconceptualizing parent roles in education through the experience of working-class families of color. *Urban Education, 42,* 250–283.

Barton, A. C., Drake, C., Perez, J. G., St. Louis, K., & George, M. (2004). Ecologies of parental engagement in urban education. *Educational Researcher, 33,* 4, 3–12.

Dyson, L. L. (2007). The unexpected effects of inclusion on the families of students with learning disabilities: A focus-group study. *Learning Disabilities, 14,* 3, 185–194.

Ferguson, D. L., Hanreddy, A. N., & Ferguson, P. M. (2013). Partnering with parents and families. In L. Florian (Ed.), *Sage Handbook of Special Education* (pp. 763–784). Thousand Oaks, CA: Sage.

Ferguson, P. (2008). The doubting dance: Contributions to a history of parent/professional interactions in early 20th century America. *Research & Practice for Persons with Severe Disabilities 33,* 1–2, 48–58.

Gibb, G. S., Young, J. R., Allred, K. W., Dyches, T. T., Egan, M. W., & Ingram, C. F. (1997). A team-based junior high inclusion program: Parent perceptions and feedback. *Remedial and Special Education, 18,* 4, 243–249.

Harry, B., Rueda, R., & Kalyanpur, M. (1999). Cultural reciprocity in sociocultural perspective: Adapting the normalization principle for family collaboration. *Exceptional Children, 66,* 1, 123–136.

Henderson, A. T. (1981). *The evidence grows: Parent participation–student achievement.* Columbia, MD: National Committee for Citizens in Education.

Henderson, A. T. (1987). *The evidence continues to grow: Parent involvement improves student achievement.* Columbia, MD: National Committee for Citizens in Education.

Henderson, A. T., & Berla, N. (1994). *A new generation of evidence: The family is critical to student achievement.* Washington, DC: Center for Law and Education.

Henderson, A. T., & Berla, N. (2002). *A new wave of evidence: The impact of school, family, and community connection on student achievement.* Austin, TX: National Center for Family and Community Connections with Schools.

Horvat, E. M., Weininger, E. B., & Lareau, A. (2003). From social ties to social capital: Class differences in the relations between schools and parent networks. *American Educational Research Journal, 40,* 2, 319–351.

Kalyanpur, M., & Harry, B. (1997). A posture of reciprocity: A practical approach to collaboration between professionals and parents of culturally diverse backgrounds. *Journal of Child and Family Studies 6,* 485–509.

Kalyanpur, M., & Harry, B. (1999). *Culture in special education: Building a posture of cultural reciprocity in parent-professional interactions.* Baltimore, MD: Paul H. Brookes.

Lareau, A., & Muñoz, V. L. (2012). "You're not going to call the shots": Structural conflicts between the principal and the PTO at a suburban public elementary school. *Sociology of Education, 85,* 201–218.

Leyser, Y., & Kirk, R. (2004). Evaluating inclusion: An examination of parent views and factors influencing their perspectives. *International Journal of Disability, Development and Education, 51,* 3, 271–285.

Lightfoot, D. (2004). "Some parents just don't care": Decoding the meanings of parental involvement in urban schools. *Urban Education, 39,* 91–107.

López, G. R., Scribner, J. D., & Mahitivanichcha, K. (2001). Redefining parental involvement: Lessons from high-performing migrant-impacted schools. *American Educational Research Journal, 38,* 253–288.

Neely-Barnes, S. L., Graff, J. C., Roberts, R. J., Hall, H. R., & Hankins, J. S. (2010). "It's our job": Qualitative study of family responses to ableism. *Intellectual and Developmental Disabilities, 48,* 4, 245–258.

Peck, C. A., Staub, D., Gallucci, C., & Schwartz, I. (2004). Parent perception of the impacts of inclusion on their nondisabled child. *Research and Practice for Persons with Severe Disabilities, 29,* 2, 135–143.

Shapiro, J., Monzo, L. D., Rueda, R., Gomez, J. A., & Blacher, J. (2004). Alienated advocacy: Perspectives of Latina mothers of young adults with developmental disabilities on service systems. *Mental Retardation 42,* 1, 37–54.

CHAPTER EIGHT

Encouraging Positive Behavior

Guiding Question
- How can you actively encourage positive student behavior?

If we stacked up all the current books giving teachers guidance and advice about classroom management, behavior management, behavior modification, and positive behavior support, the pile would undoubtedly reach the moon. There is no shortage of sage advice about how to prevent and resolve behavior issues in the classroom. There is also no paucity of resources about dealing with behavior problems of students with specific types of disabilities.

The challenge for the inclusive educator is not to find useful behavior improvement programs, systems, and interventions for use in the classroom. The task is to sort through it all in order to select the best practices for use given the ethical and practical priorities of inclusion. Which effective practices blend well with the values and goals of inclusive schooling?

Leslie Soodak (2003, p. 328) advises inclusive teachers to develop classroom management practices "specifically aimed at promoting *membership*" in the democratic classroom community.

Soodak (2003, p. 328) defines membership as:

> a child's right to belong and to have access to the same opportunities and experiences as other children of the same age. In schools that effectively include all students, membership

is promoted by educating all children in their neighborhood (i.e., local) schools, assigning students to classes heterogeneously within those schools, and avoiding policies and practices that exclude students from programs, settings, or events.

At first glance, it seems that membership is merely a synonym for inclusion. But Soodak intends much more. Membership is not achieved by individuals who might be excluded. It is created by classroom and school communities as an equal benefit for all the young *citizens*.

Chris Kliewer (1998), in his book *Schooling Children with Down Syndrome*, helps us to understand this same notion. Instead of using the term *membership*, he writes about educational *citizenship*. Drawing from his ethnographic research, he offers three different descriptors for the included/excluded status of individual children in the general education classroom.

1. *Alien*—"The alien represents community membership overtly denied" (Kliewer, 1998, p. 11). The excluded child is generally viewed as defective, lacking something essential that is considered necessary to participate and belong in the general classroom. This child is viewed as a burden to the general classroom and is schooled in a separate special education location.
2. *Squatter*—The squatter is constructed with many of the same burden and defectiveness meanings attributed to the alien, perhaps with some reduction of intensity. The squatter generally occupies a space at the periphery of the general classroom community. The squatter is *physically* included in the general classroom, but he or she is not treated as truly belonging to the community. The individual child may be seated at the side of the classroom or concealed behind a human barrier of a teacher's aide assigned to the student. This form of unsatisfactory inclusion "effectively creates a new border within the general classroom" (Kliewer, 1998, p. 11) that isolates rejected defectiveness *within* general education.
3. *Citizen*—The citizen is a human being who is fully valued as a member of the learning community. The community itself is viewed as a web of human relationships that requires the participation and contribution of all members. Community is both the location and the social process whereby individuals become themselves and democratic values such as equality and freedom are enacted.

The two goals of classroom management and behavior problem solving are to support all students as citizens, as valued community members, while creating a respectful and peaceful classroom climate conducive to learning. The classroom becomes both a social space where individual members experience belonging and a productive learning space where the student make substantial academic progress. Hmmm, you wonder […] […] […] how?

In 2004, when the United States Congress reauthorized the Individuals with Disabilities Education Act (IDEA), they added a recommended practice intended to create more support for students struggling academically or behaviorally in general education. They gave this practice the awkward name *Response to Intervention (RTI)*. Their concern was that many students only received special education supports and assistance after lengthy, soul-damaging experiences of failure. In many cases, the cumbersome bureaucracy of special education was kicking in to provide support to struggling students years after their difficulties learning to read or learning to interact peacefully with classmates first began. Sadly, this assistance was often too little too late.

RTI is a systematic framework that organizes early support for struggling learners in general education classrooms, a way of bringing the best efforts of teachers and other support professionals to assist students prior to and at the first sign of difficulties. The main goal of RTI is the prevention of enduring, painful problems of learning and behavior. This is analogous to the growing emphasis in healthcare to give people access to in health-promoting services and supports—nutrition, exercise, stress reduction, health screenings—that prevent the development of sickness and disease. Similarly, RTI involves general educators, special educators, counselors, school psychologists, and other professionals in providing what all students need to be successful in general education, thereby preventing the kinds of learning or behavioral concerns that often result in special education labels and segregated schooling (Bryant & Barrera, 2009; Hawken, Vincent, & Schumann, 2008; Meadan & Monda-Amaya, 2008).

RTI is often described as a model consisting of three tiers of support for students.

Tier 1 is universal—what every student receives, the very best instruction, behavior guidance, and social support. But some students need more or different assistance, instruction, or support in the general classroom. Tier 2 is the additional, focused instruction for students who struggle academically or behaviorally (Meadan & Monda-Amaya, 2008; RTI Action Network, 2013).

If the instruction, support, and interventions offered under Tiers 1 and 2 are not successful, then the most intensive, focused forms of professional support are offered as Tier 3. Often this means small group instruction or individualized plans of behavioral support. Tier 2 and 3 interventions frequently involve consultation and support from other professionals, such as counselors, school psychologists, and special educators. Certainly, in a co-teaching arrangement involving a general and special educator, both collaborate on all three tiers.

According to the RTI model, students who do not make good progress with Tier 3 interventions are often referred for assessment for special education services.

Special education services are the final set of systematic actions, after the educators have made extensive problem-solving efforts.

Unfortunately, while the RTI model brings a host of potentially wonderful supports and assistance to students in the general education classroom in a way that is conducive to the success of inclusion, it also has an ugly side that continues the ideological tradition of stigmatization that the disability rights movement has tried to eclipse. RTI is often described not just as way of getting students more and better help earlier. It is also viewed by many as a method of diagnosing an impairment such as a learning disability or emotional-behavioral disorder (Gresham, 2005; Reynolds & Shaywitz, 2007; Reynolds & Shaywitz, 2009). The diagnosis idea works like this. Teachers and other professionals utilize research-based interventions, the best instructional and behavior change practices that researchers have found to be successful. A child who has received three full tiers of scientifically validated professional interventions but still does not make satisfactory progress is viewed as having a "resistance to intervention" (Christ, Burns, & Ysseldyke, 2005, p. 4). That "resistance" is a taken to be an indication of a within-child impairment of learning or behavior (Fuchs & Fuchs, 2006). Rather than admitting that the educators' knowledge of how to teach reading or how to improve behavior is fallible and limited, that school-based interventions are an inexact science and an uncertain practice, the failure of the adults' efforts is translated into a declared deficit in the child. This weakness of the RTI concept diverts our attention from working closely with students and families to achieve the most learning and growth possible to a stance of professional arrogance that blames the child for the failures of our teaching.

Moments of failed teaching are challenges to our creativity and skill as educators, not invitations to pigeonhole individual students as pathologically unteachable. We educators need to remain focused on improving teaching and learning, doing our best each day to support all students as they learn and develop. Pushing the unfortunate diagnostic notion off the edge of our page, we can focus our thoughts and actions on the more useful aspects of the RTI model. While rejecting RTI's failure as a system of diagnosing individual deficits, we can embrace the RTI goal of bringing more and better assistance to students in the general classroom.

SUGGESTIONS AND ADVICE

Suggestion 1 (Tier 1): If an inclusive teacher is going to learn one (don't stop at one!) best practice of that will promote positive behavior and reduce disrespectful behavior, that best practice is classroom meetings. Specifically, learn how to facilitate problem-solving meetings with your students on a regular basis. Classroom meetings, if done well, can have a profoundly positive effect on student attitudes, relationships, problem-solving, and the quality of the overall climate in the room.

Problem-solving classroom meetings are a structured discussion format designed to allow students to work together in a constructive, respectful way to solve conflicts and improve the quality of social interactions in the classroom. With adult support, students provide the leadership and the practical ideas to improve their own community. The classroom teacher supplies the structure for the process of deliberation and facilitates the work of the students as they make it happen.

Elementary teacher Donna Styles (2001) and middle and high teacher Jonathan Erwin (2004) recommend using regular classroom meetings as a way of solving behavior problems, resolving social conflicts and misunderstandings, and empowering students to take greater responsibility for their behavior. They tout the capacity of effective classroom meetings to achieve the following positive results:

- Creating a trusting and supportive classroom community
- Resolving and reducing interpersonal conflicts and tensions
- Improving the learning environment
- Developing a greater sense of unity among the students
- Building a wide variety of individual social and emotional skills, including
  o Empathy for the feelings and perspectives of classmates
  o Listening and public speaking skills
  o Ability to communicate thoughts and feelings effectively
  o Critical cognitive skills such as analysis and evaluation
  o Leadership skills such as decision-making, goal-setting, and planning
  o Pro-social skills such as encouraging and supporting others
  o Self-confidence

Classroom Meeting Basics

Successful problem-solving classroom meetings typically involve:

1. *Regular, scheduled meetings*—Styles (2001) recommends once per week. Certainly, the timing can vary depending on the needs of the group. The meetings have to occur with enough regularity so that the issues addressed by the group are fresh and alive.
2. *Problem submission form and box*—Create a brief form for students to fill out explaining the problem they are confronting. Completed forms are placed in a box that is opened up at the start of each meeting. These supply the issues to be resolved by the group.

3. *Sit in a circle*—Seats cannot be arranged in traditional rows. The students should sit in a large circle that allows every student equal opportunity to participate.
4. *Student leader*—A student serves as leader of the meeting. This role should rotate so that as many students lead as possible. In some cases, student leaders may need training on how to run the meeting. (With very young children, it may be necessary for the teacher to lead the group.)
5. *Teacher as secretary and facilitator*—The teacher plays two roles. First, she is the secretary keeping the records of problems discussions, plans made and implemented. Second, she is the facilitator who provides support, as needed, to the student leader and to other students about how to participate.
6. *Teach process early*—Use the first one to three sessions of the year as opportunities to teach the group how to do a classroom meeting. Once the students have learned, decrease your role and allow the students to take greater responsibility. The more the students run the meetings, the greater the positive impact on them.
7. *Frame problems as shared*—A student may write the issue in a personalized way: "Jose is acting like a jerk. He keeps insulting everyone." But the problem should be framed as communal, as shared by the whole group. For example, in this instance, "how can we have a class where insults don't happen, where no one insults anyone?"

Structured Meeting Process

Students at different levels of cognitive, emotional, and linguistic development require different amounts of structure. Generally speaking, the younger the students the more structured the process should be. Also, the younger students often require procedures that call for them to make positive, supportive statements about one another.

The following two processes are designed for use in (1) elementary (Styles, 2001) and (2) middle or high school classrooms (Erwin, 2004). Modify and personalize these to your students as needed.

Elementary Meeting Agenda

1. *Encouragement Circle*—Raise hands and go around group. Students offer compliments (what he/she is good at) to the leader. This encourages the leader and sets positive, supportive tone.
2. *Old Business*—Secretary reviews problems and solutions from the prior meeting. How is each solution plan going? When problems from prior meeting are unresolved, they go into agenda of current meeting.
3. *New Business*—Leader reads each problem form out loud. Is this still a problem? If resolved, how? If still a problem:
   - *Gather Facts and Perspectives*—Students contribute information about the problem.
   - *Brainstorm Solutions*—Gather all ideas without evaluating them.
   - *Discuss Proposed Solutions*—Talk about and evaluate each. Will it work?
   - *Choose Best Solution*—May need to vote.
   - *Create Plan*—How do we carry out this solution?
4. *Thank yous and Compliments*—Conclude meeting by raising hands and going around circle with students giving compliments to any person in group, stating what that person did well.

Secondary Meeting Agenda

1. *State the Problem*—Keep in mind that the "problem," as phrased by the student who submitted the issue, may need rewording or reframing so that the problem is both shared and respectful.
2. *Set a Goal*—How do we want this to change or improve?
3. *Examine Current Situation*—What are we doing right now about this problem? How are we handling this now?
4. *Brainstorm*—What might we do to handle this issue in a better way? How can we resolve this? (Don't evaluate at this stage. Just gather ideas.)
5. *Make a Plan*—Which proposed plan is most likely to succeed? (Might need to vote.) How do we put this into action?

Suggestion 2 (Tier 2): If an inclusive teacher is going to learn one best practice for helping students who need more behavior guidance than what is offered in Tier 1, that best practice is Check In Check Out (CICO).

Adults—teacher and parents—have a set of expectations for the behavior of young people at school. Some of these expectations are formally codified into rules that are clearly articulated to the students. Most of these expectations are communicated to students in less formal and less consistent ways. For most children and adolescents, this hodge-podge of clear rules and somewhat ambiguous informal communications about how to behave in school offers sufficient guidance, at least enough to keep out of chronic trouble. But some students may require more clarity and guidance about what the adult authority's expectations are and how to successfully meet them.

CICO is a practice that provides students with clearly defined expectations for behavior in school and an intensified system of adult supervision. It also offers regular opportunities for behaviorally struggling students to receive encouragement, feedback, and coaching about their behavior. Researchers have found that CICO can be an effective, relatively simple way for teachers at the elementary and secondary level to help students reduce problematic behavior in school (Filter, McKenna, Benedict, Horner, Todd, & Watson, 2007; Mitchell, Stormont, & Gage, 2011; Todd, Campbell, Meyer, & Horner, 2008).

Keep in mind that CICO focuses only on teaching students how to comply with the expectations of the adult authority figures. In this sense, it is very limited. It does not attempt to support young people in developing a deeper, more lasting form of character based on ethical values and moral reasoning (e.g., Lickona, 2004). It is focused on getting students to comply with the rules, follow adults' directions, and stay out of trouble.

Check In Check Out Basics

Setting up and carrying out effective CICO typically follows a sequence of steps (Crone, Hawken, & Horner, 2011):

1. Teachers, student, and parents work together to craft a short list (3–5) of individualized behavior goals. These should be designed specifically to address the difficulties that the student has been experiencing in school. These goals should clearly state the desired behavior. Be sure that all three parties—educators, student, and family—agree to the goals. Agreement from the start will increase the chances that all three groups will uphold their side of the bargain.
2. Create a daily behavior rating sheet (sample below) that allows for the evaluation of each goal during periods or blocks of time during the school day. The rating sheet may be written in multiple languages, as needed. A rating system from 0 (low) to 3 (high) is common. More complex, refined rating systems may be used with some older students. For students who would benefit from the use of symbols, a rating system consisting of different numbers of thumbs up, check marks, or other icon are useful.
(I discourage the use of smiley faces as icons for behavioral performance because it confuses emotions and behaviors. Often when working with students who struggle behaviorally, we want to teach them the difference between emotions (how they feel) and behaviors (what they do). Many students need to learn, for example, that angry or sad feelings are natural, but they don't

require violent or cruel behavior. A person can experience strong feelings while choosing to act in ways that do not put those feelings into action. Learning that emotions and behavior are different is not easy when the teachers confuse the two on the rating sheet.)

3. The student "checks in" at the start of the day with an adult that the student views as caring and trustworthy. The adult gives the student a fresh behavior rating sheet and encourages the student to do well.
4. At the end of each period or block of time, the teacher and/or students completes the evaluations of each behavior goal. Initially, in most cases, the teacher completes the evaluation of student behavior goals. As soon as possible, we want the student to evaluate his or her own behavior, facilitating thinking about his or her own actions. This moves this practice from mere compliance with authority to a deeper and more lasting ability to monitor, control, and take responsibility for one's behavior. You may find it useful for both the student and the teacher to complete the ratings. When there are discrepancies, this promotes fruitful discussion about differences of perception and questions of honesty. For many students, you may be able to fade off the teacher evaluations and continue the system with only student self-evaluations.
5. At the end of the day, the student "checks out" with the same adult who conducted the morning "check in." The educator and student discuss the rating sheet, how the student did that day, what went well, how to improve. The Check Out is a time for coaching and guidance, when a trusted adult can help a young person look closely at his or her own actions, celebrate success, and plan for possible improvements.
6. The rating sheet goes home (with the student or electronically) to the parents/family as a way of communicating to parents or guardians. Typically, the parents sign and return the sheet or use email or text to communicate back to the school that they have read and understood the rating sheet. Some teachers and parents work together to set up reward systems whereby students can earn prizes based on ratings and points.
7. Many teachers and schools count the rating points earn and keep daily data as a handy means of evaluating behavior improvement. For example, on the sample behavior rating sheet provided below, a total of fifty-four thumbs up are possible during a school day.

Sample Check In Check Out Behavior Rating Sheet

	Early morning	Morning recess	Late morning	Lunch	Afternoon recess	Afternoon
Speak respectfully	👍👍👍	👍👍👍	👍👍👍	👍👍👍	👍👍👍	👍👍👍
Organize my materials	👍👍👍	👍👍👍	👍👍👍	👍👍👍	👍👍👍	👍👍👍
Follow directions without argument	👍👍👍	👍👍👍	👍👍👍	👍👍👍	👍👍👍	👍👍👍
Comments						
Parent signature:						

Suggestion 3 (Tier 3): If an inclusive teacher is going to learn one best practice for helping students who need more behavior guidance than what is offered in Tiers 1 and 2, that best practice is Collaborative Problem Solving.

Greene's (2008) *Collaborative Problem Solving* picks up where CICO leaves off. It begins at the point of frustration and exasperation experienced by teachers who are at the end of their rope, who feel like they have tried everything they know to help a student behave better in school and don't know what to do next. It begins at the point where the typical public school practices end.

For the most part, the disciplinary practices of public schools and teachers involve attempts to get students to comply with adults' expectations. The primary two devices used are rewards and punishments. Schools reward students for behavior that meets expectations and punish students for failing to meet those expectations. The narrow behavioral basis for these practices is the subject of much criticism (Kohn, 1999; Danforth & Smith, 2005). But Greene's pragmatic approach simply accepts that the first goal of most public schools is to enforce or entice compliance with adult authority. He asks, what do we do with children and adolescents do not respond to our efforts to gain their compliance? What do we do when rewards and punishments, tried again and again, often over many years, have failed?

Collaborative Problem Solving

"Kids do well if they can," Greene (2008, p. 10) plainly proclaims. Children and adolescents want to succeed. In fact, they try to do well in school, to get along with others, to follow the rules, to stay out of trouble. The most troublesome students are not simply manipulative, attention-seeking, or dishonest. While many who chronically misbehave appear to be unmotivated, Greene explains, they actually lack the cognitive skills necessary to be effective in handling the social situations that confront them in school. They do not have the cognitive and social skills to adapt to what the school and the classroom is requiring of them. What they truly need is not more punishments or rewards but structured, supportive opportunities to learn the specific cognitive and social skills required to be successful in their school setting.

Unlike the common approach of many social skills training programs, Greene does not prescribe a skills training curriculum filled with lessons and role plays carried out in an artificial context. To oversimplify, you can't learn to swim by waving your arms and kicking your feet in the air at the side of the pool. You have to learn in the water. Green's approach takes advantage of the very real situations that struggling students face every day as opportunities for students to learn and teachers to teach. He simply describes these challenging situations as "unsolved problems" (Green, 2008, p. 38). What is needed is collaboration between caring adults and students to solve these problems. Through solving social problems together, students gain the skills of cognition and behavior that allow them to grow and develop (Greene, Ablon, & Martin, 2006; Greene, Ablon, Monuteaux, Goring, Henin, Raezer, Edwards, Markey, & Rabbitt, 2004; Greene, 2008; Martin, Krieg, Esposito, Stubbe, & Cardona, 2008).

For example, imagine a second grade student who frequently has difficulty lining up for recess or lunch. The student pushes and elbows her classmates. They respond angrily, complaining and maybe pushing back. The scene often escalates verbally and physically into a messy fracas. Greene (2008) advises us that there are three possible solutions to this problem.

- Plan A—Adult uses authority to enforce order upon the situation. The teacher demands compliance. This may involve overt use of rewards or punishments. It may simply involve the unmentioned threat of punishment. Do this […] or else.
- Plan B—Collaborative Problem Solving. The student and teacher work together to understand the perspective of both persons. They then develop a plan for how the student (and teacher) can best handle that problem situation the next time it arises.
- Plan C—Intentionally taking no action at all. Teachers often choose when to step in and when to allow a situation to resolve itself. Plan C is when you decide to leave the situation alone and not intervene.

Learning how to work in a mutual fashion to effectively solve the second grader's problem lining up peacefully means developing the professional skills of Plan B. Becoming a highly skilled practitioner of Plan B requires practice and persistence.

In the case of the second grader struggling to behave well in the line for recess or lunch, Collaborative Problem Solving asks that the teacher meet individually (typically later in the day) with the student to talk about what is happening in line and how to solve it. This discussion is the opportunity for social skills teaching and learning. The process of this *Collaborative Problem Solving* teaching session involves three basic steps.

1. Empathy—First, you solicit and listen to the student's version of the problem. Without judgment or correction, you simply ask questions and listen. Gather information from the student so that you understand her concern about the unsolved problem. This gives the student an opportunity to be heard. It helps you understand how she thinks and feels about the issue. Keep in mind that the solution that the two of you develop must be acceptable and realistic given the concerns of two people, the student and you. If it only satisfies your concerns, the solution fails.
2. Define the Problem—Next, express your own concerns. Articulate your perspective about the problem. Here is what I see going on. Here is what I need to have happen in this situation. This step allows you and the student to have two sets of concerns or needs placed on the table. Both the student's and the teacher's concerns will need to be satisfied in order to solve the problem effectively.
3. Invitation—Once the concerns and needs of both the teacher and the student are presented clearly, the final step is to brainstorm possible solutions that address both child and adult concerns. Work together to make a list of possible solutions. Then evaluate each option. Select the most realistic. This step must be collaborative, facilitating the contributions of both participants, in order to be effective.

As you may imagine, the best-made plans often fail. Solutions frequently do not work. What do you do? Not to fret! Many problems take multiple meetings to solve. The beauty of the Collaborative Problem Solving approach is that each attempt to solve a problem leads to another Plan B meeting, another three step problem solving discussion. Over time, the repeated sessions advance the working relationship of the teacher and student as a collaborative team while developing the student's problem-solving abilities. The process is iterative and developmental in nature, leading gradually upward in terms of skill building and growth.

The great communication theorist Marshall McLuhan (1964/1994, p. 7) wrote, "The medium is the message." He meant that the way an idea is conveyed, the social process that delivers a message, is part of the meaning of the message itself. In the case of Collaborative Problem Solving, the way we hold each problem-solving meeting, the kind of supportive interaction and the process of cognitive problem-solving, is both the medium and the message. We are very carefully, caringly, teaching that the problems of social interaction are best resolved through patience, working together, thoughtful planning, and effort. Through this process, we are communicating our enduring support for a student who is experiencing difficulties. We are building a stronger, more trusting relationship with a student who may have very few reliable connections to adults or peers. We are embodying the very best of teaching through repetition, creativity, and interpersonal solidarity. The message is, "We will continue to work on this together. It is not easy, but we will make progress. Putting our heads and hearts together, you will learn and you will improve."

REFERENCES

Bryant, D. P., & Barrera, M. (2009). Changing roles for educators within the framework of Response-to-Intervention. *Intervention in School and Clinic, 45*, 72–79.

Christ, T. J., Burns, M. K., & Ysseldyke, J. E. (2005). Conceptual confusion within Response-to-Intervention vernacular: Clarifying meaningful differences. *NASP Communiqué, 34*, 3, 1–10.

Crone, D. E., Hawken, L. S., & Horner, R. H. (2011). *Responding to problem behavior in schools: The behavior education program* (2nd ed.). New York: Guilford Press.

Erwin, J. (2004). *The classroom of choice: Giving students what they need and getting what you want.* Alexandria, VA: ASCD.

Greene, R. W., Ablon, S. A., & Martin, A. (2006). Innovations: Child psychiatry: Use of Collaborative Problem Solving to reduce seclusion and restraint in child and adolescent inpatient units. *Psychiatric Services, 57*, 5, 610–616.

Greene, R. W., Ablon, J. S., Monuteaux, M., Goring, J., Henin, A., Raezer, L., Edwards, G., Markey, J., & Rabbitt, S. (2004). Effectiveness of Collaborative Problem Solving in affectively dysregulated youth with oppositional defiant disorder: Initial findings. *Journal of Consulting and Clinical Psychology, 72*, 1157–1164.

Greene, R. W. (2008). *Lost at school: Why our kids with behavioral challenges are falling through the cracks and how we can help them.* New York: Scribner.

Filter, K. J., McKenna, M. K., Benedict, E. A., Horner, R. H., Todd, A. W., & Watson, J. (2007). Check in/Check out: A post-hoc evaluation of an efficient, secondary-level targeted intervention for reducing problem behaviors in schools. *Education and Treatment of Children, 30*, 1, 69–84.

Fuchs, D., & Fuchs, L. (2006). Introduction to Response to Intervention: What, why, and how valid is it? *Reading Research Quarterly, 41*, 1, 93–99.

Gresham, F. M. (2005). Response to Intervention: An alternative means of identifying students as emotionally disturbed. *Education and Treatment of Children, 28*, 4, 328–344.

Hawken, L. S., Vincent, C. G., & Schumann, J. (2008). Response to intervention for social behavior: Challenges and opportunities. *Journal of Emotional and Behavioral Disorders, 16*, 4, 213–225.

Kliewer, C. (1998). *Schooling children with Down Syndrome: Toward an understanding of possibility.* New York: Teachers College Press.

Lickona, T. (2004). *Character matters: How to help our children develop good judgment, integrity, and other essential virtues.* New York: Touchstone.

McLuhan, M. (1964/1994). *Understanding media: The extensions of man.* Cambridge, MA: MIT Press.

Meadan, H., & Monda-Amaya, L. (2008). Collaboration to promote social competence for students with mild disabilities in the general classroom: A structure for providing social support. *Intervention in School and Clinic, 43,* 3, 158–167.

Mitchell, B. S., Stormont, M., & Gage, N. A. (2011). Tier two interventions implemented within the context of a tiered prevention framework. *Behavioral Disorders, 36,* 4, 241–261.

Reynolds, C. R., & Shaywitz, S. E. (2007). Response to Intervention: Prevention and remediation, perhaps. Diagnosis, no. *Child Development Perspectives, 3,* 44–47.

Reynolds, C. R., & Shaywitz, S. E. (2009). Response to intervention: Ready or not? Or, from wait-to-fail to watch-them-fail. *School Psychology Quarterly, 24,* 2, 130–145.

RTI Action Network (2013). Tiered instruction/intervention. http://www.rtinetwork.org/essential/tieredinstruction.

Soodak, L. C. (2003). Classroom management in inclusive settings. *Theory into Practice, 42,* 4, 327–333.

Styles, D. (2001). *Class meetings: Building leadership, problem-solving and decision-making skills in the respectful classroom.* Markham, Ontario: Pembroke Publishers Limited.

Todd, A. W., Campbell, A. M., Meyer, G. G., & Horner, R. H. (2008). The effects of a targeted intervention to reduce problem behaviors: Elementary school implementation of Check In-Check Out. *Journal of Positive Behavior Interventions, 10,* 1, 46–55.

CHAPTER NINE

Differentiated Instruction

> **Guiding Question**
> - How can you differentiate instruction to meet the needs of a diverse group of learners?

When I teach about differentiated instruction in my university course on inclusion, I often begin with a scenario that serves as an analogy to classroom teaching in a public school. Imagine that you sign up at your local fitness center for a class devoted to physical strength and conditioning. The advertised description of the course says that you will be working on increasing strength and stamina in all of the major muscle groups. When you arrive, you find that the class has thirty students, men and women of a diversity of sizes and shapes, ranging in age from early twenties to mid-eighties.

The instructor begins the first class session by posting an enormous chart on the wall. As he speaks, he points to the graphic with a long wooden pointer. "Being truly fit means achieving high standards. The National Committee on Fitness (NCF) has set standards for the muscular fitness of all Americans. In each of thirty-seven muscle groups, as you can see on this chart, the NCF has scientifically determined the optimum amount of muscular strength for an American adult. At the conclusion of this course, you will take the NCF comprehensive bodily fitness examination. This exercise program will successfully prepare you to pass all thirty-seven national standards on the NCF exam."

Just as you expected, the instructor guides the class through a weight-lifting program consisting of exercises such as bench press, arm curls, etc. But the program has four requirements that quickly become problematic.

First, everyone has to do the same exercises. For example, the instructor tells every student to do the same triceps exercise, lifting a barbell overhead, lowering it back behind the neck. Many students find this motion very uncomfortable. You imagine that there must be more than one way to work out your triceps. But the instructor only offers one way.

Second, the program requires that every student exercise with exactly the same amount of weight. On the bench press, for example, everyone must lift 150 pounds. A few of the more athletic students toss the bar into the air like it is a child's toy. For other participants, this exercise quickly becomes dangerous as the heavy bar squeezes down on their chests.

Third, the instructor mandates that all students must complete three sets of ten repetitions for each exercise. Not matter how strong or weak, large or small, experienced or inexperienced, this is the standard expectation. As you can imagine, this is overwhelmingly difficult for some students and incredibly easy for others.

Finally, the instructor is a stickler for a certain concept of fairness. He reasons that every student should receive the same amount of his time and attention. The result is that some of the students who require more instruction and support are neglected while students who can work out fairly independently get the instructor's attention whether they need it or not.

No surprisingly, many students reach a point of exasperation with this one-size-fits-all approach to muscle development. The frustrated students raise a variety of critical questions about the fitness program. To each, the strength training instructor replies, "Our purpose in this class is to meet the National Committee on Fitness standards. Since everyone is working toward the same high standards, it only makes sense that every student completes the same exercise program."

Frequently, in our university class discussion, students point out a series of instructional mistakes made by the fitness instructor. They then create a list of corrections to his mistaken assumptions that would allow him to better serve his students and their desire to increase their physical strength.

MISTAKEN IDEAS

1. Holding *high* performance standards for all means holding the *same* standards for all.
2. Since all the students are working on the same standards, every person should do the same exercises in the same way.
3. Ideally, all students will achieve the same outcomes.

4. Fairness means that every student gets the same amount of time and attention from the teacher.

CORRECTED IDEAS

1. Students begin at different levels of skill and development in relationship to the goals. Holding *high* performance standards for all persons means starting instruction for each student where he or she currently is. Then the lessons should move each person forward, making as much progress on the instructional goals as possible (Broderick, Mehta-Parek, & Reid, 2005; King-Sears, 2008; Lawrence-Brown, 2004).
2. Even though the students are pursuing the same general set of goals, the best way for them to be successful is to design a variety of different pathways to the goals. This requires a degree of personalization, tailoring the exercises to individual needs, creating comfortable ways for each person to exercise and progress (Stanford & Reeves, 2009; Tomlinson, 1999, 2000, 2001).
3. Achieving precisely the same outcomes is neither possible nor necessary. People vary in their abilities and interests. No matter what the content of the course, they won't all end up at exactly the same place. Further, in a democratic society that respects diversity, why would we even desire everyone to think or behave alike? (Broderick, Mehta-Parek, & Reid, 2005)
4. Fairness means that every student receives the time and attention that she needs to succeed, to make excellent progress in the goals of the course (Tomlinson, 1999, 2000, 2001).

Differentiated instruction is an approach to teaching that fully accepts and attends to the diversity of talents, skills, interests, and desires of the students. Every dimension of human and cultural diversity is appreciated and accepted as natural. Since students learn, participate, and display their knowledge in many different ways, differentiation means offering multiple paths to learning success in the classroom. Because humans vary from one another in so many ways, creating numerous avenues to learning and achievement is central to the challenge and joy of teaching.

What does this mean in terms of instructional practices?

Students in the same grade level or classroom differ greatly in terms of academic skills, interests, styles of learning, and life experiences (Tomlinson, 1999, 2000, 2001). Some third graders want to read, write, and study about rockets and space travel while others would prefer to learn about oceans and sea creatures. Some third graders have travelled extensively across the United States and even abroad. Others have an intensive, powerful knowledge of the homes, families, shops, and businesses of their own neighborhood.

No matter what subject matter or academic skill, at any grade level, teachers find a wide variability in the students' skill levels. Most notably, teachers observe that reading skills differ greatly among classmates. For example, Lawrence-Brown (2004, p. 36) states, "In a traditional class of fifteen-year-olds a teacher should expect a ten-year range of reading levels." Differentiated teaching plans for and strategically utilizes these natural differences between students.

Students progress toward content mastery at different speeds, and they require different levels and forms of support (from teachers, paraprofessionals, parents/families, and classmates) to be successful (Tomlinson, 1995, 1999, 2000). Further, students of varying abilities working on the "same" content may not understand or perform at the same level of depth and detail. Teachers should know how to teach the ideas, concepts, and skills in the curriculum are most important, a baseline of essentials that Lawrence-Brown (2004, p. 38) calls the "prioritized curriculum." Some students reach these essential priorities, and others exceed them to develop advanced skills and understandings.

Student variation in styles of learning—the ways they learn best—requires instruction that presents content in multiple ways. Universal Design for Learning (UDL) is an approach to creating access to successful learning for all persons. The principles of UDL were originally formed in the fields of architecture and building. The goal was to design homes, offices, and other aspects of the built environment to meet the physical needs of persons with greatly varied bodies and physical abilities, including people with disabilities and senior citizens. For example, many home builders now create shower stalls with easy access for wheelchairs. These universal design showers are functional for persons with and without disabilities.

UDL applies three basic universal design principles to activities of teaching and learning (CAST, 2013; King-Sears, 2008; Stanford & Reeves, 2009).

1. *Multiple Kinds of Representation*: When information or ideas are presented in a variety of ways, the many students will find a comfortable and useful way to access and understand the content.
    a. Written texts—Reading is an important way to access information. Keep in mind that student vary widely in both how well they read (i.e., reading level) but also the genres or forms of language they appreciate and learn from. Different written forms include school textbooks, academic reports and books, newspapers, magazines, biographies, novels, nonfiction books, blogs, and poems). Employ a variety of written texts, both in terms of reading difficulty and forms or genres.
    b. Neurological access—The primary neurological channels that the brain employs for learning are visual and auditory. At minimum, teachers should present information in multiple versions for auditory and visual access. For example, auditory forms of information delivery may include web

podcasts, radio broadcasts, and recordings. Representations that combine auditory and visual information include Powerpoint or Presi presentations, multimedia performances or presentations, and videos (with sound).
2. *Multiple Kinds of Engagement*: Learning is always experiential, the outgrowth of students experiencing—living in and through—activities rich with meaning. Additionally, we know that students find some learning experiences more appealing, energizing, and motivating. When a teacher provides students with a wide variety of learning activities, in particular those forms of activity that they find stimulating and meaningful, this creates multiple opportunities for learning. For example, students can learn in a variety of social configurations, including individual study and small groups. Varied social arrangements allow for modeling and guidance from the instructor and classmates as well as opportunities for individual responsibility and self-direction. Activities designed to facilitate student learning should maximize access to the knowledge or skills and social support from the instructor and peers.
3. *Multiple Kinds of Expression*: Students have multiple options for demonstrating what they know and how they know it. Choices may include presentations, performances, creative or constructed products, written reports, or tests and quizzes. This aspect of UDL is directly parallel to Representation. While Representation emphasizes how instructors present knowledge, Expression entails how students communicate what they know and can do. Both Representation and Expression necessarily involve flexibility and multiplicity. When knowledge is communicated in a variety of ways, more students will have access to learning and success.

Carol Ann Tomlinson's (1999, 2000, 2001) has developed a useful framework for differentiation involves matching the design of the instructional lesson to the diversity of student talents, needs, interests, and styles. She emphasizes thoughtful lesson and unit planning. Her model consists of three dimensions related to the learning activity: *content*, *process*, and *products*. Effective planning for differentiation involves purposefully modulating these three aspects of the instructional lesson in relation to three specific dimensions of student variability: *readiness*, *interests*, and *learning profile*. Table 9.1 presents Tomlinson's framework in the form of questions that teachers can ask while planning for instruction.

Planning differentiated lessons with content, process, and product in mind allows teachers to think strategically about tailoring the entire lesson to the lives of the students. The metaphor of "tailoring" helps us think about this as crafting lessons that actually fit. Instead of pulling learning activities off the rack and hoping the sleeves aren't too long, this process of developing lessons involves forming the fabric to the bodies and minds of the students. *Content* means the instructional goals of the lesson, the knowledge and/or skills that students learn. Differentiated lessons often pursue a range of closely clustered or topically organized learning goals for the range of different learning styles, abilities, and interests in the class. *Process* points to the learning activity itself, what the students actually do. Prominent features in process are the social arrangement of the learners and materials and technologies employed. Differentiation frequently calls for purposeful social grouping (such as cooperative learning groups or learning partners) matched with a carefully selected variety of materials (such as readings, videos, etc.) that provide multiple opportunities for learning engagement. Learning *products* are the significant objects or results produced by the students in the learning activity. Often these objects—reports, presentations, essays, examinations, performances—are used as the primary focus for the assessment of learning. The products are intentional displays of student learning that serve as a culmination of the lesson.

By focusing on the three dimensions of student variation, teachers mold the learning activity around the students, who they really are as persons and as learners. *Readiness* is a student's level of development, what a student knows and can do, in relation to the particular knowledge and skills required for the lesson. What knowledge and skills does each student bring to this learning activity? *Student interests* are the emotional and experiential connections to (or disconnections from) topics of study. What do students care about? *Learning profiles* are the ways of learning (including learning styles, multiple intelligences) that work best and worst for individual students. What are the most successful ways for individual students to access knowledge and develop skills?

Table 9.1. Questions to Ask When Differentiating Instruction

	Content	Process	Products
Readiness	What level of knowledge and skills do various students have in relation to this content? How can we arrange for all students to access this content in a meaningful way?	What knowledge and skills does the learning process require of the students? How can we engage and support all students?	What products will best allow all students to show their knowledge and skills in this content area?
Interests	What relevant prior school or home experiences do the students bring to this content? How is this content personally relevant for these students?	What relevant interests or preferences do students bring to this learning process? How should we organize the learning activity to build on student interests?	How can the products of this lesson engage and demonstrate the interests of students?

	Content	Process	Products
Learning Profiles	How can the content be presented in ways that engage student strengths or preferred ways of learning?	How can we design the learning process to match areas of student strengths and preferred ways of learning?	How can products (1) build on strengths and (2) develop areas of weakness?

Each of the three suggestions in this section takes up one of Tomlinson's three areas of instructional design emphasis: content, process, and products.

Suggestion #1: Become a hoarding librarian. The most common way to modify, mold, and tweak the content of a learning activity to yield greater access for students is to provide students multiple text options that address the many reading levels in the classroom. In preparation for teaching a lesson or unit of study, gather a rich and assorted buffet of written documents on topic, varying in terms of both reading level and genre.

The key to this suggested practice is purposeful hoarding of reading materials. Look closely at the list of topics and subjects that you teach during an academic year. It is likely that a central way that students gain knowledge about each topic is through reading. In many classrooms, this reading is limited to a single textbook written in dry, unappealing language. For example, if you are teaching seventh-grade social studies, you have a state-approved text book that is aimed toward readers who read at the seventh-grade level. The students in the class probably have reading comprehension levels ranging from about third grade to eleventh. The official textbook presents facts in a direct fashion, but it lacks the compelling allure of rich, well-written narrative. It is too easy for some students, too hard for others, and likely to induce a tedious state of coma for all of them.

Let's say that one of the topics your students learn about is the life and teachings of Confucius. Here is where the scholastic hoarding comes in. You need to compile a bloated smorgasbord, an overstocked cupboard, a bursting-at-the-seams library of readings on the topic. The range of readings should follow these rough guidelines:

1. Multiple genres—Fiction and nonfiction, including reference texts, diaries, travel books, maps, autobiographies and memoirs, historical fiction, realistic fiction, journalistic accounts, etc.
2. Multiple sources—Academic or curricular materials, newspapers, magazines, middle grade and children's literature, websites, etc.
3. Multiple levels of difficulty—Ranging from picture books designed for the primary grades up to high school level or adult materials.

This broad and diverse library allows you to do incredible teaching. You can ask individual students or groups of students to select their own reading materials, allowing them to find texts suitable to their interests and abilities. You can also, like a good librarian who knows just the right text for the right person, suggest specific articles, books, or websites for the needs and wants of individual students. If you undertake literary hoarding across all of the topics that your seventh-grade social studies curriculum explores, the classroom will be rich with language and thought while promoting access for all readers.

Suggestion #2: Creating a rich and flexible social process in the classroom, a way for students to work together and engage in accessible and challenging learning activities, is no small task. But there is one skill that every teacher, no matter what grade levels you teach, regardless of the subject matter, should develop. Learn how to create learning centers. If you learn how to build learning centers that support both individual and group learning activities at multiple levels of student readiness, you have the Swiss pocket knife of instructional techniques, a gift that will keep on giving throughout your career.

Learning centers are clusters of learning activities that run concurrently, creating a rich and buzzing classroom atmosphere, an experience akin to the sights, sounds, and tastes of a food truck park or an urban farmer's market. Many foods for many palates: lumpias filled with pork and cabbage sizzling, carne asada grilling next to fresh corn tortillas, beer-battered fish with thumb-thick chips, small mountains of juicy strawberries and oranges, and breads and cakes from around the world. At every turn is a different opportunity, a new option, another chance for delicious nourishment.

Learning centers are typically physical locations in the classroom, such as tables, lab stations, or study carrels where materials, directions, and assessments are organized together in ready-to-use fashion. Packaged neatly within a learning center are educational activities that focus on a specific academic theme (e.g., the Civil War; Photosynthesis; Animated films) or set of skills (e.g., Writing persuasive letters, Geometry proofs using the law of syllogism, Copyediting creative nonfiction) and assembled around a compact bundle of learning objectives.

Learning centers are, by design, social spaces where interaction and cooperation are often part of the formula. The activities may be designed for individuals, pairs, or for small groups. Students may work with very little teacher support. Or center activities may be developed for use with the supervision and leadership of a teacher or teacher's aide (Kapusnick & Hauslein, 2001; King-Sears, 2007; Tomlinson, 1999).

For example, in a classroom co-taught by a general teacher and a special educator, five different learning centers might operate simultaneously. Imagine a class that is reaching the end of a lengthy curriculum unit, completing some final assessments, and preparing to transition to the next unit.

1. Teacher A provides targeted pre-instruction to a small group of students in preparation for the new unit of instruction that starts the next day. The students have been selected because, based on assessments and the teacher's knowledge of the students, they will benefit from preview instruction on complex new concepts and terminology.
2. Students complete a series of assessment activities to evaluate their learning on the last phase of the curriculum unit. Assessments include a multiple choice test, a short answer test, an oral examination, an essay test, and an option to create and deliver a Powerpoint presentation. Students must choose two of the five optional assessment exercises.
3. Teacher B guides a small group through a structured review activity in preparation for completing the assessment activities in Center 2.
4. Students who have completed the assessment activities in Center 2 watch a video (with closed captioning) that provides additional information that extends and enriches knowledge learned during the curriculum unit.
5. Students with advanced knowledge and skills work in pairs on research projects, conducting inquiries into probing questions that they have posed. They have been working together since the second week of the curriculum unit. They are putting the final touch on their papers, websites, and presentations.

Notice how this example configuration of learning centers provides structures for teacher-led instruction as well as independent learning by individuals, pairs, and small groups. Differentiation is provided both by the range of activities across the centers and by the variability of student options within each center.

Learning centers may also play multiple roles at different phases of the instructional sequence, from the initial presentation of new academic content to the final evaluation of learning. Students can access new information, work alone or with classmates in guided practice, and leap forward into independent practice and in-depth investigations. Further, learning centers may be used to strategically supplement or augment instances of whole-class instruction.

As you might imagine, teaching with learning centers relies heavily on your ability to design learning activities. Well-designed activities provide students with the structure and materials necessary for engagement and success.

The biggest challenge in designing learning centers is organization and clarity of purpose. The teacher must fully understand the learning objectives pursued in the center activities and how students of different levels of ability or skill can successfully complete the activities. A purposeful variety of options (materials, assignments, products) must be available to meet the needs of different students or groups of students.

Margaret King-Sears (2007) warns that having a clear sense of the instructional objectives and the forms of differentiation is crucial to the success of learning centers.

> To design such activities, educators must first have a firm grasp on what they want their students to learn (i.e., learning outcomes), how students can practice information taught, and what the students' learning levels are. Without having clear direction on these aspects of instruction (e.g., "Where are we going? Who needs to practice what? What kinds of activities enable students to meaningfully practice and/or apply information learned?"), educators may find themselves overwhelmed with the prospect of designing learning centers responsive to students' needs (King-Sears, 2007, p. 138).

Developing effective learning centers requires a strong understanding of both curriculum and the students. You have to understand the purpose of each center activity and how each student can access and succeed by way of your activity design.

King-Sears (2007, p. 142) suggests that the starting point for designing learning centers is the question, "What content and types of practice do I already know students need but cannot find enough time to work on?" Think about kinds of learning and teaching opportunities that are not currently available. Think about content students are not currently engaging in meaningful and satisfactory ways. Also think about different kinds of learning activities that students might benefit from. Learning centers allow teachers and students to radically diversify the kinds and numbers of activities that take place simultaneously. If you could teach in a greater variety of ways, and if students therefore learn through numerous opportunities, just imagine what is possible.

The two main factors in designing a configuration of learning centers that operate simultaneously are *teacher time* and the *social arrangement of students*. The question of efficient and effective use of teacher time involves considering how much leadership, supervision, or guidance students at each learning center will need. Some centers require a teacher to serve as leader of the activity, devoting his full attention to the group's work. Other centers need only monitoring and supervision from the distance. An occasional question may arise, but the activities are designed for students to work with a minimum of teacher assistance. Other centers place students in fully independent mode. You will need to evaluate work quality and progress on a daily or weekly basis, but the center pretty much runs on its own steam.

Intertwined with questions of teacher time is the social configuration of centers. A center may be designed for individual work, pairs working together, or small groups of students completing tasks. Ideally, all students get the opportunity to work in all (or at least, most) of these arrangements. But teachers should use their judgment about how individual students learn best.

When you begin, be aware that many students will have to learn how to utilize the learning centers. If learning centers are a new way of learning for the students, they will need to learn the sequences of behaviors, rules for participation, and the procedures involved. It is typically helpful, at first, to give explicit instruction to students on how to work in learning centers; how to follow the written instructions, how to work independently, in pairs, or in groups, how to seek teacher assistance, etc. When students are taught expected routines and the social skills necessary for success in learning centers, then they become comfortable and capable in using centers.

Suggestion #3: No matter what your students are learning, two facts are always true. First, they will produce something—a document, object, or performance—that shows what they have learned. It may be a single item, or there may be multiple products. Second, you will examine the quality of the product(s) for the purposes of evaluation, as a way of gaining insight into what each student learned, what each student did not learn, as well how each student learns. For every lesson or unit of study, develop a useful, practical menu of products that allow students to fully show what they know and offer you a reliable way to evaluate student learning.

Let's begin our examination of the use of multiple products (or product options) with a quick look at a common teaching format that is not differentiated. The students undergo a curricular unit consisting of a series of opportunities for the students to learn a specific batch academic knowledge and skills. At the conclusion of the unit, the students take an evaluation—a test, quiz, or other assessment—that is viewed as comprehensive in relation to the learning objectives of the unit. Every student takes the same assessment because that sameness is viewed as central to the fairness of the evaluation. The assumption is that all students will display what they have learned in the same way.

The problem here aware that the performance of students on that evaluation is a function of both the quality and quantity of learning the students have experienced and the alignment of each student's talents and interests with the requirements of the assessment. For example, a written essay test examining the causes and effects of the decline in honey bee colonies demonstrates a student's scientific knowledge of the ecology of bees as well as her talents in expository writing.

The solution is to retain the intense and purposeful focus on the content of the curricular unit while creating flexibility in the ways that students can demonstrate what they have learned. This is not a call to allow students to cook up ridiculous products that are fun to make but fail to display knowledge and skills. The goal is to create useful, rigorous ways for students to display mastery of content.

How? Here are a few ways that teachers have differentiated student products. Remember that these (and other products) may be completed individually, in pairs, or in small groups.

- *Portfolios*—Think of the work of a photographer. Rather than work for a month taking and developing pictures only to take an artificial test of photography skills at the end of the month, the photography gathers a portfolio of her work that displays her talents. The portfolio may include all of her photos during a specific period of time, or it may include a purposeful selection of different types of pictures. The portfolio is a gathering of artifacts drawn from daily work (Danielson & Abrutyn, 1997; Johnson, Mims-Cox, & Doyle-Nichols, 2010). Teachers can have their students gather portfolios by providing structured guidelines detailing what to collect. The portfolio might even call for students to include written, audio, or video reflections explaining or analyzing the work, an act of self-evaluation that increases student's self-understanding and awareness of how he learns best (Grumbine & Alden, 2006).
- *Rubrics*—Evaluation rubrics may be applied to almost any student work product (including portfolios). The rubrics communicate priorities and standards of quality to the students. They also provide a framework for both students and teachers to evaluate work. Most rubrics consist of rating scales based on observable performance criteria that align with the learning objectives of the activity (Mertler, 2001).
- *Tests, exams, and quizzes*—All of the traditional approaches to assessment, including the many formats (multiple choice, short answer, essay, problem-solving, etc.) are suitable as product options. Be sure to include extended time allotments for students who need more time to demonstrate their knowledge.
- *Take-home tests*—Whenever an assessment is sent home, students have more time to complete the work and they have opportunities to utilize a variety of resources (books, internet, etc.). The factors of expanded time and additional resources raise the standards for the expected quality of the work. The take-home begins to look less like a test and more like a project. Be sure to provide clear guidelines and rules for completing the work, detailing which resources (library books? websites?) and interactions are allowed (compare notes with a classmate? phone call to Uncle Fred the Princeton professor?).
- *Oral tests, exams, and quizzes*—How many times have parents or teachers told the story of the student who could provide accurate oral answers to every bit of content on the test but performed poorly when taking the pencil-and-paper exam? Some students perform poorly on written evaluations but do well when offered a chance to answer questions aloud. Oral tests need not be time-consuming for teachers. A peer can read the questions, and the entire Q and A can be recorded on a smart phone or tablet.
- *Artistic products*—A variety of artistic media may be used to capture and express knowledge. Visual representations include drawings, paintings, photographs, video and digital media. Three-dimensional representations may

involve sculpture, architecture, design, or building. Audio representations consist of varieties of music, recordings, and voice.

- *Performances and productions*—Imagination, time, and resources are the only limits. Maybe students do presentations using Powerpoint or other visual representation technology (Doyle & Giangreco, 2009). Perhaps they engage in a formal debate on a provocative issue or dilemma. Or they may create more elaborate stage productions, employing elements of dramatic theater, music, spoken word, and comedy.

This brief smattering of product examples is intended to stir the pedagogical imagination, not to offer a complete and definitive list. Good teachers create new product options frequently as a way of both supporting students' acts of representation and facilitating good evaluation of learning.

REFERENCES

Broderick, A., Mehta-Parek, H., & Reid, D. K. (2005). Differentiating instruction for disabled students in inclusive classrooms. *Theory into Practice, 44*, 3, 194–202.

CAST, 2013. About UDL. http://www.cast.org/udl/

Danielson, C., & Abrutyn, L. (1997). *An introduction to using portfolios in the classroom.* Alexandria, VA: Association for Supervision and Curriculum Development.

Doyle, M. B., & Giangreco, M. (2009). Making presentation software accessible to high school students with intellectual disabilities. *Teaching Exceptional Children, 41*, 3, 24–31.

Grumbine, R., & Alden, P. B. (2006). Teaching science to students with learning disabilities. *The Science Teacher, 73, 3*, 26–31.

Johnson, R. S., Mims-Cox, J. S., & Doyle-Nichols, A. (2010). *Developing portfolios in education: A guide to reflection, inquiry, and assessment* (2nd ed.). Thousand Oaks, CA: Sage.

Kapusnick, R. A., & Hauslein, C. M. (2001). The 'silver cup' of differentiated instruction. *Kappa Delta Pi Record 37*, 4, 156–159.

King-Sears, M. E. (2007). Designing and delivering learning center instruction. *Intervention in School and Clinic, 42*, 137–147.

King-Sears, M. E. (2008). Facts and fallacies: Differentiation and the general education curriculum for students with special educational needs. *Support for Learning, 23*, 2, 55–62.

Lawrence-Brown, D. (2004). Differentiated instruction: Inclusive strategies for standards-based learning that benefit the whole class. *American Secondary Education, 32*, 3, 34–62.

Mertler, C. A. (2001). Designing scoring rubrics for your classroom. *Practical Assessment, Research & Evaluation, 7*, 25. Retrieved March 3, 2004 from http://PAREonline.net/getvn.asp?v=7&n=25.

Stanford, B., & Reeves, S. (2009). Making it happen: Using differentiated instruction, retrofit framework, and Universal Design for Learning. *Teaching Exceptional Children Plus, 5*, 6, Article 4. Retrieved June 24, 2013 from http://escholarship.bc.edu/education/tecplus/vol5/iss6/art4.

Tomlinson, C. A. (1999) *The differentiated classroom: Responding to the needs of all learners*. Alexandria, VA: Association for Supervision and Curriculum Development.

Tomlinson, C. A. (2000). Reconcilable differences? Standards-based teaching and differentiation. *Educational Leadership, 58*, 1, 6–11.

Tomlinson, C. A. (2001). *How to differentiate instruction in mixed-ability classrooms*. Alexandria, VA: Association for Supervision and Curriculum Development.

CHAPTER TEN

School Reform

> **Guiding Question**
> - How can you participate in a school-wide inclusive education reform effort?

But how do I get my whole school to do inclusion [...] *together*?

I have heard this question many times from valiant teachers who have labored in the hidden shadows, who have tried to create more inclusive classroom opportunities for students in a school where resource rooms and self-contained special education classes are still the customary location for disabled students. Often one or two general classroom teachers pair up with a special education colleague to do some co-teaching, creating a counter-cultural, mini-inclusive revolution (almost) beneath the radar of colleagues and administrators. There are also countless special and general educators who advocate fiercely for inclusive placements at IEP meetings, often volunteering their own time and classrooms to make it happen. In schools where the overall commitment to inclusive education is ambiguous, half-hearted, or altogether absent, there are small bands of ambitious, progressive educators who want to change the world. Or, at least, change their school.

Many inclusive education researchers contend that inclusion can only be truly successful and sustained over time if individual schools go through a process of dramatic change, involving a transformation of the principal's responsibilities, school policies, curriculum, and the daily practices of teachers. "Comprehensive school change is required to develop effective, inclusive schools" (McLeskey & Waldron, 2011, p. 54).

Inclusion, when viewed in this light, is not a program that is added to what schools and teachers already do. It is a wholesale change in the purposes of schooling and the daily activities of teachers and leaders. It requires a "profound shift" (Deering, 1998, p. 13) in the attitudes, behaviors, and interactions of administrators, teachers, and other educational professionals (Dukes & Lamar-Dukes, 2009; Fisher, Sax, Pumpian, Rodifer, & Kreikemeirer, 1997; Kilgore, Griffin, Sindelar, & Webb, 2002a, 2002b; Kugelmass, 2001; McLeskey & Waldron, 2006; Roach & Salisbury, 2006; Ryndak, Reardon, Benner, & Ward, 2007; Sailor & Roger, 2005).

Research analyses of successful and unsuccessful attempts to transform public schools from traditional practices of disability segregation into inclusive education have yielded practical guidance for schools seeking reform. Kilgore, Griffin, Sindelar, and Webb (2002a, 2002b) offer the most cogent advice in the form of five basic features of successful inclusive school reform that draw support not only from their research on reform in a Florida middle school but from multiple other studies of inclusive school reform activities (e.g., Jorgensen, 2004; Sailor & Roger, 2005; Zollers, Ramanathan, & Yu, 1999).

First, the school must operate by a "system of democratic governance" (Kilgore, Griffin, Sindelar, & Webb, 2002b, p. 10). School principals, teachers, and other professionals need to work in a system of shared decision-making that actively values the input of all persons. In order to develop the necessary level of commitment among all of the teachers, processes of decision-making cannot simply be top-down (Jorgensen, 2004; Sailor & Roger, 2005). Zollers, Ramanathan, and Yu (1999, p. 164) explain:

> School reform measures that are imposed upon the classroom teacher may not be readily adopted. If inclusion is adopted in a school in a hierarchical way, there is the risk that it will not be fully embraced by the staff and the student body. Moreover, if inclusion is imposed on staff who feel powerless, the staff may not wrestle with and solve the difficult issues that arise from school-wide changes in curriculum, staffing, assessment, and instructional practices. Within a democratic and empowering culture, teachers have the opportunity to contribute to the implementation of inclusion and, thus, will be invested in the complex process of making inclusion successful.

School reforms that are forced upon teachers without their involvement and commitment often suffer from insufficient or distorted implementation (Tyack & Cuban, 1995). When teachers actively participate in the decisions that inform and drive the reform process, they are more likely to be invested in the effort and effective in implementation.

Secondly, the school needs to develop and maintain a "culture of collaboration" (Kilgore, Griffin, Sindelar, & Webb, 2002b, p. 10), a social environment of interpersonal relationships and interactions whereby teachers and administrators work closely together. The professionals fully share the responsibility for the success of the education of all students (Deering, 1998). The work is viewed as an ongoing, mutual learning process for the entire school, an adventurous path of learning and growing together (Hyatt, DaSilva Iddings, & Ober, 2005).

For example, in Judy Kugelmass's (2001) study of the development of an inclusive elementary school, she found that a process of teamwork and shared growth encompassed virtually all of the activities of the teachers and school leader. "Collaboration emerged as the central theme at the core of everyday operations" (Kugelmass, 2001, p. 53). The teachers described their work together as "in process" (p. 59), an open-ended, continuous venture of professional experimentation and learning. The work took place within a complex and rich "collaborative community" (p. 59) involving a variety of opportunities for constructive sharing; workshops, whole faculty meetings, topical discussion groups. A wide variety of communication frameworks, some permanent and some spontaneously arising, all supported by the principal, sponsored collaborative interactions among the professionals.

> The story of this school's evolution demonstrates that no individual can be responsible for creating or sustaining an inclusive school. A commitment to supporting diversity among students requires the development of collaborative processes that, in turn, require internal and external compromises by teachers. As one teacher explained, some of her colleagues were initially 'very territorial, my kids and your kids'. However, through an ongoing and collaborative process of critical self-examination, they realised both that any teacher could teach any child and that collaborative teaching could enhance what went on in every classroom. Student and teacher autonomy was not diminished in the process, but rather, enhanced. The teachers at this school believe that collaboration enriches individual teaching. Their collective strength was most evident in their ability to negotiate with the central school district administration. With the support of their principal, they were able to create and then, on their own, sustain a collaborative culture that empowered both children and adults. (Kugelmass, 2001, p. 62)

When collaboration among educators is the social norm, when it becomes simply a valued and central dimension of everyday school practice, then individuals and the entire school team reap the numerous rewards.

The third basic principle is closely related. The faculty and administration should embrace and enact a full "commitment to and capacity for professional growth" (Kilgore, Griffin, Sindelar, & Webb, 2002b, p. 11). The school reform literature is filled with the idea that teachers and leaders must view themselves individually and as a group as inquiring, learning, changing, figuring things out. Not only does a career of teaching require that the individual instructor view himself as learning, changing, and adapting to new situations over time. Further, the school as a social group should understand itself as a learning organization, as a pedagogical knowledge and skill team that develops and changes over time. Peter Senge (2006, p. 3) defines a learning organization as an organization

> where people continually expand their capacity to create the results they truly desire, where new and expansive patterns of thinking are nurtured, where collective aspiration is set free, and where people are continually learning how to learn together.

With thoughtful leadership and serious effort, the organization sets out on a path of improvement, becoming more capable and effective through a process of individual and group learning (Brandt, 2003; Fullan, 1995).

Waldron and Redd (2011) describe this kind of growth as an entire school building greater capacity through professional development and learning in order to more effectively meet the needs of a diverse population of students. This is like a fisherman crafting a larger, stronger net; a tennis player working to increase the speed and accuracy of her topspin backhand; an artist expanding his aesthetic reach by incorporating new materials, colors, and techniques; an orchestra extending its musical repertoire by practicing works from untried genres and traditions; a football team adding an updated set of complex plays and formations in preparation for the big game; a ballet company courageously mixing classical techniques with contemporary music and narratives. This is not about showing up to work each day to essentially do what you did the day before. The group ambitiously charts a rising trajectory of performance and then learns together the knowledge and skills required for the climb.

The fourth principle *is* the principal. The school leader must provide "strong leadership" (Kilgore, Griffin, Sindelar, & Webb, 2002b, p. 11) that communicates unequivocal dedication to the goals of inclusion while providing a supportive environment where teachers can learn new ideas and skills. Waldron and Redd (2011, p. 61) describe the building principal as the "keeper of the vision" of inclusive education, the person who safeguards and maintains the focus on "inclusive practices that result in positive achievement outcomes for all students, while continually prodding teachers to take the next steps toward improving instruction." Zollers, Ramanathan, and Yu (1999, p. 165) describe one successful inclusive school principal as "values-driven," articulating and demonstrating "a strong belief in inclusion." The school leader must take a prominent role as the main person who actively cultivates and maintains the culture of collaboration, innovation, and professional learning.

Finally, from administrative actions to policy documents to the daily actions of teachers in classrooms, the school must enact a wholehearted "concern about equity and success and well-being of students" (Kilgore, Griffin, Sindelar, & Webb, 2002b, p. 11). Effective inclusive teachers are very aware that inclusion "is not about students with disabilities—it's about whether educators are willing to accept responsibility for educating all students in a personalized and motivational way" (Kilgore, Griffin, Sindelar, & Webb, 2002b, p. 11). Superficial efforts at inclusive schooling focus explicitly on meeting the needs of students with disabilities. Deeper, more mature, and enduring inclusive schooling reforms embrace focus on supporting the well-being and learning of all students. Furthermore, the educators maintain a critical vigilance concerning the tendency of public schools to marginalize a number of groups, including students of color, students with disabilities, and LGBT students.

Suggestion 1: Begin with a serious, honest self-evaluation of how inclusive your school really is. This activity should be a frank, non-judgmental conversation among the teachers and the school principal. Admit where you are, what you are doing well, what you are doing poorly. Perhaps most importantly, talk about where you really want to be. Repeat the self-evaluation as often as necessary in order to stimulate thoughtful discussion about the challenging road of improvement that all are sharing.

Any path of ambitious and hopeful improvement must involve an element of brazen, piercing honesty that fully acknowledges the strengths and weaknesses of the school's approach to inclusive education. The purpose is not to throw the entire faculty into a spiraling bout of self-deprecating depression. The purpose is not to engage in acrimonious finger-pointing. The idea is to acknowledge the starting point, where we are, in order to then begin to develop a consensus picture of where the group wants to go.

I have expanded a three-level scheme (see Table 10.1) developed initially by Howard M. Weiner (2003) for this purpose. The progressive, three-step structure of Weiner's model allows schools to both identify where they are in the process of inclusive school reform and then envision how they can improve. Level one schools do some things well, but inclusion is not a high priority to the principal or the teachers. Instructional practices overall are stagnant, lacking an explicit focus on improving learning and support for diverse students. Level two schools are ambivalent, a mixture of strong teaching for diverse groups of learners and unimpressive practices of disability segregation. Level two schools often have many of the ingredients of a successful inclusive school, but the commitment is uneven and uncoordinated. Level three schools are the exemplar, the outstanding, innovative, effective inclusive schools we all want to be part of.

Table 10.1. Levels of Inclusive Schools Culture and Learning Environment

	Level 1	Level 2	Level 3
Teacher commitment	Teachers lack an active commitment to struggling learners or students with disabilities. Teachers seek specialists to deal with students who do not learn in their class.	Some teachers enact a commitment to diverse learners and disabled students. Others do not feel responsible for the learning of all students.	Teachers evidence a strong dedication to ensuring that all students learn and feel supported. Teachers assume that all students are competent learners.
Pedagogy	Instruction is targeted toward the middle of the class, offering one activity for all students regardless of abilities or interests.	Some teachers differentiate instruction to meet the needs of many learners. Other teachers ignore variability in students' needs.	Instruction is differentiated on the basis of variation of abilities and interests. Students often work in cooperative, heterogeneous groups, assisting one another.
Leadership	The school principal lacks knowledge about and/or commitment to inclusion. The leader does little to foster organizational learning and instructional improvement for all students.	The school principal is inconsistent in terms of knowledge and support for inclusive schooling. The leader provides some support for improving pedagogy for all students.	The school principal is a knowledgeable, capable, and consistent supporter of the entire school's path of learning and growth toward increasing inclusive effectiveness.
Relationships with students	Teachers have a superficial understanding of students' lives. They maintain restricted, limited relationships with students.	Some teachers are committed to caring relationships with students that cultivate a strong sense of understanding. Others remain somewhat detached and have limited understanding of their students' lives.	Teachers have a complex and deep understanding of their students' lives. They are deeply invested in building caring, supportive relationships with students.

	Level 1	Level 2	Level 3
Use of data	Teachers utilize a limited set of data (e.g., only standardized test scores) or they misuse data to confirm prejudices about students deficits and limitations.	Some teachers use a wide variety of data to enrich their understanding of students. Most use data in restricted or biased ways.	Teachers employ a wide variety of quantitative and qualitative data, formal and informal assessments, in order to understand student learning and needs.
Professional development	Professional development is limited, lacks a research basis, or fails to support improvement of practical skills. The school lacks an explicit focus on learning as a purposeful organization.	Professional development is hit or miss, providing an inconsistent foundation for the improvement of practice. The school has an unreliable focus on working as a learning organization.	Professional development is based on research and relevant to the improvement of classroom practice. Professional learning is explicitly strategized to improve the teaching and student support capacity of the entire organization.

How do you use this three-level scheme? If there is sufficient trust and honesty in the communications between teachers and administrators in the building, then you can leap right into an open conversation about each of the six criteria in the rubric.

But [...] if there is discord, tension, and a lack of trust among the teachers or between teachers and the principal, then you should begin with a private survey. Provide an opportunity for all of the professionals to anonymously evaluate your school (there are easy, free web-based tools for this). Distribute the findings of the survey to all of the professionals. The findings can stand as an objective report reflecting the overall beliefs of the entire faculty. Then you can hold a meeting of all teachers and the administrators to discuss the findings of the survey.

Suggestion 2: Develop a consensus statement that reflects the unyielding, shared beliefs of the entire faculty and administration of the school. Do this as early as possible. If you have a clear statement of what the school is trying to achieve, and that statement has the support of the educational professionals, then you have a shared mission that you can repeatedly return to and refer to. Here is our mission. How are our actions fulfilling this mission? How are they falling short?

"Effective inclusive practices require a school vision focused on meeting the needs of all students" (Waldron & Redd, 2011, p. 59). The research literature on inclusive education reform repeatedly and emphatically points to the need for a shared mission that supports teaching all students in general education classrooms.

Hyatt, DaSilva Iddings, and Ober (2005) examined the successful inclusive reform in a large, urban elementary school. The first step in the process was a discussion of values. What do we value? What do we as a school believe in? This discussion led to the adoption of a motto for the school: "We Celebrate All Children" (Hyatt, DaSilva Iddings, & Ober, 2005, p. 5).

Of course, a brief motto, even if it is glowing and wonderful, can quickly turn into a trite bumper sticker with no relationship to the daily practices occurring in the hallways and classrooms. In order to put committed action to this motto, a number of the professional development workshops offered by university faculty partners provided a genuine focus on instructional practices appreciating and supporting all students in general classrooms. The learning trajectory of the organization was matched to the motto, creating opportunities for the teachers to bring the mission to life.

Similarly, Zollers, Ramanathan, and Yu (1999, p. 170) describe one inclusive school that rallied around the maxim "We are all special." The researchers "found a remarkable amount of shared language" at the school, frequent and specific communications enacting the collective values and mission of the organization. The consensus of purpose among the professionals was evident in the words they often used to narrate their work with students and families.

Causton-Theoharis, Theoharis, Bull, Cosier, and Dempf-Aldrich (2011) provide a cautionary tale about what happens when reformers do not share a clear understanding of inclusion. In a study of the first year in the inclusive reform of an elementary school, they found that the school achieved a fair degree of improvement. Approximately eighty-five percent of all students with disabilities were educated in the general classroom for all or part of the school day. But doubts and hesitation remained active among the teachers. A small group of very resistant teachers comprising less than ten percent of the total faculty stood as a negative, powerful barrier to further progress. The teachers generally acknowledged that a weakness in their reform efforts was a lack of an identifiable, shared philosophy. While the school had taken significant steps forward toward inclusion, the future was uncertain due to the absence of a consensus mission articulating the commitments of the professionals.

Suggestion 3: What do you do if there is no real opportunity to develop a consensus mission? Perhaps the school principal does not hold a strong commitment to inclusion. Maybe the teachers are very doubtful and hesitant. There is some evidence in the research literature to indicate that building an inclusive school very gradually, perhaps starting with just one integrated classroom co-taught by a special and general educator, can be a successful path to whole school reform. Start small. Document and demonstrate success. Invite other teachers to join in. Create a positive conspiracy.

Everett M. Rogers (2003) is a sociologist who has spent his entire career studying the diffusion of innovation, how new ideas and practices are spread, gain or loss acceptance, and either become a part of conventional, everyday activity or tumble into the dust heap of history. His scholarship examines the dissemination of a wide variety of innovations: how new agricultural practices, seeds, and pesticides gain acceptance among farmers, how HIV and AIDS prevention ideas and behaviors achieve credibility and utility, and how scientific companies develop, communicate, and ultimately convince the public to buy and use advanced computer technologies.

In his research, Rogers has discovered a general set of characteristics that help explain why some innovations are adopted quickly, others quite gradually, and others not at all. These characteristics apply very neatly to the efforts of any teacher or group of teachers who want to convince their colleagues to embrace inclusive education. If you want to start a small-scale, inclusive education school reform revolution, here are five characteristics to consider (Rogers, 2003, pp. 15–16).

Relative advantage—When people, in their subjective understandings, believe that a new idea or practice is better than the current way of doing things, then they will be ready to make a change. Their perception may be based on a variety of factors, including convenience, social prestige, and personal satisfaction. "The greater the perceived relative advantage of an innovation, the more rapid its rate of adoption will be" (Rogers, 2003, p. 15). Convincing teachers of the many benefits of inclusive education involves addressing how students with and without disabilities win in inclusive classrooms as well as the many benefits to teachers. Educators select classroom practices not only because they seem to help children but also because the teachers themselves experience those practices as satisfying and rewarding.

Compatibility—To what extent is inclusive education "perceived as being consistent with the existing values, past experiences, and needs" (Rogers, 2003, p. 15) of the teachers? The more the educators perceive inclusive education as aligning well with their beliefs, ethical commitments, and desires, the more quickly and completely it will be adopted. This is a challenge in many schools. Many teachers hold strong ethical commitments about social justice and providing high quality instruction and social support for diverse populations of students, including students who come from marginalized or oppressed groups in society. But many of those same teachers do not view disability and disabled students as part of their social justice orientation. How can we help them expand their concept of social justice to include disability?

Complexity—If a concept is too difficult to understand, or if the practical application of that concept is too hard for people to gain competence and confidence, they are likely to reject the innovation. When new ideas are simple and comfortable, then people tend to be more ready to adopt them. In the case of inclusion, the ideas and the practices are relatively complex. Effective inclusive teaching is only achievable by highly dedicated, talented, and hard-working teachers. Learning the knowledge, skills, and practices undoubtedly takes time and effort.

But then again, is high quality teaching in a non-inclusive format really easy? Isn't all excellent teaching in any approach, by any theory of instruction, harrowing?

Trialability—People tend to like to try out a new innovation on a small scale before leaping into full adoption. For example, when farmers are introduced to a new corn seed that appears to have great benefits over the seed they typically use, many test the innovation on a single acre, giving the see a practical trial before deciding whether to progress to a larger scale adoption (Rogers, 2003). In the public schools, it is possible for teachers to try out co-teaching and inclusion for a fraction of the day, perhaps one lesson or one class period, in order to evaluate the innovation. It is not uncommon for schools pursuing inclusive education reform to progress incrementally over the course of three to five years by adding more inclusive classes and grade levels each semester or year (Fisher, Sax, Pumpian, Rodifer, & Kreikemeirer, 1997; Hyatt, DaSilva Iddings, & Ober, 2005; Ryndak, Reardon, Benner, & Ward, 2007) This allows teachers to gain skill, comfort, and confidence over time.

Observability—"The easier it is for individuals to see the results of an innovation, the more likely they are to adopt" (Rogers, 2003, p. 16). If two teachers take up co-teaching and inclusion for one period each day, and they vigorously publicize their efforts and the student learning and behavior outcomes to their colleagues, then the other teachers in the building may begin to see inclusive education as not only feasible but advantageous. If they see those teachers as credible yet no more brilliant or capable than themselves, then they begin to envision themselves enacting the same practices. They think, if he can do this, and if it goes well, then I can, too.

REFERENCES

Brandt, R. (2003). Is this school a learning organization? 10 ways to tell. *Journal of Staff Development*, 24, 1, 10–16.

Causton-Theoharis, J., Theoharis, G., Bull, T., Cosier, M., & Dempf-Aldrich, K. (2011). Schools of promise: A school district-university partnership centered on inclusive school reform. *Remedial and Special Education*, 32, 3, 192–205.

Deering, P. D. (1998). Making comprehensive inclusion of special needs students work in a middle school. *Middle School Journal*, 29, 3, 12–19.

Dukes, C., & Lamar-Dukes, P. (2009). Inclusion by design: Engineering inclusive practices in secondary schools. *Teaching Exceptional Children*, 41, 3, 16–23.

Fisher, D., Sax, C., Pumpian, I., Rodifer, K., & Kreikemeirer, P. (1997). Including all students in the high school reform agenda. *Education and Treatment of Children*, 20, 59–67.

Fullan, M. (1995). The school as a learning organization: Distant dreams. *Theory into Practice, 34,* 4, 230–235.

Hyatt, K. J., DaSilva Iddings, A. C., & Ober, S. (2005). Inclusion: A catalyst for school reform. *Teaching Exceptional Children Plus, 1(3)* Article 2. Retrieved July 9, 2013 from http://escholarship.bc.edu/education/tecplus/vol1/iss3/2.

Jorgensen, C. (2004). Essential questions—inclusive answers. *Educational Leadership, 52,* 4, 52–55.

Kilgore, K., Griffin, C. C., Sindelar, P. T., & Webb, R. B. (2002a). Restructuring for inclusion: A story of middle school renewal (part 1). *Middle School Journal, 33,* 2, 44–51.

Kilgore, K., Griffin, C. C., Sindelar, P. T., & Webb, R. B. (2002b). Restructuring for inclusion: Changing teaching practices (part 2). *Middle School Journal, 33,* 3, 7–13.

Kugelmass, J. W. (2001). Collaboration and compromise in creating and sustaining an inclusive school. *International Journal of Inclusive Schooling, 5,* 1, 47–65.

McLeskey, J., & Waldron, N. L. (2006). Comprehensive school reform and inclusive schools. *Theory into Practice, 45,* 3, 269–278.

McLeskey, J., & Waldron, N. L. (2011). Educational programs for elementary students with learning disabilities: Can they be both effective and inclusive? *Learning Disabilities Research & Practice, 26,* 1, 48–57.

Roach, V., & Salisbury, C. (2006). Promoting systemic, statewide inclusion from the bottom up. *Theory into Practice, 45,* 3, 279–286.

Rogers, E. M. (2003). *Diffusion of innovation.* New York: Free Press.

Ryndak, D. L. Reardon, R., Benner, S. R., & Ward, T. (2007). Transitioning to and sustaining district-wide inclusive services: A 7-year study of a district's ongoing journey and its accompanying complexities. *Research and Practice for Persons with Severe Disabilities, 32,* 4, 228–246.

Sailor, W., & Roger, B. (2005). Rethinking inclusion: Schoolwide applications. *Phi Delta Kappan, 86,* 7, 503–509.

Senge, P. M. (2006). *The fifth discipline: The art and practice of the learning organization.* New York: Doubleday.

Tyack, D. B., & Cuban, L. (1995). *Tinkering toward utopia: A century of public school reform.* Cambridge, MA: Harvard University Press.

Waldron, N. L., & Redd, L. (2011). Providing a full circle of support to teachers in an inclusive elementary school. *Journal of Special Education Leadership, 24,* 1, 59–61.

Weiner, H. M. (2003). Effective inclusion: Professional development in the context of the classroom. *Teaching Exceptional Children, 35,* 6, 12–18.

Zollers, N. J., Ramanathan, A. K., & Yu, M. (1999). The relationship between school culture and inclusion: How an inclusive culture supports inclusive education. *Qualitative Studies in Education, 12,* 2, 157–174.

SECTION THREE

Narratives of Inclusive Education Struggle and Success

"Their story, yours, mine—it's what we all carry with us on this trip we take, and we owe it to each other to respect our stories and learn from them." (William Carlos Williams, as quoted by Coles, 1989, p. 30)

It is not uncommon for books about effective pedagogy to tout a series of instructional methods and then illustrate those teaching activities in the form of descriptive cases or narratives. Typically, these accounts are presented in an authoritative style, as large stone statues built into impressive shrines of professional knowledge. The message is, we have told you quite masterfully what to do, how to teach, and these narrated examples clearly demonstrate the best practices. So imitate the expertise exemplified in these narratives.

Undoubtedly, there is something valuable in reading the stories told by persons who have achieved a fair degree of effectiveness. I don't want to downplay how important it is for teachers to have access to experiential stories told by highly successful colleagues. Often these stories provide both inspiration and illustration, nudging the reader forward to try better practices while offering some element of guidance on that improving path. Often these stories help us to envision what is possible. *If those people can do it, why can't we?*

But the typical professional book that provides stories or case studies of effective practice is also quite artificial, presenting the complex, interpersonal art of teaching in clarified and authoritative terms. The plot and characters of the story are manufactured with professional jargon, the most popular or scientific theories and formulations, all duly noted with recent citations from the literature. But the result is too perfect and clean. When the cases or narratives of best practice are populated with all the right vocabulary and theories, one must wonder what aspects of real life and genuine teaching are left out.

Often researchers and experts supply narratives demonstrating teaching excellence with great clarity by representing teaching, learning, and classrooms in clean and unproblematic terms. The ambiguities and messiness of the daily work of teachers and students are left out of the neat equation. When narratives fully and precisely demonstrate best practices in action, often there is something of the vital untidiness of everyday life that is sacrificed. We so-called educational experts pat ourselves on the back for using all of the most revered terms and concepts of our profession, thereby securing our position as experts, while leaving most of the authentic muddiness of life on the cutting room floor.

Irving Yalom began his classic book *Existential Psychotherapy* with a story about cooking. He recounted an experience taking a cooking class taught by a noted Armenian chef and her skilled assistant. The culinary instructor methodically demonstrated each step in the preparation and cooking of the meal. Yalom and his classmates followed her model faithfully, yet their dishes turned out nothing like the instructor's delicious concoctions. Yalom was puzzled. What made the chef's dishes so special?

> The answer eluded me until one day, when I was keeping a particularly keen watch on the kitchen proceedings, I saw our teacher, with great dignity and deliberation, prepare a dish. She handed it to her servant who wordlessly carried it into the kitchen to the oven and, without breaking stride, threw in handful after handful of assorted spices and condiments. I am convinced that those surreptitious "throw ins" made all the difference. (Yalom, 1980, p. 4)

Yalom concluded that great psychotherapists, like master chefs, have the wonderful talent of "throwing in" extras here and there, creating an effective technique that goes far beyond any professional training. These extra elements were off the record, untaught, yet crucial to the fantastic flavor of the food.

Reforming public schools from segregating practices to inclusive education is much like Yalom's tale of cooking and psychotherapy. The research literature is replete with very reasonable formulas, recipes, and recommended action steps telling how you can methodically improve the quality of instruction in your inclusive classroom. Often, the experts and researchers provide a detailed list of guidelines, essential features, or comprehensive principles that neatly outline the best inclusive practices.

But the extra throw-ins, the informal and often unacknowledged practices that actually make teaching successful, do not appear in the research and practical literature. The ingredients that can make or break any teacher's effort to fully embrace and practice inclusion are often missing from the sage advice on effective inclusive practices.

These narratives are not standardized, cleaned up, and purified in order to only serve as illustrations of pedagogical best practice. Certainly, I have gathered tales of "successful" inclusive education, of inclusion gone generally well. Undoubtedly, there are lessons about great teaching captured in these descriptions.

The most obvious reason for gathering and presenting this rich batch of stories is to provide teachers with access to the successful inclusive education experiences of educators and parents. The authors are people who have been there, struggled through the sleet and rain, and have come away feeling a fair degree of satisfaction about what they and their colleagues achieved. These stories demonstrate hard journeys that, for the most part, end on high plateaus.

But these stories have not been written in formulaic fashion, stitched at the hems with proper educational theory and terminology. They are not recipes for success that any person can simply pick up and follow. They are genuine descriptions of human experiences, guided and limited by the perspectives and priorities of the authors, elevated by their wisdom and insight, restricted by their fallibility and partiality. In Yalom's language, they include both the recipes and the "throw-ins" that make teaching real.

Further, I advise you not to read the stories seeking clear and firm directions about what to do. While valuable to practitioners, narratives do not really tell us to insert Tab A into Slot B.

In their classic song "Terrapin Station," the Grateful Dead offer insight into what we can hope to gain from stories. The narrator relates a story of a soldier and a sailor vying for the affection of a fair lady. The lady offers a deadly challenge to each. At the conclusion of the story, it is unclear whether the sailor or the soldier made the wiser decision. The narrator refuses to offer an opinion. "The story teller makes no choice," the singer explains. "His job is to shed light, and not to master" (Garcia & Hunter, 1977). The narrator is not the knowledgeable master of all, the one who understands and can explain completely. Perhaps there is no one who holds such a comprehensive and assured knowledge. The narrator's task is to shed light, to bring what previously remained in the darkness, out of our awareness, into the space of appreciation and thoughtful examination. The narrator and the story facilitate greater awareness, deeper sensitivity, and intellectual facility. But they will not tell you what to think or what to do.

Finally, the stories provided in this book are not the only stories that matter. As readers, as educators, you bring your own life stories to the task of interpreting and making sense of these accounts. Your own reading of these accounts—how you hear these tales—is influenced by your own storied experiences, both personal and professional. In that act of interpretation, you make each story your own, taking it into your thoughts and beliefs, modifying and molding it to the contours of your own life and experience. You highlight what you feel and believe deserves emphasis. You skate past what, by your thinking, is less salient or important.

Some of the narratives will strike you as crucial to your own teaching practice, to what you have experienced and what you confront each day in your own classroom and school. Those narratives will stand out as most relevant and useful to you. Others will seem less pertinent. Perhaps they will appear to be written for another teacher who works in a different school.

But if you pick up this book years later and reread the same bunch of stories, you may find that narratives previously overlooked then rise to the top. As your life progresses and your professional experience evolves, your priorities and interests change. Suddenly a story that seemed less germane years ago speaks directly to you in the present moment. That is not only the power of stories but the dynamic of the interaction between your stories and these, between your life experiences and the experiential accounts written by the many authors who have contributed to this book.

REFERENCES

Coles, R. (1989). *The Call of stories: Teaching and the moral imagination.* Boston: Houghton Mifflin Company.
Garcia, J., & Hunter, R. (1977). *Terrapin Station.* New York: Arista Records.
Yalom, I. (1980). *Existential psychotherapy.* New York: Basic Books.

CHAPTER ELEVEN

A Journey into Inclusive Education

CARRIE D. WYSOCKI

THE MEDICAL JOURNEY

As a mother of three, I have experienced the moment when someone asks you if you want to have a boy or a girl. Naturally, the standard answer always came "I don't care, as long as it's healthy." Well certainly, who would ever say they "want" a disabled child? I am certain that if I were to be able to have a child again, I would certainly not suddenly say I would want a child with a disability, but my perspective and view on people with disabilities has ultimately changed beyond my wildest assumptions now that I have Gabby. But being a mom to a child with disabilities not only altered my views of parenting, even more so to my ideas as an educator, and the discovery of my hopes and dreams for my disabled daughter's education.

I began my journey in teaching before I had children. I was fortunate to attend a university where the ideas of constructivism and collaborative ways of teaching and learning were espoused, but to be honest, these theories and ideas did not match the way I had grown up to know and understand teaching. When I began my first year of teaching in a middle school, I felt my theories and philosophies contradicted those of the school and other teachers, so I began to resort to standard, top-down model approaches to teaching. My first interaction with special education was the day I was asked to cover a class during my planning period. The multiple handicapped teacher had to leave, and I spent a forty minute block of time in a room full of students with moderate to severe disabilities. I was mortified. My first reaction was "why are these kids even here? What is the point? I wonder if their Moms demanded they be here."

The shame in thinking those beliefs, I hope, will be redeemed as I share my journey of educating Gabby. Although sadly, I feel my views are not uncommon to the theories a majority of educators ascribe to in our schools. It seems the average teacher believes students like these should be separated and focuses primarily on developing basic life skills. I knew that all too often special education classrooms "lack thoughtful or recognizable academic opportunities" and that the practices of working with students with disabilities "reduce the whole of a child to the deficit contours associated with various categories of impairment" (Kliewer, 2008, p. 14). Today my context for asking the same question has shifted to why *were* those students in a multiple handicapped classroom and not in the general education classrooms? It has taken several years to begin asking that question when it comes to educating students like my Gabby.

It seems many parents of children with disabilities, ultimately given a diagnosis, seem to concur they just "knew" something was not right with their child. When my third daughter was around the age of two, I had a distinct impression something was not typically developing. She had crossed eyes, and after an eye alignment surgery to correct the issue, I thought she would be "normal." Yet I had begun to ponder by whose impossible standards gets to decide what is normal? I already knew that culture shaped "our perspectives about the world and the people around us," so it was evident that my daughter was not normal like her sisters (Baglieri & Shapiro, 2012, p. 5). By age three, when development was still significantly delayed, I began to push for services and intervention. Unfortunately, the first step most parents have to take is through the medical world and obtaining a diagnosis. It was assumed that my daughter was autistic, and thus began a series of tests that would provide information to the behavioral and developmental facility that examines autism. An appointment was made, and in the interim, an MRI was scheduled to review the brain. The process was emotional and frustrating to enter a new world of medical terms and specialists that was otherwise so foreign. The events that transpired following the MRI could be a book in itself. In a brief summary: a brain tumor was found, resulting in DNA testing discovering a chromosome deletion on the short arm of chromosome eight, followed by a nondiagnosis of autism because of the deletion. When I have met other parents that have faced such harrowing "diagnosis days," they would also share that it is a moment in our lives that it is not easily forgotten.

I also share with parents that the day we learned of my daughter's brain tumor was obviously a terrible day. Yet, the day a clinical psychologist announced to us that based on my daughter's behavioral and intellectual scores, our daughter was "mentally retarded," was even harder news to accept. I remember somberly getting in to our car to head home, and my husband and I sat there dumbfounded by the news. He finally spoke what was already on my mind, but too afraid to admit: "Well, maybe we can hope the brain tumor will take her." I was guilt ridden and devastated that we felt that way. Yet, what I discovered later in my journey of acceptance to appreciation; was we were residing in a place where we knew brain tumors could be fixed, but "retarded" cannot be.

The research in to disability studies in recent decades has revealed much about why believe this way to begin with. At this moment in time, we were thrust in to a medical model of approaching how we raise our youngest daughter. According to Siebers (2008), "the medical model defines disability as an individual defect lodged in the person, a defect that must be cured or eliminated if the person is to achieve full capacity as a human being." The struggle to understand the notion that Gabby was "not normal" was glaring, and confusing. But "the concept of normalcy has been used to justify the differential treatment of society's 'undesirables' throughout history" (Baglieri & Shapiro, 2012, p. 80). The realization that these new diagnosis' were going to impact Gabby's education consumed us. Educating students with disabilities was already synonymous with the dominant cultural view. Danforth and Gabel (2015) depict the methods to describe students with disabilities in education is based on a deficit model approach. In this model, disability becomes something to overcome, but because it is a medical problem, it can never be completely repaired (Coopman, 2003). As parents, it was evident by our reaction, that we had already been accustomed to a system that experiences pity and sadness for those that are cognitive disabled. It was in the moment the news of our daughter's cognitive disability that somehow our hope in a bright future for her was instantly dashed.

SEPARATE IS NOT EQUAL

Thankfully, the story does not end on that depressing point. It becomes a story of inspiration and hope. Gabby was enrolled in preschool, and we were very fortunate to be in an environment that was already inclusive. The school was designed to have a majority of typically developing same-age peers taught alongside children with disabilities. We were thankful to have this service provided by our local school district, and Gabby qualified for special education services based on her evaluations and brain tumor. Her preschool experience was positive and engaging. Preschool simply seemed naturally inclusive and we observed our daughter thrive. Chemotherapy treatments for her brain tumor inopportunely stalled this progress for over a year, but by age six, our daughter had completed her treatments and was ready to begin her journey into elementary school.

There is some hesitation in sharing the unfavorable experiences of the next part of the journey into educating Gabby. However, if it were not for the learning opportunities they provided, I would not be the parent, educator, researcher and advocate I am today. The inclusive preschool had been such a positive experience for Gabby. I learned that the elementary school Gabby would be attending had a multiple handicapped classroom, and all I could think of was how desperately I did not want Gabby in there. Suddenly, I felt myself face to face with the middle school classroom again and wondered if I was somehow like "those Moms," demanding for a "normal" education for my "abnormal daughter." At this crossroads, the discourse of what is normal and abnormal had already become apparent in my quest for normalcy for my daughter. I had not begun to realize that the words that define this point is a social construction to begin with.

Certainly I recognized my daughter's needs, but I was not sure any general education teacher would want Gabby in his/her classroom. I was becoming more aware that including children with significant cognitive disabilities in the general education classroom is hindered by the assumptions teachers have that these children cannot succeed, as supported by the deficit-based paradigms and medical models that are the foundation of special education practices (Kugelmass, 2001). Thus, there are significant tensions between a goal of full inclusion and the mainstream deficit approach to education in which the type and severity of a disability becomes the primary measure of a child's access to a regular education setting.

Throughout that third year of preschool, I would consider myself an involved parent. I would visit daily, ask questions and make sure I was ensuring my daughter was having access to interventions and therapies that she was entitled to. I would discuss with her preschool teacher the idea of having Gabby in a regular education classroom, wondering if it was something she could handle. I was told numerous times that is exactly where they believed Gabby belonged, with typically developing students as a model. My fears were beginning to increase as the year concluded because Gabby was not toilet trained, and I was led to believe that achieving this basic skill was her ticket in to the regular classroom. It was overwhelming. To my dismay, at the end of the year's individual education plan (IEP), the meeting to plan for Gabby's education placement for the following year; Gabby's IQ scores were determined to still be significantly low and the educators and therapists present at the meeting all agreed that Gabby should be placed in the multiple-handicapped classroom.

It was too devastating at that time to consider as her parents, we had a role to play in this decision process. The only challenge I made to the decision was requesting that my daughter be provided time in the general education kindergarten classroom, with aide support, so that she might have access to typically developing students. It was decided she would be supported an hour a day in the kindergarten classroom. Surprisingly, I deferred to the "educational experts" there, and agreed that placing Gabby in a room devoid of typical students, would be the least restrictive environment for my daughter. The placement not only proved to be restrictive, but also a tremendous opportunity to learn of the power of inclusion and my foray into this field of disability studies and inclusion.

Gabby began the kindergarten year with less fanfare than her older sisters did in their kindergarten years. We entered a self-contained classroom, with twelve desks, sitting in rows, to meet the special education teacher and two educational aides that would be there to assist the ten students assigned to the room. The year started on a sour note when the teacher was immediately accused of restraining two nonverbal students in the room. A series of investigations and pleas from the teacher to me were made to support her in the midst of educating Gabby. The challenge I faced in my relationships with teachers was the burden of having aggravations can often produce a feeling that my child might be treated differently if I raised an issue. There is also the added burden of knowing my daughter would have no way to articulate frustrations, other than her behaviors. Needless to say, these feelings consumed any disposition to raise concerns of the environment and/or way Gabby was being taught.

The ten students Gabby spent her day with ranged in disability and severity. Other than the desks in rows, there were chairs with straps, and a preschool-designed play area that students were permitted to play in if they accomplished their "work." Gabby was given a stack of worksheets each and every day that she was expected to complete in order to receive any privileges. Some of the worksheets were tracing lines; others were coloring pages of letters and numbers, and so forth. Often, Gabby would go to sleep instead of doing her daily work, and her lack of attention or focus was reported in a daily communication notebook. I had requested the notebook as a means to gain information on Gabby's day, but I was most interested in her time in the typical kindergarten classroom.

One day, I visited the multiple-handicapped classroom. The door was blocked to prevent students from "running out," or, I believed, people coming in. I remember gazing around the room, and I was suddenly looking at the same students that were in that middle school classroom, devoid of life or engagement in learning. Exasperated, I stated how I just did not believe Gabby belonged in this room. Immediately I was told that she definitely belonged there, and I needed to accept that. It was then that I realized I did accept my daughter's differences, but I was not willing to accept that because of those differences Gabby was predetermined to have limited access to learning opportunities. Suddenly every day was a hope she would go to the kindergarten classroom, the teacher would see her potential, and say she could "stay there" instead of returning to the multiple-handicapped classroom.

DECISION-MAKING

Time went on, and four months into the school year, I learned Gabby had only been to the kindergarten room an average of one hour per week. Every week when I would follow up with her time in the kindergarten room, there was always an excuse as to why it did or could not happen. The most common reason from the teacher was my daughter could not demonstrate behaviors that she was "ready" to handle the typical classroom. It was evident that the multiple-handicapped classroom teacher and aides were operating under the assumption of what Siebers (2008) calls the ideology of ability. They had created a "baseline by which humanness is determined" (p. 8) and used my daughter's measure of her abilities in mind and body to exclude her from the classroom with her peers. Frustrations mounted and I spent weeks trying to ensure Gabby could get her time in the kindergarten classroom. Finally, I arrived at a decision that I had to hold the school accountable for the goals and plan set forth in Gabby's IEP.

The meeting to request that the IEP be modified for Gabby to receive a half day placement in the kindergarten classroom was met with annoyances on behalf of the special educator and aides. I had expressed to the special education director, that upon learning the district was responsible for "making up" the hours that my daughter was entitled to as stated in her IEP, and I could essentially request all of those hours in additional tutoring hours; I shared with the director I was willing to overlook those hours if changes could be made immediately. Gabby was thus placed all morning in the kindergarten classroom, but that meant one of the aides had to leave the self-contained multiple handicapped classroom. Needless to say, this was met with resentment by the multiple-handicapped teacher and aides as this left them short-handed for the remaining special needs students. The extent of this anger was met fully at the parent teacher conference in February when I was informed that I was making their job of achieving Gabby's IEP goals impossible. I endured a lengthy meeting of how my outlook for Gabby's future was not as positive as theirs because I was allowing her to "waste time" with children that she would never be like. I was limiting her progress on learning letters and her address, achievable goals that she will need in life. Instead, Gabby was wasting her time on learning things like habitats of animals. I was told it was also pointless to have books sent home from school because she could not read. Finally, the aspect the aides were most frustrated with was that other students were "doing Gabby's work for her" in the typical kindergarten classroom. Essentially, I was asked to let this idea go that Gabby could perform in a regular classroom and place her back in the multiple-handicapped classroom full time if I truly cared about her "academics" and not simply her social life.

THE TURNING POINT

I left the meeting fuming, devastated and utterly confused as to what was best for my daughter. Like a classic narrative, this would be the climax, the pivotal moment at which a crucial decision must be made deciding the fate of the protagonist. As I was leaving the building, with tears in my eyes, the kindergarten teacher stopped me. She exclaimed she was thrilled to find me because she wanted the chance to share with me how wonderful the experience with my daughter was going. She stated that her students loved Gabby, and that Gabby had recognized and remembered songs they were singing, and was noticing concepts that even her typical kids had overlooked. Her teacher noted that Gabby was energetic and happy to be there every morning, quite the opposite information I had just received from her special educator. I was astonished.

But the story she subsequently shared was equally as revealing. She explained she had a student that was having difficulties staying on task and completing her individual work. This young girl desired to assist Gabby like other students were doing. That day, this little girl completed her own work with success, and was given the opportunity to work with Gabby on her letter identification work. The classroom teacher indicated that she had to request the aide to give them some independence, which she reluctantly did. But, as this little girl beamed with pride assisting Gabby, the teacher witnessed a difference in them both. With tears in her eyes, this twenty year veteran teacher, having never taught in an inclusive environment, shared with me that she was able to deliver a positive conference to the parents of this little girl, and that Gabby had given her a new perspective of the power of having students with varying ability levels and diverse needs in her classroom alongside typically developing peers. She simply stated "I had no idea what my classroom needed until I had a student like Gabby."

As I left the school, there was no doubt in my mind what I needed to do. I did what any rational parent would do, and called the director of special education for the district at his home and demanded that my daughter be removed from the multiple-handicapped classroom as of the next day and she be placed full time in the kindergarten classroom, with the oversight of a classroom aide. He agreed, and said it would be done the very next day. Meanwhile, I was exploring even further the topics of inclusion and finding sources available to parents like Kids Together, Inc., and other parent advocate groups that demonstrated success in inclusion. I was dumbfounded by the amount of limited resources, but excited by the prospects of what inclusion had to offer! My research into this area of disability studies and inclusion had serendipitously begun.

I was fully aware that what I was requesting for Gabby did not entirely match the philosophy of many of the classroom teachers in the building. In my research, I was learning that including children with significant cognitive disabilities in the general education classroom is hindered by the assumptions teachers have that these children cannot succeed, as supported by the deficit-based paradigms and medical models that are the foundation of special education practices (Kugelmass, 2001). Thus, there are significant tensions between an education system consistent with the goal of full inclusion and the mainstream deficit approach to education in which the type and severity of a disability becomes the primary measure of a child's access to a regular education setting.

After Gabby was placed in the kindergarten classroom full time, I received multiple letters from Gabby's special education teacher stated that I clearly did not care about educating Gabby in the most productive way based on academics and acceptance. It was difficult to focus on my philosophy in the midst of the animosity. I knew that inclusion in the regular education classroom does not guarantee acceptance. There is also a long history of supporting segregation as providing a place for students with disabilities to be accepted (Osgood, 2005). I was also fully aware that another reason in support of segregation was the belief that students with disabilities could not keep up academically in the regular education classroom and thus would suffer another form of labeling, as a failure (Osgood, 2005). Although I felt that my decision was in Gabby's best interest, I still struggled with the decision my husband and I had made. Furthermore, my husband was even more apprehensive because his natural instinct was to protect Gabby from being harassed or bullied.

During this time, another teacher in the building learned of my frustrations, and she informed me she was working on her master's thesis on inclusion. She was hoping to present her findings in a meeting with the school principal on the advantages of the building moving to a full inclusion model for educating students. Immediately I was able to participate in this process, and witness an elementary school declare its philosophy that students should not be separated based on cognitive ability. The inclusion model that was adopted involved the elimination of the traditional multiple handicapped, self contained classroom and integrating the students with disabilities into their same age peer classrooms. Thus, not only was Gabby included the following year, but all of the special education students were as well. Some of the parents were not pleased, and removed their children. Still others were beyond thrilled, and shared in some of our meetings that following year how profound the change had been to their child.

GABBY'S SUCCESS

While I was reading and researching about inclusion, I was simultaneously witnessing the amazing impact it was having on my daughter. She was not only making friends, but she had learned more letters and other skills during the last three months of school than in the previous six months segregated environment. The communication journal we had used in the multiple-handicapped classroom was also utilized daily by the classroom aide and I was astounded at how positive the comments were as compared to the previous six months in the self-contained classroom. In the first six months of school, over seventy percent of the comments in the notebook were negative and only ten percent could be considered positive comments of how Gabby would perform or interact. Beyond that, Gabby was happy, sleeping better, and smiling so much more. No intelligence test or scoring system could convince me of anything other than inclusion was the dynamic difference in my daughter's life.

The following few years, Gabby has remained in inclusive classrooms at the same school. Her first- and second-grade years enabled her to learn and develop with the encouragement of her general education teachers, intervention specialists and her additional therapists. Our daily communication journal has served as a written document of the power of inclusion. Certainly not every day was or is a success, but I have been able to fully witness the academic and social successes of my daughter on a daily basis. In my studies, I discovered an idea through the research of Christopher Kliewer (2008) on inclusive preschools and the focus of literacy. He shared that a co-constructed journal was utilized with a non-verbal student to create a "message to his parents describing the important moments from his day" (Kliewer, 2008). This process has become a teacher-guided daily ritual as "an active means of retaining a consistent connection" with us as parents. The most important aspect has been the notion that Gabby participates in the authorship of the notebook, and the journal transformed from the "bad book" as she once called it, to a means to demonstrate her progress. For Gabby's teacher, the process became revealing. Her teacher scribes for her and writes down exactly what she says and she stated that the length of Gabby's responses can be very telling. She is honest if she has had a bad day, but furthermore I can observe what she has enjoyed or found interesting because she will reveal those aspects of her day without prompting.

In Gabby's second-grade year, she learned to read and complete basic math skills. I imagine special educators would indicate that she could have learned this and maybe more in a resource room designed for students like her. Although, I would argue, that she would not have learned about a whole host of other content areas like the planet Saturn or about Grey Wolves. Like her typical peers, Gabby was assisted in constructing independent research projects. I am also willing to argue if Gabby had remained in the resource room, she would not have been invited to her first birthday party this past year. She was invited not because I arranged it, but because her friend from her class requested she be there! It is challenging to find a word to express the joy of that moment.

But the remarkable moments of inclusion for Gabby are not limited to these brief examples. For me, I embarked on a journey beyond the inclusive classrooms into a doctoral program where I have become a scholar, a researcher and professional in to the realm of Disability Studies and Inclusion. I have been able to research one of the inclusive classrooms at my daughter's school and examine what makes an inclusive environment and the attitudes surrounding teachers, parents and people in our culture regarding those with disabilities.

WHAT IT MEANS TO BE HUMAN

The irony is not lost on me that the topics I spend significant amount of my time reading and writing about intersects with my own participation in the process of educating a child with cognitive disabilities. During my education, I have been immersed in theories of teaching and learning and drawing connections to children with disabilities in learning. I have discovered in education, we ascribe learning to theories that reduces learning to individual mental capacity, thus blaming marginalized people for being marginal. I am also exploring how society, including our education system, defines students with disabilities by the labels given to them. The resulting stereotypes then look at students with disabilities through a deficit model, perpetuating the notion that students with disabilities are not-able to participate in learning adequately, and thus require a special plan for receiving education.

As I attend the IEP meetings for Gabby over the past six years, I am a willing and active partcipant in the mediating event that describes my sweet girl in academic, medical and statistical terms used to portray the deficits she possesses, thus limiting her learning. Furthermore, I am truthfully pleased to create a plan of individualized instruction that will ensure her success. I know I am already more than satisfied with the teachers and staff of her inclusive school. We have been thankful to have teachers that are willing to accodomate my daughter in the mainstream classes with her same age peers. However, participating in my daughter's individual education meetings is also bittersweet, because I will listen and read the phrases "Limited Progress" over and over again, only to be reminded of that day we were told our daughter is "mentally retarded." I will recall hearing that news, more painful, terrifying and defeating than the news of her brain tumor. I will ask myself "How in the world could I have once thought that way?!" I often relive that moment when my heart literally ached because of the vulnerable, socially constructed, naïve thoughts that crept into my mind as I considered how "brain tumors can be fixed [...] retarded can't." I have come so far from my ignorance that allowed me to believe being differently abled meant my daughter needed to be "fixed."

During Gabby's IEP meetings, my mind often wanders as I listen to the well-intentioned educational experts (of which I am one of them!) describe and delineate the learner my daughter is, yet overlook the actuality of the amazing teacher she has truly become. Gabby has taught me FAR more than any book, theorist, college course, teacher, or professor has ever taught me. Even Gabby's teacher and building principal have concluded Gabby teaches them more than they believe they are teaching her. Gabby has also revealed to me that the primary problem of a disability is the social implications that come with it, not because SHE sees herself as handicapped, but because everyone "normal" does.

Gabby has taught me the "value" of a dollar when today she found the dollar the tooth fairy left her, and she exclaimed she would buy us all something with it. She has taught me the power of words when she stated that "I don't like angry words when I'm in trouble." But Gabby is also a philosopher of love when she said to me: "I know how love works. I say it out of my mouth and I hug people and say sorry. You know what else I do when I love people? I tickle!" But most importantly, Gabby has taught me how to laugh, literally every day, because there is always something to laugh about. In one of my doctorate courses, my professor concluded each class with a statement that our research and studies should force us to ask ourselves, along with our other theoretical questions; "What does it mean to be human?" I have come to the conclusion, that *Gabby*, and everything about her, is what it means to be human.

We never know what a child is capable of unless we find ways to unleash their potential. If I had allowed the "experts" in special education continue to hide Gabby away to learn only her name, address, and phone number, then that is all she might have ever learned, in between her naps out of frustration and boredom. Education and learning is so much more than worksheets and flash cards. It is social, it is interacting with same age peers, and so students like my Gabby can live among them and not just be released from the multiple-handicapped classroom only for assemblies, ultimately separate from the rest of the student population. Thanks to inclusion, I believe my daughter has been given not only a lot more social interactions, but she has also had access to academic opportunities that she would have previously been denied.

There are teachers, and I have been blessed to observe several, that create a successful, inclusive, child-centered learning environment. Instead of asking the question "Do you really belong here?" they change it to "How do we support your belonging here?" (Kliewer, 2008). The routine of separating students based on ability exists in far too many school districts. It only serves to fuel segregation and teasing from the "typical" students who will grow up believing it is quite alright to poke fun at those who are learning disabled. With the guidance of an inclusive teacher, "children's development of positive attitudes toward persons with disabilities may be influenced by having many and varied experiences with diverse peers" (Baglieri & Shapiro, 2012). I have experienced in my own life, when students get to know their disabled peers, they learn to appreciate them and then they too have the opportunities to learn what it means to be human.

Probing Questions

- Carrie changes from being a teacher who thinks "why are these kids even here?" to a mother who knows that her disabled daughter deserves and needs an inclusive education. Not all parents (or teachers, for that matter) go through this dramatic shift in beliefs. Why does this author experience a 180 degree turn in her beliefs about inclusion?
- Carrie describes herself reach a crossroads of "the discourse of what is normal and abnormal." She comments that this distinction "is a social construction to begin with." What does she mean? And how does knowing that it is a social construction matter for inclusive education?
- It seems counterintuitive to discover that the special educators were not pleased when Gabby's IEP calls for more time in general education classrooms. Is the purpose of special education to move students into general education? Or is segregated special education somehow self-perpetuating?
- How did the communication journal work? How did this device improve the quality of Gabby's inclusive education?
- Although this story ends in triumphant fashion, we really have to wonder if all this successful inclusion would have occurred without the knowledgeable and active participation of Gabby's mother. Many parents who love their daughter dearly do not have the time, expertise, or energy to participate in the ways that Carrie has. To what extent does inclusion rely on parents to drive the school forward to best practice?

REFERENCES

Baglieri, S., & Shapiro, A. (2012). *Disability studies and the inclusive classroom*. New York: Routledge.

Coopman, S. J. (2003). Communicating disability: Metaphors of oppression, metaphors of empowerment. In P. Kalbfleisch (Ed.), *Communications Yearbook 27* (pp. 337–394). Mahwah, NJ: Lawrence Erlbaum.

Danforth, S., & Gabel, S. L. (2015). *Vital questions facing disability studies in education* (2nd ed.). New York: Peter Lang.

Kliewer, C. (2008). *Seeing all kids as readers: A new vision for literacy in the inclusive early education classroom*. Baltimore, MD: Paul H. Brookes.

Kugelmass, J. W. (2001). Collaboration and compromise in creating and sustaining an inclusive school. *International Journal of Inclusive Schooling, 5,* 1, 47–65.

Osgood, R. L. (2005). *The history of inclusion in the United States*. Washington, DC: Gallaudet University Press.

Siebers, T. (2008). *Disability theory*. Ann Arbor: University of Michigan Press.

CHAPTER TWELVE

It Takes a Whole School

KIMBERLY MILLSTEAD

I began my career as a special educator in what some would describe as a kind of hell. To me, it was an extraordinary experience, just exactly the place in which I wanted to be—but I have kind of a skewed perception of what is important in the world. I started teaching in Highland Park, Michigan, in 2005, working with elementary students with intellectual disabilities. Highland Park is a small, 2.97 square-mile city completely surrounded by the much larger city of Detroit. Many do not even realize that Highland Park exists, until they see a news report about a murder or an abandoned building that burst into flames in the early morning hours. The 2010 census reports that the city is made up 11,500 people—ninety-five percent Black, four percent White, and one percent other. In the city's schools, though, the student population is 100 percent Black. In 2005, there were around 3,000 students in the district; in 2012 there are under 1,000. The city is poverty-stricken, drug-ridden, and some would say corrupt.

In spite of this, the community of Highland Park is pretty amazing. The folks who live there identify themselves as Highland Parkers, not Detroiters. They love their little city, even as they wish it could function properly to meet their needs. Everybody knows everybody in Highland Park—it's like a small village in a very urban setting. People look out for one another—they help raise each other's children; they lend each other food stamps and money; those with cars give rides to children on their block who don't have a ride home in the winter. If you can learn to see through the poverty, abuse, corruption, drugs, and abandonment, you can find a real sense of community.

Still, almost all of my students came from a single parent household. Many of them lived in foster homes, or the homeless shelter just down the street from the school. The illiteracy rate in Highland Park is astoundingly high; the high school graduation rate is astoundingly low. Many of my students, I felt, were wrongly diagnosed and labeled. In my view, they were only behind academically because someone decided they had a disability long before they had the chance to develop the skills needed to be an independent learner. As a result, they were placed in a segregated, special education classroom, where expectations were low.

The students with whom I worked had been taught by multiple substitute teachers—teachers with inadequate training, some without even a bachelor's degree. Some of the substitutes were tired, worn out from years of teaching. Few of these teachers lasted more than a couple of months. My students were used to being excluded. They had no idea what it was like to be part of the school community. When announcements were made over the public address system to come to all-school assemblies, they were told "special education students come to the gym." They could never just be "students."

They weren't just children with disabilities. They were children with disadvantages—children with life circumstances that prevented them from not being labeled unfairly. They lived in poverty, in crack houses, in half-burned buildings, in homes without heat or electricity. They lived in vans and in homeless shelters. They lived in places riddled with bedbugs, roaches, rats, disease, drugs, and abuse. Their parents—or, for many, foster parent or aunt or grandmother—were illiterate, themselves disabled, adults who couldn't take care of children in ways in which they deserve to be taken care of. I could say they were children that had it rough. That would be a huge understatement.

Given the circumstances of the community, inclusion seemed like the last thing to be on people's minds. But I decided that I had to start somewhere, and since I had specialized training in inclusion, I would give it all I had. It was a major struggle: relationships were on edge, students were confused, parents weren't satisfied. Through all these struggles, there were many lessons to be learned. At the end of the day, we made it happen.

I worked in a public elementary school, and things did not always run smoothly. During the five years that I was in the district, I went through seven principals, two school buildings, three special education directors, and countless other staff. Many who applied for positions we either could not hire or ran the other way when they saw what they were getting into.

I took over for a long-term substitute teacher (she was studying fashion design) that had been in the position for a year. Vix and Sierra were the first students that I managed to include in the general education curriculum. When I started there, the district did not have any policy about inclusion, nor was it written into any of the students' educational plan that they be included during the school day. These third-, fourth-, and fifth-grade students were labeled as having mild to moderate intellectual disabilities, emotional-behavioral disabilities, and learning disabilities. They had been stuck in the bottom corner of the school for the first few years of their schooling, with no access to general education. They were scared to go out of the special education classroom. I was scared to let them out. Sending them out into general education seemed like a crazy idea to the students, me, and the general education teachers, but I was determined to at least try.

I made friends with some good teachers, and began the process of introducing my students into their rooms. Some were prepared for my requests, willing to take on the challenge with open arms; some were not. So, often, I had to work my way in. Fortunately, my principal at the time was very open to the idea of me starting the process of inclusion.

*

In my first classroom, I set the desks up in a kind of semicircle, the best I could manage with nineteen students in a small room. I had tables around the room for different activities—a listening center, a writing table, a math manipulatives table. I also had a cozy corner with lamps, rugs, and beanbag chairs. For many, this wasn't the type of environment they were used to—desks in rows, no learning centers, no touch of comfort or calm.

All of my students—every single one—were on free and reduced breakfast and lunch programs. They ate breakfast in the classroom, and when they had cereal, they were to pour the leftover milk in a huge bucket that sat in the corner by the door of the classroom. The milk sat there all day, becoming rank and rotten, waiting for the janitor to dump it down the drain in the maintenance room that evening—sometimes it got done, sometimes not. On evenings when it didn't get done, the next morning, two students would take the milk across the hall into the stench of the maintenance room and dump it themselves. We would later get in trouble if even one morsel of cereal was in the drain.

That first classroom had quite a large hole in the wall to the outside, about the size of a basketball. So we had critters coming through constantly, mostly mice. We'd chase them out the door, put them in an upside down bucket and scoot them down the hall back outside, where they were free to run around and come right back inside. They joined us for reading time, again and again, along with the roaches that climbed up our door, or across the floor.

When winter came, the heat in the classroom worked only sporadically, and with the hole in the wall, even on the warmest days, you could see your breath in the air. We all wore coats and hats and mittens. All day. Every day. And in these circumstances, the students in my classroom—all students with disabilities, labels, disadvantages—struggled to learn. And I was to be held accountable for their learning.

In spite of all of this, my students truly loved coming to school. I got hugs all the time, and, in a school district in which nearly EVERYONE except me was Black, these African American students were fascinated with my hair, which is down to my waist—they touched it constantly, usually with dirty fingers. They craved the exciting projects, the personalized books I made for them with their names in them, and using math manipulatives to learn. Games, a spelling bee, class performances at assemblies—they genuinely loved school, although "learning" was usually a struggle.

They asked me why they weren't in regular classes, why they were special education kids, why they didn't get to go on field trips with the other classrooms. After all of my formal education (at that point, I had an undergraduate degree in special education, and was working on a masters in inclusion), I hadn't been taught how to handle situations like this. I knew how to write an IEP, give the Woodcock Johnson, follow a teacher's manual, write a lesson plan—but dealing with this, well, it wasn't covered in any of my classes. I told my students that we were in a multi-age classroom that was called "special education" because we got to learn in different, exciting ways. I told them that they, unlike other students in the school, got to learn at exactly the level they were at, and progress at a rate that was comfortable for them. The field trip question was hard to answer—I didn't know why the other teachers wouldn't invite us. I'd mentioned at several staff meetings that my students would like to go on their respective grade level field trips, and that I thought it very appropriate for them to do so. I was kind of a bigmouth at staff meetings, tried to be an advocate for my students, and they weren't used to that. So I got shut down, more than often.

*

Some of the few, select teachers with whom I collaborated were outspoken about things pertinent to their students too, and so I made an effort to befriend them. It turned out they were wonderful, some of the best teachers around, all with their own unique styles of teaching. I became very close to them, close enough that I could tell them about my worries about my students, my hopes and dreams for them, my take on their labels and disabilities. I even got permission from the special education department to attend a conference on co-teaching with Mrs. Bray, who was becoming a very dear friend of mine.

She believed, as did I, that every child could learn, and she was willing to put in the effort to make that happen. She modified lessons for students in her own third-grade class who were falling behind, and was wonderful about keeping in touch with parents. She came early and stayed late, checking papers, trying to understand where a student might have missed something, and how she could catch them up. She was one of the hardest working teachers I knew, and I didn't want to put more work on her.

Eventually, I asked her if she would accept some of my third graders into her classroom for reading or math, and if not that, then maybe just some social time for them to be around their typically developing peers. She immediately accepted, put them in groups with her students, gave them name tags, pencil boxes, their own desks, and introduced them to students she knew would be gentle with them. She expected them to pay attention and try their best, to follow classroom rules, and to function as a part of her class. She gave them modified assignments, made them feel comfortable coming into her classroom, made sure they were safe from the harsh stigma that comes from being labeled. We talked every day about who had done what, how I could help her, what we could do to be more effective in this new effort. And most of all she helped my students feel a sense of belonging, which made me feel as if we were changing the world, one student at a time, together.

I challenged Mrs. Bray with some of my students who struggled with behavior issues. I purposely gave her Keke, who didn't have many friends and a bad attitude to go along with it. She was a sweet girl, but one of few girls in my classroom, as I had mostly boys. She didn't like anyone or anything, and most certainly gave the impression that she wasn't in school to learn. Keke was quiet in my classroom, she was small, pretty light brown eyes, shy, with an attitude, and unmotivated. After a few months, she grew very attached to me. She wanted to be by my side all the time, and she was the first of many students in the past eight years to mistakenly call me mom, and eventually she did it on purpose. She was a paper and pencil girl and certainly did not want to be the center of attention or be seen jumping around acting silly, that just wouldn't be cool. Because she had opened up so much to me and (as I was finding out) was one of my top students, I wanted her so desperately to go to Mrs. Bray and make friends with the other students, and become caring with another teacher. We put her into the classroom slowly (which is not the way I would typically do things, as I feel that students should feel part of the classroom from day one).

We had our fair share of bad days, attitude problems, hunger, swearing, fighting, sadness; I was not the one having the bad days, it was Keke, and I was where she came to get away from it all, so why wouldn't she have an attitude problem, want to fight or hit something, swear and scream at the top of her lungs? I would, if I had to deal with what she were dealing with.

She went for reading first every day, then a few weeks later for math, and began to "lighten up" when it was time to go to Mrs. Bray's class. We accommodated her, gave her a sense of belonging, and eventually she came around and broke free of whatever was holding her in. I have a feeling it was standards set in place from home for her to look pretty, and have an "I don't care what you have to say" attitude, because she was never going to be anything anyway. Mrs. Bray and I didn't feel this way about her, we knew she could do more and began to instill in her that she was smart, brave, and friendly. We began to sit down after school and talk about the next day's or week's lessons, we came up with different ways she could teach all of the students, and ways that I could reinforce what she taught Keke, while she was in my classroom. We had to be a team, especially for Keke, who came with this attitude of uncaring, we had to be a strong team. We found passages that she could read in front of the class, we worked on math the day before she was going to learn it, we challenged her with the same spelling words as the others, only slightly fewer, we did peer helpers, and everything we could think of to do. I truly believe that the most important thing we did for her was to challenge her. She needed to know, as all students do, that she is capable of doing something, going somewhere, being someone. Challenging students, especially students with special needs is by far the most important thing one can do to help a child gain confidence. Initially, they will feel like they can't do what you are asking them to do, they may get angry or frustrated with you, but each time if you make sure there are small accomplishments on the way to a big milestone, they will forget that they ever "couldn't" do it in the first place. All students can learn, in their own place, at their own pace, in their own time, but the challenge of learning and expressing something new is something that can take place between a teacher and a student, learning to challenge yourself is one of the best lessons a student can learn.

A fifth-grade teacher, friends with Mrs. Bray, saw what was going on and told me she'd be willing to take some of my "higher level" students. She was a very tough teacher—tough attitude, tough work, tough behavior policy, tough everything—but I decided it was worth it for my students to get the exposure, so I sent her one or two students who I thought could handle her, and that she could handle. They went for science, which was complicated, because the vocabulary was hard, the concepts were high order, critical concepts; but there were labs and experiments, lots of hands-on group work, educational films—all things that my students enjoyed, so, they stayed for science.

Another wonderful teacher, a native of Highland Park and whose mother had also been a teacher in the district, knew everyone—families, neighbors, cousins, uncles, brothers, aunts. She was a great teacher and could handle any type of student, knew exactly how to handle students of all shapes, sizes, backgrounds, ability level—everyone. She opened her arms and her classroom door to my students, no matter who they were.

I was unable to include all of my students due to lack of support, and lack of staff, I had third through fifth-grade students so I was unable to co-teach in all grade levels. My option was to be a support to those amazing teachers who were supporting my students. I would ask for the work they were doing that week, I would modify it or give suggestions on how they could include my students in the classwork. We modified quizzes and tests together, wrote lessons together that were scaffolded to meet the needs of every student. It was difficult because we didn't have the same planning times, but these teachers were as dedicated as I could ask them to be. They came in early and stayed late with me in order to do what was best for our students.

Vix was in fourth grade the year I started including my students. He had been in a self-contained, segregated classroom his entire school career. He had an older brother who was a very big influence on him, was in general education classrooms, and was very popular at the school. Vix knew some students in general education classes through his brother, and so he was excited to go into the new classes. He read at a pre-school level, did math at around a first-grade level, and was as street smart as you can be. Vix took the city bus alone, walked the streets until late in the night, hung out with an older crowd, smoked, had sex, and knew more about the world than most teenagers do. I was nervous to send him out, but he deserved (and had the right to have) the opportunity to explore and learn in a different context. He struggled, and couldn't keep up with the fourth-grade work, so I modified it, found some students with whom Vix could work (some who also needed additional help, and some who could keep up with the teacher) and tried to set him in a successful direction. The students took notes for him, they worked in collaborative groups with him. In class they helped him read his questions or volunteered to work with him as a partner. Socially he was making not great, but better choices, sitting with these students in the lunchroom, hanging with them on recess (there was no functioning playground equipment) so the kids just "hung out."

Sierra was in third grade and hated school as much as any red-blooded American could. She was smart and hard-working, and I knew she belonged in Ms. Bray's class, learning the great third-grade curriculum. I also knew that her behavior would be a challenge, especially because she didn't want to be the "special kid" in class—and that is what she feared she would be. She and I spent many days—weeks—talking about self-advocacy, being part of a new group, understanding a new teacher, making new friends, and how different classrooms work. Sierra and I spoke about her disability, and she really was very intelligent, and her behavior came from a place deep inside her that was angry and sad that she had to be different, along with her life situation. I talked to her about what it meant to be able to tell her "other" teacher that she needed a little extra time, or that she'd like to be paired up with someone for an assignment, or that she would be able to follow along better if she could have the work the day before so she and I could go over it ahead of time. I told her this was called advocating for herself and that I'd help her through it until she came to do it on her own. As a third grader, I was SO proud of her, she did a wonderful job of speaking to her other teacher and stating her needs. We had meetings with her other teacher and talked about the same things Sierra and I talked about so she would understand what Sierra was trying to accomplish. We also talked about disabilities in general, and that really, everyone learns in a different way, she was in a special education class because she didn't do well on some tests, and I would be able to teach her in different ways, but that I believed she should be with her third-grade peers, and that I would always be there to support her, I wouldn't let her fall unless it was a learning experience for her. I was very honest with her, and as I believe my students should be challenged to understand everything they can, I spoke to her as I would to any student in third grade and made sure she could comprehend what I was telling her. Our conversations made a huge difference in her attitude, behavior, and success in her general education classes. I strongly believe that having whole class conversations with students and one on one conversations with students are the greatest ways to build confidence and success in them. These are things I have always done and will continue to do. Mrs. Bray and I found a girl that Sierra knew from the neighborhood and sat them together. Soon, Sierra was getting in trouble—just like the rest of the class—for talking too much, or giggling at something silly during instruction. She did great in class and often requested extra homework, so she could show off what she could do.

*

I worked with teachers in that school day after day to help them create, and, maintain an inclusive learning environment. Some of the other teachers I tried to work with just wouldn't accept inclusion as an option, but I was persistent with them. They got sick of me, talked about me behind my back—I was, after all, just some dumb, uppity, first-year teacher. They didn't want to modify lessons, or make accommodations for the students in our school with disabilities. They weren't willing to budge on their perception of and expectations for what a student with a cognitive impairment might be capable of. I decided that just including my students in these classes wasn't enough. Yeah, access to the curriculum was great, modified work was great, being with typically developing peers was great—but I needed to turn my students into our students. I needed the educators in my building to build relationships with ALL students, just like I had. They didn't have to be the same kind of relationships that I had, but there had to be something there.

I began to ask teachers to write in daily notebooks that I kept for each student, call home and inform parents of what they were working on in their classes, take the students with them to recess, and most of all, just have conversations with them to get to know them. I asked an awful lot of the teachers who were helping me with this process. I was convinced, though, that if relationships could be built, that learning could take place. I discovered that it was easier to convince general education teachers to build relationships than it was to convince them to try a new method of teaching. I got on a lot of people's nerves, and had quite a few battles. But when they agreed to simply get to know my students just as people, the amazing children that they were, they suddenly became our students. Eventually they were just, well—students, children in the community, friends with non-disabled and disabled peers alike, all attending classes with teachers with whom they had real, meaningful relationships. Most importantly, they felt a sense of belonging.

While I worked at Highland Park, I accomplished something that hadn't been done there before: I introduced students without disabilities to students with disabilities. I introduced teachers to the notion that all students have a right to learn with their peers, to have access to the general education curriculum, just like everyone else. I showed teachers that the curriculum might be very challenging for students with disabilities, but that they had a right to it, and could learn from it. I helped students who had never been part of the broader school community feel like they belonged. I taught them to advocate for themselves, and helped them make friends with their peers without disabilities. In the process of this work, I changed the school's climate, the community's view of students with disabilities, and teacher's perspectives on teaching and learning. Perhaps most importantly, I helped all students to accept others, and to believe in themselves. If that's the meaning of inclusion, then it was successful.

But I didn't do it alone—really, I couldn't have. Without the collaboration of the teachers with whom I worked, none of it would have been possible. Sure, I was the lightning rod, bringing the spark into the school. But others took up that spark, and made it their own—made it OUR own. We all changed, and learned, and grew, as a result. This experience made me realize what could be accomplished by a small group of determined people, committed to changing the lives of students, and the community.

I did OK. We did OK. We had about forty students with disabilities in a small school of less than 300 students. By the time I was laid off, we had about fifteen students included, ten of them full time. After my presentations to the district, I believe much more inclusion took place in the middle and high schools too, although I can't be sure as my focus was in my school at the time. It wasn't perfect; the world wasn't changed overnight. I still have friends in Highland Park, and I've been back to visit a few times. The community, and the schools, have changed a lot since I left, and not for the better. But for a few years, in one small, poor, urban community, some good things happened. I'm good with that. I'm down with that—for reals.

Probing Questions
- Kim comments that, in an urban, impoverished community, inclusion seemed like the last thing to be on people's minds. Inclusive education certainly has the reputation of being a reform undertaken by affluent, suburban districts. Is inclusion really a luxury item appropriately suited for wealthy schools? Or is it best viewed as a way to improve instruction and outcomes for all students in culturally diverse, low income schools?
- The path to more inclusion in this one elementary school begins with the friendship between two teachers (Kim and Mrs. Bray). What role can friendships between teachers play in the growth of inclusive education in a school?
- At one point, Kim shifts her role from providing support to students with disabilities in general classrooms to providing assistance and support to general education teachers. What do you think of her change in strategy? What roles and functions should a special educator assume in support of inclusion?
- Kim concludes that "I was the lightning rod, bringing the spark into the school. But others took up that spark, and made it their own—made it OUR own." How can one person or a small group of persons be the spark to get inclusion started in a school? What are the challenges to this kind of bottom-up reform effort?

CHAPTER THIRTEEN

Using "Numbers and Narrative" to Support Inclusive Schooling

MEGHAN COSIER

When schools move toward inclusive models of supporting students with disabilities, it can be very difficult to sustain (Jerald, 2005; McLeskey & Waldron, 2006). Change can be a complex and overwhelming task, and teachers and staff may not be "sold" on the idea of inclusion. Many teachers and staff may question whether this is the "right thing" for students with and without disabilities (Sindelar, Shearer, Yendol-Hoppey, & Liebert, 2006). They are also concerned with student achievement; and more importantly, student standardized state test scores. Furthermore, it seems that their assumptions about inclusive education are often rooted in myths or misunderstandings. Thus, they are understandably concerned about such a shift in service delivery. Specifically, teachers and administrators want to know if the inclusive model is working for all students. Moreover, they want to be sure that they are providing students with and without disabilities a quality education that supports student achievement (Frattura & Capper, 2007). As a team at an elementary school trying to move toward more inclusive supports and services for students with disabilities, we (special educators, general educators, a school psychologist, and special educator turned university professor) tried to systematically collect and share data throughout our first two years as an inclusive school in order to support and sustain the new inclusive model. This is a story about how we used data including both "numbers and narrative" (Light & Pillemer, 1982; Nash, 2002) to facilitate a consistent dialogue about the impact of inclusive supports on students, teachers, parents and administrators in an effort to strengthen the base of support at the school and sustain the inclusive model.

We used a variety of data including standardized test scores, benchmark assessments, readings assessments, individual student portfolios, and student, teacher, and parent interviews. We used this data to do the following: (a) create teacher, administrator, and parent "buy-in," (b) dispel myths about inclusive education, (c) identify areas in need of improvement or problem solving, and (d) celebrate the hard work of teachers, staff, administrators, students, and parents. We shared this data in variety at staff meetings, grade level meetings, individual meetings with teachers and parents, and with school and district level administrators.

THE SCHOOL

Roosevelt Elementary School is a large elementary school in a large urban school district in the southwestern United States. The school has about 800 students in grades K–5. Almost all of the students (ninety-eight percent) receive free our reduced price lunch and most students speak a primary language other than English (e.g., Spanish, Vietnamese, Somali). At the time we began this school reform effort, the school housed three self-contained classrooms and two full-time resource specialists operating mainly "pull-out" programs to support students with disabilities. From the time the school opened twelve years ago, they used a model typically known as "mainstreaming." In this model students with more "mild" disabilities who received support from a resource specialist were "pulled out" of their classrooms for a certain period of time each day (about thirty minutes to an hour and a half) to receive tutoring or instruction in an area identified in their Individualized Education Program (IEP) goals. Students with more significant disabilities were educated in one of the three self-contained classrooms and spent about an hour each day in a general education classroom in the afternoon. There was certainly a culture of "us" and "them" (Linton, 1998). It was as if the general education teachers were "allowing" *our* students into *their* classrooms. If the "visitors" (aka students with disabilities) were disruptive or "got in the way" of other student's learning, they could be sent out at any time. Similarly, if students with disabilities who were receiving resource support were "too low" academically or exhibiting problem behaviors they were then moved to a self-contained classroom.

A core group of special education teachers, general education teachers, a school psychologist, and me (a former special educator at the school turned university professor) felt strongly that students with disabilities could benefit more socially and academically from an inclusive model of service delivery. At lunch and happy hours, we began to discuss how to move inclusion forward. I had some experience with inclusive school reform (Causton-Theoharis, Theoharis, Bull, Cosier, & Dempf-Aldrich, 2011) and felt I could at least guide the group in some way. So, we decided to go for it and began our journey toward a more inclusive school.

YEAR 1

Creating "Buy-In"

In our first year, moving toward more inclusive supports and services not all students with disabilities were fully included in general education classrooms. When our team tried to pitch the idea of a fully inclusive school to the principal, Dr. Fuller, she was a bit hesitant. It was her first year at the school and she seemed to just want to get the lay of the land before making such a big decision. We got the same hesitant response after introducing our idea to the staff. Although some teachers were quite positive about including students with disabilities more authentically, many were quite leery about any change. At that point, we realized we needed to garner support for this move toward inclusive education in order for it to be successful. Therefore, we chose four students who were educated in self-contained classes and included them full time in general education classrooms across grade levels, as part of an inclusion "pilot." We felt that this would help us create some "success" stories and gain more support.

Throughout this first year, we collected data on individual student progress for just students with disabilities using student portfolios, standardized test scores, and parent and teacher interviews. The students had many successes and some struggles along the way. We saw significant improvement in academics and/or behavior from students. Moreover, a majority of teachers were positive about the experience. The teachers also expressed concerns such as the need for more assistance with behavior support and modification of assignments, which we felt could be addressed in the upcoming year. Furthermore, the parents recounted many positive experiences and recognized the impact inclusive schooling had on their children. We did not share any of this data until we neared the end of the school year. We compiled the data into a PowerPoint presentation and set up a meeting with the principal. Before the meeting we met with the assistant principal who we felt was overall more supportive of inclusive service delivery than the principal. We showed her the data and asked for her support at the meeting. After seeing our data, she agreed to support the move toward more inclusive services at the meeting.

At the meeting with the principal, we presented our data. We included test scores that showed students moving from "far below basic" to "basic" or "proficient" in just a year. We showed a video of a second-grade girl who had significant behavior difficulties in her special day class, participating in the general education class, following directions, and interacting well with peers. We also showed her video clips of parents and teachers talking about the positive experiences they had with inclusive education. In hindsight, although the test scores and student achievement were important, it seems that it was the stories that really moved her. Seeing a parent become emotional when she recounted how her son's self-esteem had improved dramatically since he had been included in a general education was very moving. We also shared the concerns or needs expressed by teachers such as concerns regarding lack of time for collaboration with the special education teachers and the need for more support with students with difficult behavior. In addition, we shared how we felt we could address these needs and concerns in the upcoming school year. After our presentation, we then asked again if she would support moving toward a fully inclusive model the following year. This time, she was more convinced. Although she was still a bit leery (presumably of the unknown), we knew we were moving in the right direction. She agreed to try this model of service delivery the following year, but indicated that we would play a major role in implementing this change. She expected us (along with the assistant principal) to move this initiative forward and indicated we could use part of the upcoming staff meeting to present this idea to the teachers and staff at the school.

Inclusion is Great [...] And, Oh Yeah, It's the Law!

Staff meetings at our school took place once a month in the cafeteria and lasted about an hour. We covered a wide range of school business at the staff meetings from new textbook adoptions to the ever-popular "how to improve test scores." We were given thirty minutes of the staff meeting to introduce inclusive education and convince a large portion of the staff and teachers that this was the way to go. While developing this presentation, we discussed our game plan. We needed to have a strategy. We decided we would share the same data we shared with the principal, but when it came to support we would not pose the issue of support as a question, but as more of a directive. Here was our strategy: (a) introduce the main concepts of inclusive education (i.e., supports and services in the general education classroom, participation is not conditional), (b) cover what research says about inclusion (e.g., Daniel & King, 1997; Huber, Rosenfeld, & Fiorello, 2001; Waldron & McLeskey, 1998), (c) present the results of our trial period such as test scores and interviews, and (d) cite the portions of the law that says we need to be providing students with disabilities access to general education curriculum and peers. After presenting our argument, we planned to tell the staff, "This is the way the district and our school are moving [...] we are moving to a more inclusive model and we hope you are with us."

Before discussing the move toward an inclusive service delivery model, we felt we had to introduce the teachers and staff to the main concepts of "inclusion." "Inclusive education" can carry a variety of different meanings (Friend & Pope, 2005). We wanted to be sure that the teachers were clear in terms of what we meant when we said inclusive education. It was important to show some examples of what inclusive supports could look like at both the school and classroom level. We showed some visual representations of staffing "before" and "after" schools became inclusive. We explained how teachers worked in collaborative teams and how students were supported in general education settings (Frattura & Capper, 2007; Villa & Thousand, 2005). To illustrate these practices, we provided some examples of inclusive education at the classroom level, describing how students who formerly received services in pull-out and self-contained settings received services in general education settings (Causton-Theoharis, Theoharis, Bull, Cosier, & Dempf-Aldrich, 2011). For example, we told the teachers about "Kenny," a student with a learning disability who read two grades below grade level and received an hour of resource specialist support per day in a pull-out setting. This meant that Kenny never participated in language arts instruction with his classmates because he was always in the resource room during that instructional time. This year, the special education teacher and general education co-taught during language arts instruction. The special education teacher saw Kenny in a small group each day with other students and worked on IEP goals. In addition, the special education teacher and general education worked together to modify assignments at other centers so Kenny could participate in the centers with the other students, even though he struggled to read some of the grade level content. We also provided some examples of students with more significant disabilities who were included in general education classrooms such as Sammi. Sammi was a second-grade girl with significant attention and learning difficulties. She had previously been educated in a self-contained classroom for students with moderate to severe disabilities. Even the special education teacher admitted she was unsure if an inclusive setting would work for Sammi. Sammi ended up being very successful in the general education classroom. We showed videos of how Sammi was included in instruction in the general education classroom with positive behavior support, peer support, and curriculum modifications. Sammi went from a student many teachers thought would never be educated in a general education setting to a student who was clearly an integral part of the learning community.

Along with some specific examples, we also shared some basic assumptions about inclusive education with the teachers. These include: (a) All means all and (b) Belonging is not conditional. We first explained that when we talked about including students with disabilities we were not just talking about students with "mild" disabilities or students who were "ready" to be included, but that our goal was to include *all* students—regardless of the severity of their disability. This was shocking to a number of teachers who had a bit of difficulty imagining some of the students they had seen in the self-contained classrooms on campus in their classrooms. Moreover, we also tried to communicate to teachers that belonging in the classroom was not conditional. For instance, we could not make statements such as, "the student can be included *as long as they* can do the work," or "the student can be included *as long as they* behave." The students with disabilities would "belong" to that classroom as much as the students without disabilities. If a student was having difficulty, then it was our job to figure out how to make it work, not to remove the student from the classroom.

After laying the groundwork related to principles and practices of inclusive education, we also shared some research related to inclusive education in order to dispel commonly held beliefs and myths and/or fears related to inclusive education. These include: (a) students with disabilities will "bring down" the achievement scores of students without disabilities; (b) inclusive education only benefits students with disabilities; (c) students with disabilities are "safer" in self-contained classrooms; and (d) teachers prefer to teach by themselves as opposed to co-teaching or collaborating. We felt that dispelling these myths at the beginning would help reframe some of the negative assumptions teachers may have held on inclusive education.

We first wanted to address some commonly held beliefs related to achievement of students with and without disabilities. We shared the overwhelming body of research with the teachers that suggests that students without disabilities are not negatively impacted by sharing classrooms with students with disabilities (e.g., Gandhi, 2007; Trejo, 2008) and that students without disabilities may benefit from the differentiated instructional strategies employed in diverse inclusive classrooms (Villa & Thousand, 2005). In addition, we shared research that suggests that students with disabilities achieve greater academic and social success in inclusive classrooms than in segregated settings (McDonnell *et al.*, 2003; McDonnell, Johnson, Polychronis, & Risen, 2002; Saint-Laurent *et al.*, 1998). Lastly, we shared some information related to the proposed academic and benefits of self-contained classrooms that researchers have proven to be false (Causton-Theoharis, Theoharis, Cosier, & Orsati, 2011). For example, proponents of self-contained educational settings for students with disabilities have contended that these programs benefit students because adaptations to the academic content are more individualized and the environment is less distracting (Kauffman & Hallahan, 2005). We shared some examples of research that suggests that the content in self-contained or pull-out settings is not necessarily more individualized and that self-contained settings are often noisier and more distracting than general education environments (Causton-Theoharis, Theoharis, Cosier, & Orsati, 2011; Vaughn, Moody, & Schumm, 1998).

In addition to deeply held beliefs about student achievement and benefits related to inclusive education, many teachers are apprehensive about/or intimidated by co-teaching and collaborative support contexts that occur in inclusive educational environments (Keefe, Moore, & Duff, 2004). Therefore, in addition to sharing information on the benefits of inclusive schooling related to student achievement, we also shared information on the benefits of co-teaching and collaboration. For instance, we shared research that suggests that students benefit from co-teaching contexts (Solis, Vaughn, Swanson, & McCulley, 2012). We also shared information from interviews with teachers at the school who had been part of our pilot project. Many of teachers felt that not only did the students benefit from the co-teaching and collaboration, but that they became better teachers through collaborating, sharing ideas, and being able observe another teacher on a regular basis.

After sharing research about inclusive education from a broader context, we moved on to share more data from our "trial period" at the school. This data included a set of "case studies" or stories related to students with disabilities and teachers. For students, the case studies included student test scores and work samples, stories about improvements in behavior, and quotes from student interviews related to how they felt about being included in a general education classroom. Most of the students improved on their standardized test scores and improved in reading and on mathematics benchmark tests throughout the year. Displaying this data helped support our points that students with disabilities benefited from inclusive education. For students who did not take these tests, we used samples of student work and progress toward goals to measure and show achievement. We then asked general education teachers who we had worked with during this trial period to talk about their experiences and how it impacted them and the students with and without disabilities. Many of the teachers saw significant improvements in student's academic achievement or social behavior. For instance, one teacher told the story of Minh. Minh was fifth-grade student labeled with an "emotional disorder" who had spent his entire school career in a segregated setting. He often exhibited "problem" behavior such as hitting other students and drawing "naughty" pictures on other student's property in his self-contained classroom and when he was "mainstreamed" the year before. Many of the teachers already knew Minh, or knew of him, as he had developed a reputation around school for being a "bad" kid. With the support of the special educator, the general education teacher worked with this student to develop more appropriate behaviors in the classroom and provide the student with a sense of belonging. Not only did this student's behaviors decrease significantly, his academic skills increased dramatically. We showed many samples of his work; comparing his work from the special day class the year before to the work, he was currently producing in the general education class. For instance, we showed a writing sample from the year before with a just a few sentences and compared it to a writing sample the current year that contained a few very well written paragraphs. The teacher talked about how she really felt this experience had changed the course of Minh's life. He no longer had to act the part of the naughty student. He felt like he belonged to the larger community and even ended up becoming one of the leaders in the classroom heading a lunchtime "flash mob" dance put on the fifth grade at the end of the school year.

In addition to sharing data about student social and academic achievement, we shared data from interviews with students, teachers, and parents about their experiences with inclusive education. One teacher stated, "I have been teaching for thirteen years and this has been my best year teaching." A parent indicated that she was not "sold" on inclusive education at first, but that she had seen her son's confidence grow tremendously since he had been educated in a general education classroom. Lastly, we shared student interview data that indicated that students were really felt a sense of belonging in their new classes with one student commenting that he loved that he "had a lot more friends" this year because there were more students in the classroom. These case studies really seemed to resonate with teachers as they knew many of these students—it became more personal.

We finished our presentation by moving from the personal to the legal. We were fortunate that at this same time the entire district was focusing on providing more inclusive opportunities for students with disabilities, and the district was also focusing on meeting legal mandates related to access to general education curriculum and peers. We highlighted aspects of the Individuals with Disabilities Education Act (2004) such as Least Restrictive Environment (LRE) that state that students with disabilities must be given opportunities to receive an education along with students without disabilities with supplementary aids and services. We discussed how many of the students in the special day classes were not being given that opportunity and thus, we were not meeting that mandate. We also emphasized that IDEA and The No Child Left Act (2001) stress the importance of access to the general education curriculum (Yell, 2006). Many of these students were not receiving access to the general education curriculum in ways that they could if they were included more in general education classrooms. We tried to make the point that there were many areas of the law related to access to general education where we were falling short. We hoped that this would resonate with some of the teachers.

We ended our presentation by stating that this is the way the school was moving—we were going to try more inclusive schooling next year. To our surprise, we got very little resistance at that meeting. Maybe it was because teachers hadn't had time to digest all that we covered, and it is likely many just didn't want to air their complaints in such a public forum. All in all, it seemed that most teachers left feeling that this was a necessary step. So, we moved forward with planning for the next year.

End of Year One and Summer ("Between" Year One and Year Two)

Toward the end of the school year and into the summer, we began planning for the following year. We put together a "larger" team including us (special educators, general educators, and school psychologist) and a few more general education teachers, a speech language therapist, and a teaching assistant. We began to re-imagine supports and services for students with disabilities and then began creating inclusive classrooms, by first placing students with disabilities in order to maintain natural proportions (Frattura & Capper, 2007) and then adding students without disabilities. After creating the classrooms, we established teaching teams of general educators and special educators for each grade level. At this same time the district was providing professional development related to co-teaching and differentiating instruction and many of the teams took advantage of this professional development during the summer and throughout the school year.

YEAR 2 AND BEYOND

For our second year, we wanted to plan which data we were going to collect and also how we were going to share this data with the teachers, parents, and administrators. We decided we were going to collect the following data: (a) all student's (both students with and without disabilities) quarterly benchmark test scores; (b) all reading scores (collected quarterly); (c) individual student portfolios for students with disabilities; (d) student, parent, and teacher interviews, and (e) state test scores for all students. We felt that by systematically collecting this data and sharing it with the staff we could establish a consistent dialogue related to student achievement and the school reform process. Therefore, we shared the data with teachers, administrators, staff and parents at staff meetings, grade level or team meetings, one-on-one meetings with teachers, and at parent-teacher conferences. This proved to be quite effective in establishing an open and constructive dialogue about what was happening at the school, how inclusive education was impacting the students, how we could go about problem solving when issues arose, and how we could improve instruction.

All students in the school aside from those with more significant disabilities who took alternative assessments or who mainly used an alternative curriculum took quarterly benchmark tests in reading and mathematics to assess their progress toward meeting grade level standards. We used this benchmark tests to assess the progress of both students with and without disabilities. Therefore, we compared the test scores of students with disabilities from the previous year when most of them were educated in self-contained classrooms to scores from the current year where they were included in general education classrooms. Furthermore, we compared the test scores of students without disabilities from one year to the next. We found that students with disabilities showed significant progress in their inclusive settings and students without disabilities showed the same gains they had the year before in their "non-inclusive classrooms (see Figure 13.1). By sharing this data with teachers, parents, and staff we were able to open up discussion about the positive impact for students with disabilities. We could also discuss the scores that suggested that the achievement of students without disabilities was not affected by the new inclusive service delivery model. We also identified some students that seemed to be struggling and then discussed how we could better support those students.

Students With and Without Disabilities: Average Percent Correct

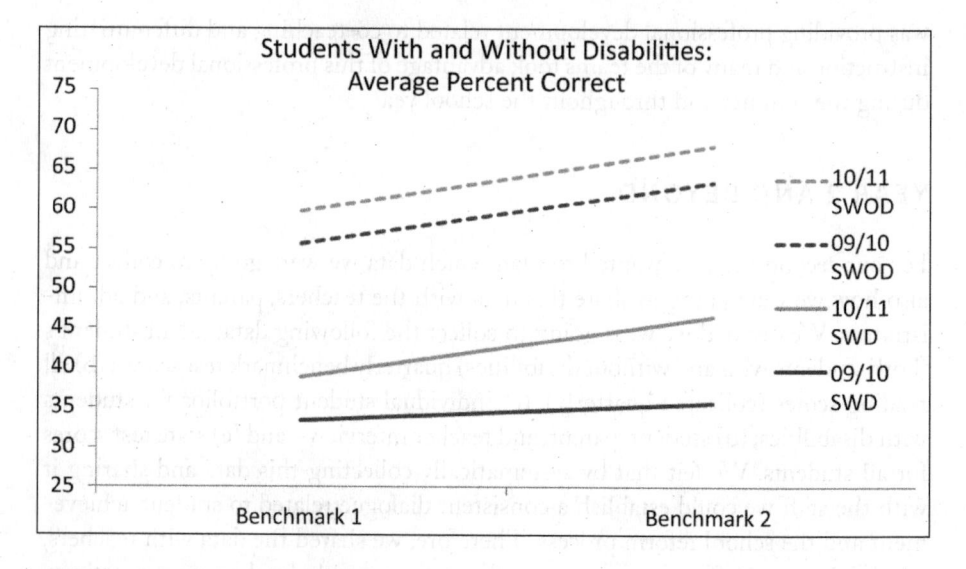

Figure 13.1. Benchmark language arts data comparing before and after inclusion.
Note. SWOD = Students Without Disabilities; SWD = Students With Disabilities.

Along with to benchmark scores, we also collected all students' scores on the Developmental Reading Assessment [DRA] (Beaver & Carter, 2005) on a quarterly basis. We used these scores to evaluate students' reading achievement "pre" and "post" inclusion, and allowed us to look at the achievement scores of entire classrooms. Since not all classes were "inclusive,"[1] we were able to compare the reading performance of "inclusive" and "non-inclusive" classrooms. We found that almost all students who were formerly educated in segregated settings made more progress in reading during their year in an inclusive classroom than they had in a segregated classroom. A few students who had only made minimal progress in segregated settings increased one or two full years of reading in less than one year in an inclusive classroom. Furthermore, we saw that some struggling students without disabilities were making more gains and that many students without disabilities were making the same steady gains they were making in "non-inclusive" classrooms. We discussed this data at grade level meetings with teachers to talk about some of the reasons for these gains and how we could continue to implement instruction to increase student achievement. We suspect that students with disabilities made such extraordinary gains because they were around peers that could support and challenge them. We also felt they were receiving much richer literacy instruction in the general education classrooms. We suspected that students without disabilities who were struggling such as some English Language Learners benefitted from the instruction and support the special educator was able to provide while co-teaching throughout the day. Many of the general education teachers mentioned that they found the expertise of the special educator extremely helpful in reaching students who were struggling in reading. Moreover, we were able to identify students who were struggling and discuss ways to improve or adjust instruction in an effort to reach these learners.

In addition to benchmark and reading scores, we developed portfolios for the students with disabilities. We wanted to focus on students with more significant disabilities who did not participate in some of the other assessments such as the benchmark assessments. We collected writing, work samples, and anecdotal notes on progress toward goals. We also took photos and video of the students to share with parents. This allowed us to keep a close eye on the students and communicate effectively with parents in terms of progress. We also had some exceptional success stories to share with the teachers and staff at meetings. We could show "before" and "after" pictures of student's work that showed they made significant gains.

Along with individual student portfolios, we also conducted interviews with students, teachers, and parents. We were interested in getting to know about their perceptions of the new inclusive service delivery. We asked students questions such as "Tell me about your classroom this year" and "In what ways do you think your classroom this year is different than last year?" We asked parents to tell us about how they felt the inclusive service delivery impacted their children. Lastly, we asked teachers to talk about their experiences in these new co-teaching and collaborative settings.

Students responded in very powerful ways during the interviews. Students said things such as, "This year is really awesome, it made me have a fantastic year" and "People are helping me achieve my goals." One parent responded that she was amazed at how motivated her son was this year and how the teachers told her he made a lot of progress in reading. Lastly, teachers provided responses such as "I felt like last year I was all alone in my self-contained classroom. This year I feel like I have colleagues. I feel more connected" and "I have learned so much this year from working more with the special education teacher." Clearly, there were many successes to celebrate.

State Test Scores and "Getting Out" of Program Improvement. In this age of testing and accountability in our schools, it is no surprise that many teachers and administrators were focused on state test scores. So, we waited with great anticipation for the state test scores from our first full year as an inclusive school. And [...] we could not have been happier upon receiving the results. As a whole, the students' scores had improved so much that the school was removed from the list of schools under "program improvement" (see Figure 13.2). Teachers and the administrator were thrilled. This gave us some momentum going into "Year 3" as we continue to work toward creating a sustainable structure of inclusive schooling.

Grade 3 / Grade 4 / Grade 5

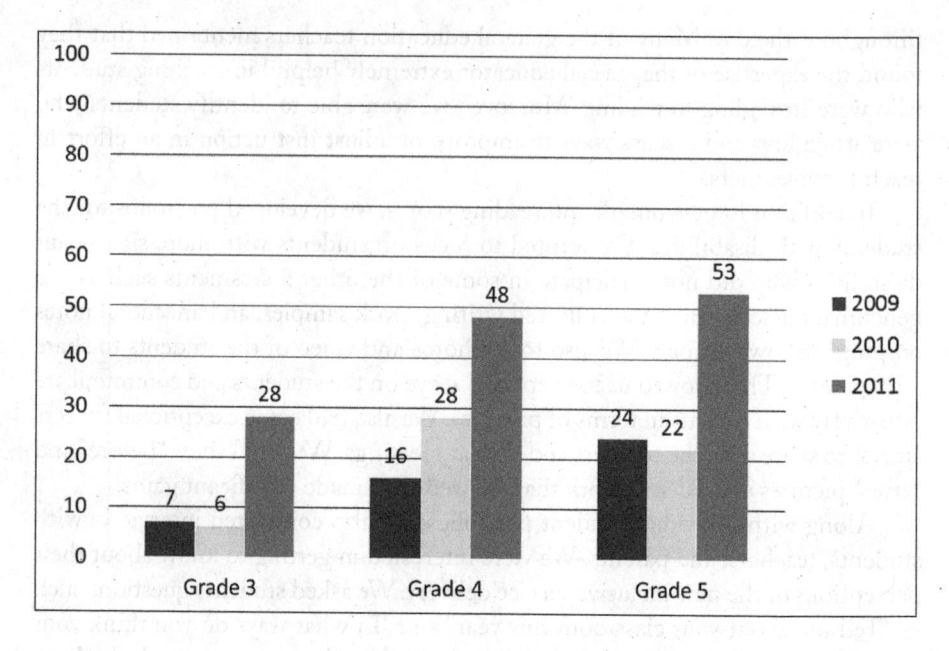

Grade	2009	2010	2011
Grade 3	7	6	28
Grade 4	16	28	48
Grade 5	24	22	53

Figure 13.2. Percentage of students with disabilities scoring proficient or advanced on the State Modified Standardized Assessment.

Note. 2009 and 2010 = Before Inclusive Education; 2011 = First Year of Inclusive Education.

Not only did we use the data to celebrate our accomplishments, we also used the data to problem solve and drive future instruction. For example, we were able to identify students with and without disabilities who needed more support academically or behaviorally. We could then brainstorm new ways to support these students. Furthermore, teachers were able to tell us their perceptions of how the collaborative teaching was going and if they felt their needed to be some changes in the ways that the teachers collaborated. If a teacher was not comfortable with the collaborative teaching models, we could then address this by offering more professional development or support in this area, or by improving or adjusting the collaborative teaching models used in the classroom.

CONCLUSION

Systematically collecting data as both "numbers and narrative" (Light & Pillemer, 1982; Nash, 2002) allowed us to create an important dialogue around our school reform initiative. We were able to use the data as a tool for critical thinking about supports and services for students with and without disabilities. By focusing on the data, we could discuss problems and concerns in a constructive manner. More importantly, we could celebrate the successes and hard work of the faculty and staff. Inclusive school reform is challenging and difficult work—it is important to find ways to celebrate successes and keep morale high through those challenging times. The team intends to continue to use both numbers and narrative to sustain inclusive education at the school.

> **Probing Questions**
> - Meghan describes a multifaceted, highly orchestrated plan to win over the teachers of this school to the philosophy and practice of inclusive education. Imagine that you were a teacher who was highly skeptical about inclusion. What might you think and feel about all of the data and stories that Meghan and her colleagues gathered and presented?
> - The data on the state standardized academic assessments are pretty clear and compelling. But a dramatic school reform like inclusion doesn't always yield such immediate and obvious leaps in measured achievement. What could Meghan do if the data was less positive?
> - The inclusive education reform in this elementary school relied on the extensive efforts of Meghan, a knowledgeable outside consultant. Not all schools can afford or have access to this kind of expertise. Can inclusive school reform happen without an external consultant? What can a school accomplish without outside support and guidance?
> - Numbers and narratives, in this story, provide for great opportunities for dialogue among the teachers. Are there other ways to bring teachers together to have powerful discussions that improve the quality and quantity of inclusion in a school?

REFERENCES

Beaver, J., & Carter, M. (2005). *Developmental reading assessment* (2nd ed.). Boston, MA: Pearson.

Causton-Theoharis, J., Theoharis, G., Bull, T., Cosier, M., & Dempf-Aldrich, K. (2011). Schools of promise: A school district-university partnership centered on inclusive school reform. *Remedial and Special Education, 32*, 3, 192–205.

Daniel, L. G., & King, D. A. (1997). Impact of inclusion education on academic achievement, student behavior, and self-esteem, and parental attitudes. *The Journal of Educational Research, 91*(2), 67–80.

Frattura, E. M., & Capper, C. A. (2007). *Leading for social justice. Transforming schools for all learners.* Thousand Oaks, CA: Corwin Press.

Friend, M., & Pope, K. L. (2005). Creating schools in which all students can succeed. *Kappa Delta Pi Record, 41*(2), 56–61.

Gandhi, A. G. (2007). Context matters: Exploring relations between inclusion and reading achievement of students without disabilities. *International Journal of Disability, Development, and Education, 54*, 91–112.

Huber, K. D., Rosenfeld, J. G., & Fiorello, C. A. (2001). The differential impact of inclusion and inclusive practices on high, average, and low achieving general education students. *Psychology in the Schools, 38*(6), 497–504.

Jerald, C. (2005). *The implementation trap: Helping schools overcome barriers to change.* The Center for Comprehensive School Reform and Improvement. Retrieved on July 25, 2009 from http://www.centerforcsi.org.

Kauffman, J. M., & Hallahan, D. P. (2005). *The illusion of full inclusion: A comprehensive critique of a current special education bandwagon* (2nd ed.). Austin, TX: Pro-ed.

Keefe, E. B., Moore, V., & Duff, F. (2004). The four "knows" of collaborative teaching. *Teaching Exceptional Children, 36*(5), 36–41.

Light, R. J., & Pillemer, D. B. (1982). Numbers and narrative: Combining their strengths in research reviews. *Harvard Educational Review, 52*, 1, 1–26.

Linton, S. (1998). *Claiming disability: Knowledge and identity.* New York: New York University Press.

McDonnell, J., Johnson, J. W., Polychronis, S., & Risen, T. (2002). Effects of imbedded instruction on students with moderate disabilities enrolled in general education classes. *Education and Training in Mental Retardation and Developmental Disabilities, 37*(4), 363–377.

McDonnell, J., Thorson, N., Disher, S., Mathot-Buckner, C., Mendel, J., & Ray, L. (2003). The achievement of students with disabilities and their peers without disabilities in inclusive settings. *Education and Treatment of Children, 26*(3), 224–236.

McLeskey, J. & Waldron, N. L. (2006). Comprehensive school reform and inclusive schools. *Theory into Practice, 45*, 3, 269–278.

Nash, R. (2002). Numbers and narratives: Further reflections in the sociology of education. *British Journal of Sociology of Education, 23*(3), 397–412.

Saint-Laurent, L., Dionne, J., Giasson, J., Royer, G., Simard, C., & Pierard, B. (1998). Academic achievement effects of an in-class service model on students with and without disabilities. *Exceptional Children, 64*(2), 239–253.

Sindelar, P. T., Shearer, D. K., Yendol-Hoppey, D., & Liebert, T. W. (2006). The sustainability of inclusive school reform. *Exceptional Children, 72*(3), 317–331.

Solis, M., Vaughn, S., Swanson, E., & McCulley, L. (2012). Collaborative models of instruction: The empirical foundations of inclusion and co-teaching. *Psychology in Schools, 49*(5), 498–510.

Trejo, C. L. (2008). *The impact of inclusion programs on the academic achievement on non-disabled learners in selected Texas elementary schools.* Retrieved from ProQuest Dissertation & Theses Database (AAT 3308913).

Vaughn, S., Moody, S. W., & Schumm, J. S. (1998). Broken promises: Reading instruction in the resource room. *Exceptional Children, 64*(2), 211–226.

Villa, R. A., & Thousand, J. A. (Eds.). (2005). *Creating an inclusive school* (2nd ed.). Alexandria, VA: Association for Supervision and Curriculum Development.

Waldron, N. L., & McLeskey, J. (1998). The effects of an inclusive school program on students with mild and severe learning disabilities. *Exceptional Children, 64*(3), 395–405.

Yell, M. L. (2006). *The law and special education.* Columbus, OH: Pearson.

NOTE

1. Due to the size of the school and the number of students with disabilities, not all classrooms included students with disabilities.

CHAPTER FOURTEEN

"It's always about the kids, not us"

Successful Elementary Co-teaching

ZACHARY ROSSETTI

I first met Crosby while supervising a special education student teacher in an inclusive kindergarten class at a nearby public elementary school. I was excited to meet him as I had heard from both the student teacher and the in-service special education teacher about the remarkable improvements he had made during just a few months. The year before had not been successful. Crosby was placed in an inclusive class, but the teachers were not experienced teaching students with autism, were not supported to do so, and, in their words, did not know what to do with him. He did not speak while in this class, and most days ended with an early call home as Crosby cried in the fetal position under his desk. Reaching crisis, Crosby's mother removed him from the public school and placed him in a private pre-school classroom with fewer students. He made progress in this class, and his mother quickly returned him to the public school kindergarten class.

When I arrived to the classroom on the day of our first meeting, Crosby sat at his desk with his head in his hands. His classmates assembled in their spots on the rug of colored squares for morning meeting with the student teacher, Ms. Banelli. I should have known not to approach him as he seemed to be "cooling off" from an earlier difficulty. As he lifted his head to watch his classmates in morning meeting, I thought it might be a good time to say hello. I slowly inched toward the sink/water area near his desk. As I looked up to greet him for the first time, he quickly glared at me and exclaimed, "Don't come close to me." Mrs. Rooney, the general educator, overheard and intervened, explaining who I was and why I was there. Crosby replied, unimpressed, "I don't want to talk to him." Mrs. Rooney then asked Crosby to help her carry the reading assessments from the closet. As he approached me, he quickly slid to the other side of her from me, shielding himself with Mrs. Rooney's legs.

Upon completing his task, Crosby returned to his seat, still refusing to speak with me despite numerous prompts from Mrs. Rooney and also from the special educator Mrs. Green. After a few more minutes, Mrs. Green asked Crosby if he would like to join morning meeting. He immediately and definitively said, "No," dropping his head back into his hands on his desk. Next in the morning meeting routine was reading high-frequency words from the class word wall. In typical fashion, all of the students read these words in unison creating a rhythmic pattern. Crosby picked up his head almost immediately, intently watching the students reciting these words. Soon he began to mouth the words silently. He slowly stood up and eventually joined the morning meeting after the word wall when it was time to sing their days of the week and months of the year songs. They sang each one twice.

Crosby plopped down in his spot on the rug, which was—and had to be—the blue square. As he took his spot he inadvertently but forcefully bumped the girl beside him with his leg. She immediately grabbed her head and said, "Ow!" She turned toward him as she fixed her braid, but he did not apologize or acknowledge her in any way. Mrs. Green, monitoring from afar, prompted him to apologize to her, "Crosby, tell Malia her you are sorry." He quietly muttered, "Sorry," quickly without making eye contact. Mrs. Green immediately called him on it, prompting him again, "Crosby! Full sentences, and say it like you mean it." He slowly turned toward her and said, "Sorry for bumping you in the head with my leg, Malia." Mrs. Green thanked him and then reminded him to be more careful of others next time.

Throughout this encounter the class had been counting the days of April by ones. Crosby counted along in between his failed apology attempt and then the successful apology. Once they finished, he asked, "Can we do the word list?"

Ms. Banelli replied, "We already did it, Crosby."

Crosby immediately responded, getting angrier with each phrase, "I didn't do the word list. It's time for the word list! IT'S TIME FOR THE WORD LIST!"

Mrs. Green knelt beside Crosby, reminding him that this was not how to speak during morning meeting, nor was it how to speak to teachers. She also pointed to his Koosh ball, nonverbally reminding him to squeeze it as part of his self-regulating strategies for when he needed to calm his emotions. He picked up the Koosh ball as he protested again, but quietly and meekly as if he had already reluctantly accepted the premise that the meeting was moving on, "But [...] I didn't do [...] the word list."

Simultaneously, Mrs. Rooney, who had been monitoring the other members of the class while Mrs. Green focused on Crosby, caught Ms. Banelli's attention. She motioned to the number wall and the pointer with her eyes and then pointed at Crosby.

Ms. Banelli, picking up on the nonverbal cueing, said, "Crosby, why don't you be the pointer for the number wall today?"

Crosby smiled and agreed, "Okay."

Ms. Banelli handed Crosby a large pointer and pointed toward the number wall which hung on the door to the bathroom in the classroom. The number wall had pockets with numbers 1 to 100 and then a piece of white chart paper taped underneath it with numbers 101 to 136 that seemed to each be drawn by different students since they were different sizes, colors, and forms. These numbers identified the number of school days, of course. The class counted by ones all the way up to 136. Crosby pointed correctly to each number as it was counted for the first two rows, but then began to point to the row of numbers directly below where the students were counting. He smiled as he did this.

Ms. Banelli, smiling, quietly said, "Crosby, don't be silly."

Mrs. Green and Mrs. Rooney looked at each other and smiled as well.

Crosby pointed to the correct row of numbers, but then pointed to the row below again, smiling. His classmates did not seem to notice this or to mind. They continued counting their numbers in order. It was more of a joke between Crosby and his teachers. When they arrived at 136, Ms. Banelli asked Crosby to write in "the number for today," and he wrote 137 in large, well-formed numbers. Crosby walked back to his spot on the rug, smiling. This time he did not bump Malia or any other classmates when he sat down on the blue square. He participated actively and without incident during the rest of morning meeting and story time.

CO-TEACHING

Co-teaching, similar to inclusion, has become a special education buzz word used frequently but often referenced and defined in multiple ways. As such, it is also implemented ineffectively. The all too common co-teaching arrangement involves the classroom teacher instructing his or her general education students while the special education teacher sits in the back or the side of the room trying to figure out how to adapt the lesson or materials on the fly for his or her students with Individualized Education Programs (IEPs) receiving special education services. In many situations, there has been no common planning time, let alone a conversation before class about the content, standards, or structure of the lesson. The special educator acts as a teacher assistant, and ultimately as a guest, in the general educator's classroom. Within the context of special education student teaching, this is especially problematic because the student teacher in such a classroom will not engage in much actual teaching. From the educators to the students, an us-them dynamic distinguishing general and special education persists in such classrooms.

Co-teaching is defined as two or more certified teachers, usually a special educator and a general educator, planning, delivering, and evaluating instruction to a class of diverse learners in a shared physical space, typically the general education setting (Cook & Friend, 1995; Conderman, Bresnahan, & Pedersen, 2009; Murawski & Dieker, 2008). The literature describes slight variations on a core group of co-teaching approaches: One Teach, One Observe; Station Teaching; Parallel Teaching; Alternative Teaching; Teaming; and, One Teach, One Assist (Friend & Bursuck, 2012). The latter approach (as well as the first) runs the risk of being implemented ineffectively when one teacher, usually the general educator, exclusively plays the role of teacher such as in the example described above. In order to improve the effectiveness of co-teaching and to ensure it is a productive use of the special educator's time, Kloo and Zigmond (2008) stressed not just helping but delivering individualized instruction to students and modeling what is special about special education to the general educator. The intended benefit of co-teaching as a general approach is not just to add a second adult to the classroom, but to utilize two separate and equally useful bodies of knowledge possessed by the general educator and special educator through planning, individualizing, and differentiating instruction to be delivered in the model that best fits the students, educators, and classroom environment.

A MODEL OF INCLUSIVE CO-TEACHING

When I first observed in their classroom, I assumed Mrs. Rooney and Mrs. Green had been teaching together for years because of the ease with which they effectively collaborated and taught almost thirty culturally and linguistically diverse (CLD) students, half with IEPs receiving special education services. Yet, it was actually their first year working together. If I had not been aware of their specific roles due to the student teaching arrangement, I would not have been able to discern them. Guests to the classroom were often unsure who the general educator was and who the special educator was.

Though they struggle with a lack of resources, a classroom designed for half their population, and challenging student behaviors and situations, Mrs. Green and Mrs. Rooney make co-teaching in their inclusive kindergarten classroom work. They make it work with efficient and effective instruction that is explicit and hands-on. They make it work with steady classroom management emphasizing clear rules that are consistently enforced within an underlying foundation of constant community building. Ultimately, their successes stem from a shared responsibility for all students. Mrs. Rooney explained their joint philosophy: "We do everything for the kids. And we work well together. It's not about, 'Well, you did this and I need more time for this.' It's always about the kids, not us."

"SURPRISINGLY, WE DID NOT HAVE ANY DIFFICULTIES"

In contrast to likely expectations and fears about this intense professional collaboration, Mrs. Green and Mrs. Rooney did not experience difficulties when they began co-teaching this classroom. One reason for this is that they were encouraged to work together by an administrator, specifically the special education district supervisor. The supervisor knew both Mrs. Green and Mrs. Rooney personally and professionally, and felt that they would make an effective team. This is not usually the situation for many teachers who are placed into a needed slot or who choose an available job.

Regarding professional experience and preparation, both Mrs. Green and Mrs. Rooney were well suited for this teaching position and arrangement, though this was a first for each of them. They each had been teaching for over fifteen years. Mrs. Green possessed K–12 special education licensure, teaching in a self-contained special education classroom at the high school level and then in resource rooms at all elementary grade levels. However, she had taught primarily in an inclusive setting only one year prior to this. Mrs. Rooney possessed Early Childhood, Elementary, and English as a Second Language (ESL) licensure and had most recently been working as a kindergarten ESL teacher for the past seven years. While they lacked formal experience with the co-teaching model, the common element of their divergent professional paths was that they valued diversity. Whether CLD students or students with disabilities (or both), Mrs. Green and Mrs. Rooney embraced teaching and reaching diverse learners, striving to support their growth as learners and as individuals.

"WE APPROACHED THE JOB WITH OPENNESS AND INTEREST"

While they experienced no significant difficulties in beginning this work, Mrs. Green and Mrs. Rooney needed to work through the inevitable early awkwardness of a new working relationship. This early stage may include personal elements of getting to know someone, as well as personal and professional reactions to the differences of style and of opinion in the decision making and problem solving this process entails. Who will teach what content? How will other tasks (e.g., assessments, meetings, duties) be divided? How will the room be arranged? Where will each teacher's desk/area be located? How will the students be grouped? Who will teach each group of students? What style and structure of classroom management will be used? What consequences for student misbehavior will be followed? What are the behavioral standards and expectations against which misbehavior will be measured? What type of classroom culture will be valued and created?

For Mrs. Green and Mrs. Rooney this early stage did not last long, about a week, and they quickly moved on to focus on the immense task at hand. "We approached the job with openness and interest." This succinct summary statement highlights two key elements of their successful approach to beginning their co-teaching. First, related to the openness of their approach, they let go of former distinctions, expectations, and preconceived notions based on their job titles to understand their positions as teaching together in a mutually shared classroom. They were not resistant or guarded. They did not ask, "*whose* classroom management style will be used?" They asked, "what style will be best for our classroom?" There were no turf battles. Mrs. Rooney and Mrs. Green each agreed that, "being territorial never works."

Their situation, unlike many others, minimized the potential for turf battles because they each left a different classroom to begin in their new classroom together. It was not the more common situation of one teacher, usually the special educator, being externally added to the general educator's domain. It is precisely in these types of situations that resistance and resentment may lead to turf battles in which there is a separation of students within the classroom based on the perpetuation of separate teacher roles and incessant jockeying for "ownership" of the classroom.

Second, since they viewed their job as working together fully, they each began with an overarching interest and belief in teaching all students, together. Mrs. Green explained their focus: "We shared the philosophy that the classroom should have an atmosphere that would motivate and nurture *all* students." What does this look like? First, they actively worked to construct a sense of community. Mrs. Green explained, "at the beginning of the year we emphasize that this class is like our family. This is our school family." Mrs. Rooney added, "and you don't always have to love someone or even like them, but you always have to be nice."

Next, they decided to accomplish all instruction, assessment, and other tasks together, opting not to separate these classroom responsibilities. The first key to the success of this approach was extensive—but efficient—weekly planning with daily updates and check-ins. During planning, they split daily jobs and areas of instruction, but most importantly, they discussed their students and ways they could better individualize or teach specific content to specific students. During these planning meetings they shared, blended, and utilized their specialized areas of expertise. In practice, they typically delivered instruction according to the co-teaching approaches of Teaming in which they shared instruction or One Teach, One Assist in which they alternated leading a lesson while the other assisted individual students. They key to the latter approach was that they equally distributed the role of lead teacher and support teacher which was reflective of their mutual decision to work together in their shared classroom.

"THEY WERE ALL OUR STUDENTS"

Deciding not to split classroom responsibilities, they then made this same agreement about their students. "They were all *our* students. There would be no distinction of mine/yours, special education/general education [...]. The 'lines' were blurred. Many times we couldn't even remember which students were on the general education list or the special education list." Any student struggling in a specific content area could be called into a skills group by either teacher. The skills groups were brief, intensive, teacher-directed sessions or mini lessons focused on particular beginning academic or functional skills. Utilizing these skill groups reflected the co-teaching approach of Alternative Teaching. Beyond sharing the instruction of all students, Mrs. Green provided extra assistance to struggling learners without disabilities while Mrs. Rooney helped with additional classroom management techniques and positive behavior supports for Crosby and several other students.

Mrs. Green and Mrs. Rooney followed this absence of distinction through all aspects of their jobs. Meetings for any child were attended by both teachers. Notes home and official school documents contained both teachers' names and/or signatures. In this manner, Mrs. Green and Mrs. Rooney delivered needs-based instruction and supports to all students, thus taking a non-categorical approach one level higher than is typical before the special education-general education split could occur.[1]

To summarize these key elements of their successful transition to co-teaching, Mrs. Green and Mrs. Rooney viewed their new jobs as teaching together in a mutually shared classroom environment. Further, as an extension of their values-based, shared embracement of diversity and individuality, they purposefully chose to teach all students together. Ms. Banelli, the special education student teacher, recognized the results of this approach: "My favorite thing about this class was the positive attitude that every student and all of the teachers possessed, and how accepting the students were of one another."

INCLUDING CROSBY: A SUCCESS STORY

The summer before Crosby returned to public school, Mrs. Green and Mrs. Rooney started working together to plan for his arrival. They learned that his prior classroom did not actually function as a truly inclusive classroom. They began to realize that at least some of his difficulties were rooted in an ineffective class environment. During these summer discussions, their similar philosophies crystallized into their own classroom culture of mutual instruction and motivation of all students. Faced with a specific task, they naturally enacted their co-teaching preferences and styles in problem solving for Crosby's inclusion. Rather than generally discussing options for how they should co-teach and arguing about personal interests or preferences, they skipped ahead past the early stage of working out differences to focus on what was best for a specific child.

They discussed Crosby's interests, strengths, and needs. They shared that they were looking forward to getting to know him. They began the year optimistic and excited. One of them monitored Crosby at all times throughout the day. By now, Crosby spoke regularly but was extremely reliant on structure and insistent on sameness. He quickly adjusted to the clear expectations, daily routines, and overall calmness of Mrs. Green's and Mrs. Rooney's classroom. However, he frequently erupted into meltdowns when he encountered any slight change or disruption to these structures and routines such as when the order of songs was changed during morning meeting. When this occurred, Crosby began to cry and yelled, "NO, YOU CAN'T DO THAT!" Instead of responding in a similarly rigid manner and focusing on teacher control, Mrs. Green reframed the situation as teaching and helping Crosby to adjust to minor changes that could occur without warning by learning strategies to calm himself during situations in which he became upset. They collaborated with the occupational therapist (OT) who explored and identified some useful tools including a weighted vest, a Sponge Bob puppet, and the Koosh ball. He eventually learned to use these on his own, requesting the weighted vest and holding the puppet or Koosh ball when necessary.

Crosby also became increasingly agitated and often engaged in tantrums when his interests could not be accommodated or he could not get his way. Examples included him needing to sit in the blue square, continually asking to be picked when he was not called on during morning meeting and lessons, crying when he did not get the plastic firefighter's hat from the bin of recess toys, and yelling when his mother differentiated her route to school or parked in a different spot. To address these behaviors, Mrs. Green and Mrs. Rooney collaborated with the speech and language pathologist (SLP) who quickly realized that social stories were effective in helping Crosby accept these changes or instances of delayed gratification. They wrote one for morning meeting: "Mrs. Rooney can switch the songs. It is okay if things do not happen the same way." They wrote another for commuting with his mother: "Mom can drive to school using different roads. Mom can park in different places. This is okay." Social stories related to the firefighter's hat and not being picked on emphasized sharing with his classmates. Despite ongoing attempts to increase flexibility while sitting on the rug, Crosby insisted on sitting in his blue square. Since some of his classmates also have their favorite spots, and they began to save that spot for him, Mrs. Green and Mrs. Rooney chose to allow Crosby's preference here.

Once he learned to utilize these tools himself and responded positively to the strategies and supports implemented by Mrs. Green and Mrs. Rooney in collaboration with the OT and SLP, Crosby completed work, participated fully, and interacted socially with his classmates. Meltdowns and tantrums became the exception not the norm. When he started to become upset he asked one of the teachers to read the related social story to him. He learned to take turns and to listen to others. He developed a close friendship with Miguel, the two playing chase and firefighters at recess most days. The friendship became so important to Crosby that he began to experience meltdowns when Miguel was absent. Mrs. Green and Mrs. Rooney wrote another social story for this situation that quickly became very useful for these situations.

Mrs. Green felt very strongly that these improvements were due in large part to their emphasis on teaching him strategies to be successful rather than punishing him or focusing on consequences for what could have been perceived as misbehavior. Both teachers saw the communicative intent and evidence of real difficulties in Crosby's behaviors, and they responded by supporting him to independently take control of his feelings and learn to adapt to change so that he could participate fully with his classmates.

REFLECTIONS ON SUCCESSFUL CO-TEACHING

Having gained several years of co-teaching experience since their initial year together, Mrs. Green and Mrs. Rooney reflected on the essential elements of successful co-teaching. They identified their essential elements, a list of characteristics and strategies that worked well for them and continues to guide their exceptional practice.

Beginning with the personal, they both described not just the importance, but the necessity of humor. Humor allows them to find a balance between work and their lives outside of work. It helps them to reframe some of the minor issues and challenges that seem major at the time. It helps them to regain their patience and to maintain their focus on supporting students to learn age-appropriate skills rather than punishing them for perceived misbehavior.

Having long since recognized what that special education administrator who placed them together did, Mrs. Green and Mrs. Rooney cited their similarities in the fundamental values with which they approach their jobs. They share a strong love of and desire to teach all children, especially the ones who tend to fall through the cracks or frustrate other teachers or struggle in their transition to school. They also share the same educational philosophies, namely celebrating diversity and holding high expectations for all learners.

As they began to work together, they each approached the new challenge with a mutual willingness to collaborate and openness to change. Most importantly, they were willing to learn from each other and to try different strategies or instructional approaches. While this can be difficult to achieve, it is crucial because it reflects one of the primary benefits of co-teaching in that each teacher brings a separate knowledge base with them resulting in a whole that is greater than the sum of its parts.

Inherent to this willingness was recognizing and utilizing each other's strengths. Mrs. Green was patient but firm in response to challenging behaviors. Mrs. Rooney explained skills clearly in her explicit instruction, and she motivated students by conveying that learning was fun and showing them all that they were indeed accomplishing. As the relationship developed, they became comfortable not only with recognizing the other's strengths but in taking suggestions from the other without taking it personally because it was based on strengths and experiences. Ultimately, the most helpful tool for reframing suggestions that could potentially be perceived as insulting was remembering that everything they were doing together was for the benefit of the child. They constantly reminded themselves and each other that it was not about them, but the children. This allowed them to really listen to hard truths and to make changes to or improve their practices when necessary.

Finally, they still feel that their initial decision to teach all students together is the cornerstone upon which their other successful practices have been built. They share responsibilities related to all students through the entire day. They prep together and they problem solve together. They have developed such comfort with each other in the context of their daily routines that they can focus even more on how the progress of each child is developing in all academic and functional skills.

> **Probing Questions**
> - One might easily conclude that Mrs. Green and Mrs. Rooney collaborate quite naturally. So it seems. But they actually have worked in a very intentional way to become a cohesive team. What have they done to develop into an effective co-teaching duo?
> - Mrs. Green and Mrs. Rooney may not be experts on autism. But they receive tremendous professional advice from an occupational therapist and a speech and language therapist. How did Mrs. Green and Mrs. Rooney use these consultations to improve their classroom?
> - Zachary describes Mrs. Green and Mrs. Rooney as sharing very fundamental values. Often two co-teachers do not embrace the same human values. How can a general educator and a special educator become an effective co-teaching team if they do not share basic ethical commitments?

REFERENCES

Conderman, G., Bresnahan, V., & Pedersen, T. (2009). *Purposeful co-teaching: Real cases and effective strategies*. Thousand Oaks, CA: Sage Publications.

Cook, L., & Friend, M. (1995). Co-teaching: Guidelines for creating effective practices. *Focus on Exceptional Children, 28*(3), 1–16.

Friend, M., & Bursuck, W. D. (2012). *Including students with special needs: A practical guide for classroom teachers* (6th ed.). Boston, MA: Pearson.

Kloo, A., & Zigmond, N. (2008). Coteaching revisited: Redrawing the blueprint. *Preventing School Failure, 52*(2), 12–20.

Murawski, W. W., & Dieker, L. (2008). 50 ways to keep your co-teacher: Strategies for before, during, and after co-teaching. *Teaching Exceptional Children, 40*(4), 40–48.

NOTE

1. By no means should this indicate that appropriate and effective, needs-based special education and related services were not provided to students with documented disabilities per their IEP goals. They were. Mrs. Green was exceptionally organized, maintaining binders on each student and aware of their strengths, needs, and goals in all areas. In fact, it is partly because of this knowledge of students and their IEP goals that both teachers were able to teach all students together.

CHAPTER FIFTEEN

Spilt Milk Counts

Belonging and Moving on Down the Hall...

STACEY HODGINS AND S. ANTHONY THOMPSON

As a Student Services (Resource) Teacher, I was co-teaching in the grade one classroom one day; the classroom teacher had stepped out. Then [...] boom! Bang! Crash! Stomp! What just happened? In that adrenaline-filled instant, I paused—or froze; I shuttered slightly. I had asked a student to check out a library book, which somehow resulted in flying chairs, tipping desks, and screaming: "I hate this school, I hate these teachers, I hate it all." In that moment, time stopped tersely, unexpectedly and unabashedly. I suddenly heard my heart beating inside my head—a baffling though perhaps predictable occurrence. Strangely and almost unknowingly, I felt like I had super powers—the unbelievable kind, like I could foster an invisible force field or morph my body or kinetically charge my brain: I needed to quickly make countless classroom decisions. Time was sprinting. I found ways to keep the other students safe while simultaneously somehow continuing a lesson. Still in this simultaneity, I distracted the aggravated booming, banging, crashing stomping student, Clark, and attempted to convince him to come to a safe area to attempt to calm down. I made many, many decisions in this strange time contortion [...] and yet the booming, banging, crashing, and stomping continued [...].

On this day in this moment of confusing simultaneities, I thought of my co-teaching partner, the classroom teacher, where was she? How might I contact her? I also thought of Bill. Could he be the distraction I needed in this crisis? Looking at the clock it is 11:50. Shortly, a student would be coming to the grade one room to deliver the milk for lunch time. I hoped and prayed it would be Bill on this day.

Thump, thump, thump. My heart raced. Suddenly, the door opened. Alas, it was Bill!

Bill is one of the grade five students who regularly and eagerly volunteers for the school milk delivery. The job encompasses picking up the order from the front office, counting the requisite cartons and delivering them to each classroom, all before the lunch bell. Although our rural Saskatchewan school is of modest size, there are over 170 students, so one person doing milk delivery for the entire school is physically challenging. Bill does not seem to mind, indeed he cheerfully distributes the cartons, and I look forward to the days when he cheerfully enters the classroom. And today, I was *especially* appreciative of his smiling and stalwart reliability. As he came into the frenzied, frazzled space with his heavy crate of milk boxes, I rushed to him for help. Without hesitation, he agreed. I asked him if Clark, our student currently booming, banging, crashing, and stomping, could accompany him to finish the remaining deliveries together. Bill intuitively went over, and with a soft, gentle, and comforting voice, told Clark he needed to calm down just a little in order to help drop off the milk. Clark, with his still scarlet face and still catching his breath, said nothing. Nothing. My heart spoke audibly, thump, thump, thump. Hundreds of thoughts fleetingly flew through my mind: How mad is Clark exactly? Will he run away? Are the other children safe? Clark is new to the school [...] what do I know about Clark? I had been warned by the previous school that he may have explosive episodes [...] what will he do now? What will he do now? Will this work? Will he go with Bill? I watched; I watched [...] as he [...] as he [...]

He went with Bill! Without a word or even a sound, Clark walked out into the long hallway with its old linoleum tiles; he waited as he watched Bill grab a milk crate, then he grabbed one himself. Clark's breathing became less intense more natural; his flushed face nonchalantly regaining composure. They continued on to the next classroom. I saw the heavy cart roll languidly down the hallway as they gently pushed it along. I was stunned. Time resumed, although it did so with great reluctance—it began with a stalled creeping as though it pondered each movie frame before advancing to the next. Thump [...] thump [...] thump. My heart rate returned to normal, although that too seemed like a struggle. Despite our school's small size, I have always felt the hallway's length as slightly claustrophobic, but not today. Today, I felt the expansiveness of it—as wide and as open as the Saskatchewan prairie itself. Relief.

Bill has such a calm, relaxed manner with younger students. Busy with dodge ball or soccer as all grade fives are at recess, Bill still manages some time, now and then, to talk or play with them. The children adore him. He is a natural leader. As I continued to watch, Bill and Clark slowly roll the cart from classroom to classroom, and as I regained my inner composure, I wondered how we could encourage this natural friendship/mentorship, between Bill and Clark.

Clark has many issues, perhaps the most burning one is the loss of his own school which had recently closed in the neighboring small town; Clark was in mourning. Indeed, Clark was one of many new students this year at Flowerville Elementary; there was much mourning. Closing schools is not uncommon here on the rural Canadian prairies, and no matter how prepared, advised, and forewarned a community may be, it always seems to happen abruptly. Closures are especially acute in rural places where the school is often the activity hub—and more significant than that, it is the town's thermometer, measuring and proclaiming the community's health and viability. So the school goes [...] so the community goes. This school closure was that of a First Nations' band school; the center of this neighboring reserve where the cultural and spiritual teachings of Aboriginal people (or First Nations) were taught and experienced. The collective experience of loss weighed particularly heavy on Clark and his peers. His was a cultural loss.

Students, staff, and parents were working through this fast moving change: one school closed, another one inflated. Indeed, it was common to hear the new/displaced students mutter, "I miss our school. I don't like this school." The staff at Flowerville Elementary felt how deeply challenging this change was—certainly, more than a simple change of venue. And seemingly at the core of this change was Clark.

After school, a few staff members and I gathered in my classroom. Certainly, we needed to figure out how to support Clark, but also how to support all the children from the closed school. Perhaps not coincidentally, we had previously planned to meet to discuss a myriad of (mostly behavioral) concerns coming my way. To use the student support (resource) teacher, clinical language, the grade one class had many diverse learning, social and behavioral needs. Six students had an individual education plan (IEP), two of which held the highest designation of intensive needs as defined by our Ministry of Education. At any other official meeting, we would meet around my large round table, let loose our frustrations, discuss and brainstorm solutions, and create an action plan. Ideally, everyone would feel ready to address the concerns—some short-term, some long-term goals and strategies identified. Luckily, we are a cohesive staff.

However, this day was different; we sat in silence—no appetite or energy even for venting. We held our heads in our hands while some descended into the couch, another declined into the boneless, over-stuffed chair, a colleague even managed to slouch into the hard spindled-back rocking chair. Couches and comfy chairs just seemed more appropriate than my official conference table for this meeting. As I gazed about, I took inventory of the expertise around me: the classroom teacher has her Master's degree and over twenty years teaching experience, my administrator, though only in her second year as principal, also had over twenty years of teaching experience, the registered social worker with five years' experience in this school and a great rapport with students, and myself a student services teacher currently in her seventh year teaching. What were we to do for Clark? What were we to do with the classroom of grade one students, many of whom were viscerally experiencing loss?

Despite these credentials and experience, the team seemed lost and overwhelmed. No one had spoken in quite some time. I was thinking about Bill and Clark; perhaps surprisingly, the image of them walking down that antiquated hall together was the highlight of the day. I was so proud of Bill for taking the leadership role when I desperately needed him. He helped out in a way that none of us could. Finally, I broke the silence and spoke; my voice seemed to bring the group out of its acquiescent trance. I shared the story of Bill taking Clark on his milk delivery and how Clark's face beamed brightly when he came back for lunch. The classroom teacher commented that the afternoon had gone better for Clark, and I wondered if it had been because of the experience. Clark seemed to feel a sense of purpose, a sense of belonging, even if it were for but a few minutes. This sparked the conversation about belonging and the *Circle of Courage* (Brendtro, Brokenleg, & Van Bockern, 2002), a First Nations inspired curricular concept and practice about which we recently learned.

The *Circle of Courage* consists of four domains: sense of belonging, mastery, independence, and generosity. If one domain is not being addressed for a child, it can lead to discouragement—a feeling with which we were all too familiar. As a group we knew that Clark and many of his peers were feeling discouraged; plainly and obviously stated, school did not provide a sense belonging. At best some students probably felt like visitors—at worst, as exiled refuges in a strange land—a land that was a larger building that housed many new faces. Who were these newly displaced students? What was their connection to this building? To this community? How was their culture reflected in this school? Where were their teachers? What does a sense of belonging mean when these students ride a bus past their abandoned school every day with its once familiar teachers and routines, to a new school with unfamiliar teachers and routines?

We realized as a group that we needed to revitalize, reinvent, and recreate our school's culture; we needed to be inclusive from our very grassland roots. We required input from all students and parents, new and old. We wondered what students, parents, and guardians wanted their school to look like? Feel like? Sound like? To create an inclusive and welcoming school, we knew we needed to act more inclusive and welcoming.

We instituted student consultation pods. These were multi-graded groups of roughly twelve students each, and included a staff member to assist the student facilitators. The pods provided an opportunity for all students to learn from one another in a peer-directed activity. The sixth-grade leaders facilitated what we called the "virtues sessions" (they had been previously trained how to do this). For example, a grade six student might explain the "golden rule" to the children. They might then ask the younger students for examples of what the golden rule looks like, sounds like, or feels like. The grade six students would record their responses on a giant pledge poster. At the conclusion of these virtue sessions, all students in that virtue group would sign the poster, pledging that they will follow, for example, the golden rule. We were specific, we asked: What would a sense of belonging look like? What would generosity sound like? What does it mean to be independent [...] and how might it feel like, look like, for different students?

At the same time, we began re-introducing our bucket wish-list; we are a "bucket-filling" school (see www.bucketfillers101.com). Each student has an invisible bucket that must feel full to support that sense of belonging. We filled their buckets with compliments and praise and favorite activities; we also taught students to fill the buckets of their peers. We taught many little things, such as saying hello, holding the door, helping someone in need, asking someone to play, telling you mom or dad you love them, and hugging your grandmother, etc. We challenged students to think about whether they were dipping or dumping others' buckets. We decided we would re-examine this concept school-wide, as a social skill lesson to each grade.

As we were instituting these school-wide efforts to foster inclusivity, the school-based team also drew its concern back to Clark. Where was his place here? What was his role here? Certainly, there was a connection between Clark and Bill; we agreed to foster it. We could at least begin there. In fact, Bill was sort of new to the school too—having moved into it only two years ago; maybe, he could relate to Clark's situation. If this acquaintanceship were to bloom into a friendship, Clark may feel connected, may feel like he has a place, and may feel like he belonged. We would begin to put things in place tomorrow.

The next morning, consistent with best practice, we prepared Clark for the change that would happen before lunch; starting today, he was helping with milk delivery. (We arranged for that student to be Bill again today.) Clark helped attach the new milk-delivery picture to his visual schedule. He counted how many changes would occur before Bill came to pick him up. A few times, that morning he asked if it were time. We pointed to his schedule and aloud, he would re-tally the changes remaining until Bill arrived. Then, right on time, Bill arrived. Grinning from ear to ear when he saw Clark, he asked him if he were ready to learn where they kept the milk. Clark's eyes lit up and he nodded, and followed Bill out of the grade one classroom. Though Bill was small for his age, he towered over Clark. They walked down the hall together as if they had done so for years.

I watched them leave the classroom, I had a satisfied ease—one of those brief time snippets where somehow everything feels right. I paused, and in my reverie, I was sure I heard the voice of a First Nations elder speaking through Bill. Bill engaged Clark in conversation as they walked [...].

"What was all that mess about in your room yesterday?" Bill asked Clark.

"I dunno [...] what mess?" Clark responded looking down.

"The chairs pushed down and the desks on the ground." Bill restated.

"I dunno [...] I was mad [...]" Clark bashfully responded.

"You can't do that here. You get in trouble. You gotta do what they tell you."

"I don't gotta do nothing," Clark said strongly.

"Well, you don't get money for making a mess." Bill stated simply.
"Money?" Clark's eyes gazed up at Bill.
"Ya […] for the store." Bill explained.
"The store? What store?" Clark questioned.
"When you do what they tell you to, you get money for your store. You get it for doing your jobs good." Bill continued.
"Your jobs?" Clark asked.
"Yeah […] like milk. If you do good, you get two bucks. 'Cause it's a big job. Or straightening up the computer lab. You can get money for that too. And then you put your money in your bank until the store is open." Bill stated.
"I want money for the store." Clark squealed.
"Ask your teacher." Said Bill.

Hearing this conversation, I quickly grabbed a plastic baggie and wrote "Clark" on the front in big red letters. It was on his desk when he returned. Next to it, I placed a plastic toonie from the math manipulatives bucket. When Clark came back, he quickly noticed the baggie and the coin. He grinned as he looked up at me. "This is to start your bank," I stated, "you did a great job delivering milk today, so you earned two dollars for your bank. When you earn more money, we can go to the store in my room and shop."

"Can I do another job?" Clark eagerly asked.
"First, it's lunch, but after lunch (pointing at his schedule) we can do another job." I explained.
"Will I get more money?" Bill questioned.
"If you do the job well you will." I responded.

At lunch, I printed pictures of the store's merchandise and with the requisite prices. I informed my staff that Clark was able to earn money for doing jobs around the school like other children. Additionally, scheduling these jobs as part of Clark's daily routine provided him with much-needed movement breaks. We planned on a job right after lunch. Settling after lunch and recess was difficult for many students, but particularly for Clark. That afternoon, we ensured Clark earned enough money to buy something. We took him down to the store, and showed him the menu of choices. He emptied his little baggie with his name proudly embossed, and counted his coins. This was a challenge for him but he meticulously touched each coin as he rehearsed the amount aloud. He had earned five dollars. He selected candy as his choice from the store menu. I took the coins from his little hand and he ecstatically selected the candies he wished to purchase.

"Can I get more money?" Clark asked as he left the room.
"You sure can!" I responded, "Keep doing the jobs well and you will keep earning more money."

Over the next few days, news of our school store was spreading in the grade one classroom. Another student, Greg, found out about the store from Clark and thought it would be a good thing for him too. He too needed breaks from his work and getting away from the stimulation that was the sounds and sights of the classroom, calmed him right down. We decided in addition to scheduling opportunities for movement, we would also try the store concept with Greg. He would learn the life skills of money management, organization, and independence, all while getting the needed break.

Clark and Greg were more motivated to be at school to complete jobs and earn money. However, and perhaps predictably, problems began to arise; the boys only wanted to do jobs outside of the classroom and were beginning to miss the lessons inside the class. They also insisted on going to the store as soon as they had enough money, which we had permitted; however, the store seemed to becoming an avoidance tactic rather than an incentive to work hard.

I wondered about the store; we were simply "bribing" students to behave? Were we contributing to, or detracting from, students' sense of belonging? Were we paying them to belong? Is that the lesson we were teaching? As I ruminated, I felt a presence behind me. Who could it be I wondered; the students were outside for recess? I turned around to find Bill glancing up at me. His cheeks were rosy but I could not help but notice his hands were pale, chapped, and a little worn.

"Hi Bill, why are you not outside for recess?" I questioned. I really was quite surprised to see Bill inside; although somewhat cold it was a blisteringly shiny prairie day.

Bill was silent; eventually his foot gently stammered. "I was just wondering if I could buy something from the store," he said. Oh no, I thought, now Bill is avoiding activities too—even something fun like recess—because of the store. Perhaps the store is more of a hassle than it is helpful. "Bill, now is not a good time to go shopping you need to be outside" I explained.

"Oh, well, I just wondered if you had any mitts at the store. I gave mine to Clark. I noticed he couldn't hang on to the teeter-totter because his hands were too cold […] so I gave him mine […] But […] […]" His voice trailed off as he looked down toward the floor. How could I have doubted this noble child? Once again the leadership, empathy and wisdom of this student amazed me. I guided him to my room where I kept a few extra pairs of mittens and gave him a pair "on the house." He cheerfully smiled and scurried back outside for the remainder of recess.

A few minutes later the bell rang and I rushed to the doorway where I was to supervise the students coming inside. As the students walked in I noticed Clark, smiling and gazing down at his hands. He caught me looking at him and explained how much fun he had on the teeter-totter at recess; he commented that his old school did not have one, and that it felt like flying. I could not help but smile as I thought about how Bill, ever the elder, was able to foster a sense of belonging for Clark. I moved to the boot room to oversee the transition in from recess, and witnessed many older students assisting the younger students. I noticed relationships blossoming between the younger and older students and the new and existing students. It was starting to sound, look and feel like the school they had envisioned.

A few days later, I smiled as I heard the children chatting away about the store and celebrating the successes of one another. The grade one children were living a kind of diversity and inclusivity a teacher can only dream of! And at 11:50, the door creaked open and Clark rushed toward it. Right on time, it was Bill. However, on this day Bill's normally happy demeanor was instead concerned and worried. He frantically waved his hand, looking at me as if he needed me to come and talk to him. I went to the door to see what seemed to be bothering him. I gently indicated to Clark that he needed to wait a moment.

"Hi Bill. Did you need something?" I asked.

Bill looked down and then away from me. There was a notable awkward pause, "I dunno, if I can do milk anymore." He finally offered.

"Why not? You are doing such a great job and Clark is learning so much from you." I questioned.

"I heard the milk prices are different soon and I can't count that kinda money." The look of concern grew on his face.

I suddenly remembered the struggle Bill had to learn the current pricings. I felt his fear. "Don't worry Bill." I said reassuringly, "You will learn new prices. Just think how difficult you thought these prices were, and you have those mastered." I responded. "Your classroom teacher and I will make sure you have lots of practice in math class with the new numbers before the change happens." Bill did not often show doubt in his abilities, but as he got older he began to notice that his math skills were different than the other fifth graders. Although he was in a fifth-grade class his math program was comparable to Clark's in grade one. The jobs selected for Bill were created to help him build his money skills. Counting the milk each day was a challenge as he worked on one-to-one correspondence. He celebrated the day he was able to read the clock on his own; he knew when to leave to be on time for the milk delivery. He had demonstrated so much growth in his two years at the school. Now, he was able to continue to grow as the milk prices changed and all through this he could teach Clark the process. The worried look began to fade.

"Oh, okay. Can I start showing Clark how I take the milk orders?" Bill's smile began to grow.

"Sure. Let's figure out the new prices together and then you can teach Clark." I suggested. They each nodded their heads and off they went together down the hallway. The teaching assistant followed the boys, and caught my eye; we smiled at each other. I knew the smile was a reflection of the growth we had seen in both Bill and Clark. We were proud of the independence Bill had gained and the growing sense of belonging in Clark.

That day after school, we met as a grade one team again. Heads were held higher I noticed as we sat around the large brown table. Sidebar conversations were aplenty as we waited for the meeting to begin. Shared stories and small giggles floated through the air. Things are coming along I thought. Each day there are challenges and new obstacles we face with the demanding job that is inclusive education. However, we see growth in the students. Fewer melt downs and longer time spent in the classroom. Better days for everyone. More belonging, more independence, more mastery, and more generosity [...] who knew that cartons of milk, milk already contained, could fill so many buckets! We were all encouraged.

> **Probing Questions**
>
> - One might criticize Stacey for putting too much faith in one young boy (Bill) to provide assistance and counseling to a misbehaving young boy (Clark). But her actions make sense given her orientation to her school as a community of belonging and support. What kind of community does Stacey envision in her school and how does that vision inform her actions?
> - What concepts do the teachers utilize to drive their thinking about creating a community where students feel loved and supported? Are these the only conceptual underpinnings that a school might use for this purpose? What other useful ideas and practices do you know that teachers can use to build a caring community?
> - At one point, Stacey questions whether the reward system and the school store contradict the school's emphasis on relationships and community. She wonders, "Were we paying them to belong? Is that the lesson we were teaching?" What do you think?
> - One can argue that the current climate of high stakes testing in the United States serves as a major obstacle to public schools having the strong emphasis on social, emotional, and moral development evident in this Canadian elementary school. Or one can also make the opposite argument, that the emphasis on measured achievement in the United States makes the creation of a healthy, safe learning environment all the more crucial. What do you think?

REFERENCES

Brendtro, L., Brokenleg, M., & Van Bockern, S. (2002). *Reclaiming youth at risk: Our hope for the future.* Bloomington, IN: National Education Service.

CHAPTER SIXTEEN

Inclusive Education

A Messy and Liberating Venture

EMILY NUSBAUM

Writing this chapter was much more difficult than I had imagined. Telling my story—the story of my work in inclusive education was challenging because it is all I've ever known, professionally. How could I tell the story of the only kind of work I've been involved in since finishing college? For me, inclusion in schools and community just *is*. Or at least is something that *should be*, for all kids. I've never had to "undo" any prior knowledge about disability, special education, or the places and ways that we teach kids with disabilities in order to open my mind to the practices of inclusive education.

I consider inclusive education to be both a civil right and a matter of social justice. And will readily acknowledge that it isn't always easy—but then again, transformative work rarely is! It asks us to consider difficult questions about our beliefs and commitments, to release ideas about individually held expertise, and to consider what it means to be human. Creating school communities that are inclusive of all students requires commitments far beyond the 8–3 school day.

The rest of this chapter is organized around three themes that have been essential, in my experiences, to the development of inclusive schools. I'll reflect on some of my most formative experiences from very early on in my career to more current ones, in order to highlight the importance of: a commitment to the "messiness" of inclusive work (and at the same time, how liberating this work is!); the need to operate from a capacity-building perspective; and finally, a belief in the human contribution that every individual can and wants to make. Beyond the impressive body of research about those practices that can best support academic and social/relational development for students with and without disabilities (for example: Halvorsen & Neary, 2009; Hunt & Goetz, 1997; Hunt & McDonnell, 2007; Jackson, Ryndak, & Wehmeyer, 2008–09; McGregor & Vogelsberg, 1998; Ryndak, Ward, Alper, Montgomery, & Storch, 2010), as well as the models of whole-school reform that can support all students in general education (Caustin-Theoharis & Theoharis, 2008; Causton-Theoharis, Theoharis, Bull, Cosier, & Dempf-Aldrich, 2011; Sailor & Roger, 2005), these three, core commitments have, at least for me, been the foundation of my work in schools and academia.

A COMMITMENT TO THE "MESSINESS" OF INCLUSIVE SCHOOLING

I graduated from college in 1994 and subsequently moved to Boston where, like many twenty-somethings, I cobbled together a living with a few different, part-time jobs while I applied to graduate school. I had been an anthropology and political science major in college—nothing related to education or disability. One of my part-time jobs was working with adults who had spent most of their lives in institutions in western Massachusetts. I was supposed to provide transportation from a sheltered workshop to their group home, in a suburban Boston town. One of the individuals I worked with, whose name was Patty, had never known her family—born in the 1940s, she was institutionalized at the recommendation of a physician soon after birth.

Patty would talk to me about hating the sheltered workshop. Knowing little about common practices for adults with disabilities, it made sense why she would hate it—she described boredom, not having anyone to talk to, and not understanding why her paychecks each month were under twenty dollars when she "worked" almost all day, every day. Patty wanted a job in the community, she'd tell me each afternoon on our drive home. A job in the community, in an office building, doing something like janitorial work, in a place that had a break room where she could drink coffee with coworkers. Over the two years I worked in that job, Patty became my friend. She would visit my apartment in Boston sometimes. We'd go walk around nearby college campuses and parks, go out for coffee, and talk about the life Patty wanted to have. She never wanted to talk about the majority of her life that had been spent in an institution, but rather about the life that she wanted to have in the community. Patty met some of my friends and sometimes a girlfriend and I would take her shopping for new clothes or we would just hang out talking, as girlfriends do.

The summer after college graduation, when I started the job and met Patty, someone (and I truthfully have absolutely no idea who) recommended that I apply to special education credentialing programs and become a teacher. I don't know that before this time that I'd ever thought of being a teacher, let alone a special education teacher, but I am eternally and deeply grateful for whomever it was that made this recommendation. My profession has shaped who I am today in profound ways and provided me with more gratitude, humility, and satisfaction than almost any other undertaking. So I applied—to every special education credential and Masters degree program in Boston! I knew nothing of inclusive education at the time and had no idea how to judge a good or better program. I chose the graduate program that offered me the most financial support, in the form of an urban-focused, teacher-preparation fellowship. On the first night of class, my advisor showed slides from the book *Christmas in Purgatory* (Blatt & Kaplan, 1974). I saw the kinds of places—institutions—that Patty had grown up in. I remember the words of the professor, who told us that if we wanted to perpetuate the continued segregation of individuals with disabilities than this graduate program was not for us. Or, she gave us the charge, we could work as advocates and be a part of creating a change in the systems that serve individuals with disabilities. I suppose I've taken those words to heart and tried to embody them over the course of my own professional development, and career as a teacher, teacher educator, and academic.

Additionally, as a part of receiving this fellowship, I got a job at The Patrick O'Hearn School (now renamed The Dr. William Henderson Inclusion School), a public elementary school in a very urban part of Boston. The O'Hearn did and does serve a very ethnically and economically diverse student body. And like my credential program at Boston College, the O'Hearn helped create who I am today. It was the first school that I worked in, and as such shaped how I think, teach, and talk about schools, disability, and what true inclusion of *all* students means. It was a community in the truest sense of the word. All individuals working at and attending the school were expected to support the mission of the O'Hearn—that children with and without disabilities, those from diverse family structures, and those with racial/ethnic and socioeconomic diversity, would learn and succeed together. The O'Hearn is somewhat unique. Each classroom has a general and special educator co-teaching all day. The percentage of students with IEPs, as well as those with significant and multiple support needs, is higher than natural proportions of those with disabilities in broader society. All therapies and services are delivered in heterogeneous groupings of students, typically within classroom and curricular contexts. And, when something isn't working, the school community comes together to solve problems, rather than assigning blame. Throughout the years since I worked at the O'Hearn I have been asked to respond to skeptics and nay-sayers about inclusive education. Each time, I return to my experiences there, as part of a school community that was led by the vision of then principal Dr. William Henderson, and in which each member (truly, *all* students, teachers, support staff, service providers, and parents) is valued for the contributions they are expected to and supported in making. I think about the O'Hearn School almost every time I teach, give a workshop, or am asked if inclusive education can really work.

Inclusive education requires a commitment to "messiness." I am talking about a "messiness" that is both literal and figurative; teaching, itself, is an inherently messy venture, despite how we're often taught to design and implement all kinds of curricula, interventions, and supports in our teacher education programs. I often use the phrase "if life were like a television show, this would never be happening" to describe messy life situations that don't resolve themselves easily and smoothly—well, teaching isn't like the textbooks or as neat and tidy as how you learn about it in your teacher education program. And, working in an inclusive school requires that educational professionals and families transcend many of the roles that textbooks teach us and school structures expect us to fulfill, in order to truly share expertise and value the knowledge each person offers. This is a messy venture and can make us feel uncomfortable and uneasy, but ultimately is the most liberating, as no single one of us needs to supply all of the answers or have some knowledge that will "fix" a child in any way. There is freedom in this messiness and the belief that each of us has something to contribute, is valued, and that no one is to blame when the work of inclusion doesn't quite work.

As an instructional aide at the O'Hearn, I worked primarily in a fifth grade and a kindergarten classroom. I also supported a group of students in managing and running a school-wide book swap program. And, like everyone at the O'Hearn, was expected to generally pitch in, fill gaps, and do whatever was necessary to support the participation and high achievement of all students. Those working at the O'Hearn didn't always get it right, but I don't ever remember experiencing, seeing, or hearing blame on a student when something didn't work. Too often, students with disabilities are the ones blamed when things don't work for them in schools. But at the O'Hearn, I only remember a sense of community, that we were *all* (students and families, included) in this together, and that the solutions were ours to create together. This was a commitment that we were each reminded of every day by the work of the principal, Dr. Henderson, who was omnipresent in the school, knew the names of every single person at the site, who remembered something important about you, and who is also blind. I rely on my few years working at the O'Hearn to remind me that it is possible to create and nurture a school environment that is responsive to the needs of *everyone*, in which there are all kinds of bodies, minds, ways of communicating, races, and ethnicities, and in which they are all valued. It is not a clean-cut venture that always looks pretty and feels easy, but I can attest to how good it felt to be a part of that place for the time I was.

A RELIANCE ON A CAPACITY-BUILDING PERSPECTIVE

> [...] To not presume competence is to assume that some individuals cannot learn, develop, or participate in the world. Presuming competence is nothing less than a Hippocratic oath for educators. It is a framework that says, "approach each child as wanting to be fully included, wanting acceptance and appreciation, wanting to learn, wanting to be heard, wanting to contribute." By presuming competence, educators place the burden on themselves to come up with ever more creative, innovative ways for individuals to learn. The question is no longer who can be included or who can learn, but how can we achieve inclusive education. We begin by presuming competence (http://www.unesco.org).

The assumption of competence of individuals with disabilities is a lens that scholars have used to critique educational approaches for students with disabilities and to assert that a student's difficulties with performance are not evidence of their *incapacity*, thus requiring these students to "prove" their capacity and worth as leaners (Biklen & Burke, 2006; Biklen & Duchan, 1994; Biklen & Kliewer, 2006; Kliewer, Biklen, & Kasa-Hendrickson, 2006). Rather, assuming the competence of all students in our schools, as the UNESCO quote above indicates, allows educational professionals to ask very different and totally reframing questions about *how* inclusive education is enacted and *who* should have access to it. How do we actively reframe those students who have typically been assumed to be *incompetent*, and through this reframing, contribute to the work of rewriting their institutional identities, and thus the education and opportunities that are created (versus constrained) for them? I have recently been exploring the use of a capacity-building framework can be used to talk about student support needs and to guide how language is used in IEPs and reports, as a way to make the presumption of competence an active practice in our schools.

The ability to operate from a capacity-building (versus deficit-finding) perspective is intrinsically linked, for me, to the "messiness" of inclusive education. A capacity-building stance allows school professionals to understand and redefine those areas typically described as student deficits and to support the assumed competence of students with disabilities, in order to look beyond what a student is "doing" (e.g., descriptions of student skills or behaviors), and to consider systems of support that develop and enhance capabilities (Maier & Nusbaum, 2012; Nusbaum & Rodriguez, 2010). Additionally, and as importantly, I believe it allows us to essentially remove "problems" from individual students, to shift them to ourselves, and to then see the students with whom we work (especially those who challenge us the most, in a range of ways) as having agency, autonomy, and purposefulness in the world.

My early and formative experience at the O'Hearn modeled for me how all individuals could be viewed through a capacity lens. Dr. Henderson embodied capacity and saw it in each person. He not only highlighted strengths and contributions of students, families, and every member of the school staff in many different ways, but he was also able to understand even the most individual and complex support needs of students and to do so by understanding them as valued members of the O'Hearn community. As a principal, he supported school staff in asking the most difficult questions about ourselves, especially in light of those students who challenged us the most. Dr. Henderson supported the school community in not asking why, but always revisiting the question of *how?*

For me, assuming the competence of students with disabilities and understanding every individual through a capacity framework, has become an essential part of myself, my teaching, and my academic work. As I share repeatedly in my courses and in workshops with parents and education professionals, to understand each individual and their needs, via capacity versus deficit, is a liberating practice that feels good! No longer are we required to hold all of the answers in our individual expertise (thus requiring blame be placed somewhere when our ideas don't yield the results we hope for). But rather, teaching becomes a joint venture between all those involved and allows for reciprocal and more human and humane interactions. Biklen (2012), Dean of the School of Education at Syracuse University stated it so simply: "If you want to see competence, look for it."

A BELIEF IN THE HUMAN CONTRIBUTION OF EACH INDIVIDUAL

Thomas Hehir, former director of the federal Office of Special Education Programs, now a professor at Harvard's Graduate School of Education, says inclusion is still a threatening concept because it forces people to confront preconceived notions about education, as well their own prejudices (Hehir & Katzman, 2012; Sataline, 2005). Inclusive education poses fundamental questions, such as: how do we authentically understand every student in our schools as full, complex, and as human as ourselves, who can contribute positively to a diverse society? This is a foundational principle that I think and teach about in most of my professional and academic interactions with colleagues and students. It requires two things, in my mind: (1) being able to relinquish the notion of expertise (expertise about a given disability label and characteristics associated with it, the expertise that we know, then, the best ways to respond to these characteristics, and the expertise that our years of schooling, graduate degrees, and licensures seem to confer on us) and (2) the ability to see ourselves reflected in another person, including those whose bodies move differently and unexpectedly, who might not use spoken words to communicate, or whose minds frame their interactions with the world differently than our own.

I often recall, in my courses, one of the experiences that drove me to pursue doctoral work. After leaving San Francisco Unified School District in 2001, where I had worked as an inclusion support teacher, I spent a number of years doing consulting work with school teams in northern California, focused on supporting the development of inclusive practices. My business partner and I called our consulting business "Forward Thinking" because we believed that school districts would be "forward thinking" about their practices related to students with disabilities and the development of inclusive schools. The majority of our work came from mediation or litigation between families and school districts that resulted in *mandates* that districts provide inclusive options, often one child at-a-time. During this time, I worked for three years in a small, urban school district through the federal court, as the result of a class action lawsuit. At the time, this district served over ninety-five percent non-White students, almost 100 percent of the student body experienced poverty, and there were high rates of gang affiliation. My business partner and I spent three years working alongside teachers, to bring all students with disabilities back into the district and support them in age-appropriate general education classrooms.

During our last year working in this district, I provided a great deal of support to an eighth-grade classroom at one school. Livy, a student in the classroom, had been in segregated settings until that year. She had a label of multiple disabilities, including cortical blindness, a seizure disorder, physical impairment, and intellectual disability, as well as no consistent mode of communication beyond how she used her body. When the school year started, we figured out that thrusting her left elbow was the motor function that Livy could control best. So we mounted switches on the left side her wheelchair so that she could learn to operate various technologies in the classroom and learn to use a communication device via her elbow. Livy was a fixture in her classroom. One day, when a substitute aide was working in the class and didn't notice some of the very small seizures that Livy experienced every day, a student turned and said, "hey, you missed some." And this student went on to fill in the data sheet that was used to record information about her seizures. Livy's girlfriends were being taught how to provide feeding support to her in the cafeteria. At recess they would hang on her wheelchair and talk about boys and their young, Teach for America teacher, who they all had a crush on.

At Livy's IEP meeting that year there were doctors from the seizure clinic in a nearby medical school present, as well as the school psychologist, Livy's eighth-grade teacher, support staff, myself, and her mother. Livy's mother was from Samoa and had not finished high school. She and Livy were often homeless and lived mostly in a community shelter. The school psychologist began the meeting by talking about all of the deficits he could muster. The Livy he detailed, through age equivalents, like "two months," was not the Livy that I saw and saw interacting with others in her classroom. When the school psychologist mentioned hearing loss, Livy's mother, teacher, and I all tried to counter this. We knew Livy had great hearing—this was obvious when watching how her whole body moved and responded differently when she heard the voice of the teacher entering the classroom in the morning or when she was asked to run classroom technology via the switch on her wheelchair, versus when a support staff told her it was time to leave the class and go to the bathroom. Livy's mom tried to share stories about how she knew Livy heard her when she sang and spoke to her. Soon after this, the doctors started presenting information about her brainwaves that they would measure when she visited the seizure clinic. In this meeting, with Livy's mom sitting across from them, they described her as "essentially a vegetable," literally stripping her humanness from her. I remember countering them—by describing the importance of Livy's presence and that kids always asked where she was when she was out sick for a few days. Livy's teacher and I tried to communicate that her presence was essential to the classroom community that had been established that year, but the doctor's kept countering us, by asking why a school would invest the effort to support her that we had, when she wasn't as fully human (according to their measures of brainwaves) as other students. This was, for me, a very defining moment. It is when I realized that this belief in *all* of us as human, and full of potential, was not universal. But, was indeed foundational when I consider places like the community that was Livy's classroom that year and the contributions she made by her presence in this community.

So, how do we as teachers and education professionals do this? To engage with this idea of humanness, our own ideas about who we consider to be as fully human as ourselves, and how these ideas might influence our work with students in schools? This is really difficult work. I continuously engage teachers in this process by nudging (and sometimes pushing!) them to articulate their ideas and frames of understanding about constructs like disability, "smartness," and who should have access to what kinds of curriculum and places in schools. As importantly, we work to identify together how their ideas have positive and negative implications in the lives of the individual students with whom they work.

This process of critical reflection is something that I start early on—in the very first session of an introduction course. Almost all states require that teacher candidates learn about the characteristics of the thirteen, federal disability categories that allow a student to receive special education services. An integral part of an assignment related to this requires students to look at representation of these categories and characteristics in IDEA, and other mainstream sources like the DSM and some of the "big glossy" textbooks (Brantlinger, 2006) that pervade teacher education. Students then engage in a series of reflection responses about how these descriptions make them feel, what their responses might be as a teacher if they were told a student "like this" would be coming to their classrooms, and to describe (honestly) their initial responses based soley on this kind of characteristics-based information. We then explore many first-person, autobiographical, and other kinds of representations of disability (e.g., as a political, minority group and through self-advocate versus expert-run organizations) in order to compare and contrast different ways of representing, or "knowing," disability, as well as discussion the implications of each.

CONCLUSION

Schools that don't include students with disability labels as members of age-appropriate, general education classrooms are often structured around deficit-based characteristics that become associated not only with disability labels, but more importantly, with the students to whom these labels are applied and the places that they are educated. I believe that because the O'Hearn was the first school that I worked in, and because it was a place where disability labels—or any other labels that are pervasive in schools (e.g., low-performing, low socioeconomic status, at-risk, gifted)—were not routinely utilized (beyond what is required by law in the development of IEPs), I never learned to think or talk about students in this way. As importantly, I never experienced that kind of talk that many teachers report fills hallways, teachers' break rooms, and meeting chatter. The kind of talk that gets framed in deficit-based characteristics, the problems that students *have* (and thus *cause*), and the myriad of reasons that school professionals can articulate for some students not to have access to mainstream spaces. The O'Hearn was not perfect, nor were any of the adults working there. Everyone lost her/his temper, sometimes reacted in ways that were not reflective of the work of the school, and, in essence, behaved like human beings. But ultimately, these moments were diffused by the leadership of Dr. Henderson and by the problem-solving nature of working at the O'Hearn. Dr. Henderson modeled and created the structures within the school that allowed for the problems that were solved to be about supporting the meaningful participation and achievement of every single student, versus the problems "created" by learning or behavioral deficits associated with a disability.

Perhaps my story is unique. I know that not very many people get to work at places like The O'Hearn School and with a principal like Dr. Henderson. Many of the teachers I have met over the last decade ask me how to remain true to the kind of commitments that I've described here, when the schools they work in don't support this kind of approach, when accountability measures add ever-increasing pressures that are linked to test scores on standard assessments, and where students who live outside a narrowing conception of normal continue to be segregated. And I don't have any easy answer for this, except to talk about the possibility for real, social transformation that lies at the heart of inclusive education, as well as, and perhaps more importantly, the very real transformation of the self. This is why I think about the O'Hearn almost every time I teach and every time I consider my own identity as an educator. And how I know that an inclusive school has the ability to be a model for a more equitable, just, and humane world.

> **Probing Questions**
> - How is Emily influenced by her friendship with Patty? Look closely at your own life. Have you had or do you have good friendships with persons with disabilities? What disabled person or persons have influenced your thinking about disability and inclusion?
> - Teaching at The Patrick O'Hearn School gave Emily a profound experience with inclusive education excellence. Have you spent significant time in a highly successful inclusive school? If "yes," how has that experience impacted your work as an educator? If "no," arrange to visit the best inclusive school in your area. Observe in classrooms. Talk to the students, parents, teachers, and administrators. What did you learn from that experience?
> - Emily describes an IEP meeting that starts off with a school psychologist "talking about all of the deficits he could muster." To most educators, this is a pretty familiar scene. How does IEP planning specifically and teaching in general change when we lose interest in the concept of deficits as defining features of who a student truly is? How does this shift toward John Dewey's "moral equality" concept change our approach to IEP meetings?

REFERENCES

Biklen, D. (2012). Personal communication.
Biklen, D., & Burke, J. (2006). Presuming competence. *Equity & Excellence in Education, 39,* 2, 166–175.
Biklen, D., & Duchan, J. F. (1994). "I am intelligent": The social construction of mental retardation. *Journal of the Association for Persons with Severe Handicaps, 19*(3), 173–184.
Biklen, D., & Kliewer, C. (2006). Constructing competence: Autism, voice, and the 'disordered' body. *International Journal of Inclusive Education, 10,* 2–3, 169–188.
Blatt, B., & Kaplan, F. (1966). *Christmas in purgatory: A photographic essay on mental retardation.* Boston, MA: Allyn & Bacon.
Brantlinger, E. (2006). The big glossies: How textbooks structure (special) education. In E. Brantlinger (Ed.), *Who benefits from special education? Remediating (fixing) other people's children* (pp. 45–76). Mahwah, NJ: Lawrence Erlbaum.
Causton-Theoharis, J., & Theoharis, G. (2008). Creating inclusive schools for all students. *The School Administrator,* September, 24–31.
Causton-Theoharis, J., Theoharis, G., Bull, T., Cosier, M., & Dempf-Aldrich, K. (2011). Schools of promise: A school district-university partnership centered on inclusive school reform. *Remedial and Special Education, 32,* 3, 192–205.

Halvorsen, A., & Neary, T. (2009). *Building inclusive schools: Tools and strategies for success* (2nd ed.). Boston, MA: Allyn & Bacon.

Hehir, T., & Katzman, L. I. (2012). *Effective inclusive schools: Designing successful schoolwide programs.* San Francisco, CA: Jossey Bass.

Hunt, P., & Goetz, L. (1997). Research on inclusive education programs, practices and outcomes for students with severe disabilities. *Journal of Special Education, 31*(1), 3–29.

Hunt, P., & McDonnell, J. (2007). Inclusive education. In S. L. Odom, R. H. Horner, M. E. Snell, & J. Blacher (Eds.), *Handbook of developmental disabilities* (pp. 269–291). New York: Guilford Press.

Jackson, L. M., Ryndak, D. L., Wehmeyer, M. L. (2008–09). Context, curriculum, and student learning: A case for inclusive education as a research-based practice. *Research and Practice for Persons with Severe Disabilities, 33*(4), 175–195.

Kliewer, C., Biklen, D., & Kasa-Hendrickson, C. (2006). Who may be literate? Disability and resistance to the cultural denial of competence. *American Educational Research Journal, 43*(2), 163–192.

Maier, J., & Nusbaum, E. (December, 2012). Using a capacity-building perspective to redefine student deficits and empower school teams to develop meaningful, effective, inclusive programs and supports for students with significant support needs. Paper presented at TASH annual conference, Long Beach, CA.

McGregor, G., & Vogelsberg, R. T. (1998). Inclusive schooling practices: Pedagogical and research foundations. A synthesis of the literature that informs best practices about inclusive schooling. Allegheny University of the Health Sciences.

Nusbaum, E., & Rodriguez, J. (March, 2010). Using a Capacity-building perspective to redefine student "problems." CA TASH annual conference, Burlingame, CA.

Ryndak, D., Ward, T., Alper, S., Storch, J., & Montgomery, J. (2010). Long-term outcomes of services in inclusive and self-contained settings for siblings with comparable significant disabilities. *Education and Training in Autism and Developmental Disabilities, 45*(1), 38–53.

Sailor, W., & Roger, B. (2005). Rethinking inclusion: Schoolwide applications. *Phi Delta Kappan, 86,* 7, 503–509.

Sataline, S. (January 30, 2005). A matter of principal. *The Boston Globe.* Retrieved from http://www.boston.com/news/education/k_12/articles/2005/01/30/a_matter_of_principal/?page=full.

CHAPTER SEVENTEEN

"I don't have a special world for her to live in: She has to adapt to this one"

On Becoming a Renaissance Middle Schooler

ALICIA A. BRODERICK

INTRODUCING KIM: A RENAISSANCE MIDDLE-SCHOOLER

Kimberly Harrison[1] is a middle-class, African American eighth grader living in a small, affluent, suburban community in the northeastern United States. Like many other middle-class middle schoolers in the United States, she leads a full, busy, interesting, and highly scheduled life. In addition to her demanding academic curriculum, she routinely engages in many extra-curricular activities as well, both school- and community-based. She identifies not only as a student who works hard and does well academically, but also as a musician (she sings and plays the cello), an actor and dancer (she is an actress in school and community theatre, and is both a jazz and tap dancer), and as an athlete (she plays the team sports of soccer, field hockey, and basketball, and is also an accomplished gymnast and horseback rider who competes and wins awards at very high levels in the equestrian sport of dressage). She is also an avid, experienced, and seasoned traveler, both domestically and internationally, where she occasionally has opportunity to use the French she is acquiring (through her middle school classes and a private tutor) as a second language (her first language is English). She is actively involved in the production of her middle school yearbook, and she is a lifelong Girl Scout and routine volunteer for a variety of service learning opportunities in her school and community.

Does she sleep, you ask? Through her mother's careful, thoughtful, and vigilant organization and oversight of her schedule, Kim somehow manages to get all the rest that a typical teenager requires (just). (Although her parents, almost certainly, get far less sleep than they require and desire most nights [...].) Add to this the fact that she is one of the friendliest, most polite, and genuinely happiest teenagers that you are ever likely to meet, and you may begin to wonder if this young woman is merely a figment of my idealistic imagination. I assure you, she is not (and anyone who knows me will also assure you that my imagination tends toward the dystopic rather than the idealistic, anyway).

She also happens to be autistic and she has received special education and related services since she was less than two years of age. I reserve this description for the close of this brief profile of Kim not because I believe it to be an unimportant facet of her identity, nor because I believe it to be incongruent with the many other facets of her identity (I believe neither of these things); rather, I reserve this description of Kim as autistic for the close of her profile precisely because it is not currently part of her identity at all; at least, not of her self-identity. Kim does not currently identify as autistic, although she would readily identify herself to others as a dancer, athlete, musician, student, etc., as described above. According to Kim's mother, Alex, "We've never used the words 'autism' or 'autistic' with her—she just doesn't think of herself as autistic. She knows that she has an IEP, and she knows that she needs some supports that other kids don't necessarily have, and that everyone learns differently, but she doesn't identify as autistic."[2] Nevertheless, Kim's "story of success" with inclusion in school is integrally bound up with the fact that she has reams and reams of files and paperwork that identify her as autistic, and therefore her "inclusion" as being a matter of concern to the school district as mediated through the spirit and the letter of the Individuals with Disabilities Education Improvement Act (IDEIA, 2004). While Kim may not identify as autistic, other people, including the many highly competent school-based teachers and other professionals who have worked with Kim during her lifetime, almost certainly identify her as a successfully included autistic student.

In narrating the story of Kimberly's successful inclusion in school, and her growth into what I call a "Renaissance Middle-Schooler," I will tell the story of supports and resources facilitating that growth that are provided by (a) her family and (b) her school-based teams. Ultimately, it is the collaborative relationship forged between these two highly interested parties, coupled with the indomitable stamina, drive, hard work, and ingenuity of Kim herself, that create the synergetic circumstances under which this Renaissance Middle-Schooler has grown and thrived. I begin by narrating the story of Kimberly's family and the unwavering strength of their supports—emotional, social, material, and otherwise—that they have always provided her with to facilitate and scaffold her growth and development into the remarkable young woman that she has become.

"I DON'T HAVE A SPECIAL WORLD FOR HER TO LIVE IN: SHE HAS TO ADAPT TO THIS ONE"

If there is one persistent theme across the efforts of Kim's parents to support her success in school, it is the repeated demonstration that they will stop at nothing, going to the proverbial ends of the earth to secure any experience, service, or perspective that will be of potential benefit to their daughter (which is an observation that can be made of most parents, within the limits of their means—informational, economic, and otherwise). For example, in the early days, Kim's autism manifested itself, as it does for many children, in significantly delayed language development coupled with difficulty tolerating, processing, and integrating sensory information. The two of these combined created behavioral manifestations that involved a lot of tantrums and other challenging behaviors. Alex and Jim decided that living their lives with these presentations simply was not an option, and aggressively sought the supports necessary to manage her unpredictable behavior and to quickly augment her language development and support her sensory desensitization and integration. Thus, very early on, her parents advocated and sought for her (as many parents do) a private, specialized, and segregated school for students with labels of autism, a school that utilized an approach to teaching and learning grounded primarily in Applied Behavior Analysis (ABA), coupled with intensive speech and language therapy, and physical and occupational therapies.

However, as Kim transitioned to first grade, her parents were already concerned about her future (limited) access to academic curriculum if she remained at the ABA school long-term, and they seized the opportunity for their school district to reclaim responsibility for Kim's education, to transition her back within-district to a local elementary school (although not Kim's neighborhood school—it was, rather, the best-resourced elementary school in the district). This decision was strategic on her parents' part, and turned out to be quite a savvy one in the long run—Kim was initially placed there because that was where the district housed a self-contained classroom for students considered to have "significant" disabilities. Almost immediately upon enrolling her in this segregated classroom, her parents advocated for her inclusion in a general education class at her grade level, with supplementary and resource supports provided by the special educator from the self-contained room, a range of related service professionals, and an inclusion consultant (me). By the time Kim was old enough to be transitioned to the district's self-contained classroom for third, fourth, and fifth graders with significant disabilities (housed in another school), her parents were able to successfully make the argument that Kim had experienced success with inclusive participation in her first- and second-grade classrooms, that she had built relationships with her peers that were a central facet of her success, and that disrupting those relationships by moving her to a different building would be detrimental to Kim's future academic success. Thus, Kim's parents successfully secured her continuing membership as a student in a general education classroom in the best-resourced elementary school in the district, which happened also to feed into the best-resourced middle school in the district.

From the very beginning, Kim's parents understood very well that she was entitled not to the best education possible (every parent's goal for their child), but rather, only to "an appropriate education" under IDEIA. Therefore, when no one in district had expertise around inclusive pedagogy and practice, they accepted this limitation and privately secured my participation on Kim's team as an inclusion consultant. Likewise, when Kim's IEP teams determined that she was eligible for a lesser degree or level of related service than her parents believed would benefit her, they secured the supplemental service provision privately, and then actively facilitated communication themselves between Kim's school-based IEP team and her private speech and occupational therapists.

None of this has been easy for Kim's parents, although they recognize how fortunate they are to have accrued the cultural and economic capital that they have in their lifetimes, and they wield it strategically and incisively in order to secure for Kim the advantages that will benefit her. Both Kim's mother, Alex, and her father, Jim, grew up solidly working class and are strong believers in the power of education to support upward social mobility, as it did for each of them (they hold several advanced postgraduate degrees between them). Alex is a physician running a small private practice as her "day job," although she also works a full-time second shift in managing Kim's schooling and other activities. Jim holds two advanced post-secondary degrees in engineering and is an elected local official, which gives their family a somewhat higher profile within the school district than many families have, something that has undoubtedly "greased the wheels" on occasion in the family's interactions with the school district around questions of securing services for their daughter. Jim works his second shift teaching classes at a local university, and this shared occupational situation (both of university teaching and of juggling more than one job) caused Jim and I to have a good laugh some years ago when he pointed out to me that, "it doesn't matter how prestigious your day job is—if you're still working more than one job, you're still working class!"

The Harrisons expect no less of Kim than they do of themselves. They have worked very hard to give her every opportunity that their resources can provide, but ultimately, they expect Kim to do her best to work and to learn and to grow and to expand her skills and her thinking and her horizons. I once asked Alex what feeds the vigor and apparent ferocity with which she and Jim have sought to actively cultivate Kim's learning and growth over the years, and she told me that she realized very early on that "I don't have a special world for her to live in. She has to adapt to this one." And that has been the goal that has been aggressively sought for Kim from the time she was a toddler—to adapt to the expectations of a nondisabled world to the very best of her ability and of the family's resources for supports, in order to hopefully mitigate the many insecurities her parents fear she may potentially face as a disabled adult in that world.

Alex and Jim also know that "autism" is probably the first word that school professionals see when they look at Kim's paperwork, before they have even met or had a chance to interact with Kim. For this reason, and knowing full well the cultural stereotypes and misinformation and stigma that can accompany this label, they have always aggressively sought to make Kim, not her autism, the center of her educational planning. For example, when working with a new school team, they bring the most updated version of an "all about me" booklet that they've put together with Kim each year to document some of her activities and accomplishments of the previous year. It's a small photo album, with captions written either by Kim or her parents, showing off significant events like musical, dance, or theatrical performances that she's participated in over the past year, her active participation in a variety of sporting events, public speaking opportunities she's had or awards ceremonies she's been recognized in, participation in family celebrations, or fun activities from her latest travel (which may include rock climbing, parasailing, scuba diving or even bungee jumping!). All of these efforts are about managing expectations, and ensuring that teachers' expectations of Kim are exceptionally high. Her parents point out to teachers that, after reading Kim's IEP files, they may not have readily imagined her (fill in the blank—scuba diving, winning a regional gymnastics competition, etc.), and yet, here is a photo of her doing just that. Their plea to her teachers is not to let the limitations of their own imaginations limit the opportunities they provide to Kim or the expectations they hold of her in terms of her academic achievement and accomplishments. It has proven to be a remarkably effective strategy over the years, as her teachers continue to expect her to reach the stars, and she continues to meet them there, with only minor bumps along the ways as the team figures out what supports she may need to enable her to get there.

A key structural support to working so successfully with Kim's school teams over the years has been the standing monthly team meeting that Kim's parents hold with her case manager, her related service professionals, her paraprofessional, and her classroom teachers—with all of these parties around the table for a forty-five-minute meeting once a month, her parents have been able to ensure that her services have been well-coordinated, that any problems are identified and responded to as soon as they arise, and that a genuinely collegial working relationship between family and school is cultivated, working as closely and as frequently as they do with one another. Kim's parents are aware that not all parents in the district would necessarily ask for such close collaborative involvement with the school, and that of those who do request it, not all of them will probably have been granted the access to their child's school teams that they have been granted to Kim's. However, this awareness of a potential inequity in the district's implementation of IDEIA does not deter them from pursuing every benefit they can for their own daughter—that is, after all, their singular goal. If other disabled students and their families benefit from the relationship they have forged with the district, and the innovations in providing her supports and services, so much the better; however, systemic change or reform of special education or of inclusive schooling is not what they seek. The prize on which they tenaciously keep their eyes is the best possible education they can secure for their Kimberly.

INCLUSIVE PEDAGOGIES AND RIGOROUS CURRICULUM

In narrating the story of Kimberly's successful inclusion in school, her supportive and devoted family is only half of the picture of the myriad supports and resources that have facilitated her growth into the Renaissance Middle-Schooler that she is. The second half of this story is the story of the school context within which she has emerged as the competent young woman that she is. I next illustrate several components of that context through the use of a composite vignette, combining elements of many of her classrooms and of her teachers into a representative illustration of several key supports to Kim's successful inclusion in both elementary and middle school.

Every classroom in Kim's elementary and middle schools is equipped with SmartBoard technology. The expenditures for installing these improvements to the physical and technological infrastructure of the schools did not come out of the district's $14,850 per year per pupil expenditures; rather, the funds were raised by the schools' Parent Teacher Associations (PTAs). In federal and state formulas designed to attempt to equalize per pupil expenditures in relatively poor districts to compete with the resources available through property taxation in a relatively affluent district such as Kimberly's, the "soft" socioeconomic resources of the families in the more affluent districts and their considerable support of their children's schools through funding mechanisms such as PTA donations is not accounted for. And although many classrooms in Title I districts are now similarly equipped with SmartBoards™ or similar technologies through government or foundation grants, a key difference that I have observed between Title I districts and districts like Kimberly's has been the education and training provided (or not) to the teachers to enable them to maximize the benefit of such technological resources. In many Title I schools equipped with projectors and touch screen technologies, the resources are underutilized by teachers who have not had adequate training to exploit the many potential benefits of using such technologies. Enter this composite vignette with me to explore the ways in which Kim's teachers were able to exploit these technologies to the benefit of all students in the classroom, including, though by no means limited to, students who may have IEPs.

It is 9:34 and the students are filing into their seventh-grade science classroom. Kim is seated at a lab-style desk with one other student. On the projector at the front of the room is a prompt listing ten abbreviations of elements from the periodic table, each of which was discussed in the assigned reading from last night's homework (NA, H, FE, O, etc.), and asking each pair of students to write out as many names of the elements as they can remember. Students have their heads together, members of each pair wracking their brains to complete the list in the time allotted. Most groups come up with seven or eight. Kim and her partner are the only group to correctly identify all ten of the elements listed—in large part due to the fact that Kim's first period resource room with her special educator is used (as it has been for years) to *preteach* today's material from her more challenging classes, rather than primarily to *reteach* things that she has demonstrated difficulty with, as resource room time is more commonly used for. The students are not aware of this pedagogical strategy; they simply know that having Kim for a lab partner is a considerable asset, and that she contributes much to the small- and large-group discussions in class.

Kimberly has some difficulty with processing auditory information, and so learns best when information is presented to her in graphic, spatial, and experiential forms. She watches intently as Ms. Austin, the science teacher, after acknowledging Kim and her partner for their ten correct responses, now displays on the projection screen an application that she is running on her (personally owned) iPad—it is an application of the periodic table of elements. She randomly selects several of the elements that the students were asked to identify from the abbreviations, and the students watch as the atomic structure of the element is rotated in three dimensions before their very eyes. After going through several of the elements, she uses the touch screen to pull up two hydrogen atoms and an oxygen atom, and the students are again able to see how the elements combine to create a water molecule. Had Kim merely read a chapter explaining this, it may have been difficult for her to maintain attention and possibly to understand the vocabulary load; had she merely listened to her teacher lecture a description of how this happens she almost certainly would have been unable to attend to and process the whole lecture; however, because these modalities have been so successfully combined (having already read about it, having already had it orally explained to her, and now having it graphically and dynamically demonstrated before her eyes), Kim is able to grasp these concepts quite solidly (as are the other students with whom she shares the classroom).

It is difficult for me to imagine a lesson of this nature being conducted with the seventh graders attending the segregated school where Kim began her school career (not because the students were not capable of benefitting from such a lesson, but simply because the school did not routinely expose their students to such a rigorous academic curriculum as this public school does theirs).

The lesson continues with the students' active and systematic exploration of the properties of water in interaction with a variety of surfaces (aluminum foil, wax paper, paper towel, and notebook paper), this time, in groups of four. Through use of the SmartBoard™, Ms. Austin next provides a sequence of instructions in enumerated visual format, in addition to her verbal issuing of those sequenced instructions for students to follow. It has been well documented that Kimberly benefits considerably (as do many students) from the provision of visual information to supplement auditory information, particularly when the information involves a sequence of multiple steps or directions. The sequence of instructions remains visible on the board throughout the experimentation period, and many students (Kim included) make reference to the sequence through the activity to make sure they are completing the required steps in the prescribed order. While the students are reporting to the class their carefully documented observations of what had happened as the water droplets interacted with these different surfaces, Ms. Austin now uses the SmartBoard™ to display her summary and documentation of students' verbal comments. This not only provides another example of Ms. Austin ensuring the provision of information in both visual as well as verbal form, it also has the added benefit of modeling for students the routine use of keyboarding skills and available technologies to enhance the instructional experiences of all students.

Had the classroom teacher not used the SmartBoard™ in these well-integrated ways, it might have been my recommendation that Kimberly's 1:1 aide make use of a laptop or other individualized form of assistive technology to list the sequence of instructions and to visually document the discussion so as to make it more accessible for Kim. However, Ms. Austin's routine use of the SmartBoard™ technology is a wonderful example of the ways in which the greater the universal design of a teacher's curriculum and instruction, the lesser the needs for individualized student supports will be. Several goals are achieved in this way: (a) the needs for individualized (and potentially stigmatizing) supports for Kimberly and other visual learners are significantly diminished, (b) the rest of the students benefit from having the provision of information in multiple modalities, even if they do not require them in order to benefit from the instruction, and (c) the technological literacy of the entire class is enhanced through such routine and well-integrated opportunities to utilize technology in their routine instructional experiences.

An additional key feature of Kim's schooling context supporting her successful experience with inclusion that this vignette illustrates involves the hands-on, exploratory, and constructivist nature of the approach to the curriculum that Ms. Austin employed. Rather than employing a textbook-based, didactic or directive approach to the concepts of the lesson, the lesson was constructed as an exploratory experience in which all students were able to fully and meaningfully participate. I was very pleased to observe, in fact, that Kimberly's participation on at least two observed occasions expanded and further contributed to her peers' exploration of the relevant concepts. For example, Kim discovered that due to the surface tension of the water on aluminum foil, a dropper could be used to "drag" water droplets from one to another in order to form a single, larger droplet. Having discovered this on her own, Kim quickly demonstrated it to her peers, who each began to explore this particular property further on their own. In addition, when making observations about what happened to water droplets on a particular surface (that of notebook paper), Kim furthered her group's thinking considerably by introducing another factor to their thinking—that of distance or height from which the water is dropped. Several students in Kim's group dropped their droplets of water from their water droppers onto a sheet of notebook paper from six to ten inches above the surface, and were unanimously documenting that the water "splattered" on the surface of the paper. Kim introduced another element to her exploration, by first "splattering" a droplet from a height similar to her peers, then by placing the dropper about an inch above the surface of the paper and releasing a single drop. Without the distance to fall, the water droplet remained as a bead on the surface, without "splattering" as it had from the previous height. Kimberly again quickly demonstrated her observation to her peers, who then joined her in experimenting with the ways in which height the water was dropped from affected the properties of the water when it hit the particular surface.

As is the case with good constructivist, cooperative learning arrangements in which groupings are purposefully heterogeneous, everyone learns and benefits from the heterogeneity of the group. Had the concepts of this lesson been presented in a didactic manner that was overly reliant on either lecture (auditory processing of information) or the reading of a textbook, its content may have been made inaccessible to Kimberly (and likely to other students) in a number of ways. However, due to the pedagogical approaches employed by Ms. Austin, not only was the lesson *not in*accessible to Kim, she also emerged as a leader and a significant contributor to her peers' learning processes. I observed in Ms. Austin a very talented, dynamic, constructivist teacher who seemed to be well-skilled in making relevant use of the available instructional technologies, making their use a routine and integral part of her pedagogy and therefore of students' instructional experiences in the classroom. Through her integrated use of classroom technologies, Ms. Austin managed to provide to all of the students a number of the individualized supports that also happen to be particularly helpful to Kimberly's learning strengths and needs.

Kimberly also routinely experiences more teacher-directed forms of instruction; however, she and her classmates are fortunate to routinely experience a balance of teacher-directed pedagogies with more student-centered, actively engaging pedagogies richly embedded with instructional technologies, inquiry, and critical thinking.

Whether it be a science lesson in which students actively explore and document their own observations of the properties of a particular substance, or a language arts lesson where the students split into groups to act out a scene from a novel from each of several characters' perspectives, or a social studies activity where students actively simulate the economic and social relations in the North and South under reconstruction, Kimberly has had the benefit throughout her elementary and middle school years of access to rigorous academic curriculum, excellent instruction and pedagogy, and whatever individualized supplementary supports and resources she has required to fully benefit from that access.

DISCUSSION: THE ROLE OF SOCIAL CLASS IN CULTIVATING A RENAISSANCE MIDDLE-SCHOOLER

When I show my teacher education students documentary films of "successful inclusion" experiences, such as *Including Samuel* (Habib, 2009) or *You're Going to Love this Kid* (Kluth, 2012), their primary and most immediate critiques are twofold (and are remarkably consistent across time and different classes): (a) the schools featured in the films appear to be very well-resourced, and not at all representative of the under-resourced urban schools in which many of them work and (b) the individual students and student bodies of schools featured in the films are predominantly White, with many fewer students and families of color represented. I thus cannot help but feel the need to preempt the "yeah, but [...]" response that I know my own students will have to Kim's narrative with a brief analysis of the ways that social class and race come into play in her successful experience with inclusive schooling.

The question of financial resources appears to me so obvious that it hardly merits mentioning—the kind of schooling experiences that Kim has had (e.g., with consistent access to rich curriculum and engaging materials, ample and current technological resources, and ample human resources [as manifested by her 1:1 classroom aide, her classroom teachers having consistent access to a coteacher certified as a Teacher of Students with Disabilities, and the "soft" benefits of very well-resourced arts, athletics, and other extracurricular programs]) are more easily facilitated in the presence of ample financial and other material resources. This is not to say that students cannot also have rich and similar experiences in under-resourced schools; merely that it is easier to create such experiences for students when resources are adequate and/or ample. However, I do not think that the material resources afforded her through her schooling experiences are the most salient manifestation of how social class comes into play in Kim's successful experience with inclusive education. A related (and arguably more significant) benefit to having access to these kinds of material resources is, for example, the general class-based presumption within the district that all students are college-bound. All of the classes in her middle school proceed from this assumption, and expose kids to and support kids to learn a rigorous academic curriculum (even kids with some significant needs for academic supports). In a more socioeconomically diverse district and/or school building, it is more likely that discrepancies among academic tracks would be greater, and that Kim would be at greater risk, simply due to her having an IEP, of being placed in a low academic track without the expectation of preparing her for the possibility of post-secondary education, should she desire it.

Thus, the successful synergy of Kim's experience with inclusive education is perhaps less about the availability of material capital and more about the presence of what Bourdieu (1986) terms "cultural capital." The brief narrative analysis offered here about Kimberly Harrison's experiences with successful inclusive schooling is entirely consistent with the in-depth sociological analyses of the ways that class and race operate in schooling offered by Lareau (2000, 2011). Drawing heavily upon Bourdieu's notion of cultural capital, Lareau (2011) argues that "organized activities, established and controlled by mothers and fathers, dominate the lives of middle-class children [...]. By making certain their children have these and other experiences, middle-class parents engage in a process of *concerted cultivation*" (pp. 1–2, emphasis in original). In this longitudinal sociological study, Lareau describes the differential logics and approaches to child rearing that emerge between middle class families and working class and/or poor families, documenting a consistent pattern of concerted cultivation across the middle-class families participating in the study, both Black families and White families. Indeed, Lareau argues that "the biggest differences in the cultural logic of child rearing in the day-to-day behavior of children in this study were between middle-class children on the one hand (including wealthy members of the middle class) and working-class and poor children on the other" (p. 241), and that the experiences of Black and White children of the same social class have much more in common than do the experiences of either White or Black children across social classes. I mentioned early on that Kimberly attended the best-resourced elementary and middle-schools in her district, but that they were not her home schools. What I didn't mention at the time was that the majority of other African American students in the district (and African American families make up only three percent of the population in this predominantly White suburb) attended what would have been Kim's home school, which she did not attend. It must have been a difficult decision for her parents to elect to put her in a schooling situation where she would so often be the only African American student in her class, but, consistent with Lareau's (2011) findings about the logic of childrearing, in most cases, "race mattered less [...] than did [...] social class" (p. 241).

However, for middle-class parents, like the Harrisons, who ascribe to the logic and practices of concerted cultivation as an approach to child-rearing, a couple of distinct advantages when interacting with schools may emerge. One distinct advantage they may experience is the relative congruence of that perspective with dominant professional standards and beliefs about child-rearing, a congruence that tends to lead to "the *transmission of differential advantages* to children" (Lareau, 2011, p. 5, emphasis in original). Thus, the logic of concerted cultivation that the Harrisons employ in their approach to rearing Kimberly to "adapt" to the nondisabled world, through countless therapies, interventions, organized activities, and extracurricular experiences, is entirely congruent with the childrearing beliefs and practices of the majority of the parents in her school, as well as with the school administration and faculty. They are all collectively engaged in the business of very actively seeking to cultivate Renaissance teenagers: Is the child a little bit shy or uncomfortable with public speaking? Put him in a drama club. Is the child's hand-eye coordination a bit of a challenge for them? Get her in a t-ball league when she's four and follow it up with organized leagues straight up through high school (and maybe beyond—could be a scholarship possibility for college). Does the child enjoy singing and dancing? Get her in private voice and dance lessons and performing publicly by the time she's a teenager. Is the child struggling a little bit with his Spanish language class? Sign him up with a private language tutor. Are you worried about your child's potential performance on standardized tests such as their SATs? Sign him or her up for classes designed to teach test-taking strategy and thereby maximize their scores as much as possible, simply through direct instruction in the "rules of the game." Kimberly's many therapies, activities, and supplemental services she receives in school are not at all out of place or out of step with this cultural ethos about childrearing. Her family is doing what every other family in the school is doing, and it doesn't necessarily look all that different just because her files say she is autistic.

Families that practice concerted cultivation also tend to already possess and exercise some sense of entitlement, particularly in interaction with social institutions such as schools, and to actively cultivate the emergence of such a sense of entitlement in their children (Lareau, 2000). Thus, while it is conceivable that a working-class family whose child attended Kim's very well-resourced school may still enjoy material benefits from access to those resources, it also seems likely that unless those working-class parents were to exercise a sense of entitlement to full access and benefit of available resources, their child may not have experienced an education quite as rich as Kimberly's has been. Coordinating schedules so that four to five school professionals can meet on a monthly basis with families, for forty-five minutes at a time, and to engage in sometimes daily e-mail and telephone correspondence in between those meetings for purposes of follow-up, is not something that is generally offered to families. Had the Harrisons not assertively asked for such arrangements to be made, it seems unlikely that Kim would have benefitted from them. Likewise for the arrangement of her resource room time being spent in preteaching rather than reteaching material: It takes more work, planning, and time on the part of teachers to organize such a use of resource time (e.g., it requires that the teachers communicate ahead of time what sorts of curricular content will need to be covered, rather than the more passive, yet more dominant, practice of letting the student bring to the resource room the assignments that were covered in class that day, where they may be retaught if necessary), and it seems unlikely to me that such arrangements would have been made, even in the presence of ample material and human resources, in the absence of the cultural capital of a family insisting that the resources be allocated in this way, because it would be of greater benefit to their child.

If there is a critique to be made of this experience, it is not of Kim, nor her family, nor her school; rather, it is a critique of the culture within which this conceptualization of a "successful" experience with inclusive education emerges. There is an element of "passing" at work here: Kimberly's experience with inclusive education may be regarded as successful in part because she has been so well "cultivated," and therefore blends in so well with the cultivated nondisabled Renaissance middle schoolers—she speaks thoughtfully and eloquently (even if her syntax and vocabulary may not always be on a par with the most sophisticated of her peers), she presents no difficult or unusual behavioral challenges, and she is a pleasant, friendly, and sociable kid—in short, she is a pleasure to be around. Her mother's clear, simple, and adaptive explanation to me for the nature and intensity of her efforts on her daughter's behalf is a supremely pragmatic one: "I don't have a special world for her to live in: She has to adapt to this one." There is not room in her calculations for ideology; there is not room for reform or cultural change—the litmus test for every decision is what will enable her daughter not only to survive, but also to thrive? It is the answers to these questions, not an indulgence in cultural or ideological critique, that guide Alex and Jim's decision-making. And access to every advantage that a family can muster—material capital, cultural capital, etc.—must be brought to bear if their child is to get the education that every parent believes their child is entitled to (the best available), even in the legal context of a law that only guarantees access to an education that is "appropriate."

Kimberly's experience highlights for us what is possible in creating inclusive educational experiences. The perennial challenge before us now, as always it has been, is to figure out ways to create the best of inclusive educational schooling experiences for *all* students, not merely for those whose parents are so fortunate as to be in a position to create them. If pragmatics must drive the decisions of parents (and they must; parents cannot wait for equity to be offered to them), then political and ideological commitments to dismantle educational inequities must be what drives school professionals. No matter how privileged a family's cultural and other forms of capital, being ideologically, rather than pragmatically, driven in making decisions about their children's futures is a luxury that most families simply don't have.

> **Probing Questions**
> - Alicia's description of Kimberly as "A Renaissance Middle-Schooler" makes it abundantly clear that this young person is highly talented and very complex. What is the broader message that Alicia is communicating about how we view disabled persons?
> - Kimberly's parents work very hard to secure an inclusive education for their daughter. Are they trying to create dramatic change in a school so that other disabled children have greater access? Or are they merely attempting to create a usable inclusive pathway for their one child?
> - The communication between parents and school in this case is extensive and very effective. Specifically, what do both sides do to make this collaboration work?
> - The politics of race, social class, disability and political privilege in regard to Kimberly and her family are complex. One can argue that her school district is offering her an education that other African American children with a disability do not receive. The author also notes that Kimberly may be "passing" as a nondisabled student in order to receive a better education. What are the complex politics that play out in this narrative of effective inclusion?

REFERENCES

Bourdieu, P. (1986). The forms of capital. In J. Richardson (Ed.), *Handbook of theory and research for the sociology of education* (pp. 241–258). New York: Greenwood.

Habib, D. (2009). *Including Samuel (DVD)*. Concord, NH: DH Photography.

Kluth, P. (2012). *"You're going to love this kid!" A professional development package for teaching students with autism in the inclusive classroom (DVD)*. Baltimore, MD: Paul H. Brookes.

Lareau, A. (2000). *Home advantage: Social class and parental intervention in elementary education* (2nd ed.). Lanham, MD: Rowman and Littlefield Publishers.

Lareau, A. (2011). *Unequal childhoods: Class, race, and family life* (2nd ed.). Berkeley: University of California Press.

NOTES

1. Kimberly Harrison is a pseudonym, as are all other names of individuals, schools, and other locations provided. Descriptive and other identifying information has been altered to protect the anonymity and confidentiality of Kimberly and her family, school district, and community.
2. I use identity-first (e.g., "autistic person") rather than "people-first" (e.g., "person with autism") language in this manuscript, in solidarity with the many autistic activists and self-advocates who claim identity-first usage as a purposeful political act, claiming their autism as an integral and central facet of their identity, rather than as an external and presumably negative appendage that one "has." I do so despite the fact that Kim does not personally identify as "autistic," in part also because I have on many occasions heard her parents refer to her as "autistic," and I know them to be comfortable with this usage, although I do not believe they use it with the same political intent as many autistic activists do.

CHAPTER EIGHTEEN

Including Talia

A Mother's Tale

KATHY KOTEL

After a busy morning of packing up school supplies, making lunches, taking pictures, and sending my three kids off to another first day of school, I realized that the anxious feeling I usually have on the first day was not there. Most mothers are somewhat excited about having some peace and quiet and the opportunity to get their houses back in order after a fun-filled summer. I feel that excitement too, but I also feel anxious at the beginning of each school year. My daughter, Talia, was born with Down Syndrome and with the start of each school year comes the fear of the unknown. Will her teachers understand her? Will other kids make fun of her? Will she receive the appropriate support, accommodations, and modifications? Will she be challenged, but not overwhelmed? Most importantly will she learn and have fun?

All the years of uncertainty led my daughter and me to that day. It was her first day of fifth grade and she was still fully included. When she entered kindergarten I hoped that she would be included through second grade. I never really thought much beyond that. That day I was so proud of her and all that she accomplished throughout the years. I felt secure and relieved knowing that the previous five years had successfully prepared her for fifth grade and as a parent I had come to fully trust all her teachers and their commitment to do whatever it takes to make her educational experience a success. The five years were not without struggles or concerns, nor was there a specific plan as to how to provide an inclusive opportunity for Talia. After all, the academic gap usually widens and the curriculum becomes a little more challenging to modify as students with intellectual disabilities progress through the school system. But over time we had built an amazing team that spent much time planning and collaborating about how to best meet Talia's needs in the general education classroom. No one had given up on her. I knew it was important to keep her in the general education classroom with her peers because I saw how many connections she made to her world after being exposed to the general education curriculum, how much she benefitted socially from being with her peers in the same classroom all day and how much they benefitted from her, and how this helped her engage with confidence in her world.

Talia's third-grade teacher, Miss Johnson, told me about a time when she asked her class what made an author a good author. Since this was the beginning of the year, she didn't know her students that well yet. Talia raised her hand but Miss Johnson was a bit hesitant to call on her. She wasn't sure if Talia understood the question or would know the correct answer and she didn't want to embarrass her. Taking a risk the teacher decided to call on her. Talia responded with something to the extent that a good author "uses a lot of words." The teacher accepted her response. From a young child's perspective, a good author does use a lot of words to communicate his or her thoughts. The teacher then went on to explain that authors use a lot of words to express their ideas with more details. The describing words authors use are called adjectives […] and so the lesson on adjectives began. My daughter probably did not know that describing words are called adjectives or that the lesson was going to be on adjectives, but she contributed to the class discussion and her response was accurate and expanded upon by the teacher. This situation not only made Talia a valued class member but it helped to create a very safe environment for all the children.

We were visiting New York City one weekend. After dinner one evening, we walked outside after dark. Talia looked up at all the buildings illuminating with the bright lights and said, "Mommy look up. It is beautiful. I drew the lights in the sky." I wasn't sure what she was talking about, but when I went to the open house a few weeks later, there were drawings of city skylines with buildings lit up in the night that she had drawn in class after studying cities in social studies. She made her own connection from classroom to real world.

If any type of situation arose throughout the school year, we had developed an open and honest communication system that allowed us to work through it together. Our conversations helped create deeper understanding of the different situations. Over time when I saw on caller ID that school was calling, the nervous feeling started to diminish. The phone calls became an invitation to work together and collaborate as a team. Some of our conversations were a bit humorous. I remember one phone call when her teacher, Mrs. Sanders, called to let me know Talia had used a cuss word. We ended up laughing because even though using cuss words are not allowed and considered inappropriate, we were so proud that she used the word appropriately within the context of the situation. Talia dropped her books and one of them landed on her toes. It hurt and she expressed her pain. She clearly articulated the new word so well that Mrs. Sanders had to make a call home to let me know that Talia had to stay in for recess as a consequence for her inappropriate use of language.

I was grateful for all her teachers, therapists, and administrators who were committed to working toward an inclusive environment. I did not want her to leave Lincoln School. The environment was encouraging and accepting of her. If there was a sixth-grade class in the same building we would just continue on with what we had been doing [...] taking one year at a time, adapting and modifying the curriculum, providing supports and opportunities for Talia to get involved in all the school activities, encouraging her to take risks, collaborating on yearly goals [...].

As much as I did not want to think about the transition into middle school, I knew it was crucial that I explore placement options and that planning for a successful transition and middle school experience would require time and team work. I would have to focus on what I wanted for my daughter and her future. I would have to communicate my desires and goals and the reasons why these goals were important to her new team.

In preparing for the transition from elementary school to middle school I was aware of some of the barriers and limitations we were up against. My first experience with our middle school was my son's sixth-grade parent-teacher conference. At that time the conferences were held in the gymnasium instead of the individual classrooms. When I walked downstairs to where the gyms were located, I was not prepared for what I saw. The two gym entrances were separated by a small wall with two signs. One sign said *general education* with an arrow pointing to the right and another sign said *special education* with a sign pointing to the left. This vision reminded me of the photograph often used in history books showing the separate drinking fountains of the 1950s. I could not believe that in 2008 I lived in a world so insensitive to disability. The thought of Talia attending middle school there made me sick. I wanted to enact my rights as a parent and take away her IEP, so that she would be denied services and would fail and Lincoln School would be forced to retain her in the fifth grade. I would have been content keeping her at her elementary school until she turned twenty-two instead of allowing her to attend a school that clearly was that insensitive. I couldn't imagine that her educational opportunities were going to be that much better. Knowing this wasn't a real option but feeling desperate, I met with our elementary principal, Dr. Kurnyn, shortly after Talia started fifth grade and shared my concerns about transitioning from a school that believed, supported, and practiced inclusion to a school that allowed such blatant separation and segregation. She recommended I observe the placement options and meet with the middle school principal.

A meeting was set up for after winter break and I was very optimistic and confident of my ability to ask questions and share my goals for my daughter in the hopes of setting a tone of team work and collaboration. I was a middle school teacher for thirteen years prior to having my own children. I was aware of many of the challenges including a child with an intellectual disability; the possible resistance from teachers whose belief system did not align with inclusive education; the lack of training and support for teachers; the lack of understanding of what appropriate modifications and accommodations would support a child's learning; the limitations with scheduling and assessment, cost etc. [...] But I also knew of the possibilities.

What I was hoping for from this initial meeting and observation was a feeling that my daughter was going to be accepted, included and a valued member of the school. Instead, I felt like she was going to be segregated, isolated from the other students, not challenged academically, left out, and not part of the school community. Throughout the meeting there was resistance toward an inclusive placement, assumptions made about my daughter, and expressions of low expectations and limitations based on unexamined beliefs about disability. At one point during the tour of the building, when we were by the PE locker rooms, I mentioned that Talia would need a few extra minutes to change. The assistant principal, Ms. Andress, responded by saying she could change upstairs in the bathroom. I was confused because I said "a few extra minutes" not "separate place." Talia did not need to go upstairs in a separate bathroom to change. She could change in the locker room with her peers. She would just need a few extra minutes to dress and undress because she has some difficulty with the fine motor skills necessary for dressing. I also mentioned she would need a little extra help at first navigating the cafeteria system and food lines. I was given a blank stare, asked if I could pack her a lunch, and told that she could eat in the classroom.

I asked about the classes that sixth graders are required to take and what electives were available. Ms. Andress said Talia would have all her classes in a "cross-cat" (cross-categorical special education) class. I did not expect that answer nor was I going to allow my daughter to come from a fully inclusive placement and be placed in a self-contained classroom. This was February. We did not have an IEP meeting yet. How could a placement have been decided? We did not have any discussions regarding placement or at least I wasn't part of any placement discussion. To my knowledge, the middle school team had not met my daughter, reviewed her IEP, or met with her elementary team. The low expectations and assumptions about my daughter's ability to learn were based on her label, Down Syndrome, not her. What about an inclusion facilitator, a co-taught classroom, a push-in program, or resource support?

When I asked about an aide, I was told students in the cross-cat class are not assigned an aide because they stay in the classroom most of the day. I asked if I could see the class hoping I might have a better understanding of why this type of placement would better serve my daughter. The classroom was located at the end of the eighth-grade wing and was segregated from all the sixth and seventh graders. With a compassionate tone, Ms. Andress told me the classroom was located at the end of the hall by the exit so the special education students had easy access to the buses. However, the exit Ms. Andress referred to was a completely separate exit. All the other students exited from the front door. Why segregated bus lines? The front door was wheelchair accessible.

Trying to re-direct my focus back to the classes and electives available for sixth graders in search of some type of inclusive opportunity for my daughter, I asked again what electives were available for sixth graders. I was told the special education students in the cross-cat classroom usually have PE and some of the students have the "Arts and Tech" rotation for half the year. The other half of the year, they have a life skills class. At this point I was shocked and hardly able to think. Even with all my confidence and expertise, this belief system colliding with my own caused such confusion that I was unable to connect what points to navigate anymore in hopes of providing an inclusive opportunity. I wasn't sure how a child could come from a successful inclusive placement and end up in such segregation when nothing about her changed. The only thing that was going to be different was that she was going to be educated in a different building, albeit the school had a completely different understanding and philosophy of inclusion. What happened to a continuation of services?

I tried to link the number of periods in the day and the different courses that I recalled from my son's sixth-grade experience. I wondered if it were possible to repeat the Arts and Tech rotation class instead of a life skills class. The Arts and Tech rotation class consists of applied technology, art, music, drama, family and consumer science, and health. In seventh and eighth grade students have Arts and Tech rotation for a full year. I also questioned why Spanish wasn't mentioned. The sixth-grade Spanish class focuses more on the culture of Spanish speaking countries than speaking the language. I remembered all the churros and empanadas I sent in for my son's class fiestas. I knew Talia would not only enjoy the class, but she would be with her peers for at least part of the day. She would learn many of the Spanish vocabulary words just by being in the classroom and hearing the repetition of them. When I asked about repeating the Arts and Tech rotation class Ms. Andress looked at me. I am not sure what she thought of me, but I knew we could not be any farther apart in our beliefs. I basically shut down mentally and emotionally.

Mrs. Sanders, Talia's elementary education teacher, attended the observation with me. So we drove together. When we arrived back at my house we sat in my driveway and tried to figure out what just happened. I was relieved to know she felt the same confusion I did, but at the same time I realized her confusion meant I was really up against a very resistant and unchallenged belief system. My job as Talia's mother was going to be very challenging. I understood from a middle school teacher's point of view how it may seem easier to educate Talia in a special education classroom and how challenging it is to include a child with an intellectual disability in a general education class. Yet as a mother, I knew how important it was for my daughter to have access to the general education curriculum, be included with her peers in the general education classroom with supports with the goal of helping her become successful in her own unique way and to be a valued member of the classroom. I have to do this every day in my own home with my family. Talia has to learn how to live as independently as she can in the world we share with others. The classroom is a great place for others to learn about and acceptance and diversity and for Talia to learn about her world, but if we take her out of the classroom what have we really taught her and our members of society?

When Dr. Kurnyn heard about the meeting, she called and assured me that we would meet as a team and discuss what we wanted for Talia prior to the IEP meeting. As a team, we discussed every aspect of Talia's day and what supports she would need to help her be successful. We made a list:

- the classes that would be best to include her
- the use of push button locks for her PE and personal lockers
- clubs and social activities and what supports she would need
- what supports she would need at first in lunch
- extra time to change for PE and passing between classes
- an aide to support her in the general education classes
- friends that would serve as natural supports to help her succeed in the new setting

With the list complete, the IEP meeting was scheduled. I felt well prepared. I knew in my heart and mind that working toward the most inclusive placement was crucial. I also knew that we couldn't just drop Talia into any old general education class. The people working with Talia had to understand the reasons and believe in them. She would need support and modifications in order for inclusion to be successful. Balancing all of this with Talia at the forefront makes it challenging. I ask myself three questions that guide my mothering. Is she learning? What is her behavior telling me? And most importantly [...] is she happy?

Dr. Kurnyn began the IEP meeting by sharing her experiences with us as a family and Talia as a student. She stressed the importance and impact that inclusion had not only on Talia, but her peers and teachers. Talia truly learns best in an inclusive environment. She is challenged. She has role models. She has access to the general education curriculum. Student work is displayed around the classroom for Talia to learn from. She participates in clubs, afterschool activities because she feels safe with her peers and she is part of the school community. The tone of the meeting was set with honesty. Every teacher and therapist that worked with Talia had information to share about Talia's strengths and recommendations for goals. We created a schedule that was not as inclusive as I would have liked it to have been, but it was acceptable considering the circumstances. She would have one period of reading, writing, and math in the cross-cat class. She would have one semester of instructional social studies and the other semester she would be included in the Arts and Tech rotation class with the general education students. She would be included in the sixth grade general education science class with a resource class the period before to review and prepare for the upcoming class. She would have PE and lunch with the general education students. In sixth grade, students can choose to have chorus, band, or orchestra in place of an advisory period. We decided to put Talia in chorus because she loves music, singing, and dancing, and we felt she really didn't need an advisory period. All in all, it was an individualized schedule that offered some inclusive opportunities for Talia.

Even though we put so much thought and effort into creating the best plan possible, I was anxious when the first day of middle school for my daughter came. She was so excited to go to her new school and see her old friends from Lincoln School. She was excited about wearing a PE uniform and having the opportunity to order junk food for lunch. She was probably one of the few students who was not worried about opening a lock. She had mastered the memorization of her combinations and the skill of opening the locks. She was confident.

About two weeks after school started, I went to parent's night with my husband. I went to Talia's classes and he went to my son's. When I looked at the copy of Talia's schedule, I noticed the schedule was different than what we talked about in our IEP meeting and the one that I had received over the summer. I didn't think much of it at the time. I went through her schedule, saw her teachers, and listened to their introductions. I was most excited to hear about the science class because this was the only general education core class that she was included in. The science teacher, Ms. Bacin, explained her course and expectations. She introduced the resource teacher, Ms. Mato, who was assigned to this particular class to assist some students. I remembered that teacher form our transition IEP meeting. The bell rang. I wanted to introduce myself to the science teacher and let her know that she could contact me any time with questions or concerns. As I was waiting for her to finish talking with other parents, I saw the resource teacher who Talia was supposed to have and introduced myself. She told me that she did not have Talia in her resource class and walked away. I was a bit stunned by her bluntness and lack of explanation as to why she didn't have Talia in the resource class anymore. She was originally scheduled to be in the resource class the period before science with the intent to review material covered the day before and to introduce new material.

When the science teacher was free, I approached her. Noticing how young she looked I had a bit of hope that perhaps she was open to the concept of inclusion and I would have less barriers to break down. I introduced myself as Mrs. Kotel. She was all smiles. When I reminded her I was Talia's mom her smile turned upside down. She explained how she wasn't sure if "this" was going to work. She said Talia seemed so tired and not interested. My heart sank. I immediately wanted to quit and pull her out of science. I told my husband what happened as we drove home.

I realized we had an inclusive placement, but not a belief. I reminded myself that most often I need to educate others about my daughter and disability. Unless people have experienced disability first hand or through a loved one, unexamined beliefs and inaccurate assumptions about disability are perpetuated and passed along. As a new teacher myself, many times I did not question what was being done in the schools. In a sense, new teachers are indoctrinated into belief systems because they don't question them. I needed to talk with the teacher and let her know why including Talia in the science class was so important not only for her but for others. I wanted her to now that Talia is capable of learning and she learns far more than we realize or that she articulates at a given particular time. Sometimes what she has learned shows up days, weeks, months, and even years later.

I wanted her to know about the time when Talia asked me if I remembered her kindergarten teacher, Mr. Collins, and the days of the week song that they sang. I remembered, but I was wondering why she was asking me about it five years later. I found out her fifth-grade aide, Ms. Guerin, was helping Talia with calendar skills. Most often, this is reviewed daily in kindergarten and as students move up grades it is taught less and less and assumed all kids know their days and months. When Ms. Guerin realized Talia still needed help recalling the days and months she started teaching her mini lessons on calendar skills. Talia recalled the song Mr. Collins taught in kindergarten. Because of her limited speech, she was not able to articulate the words as clearly and as quickly as the other students at that time and it could have been assumed she wasn't learning. But she was. Five years later, she remembered the song and applied it. She learned the days and months that same week.

I wanted Ms. Bacin to know that Talia may not learn everything her peers are learning but that's OK. She can learn the same curriculum with modifications. I wanted her to know about the list she and her older brother created with all the science topics the sixth-grade curriculum covers and how excited she was. I wanted her to know that Talia turns her bathroom into a science lab creating all kinds of experiments on her own. I wanted her to know that the only thing that motivated her to leave her grandparents' summer cottage was that she would be able to go home and start fourth grade. She was going to have Mr. Williams who was known for his science experiments and starting the year off with his soda pop and Mentos explosion. I wanted her to know Talia will learn far more about life being with her peers in the general education science class than she would learn being in a cross-cat class all day.

I wanted Ms. Bacin to know that any behavior issues that may arise will be a message from Talia to let you know she is frustrated in some way. Call me and we can figure it out together. I wanted her to know we can't give up just because there is a special education classroom available. We have to work together. I wanted her to know that Talia should be tired at the end of the day at the beginning of sixth grade. Sixth grade is a big adjustment for almost all sixth graders. She was exhausted when she started kindergarten, but we didn't change her placement.

So I shared my concerns with Mrs. D'Angelo who was the cross-cat special education teacher and case coordinator. She spoke with Ms. Bacin and explained the reasons why Talia was in the science class. I waited a few weeks for parent-teacher conferences to meet with Ms. Bacin. I wanted to allow for some time to pass. Once again, I went downstairs to the separate gyms where the parent-teacher conferences were held. I waited in line not sure what I was going to hear. Ms. Bacin started out with a big smile and said she couldn't believe how well Talia was doing since she spoke with Mrs. D'Angelo. She told me they were studying tornados: vortex, wind speed, and tornados ratings etc. She asked the class why tornados are dark in color. Talia raised her hand. Ms. Bacin called on her, and like Ms. Johnson, the third-grade teacher, she was not sure what Talia was going to say and if she would understand her. Talia responded something to the extent that tornados are dark because of all the "debris" flying around. She was right tornados are dark because of the dirt and dust pulled up from the ground into it. The mess left behind is called a debris field. A few months later Talia was the one to tell her siblings they needed to go to the basement for "protection" because she heard the tornado sirens. After studying earthquakes in class, she made connections with the news reports she heard at home about the earthquakes in Haiti and Chili. She learned about hurricanes and fires. She learned vocabulary words like destructive and constructive. She learned science skills such as measuring and observing and data collection.

The sixth-grade end of the year IEP meeting seemed to arrive quickly and was a turning point for me. I went in expecting a collaborative environment. I entered the meeting with a sense that things were going well and I was hoping to increase the amount of classes that Talia was included in. I had many ideas and was hoping to hear some options. The meeting started off with a printed agenda generated by the school. I did not have enough time to put my glasses on to review the agenda and the meeting started without introductions. I knew everyone at the meeting, but my husband had not met everyone. The principal was not in the room. The psychologist walked in late. The updates were given rather quickly, and there was a moment when I was asked if I had any questions. Later, I realized that was my official time for parent input. In the past both as a mother and as a teacher, IEP meetings were a collaborative process. A time to discuss, take turns, bounce ideas, share thoughts and ideas. This meeting was an agenda following meeting […] no time for collaboration.

I had asked for a draft of the IEP goals prior to the meeting. I had time to review it and I had some questions. One of the concerns the teacher had was in regards to Talia transitioning from study skills to science. Mrs. D'Angelo had reported to me that there were times when Talia "refused" to go to science. I was concerned about this too, because I wasn't sure why Talia would "refuse" to go. Did she not like science? Was it too challenging? I needed more information. Mrs. D'Angelo told me she was going to write a transition goal. I thought that was a great idea and we would discuss it at the IEP meeting. To my surprise after listing the academic and speech goals, the psychologists presented a copy of a Behavior Intervention Plan (BIP) for Talia. Once again I was stunned, not sure what to do or say. I knew from my professional experience that good practice is to notify the parent of a concern and to let them know a Functional Behavioral Analysis (FBA) would be needed and then a draft of a BIP would be completed and discussed. Not sure how to process my own thinking, I looked over at my husband who did not really know what was going on. I thought about how other parents who are not educators might not understand what was really going on either: the lack of collaboration, the power held by the professionals, the separation between team members [...].

After a few days of processing, I called the teacher and told her I wanted to schedule another meeting. I did not think we really discussed Talia's needs, and as parents, we did not have input. I mentioned that we were surprised when a BIP was presented. She asked that I send my concerns in writing, so I did. I needed to advocate for my daughter. At the follow-up meeting, I explained to the entire team our goals and the reasons for them. I realized they never heard our views directly from us, the parents. They were not at the transition meeting the year before nor did we meet together as a team.

We spoke at length regarding the BIP. It wasn't clear if Talia was refusing to go to science because she didn't like science or she didn't want to stop what she was doing because she had to go to science. I found out that Talia really enjoyed science and was doing well when she went. I asked what happens when she "refuses." Mrs. D'Angelo told me she would argue and say she wasn't going. We talked more and I asked about the resource class that Talia was supposed to have prior to science that would allow for review and preview of upcoming material. I found out that the resource class was changed without my knowledge to a study skills class. The study skills was supposed to be a class to work on study skills but really was an opportunity for the cross-cat students to cash in their reward tickets for the day and choose different activities depending on how many reward tickets they had. So, Talia was able to go to the study skills class after a long day, get relaxed, play a few computer games and then she was expected to transition to general education science. No wonder she had transition issues. Some days she did not want to leave that fun environment. I checked to make sure that on the days she didn't refuse to go to science that everything was OK. They said she was fine and no behavior problems. She participated in class. I asked what the consequence was when she refused. There really was not a consequence. She was allowed to stay in Mrs. D'Angelo's class and play computer games. So what was really happening is Talia got to pick and choose when she went to science. When she "refused," she was actually rewarded with the opportunity to play computer games or relax. We talked about having the same expectations and consequences for Talia that they would have for any other student who refused to go to class. Overall, the meeting was successful in terms of collaboration and I realized how much is not understood about disability and how important it is for me to be more of a voice for my daughter.

Seventh grade was a year of pushing the boundaries and expectations. I realized that I was going to have to advocate for my daughter directly. I went to Back to School Night and introduced myself to all of Talia's seventh-grade teachers. I explained our reasons for including her and our desires for high expectations. At parent-teacher conferences, I questioned the life skills class. We agreed Talia was not being challenged. I made some suggestions about what some of her real life skills might be. For example, she could work on keyboarding, keeping her own calendar and schedule on the computer, check and answer emails, research different apps on her itouch that would help her in the real world, practice using a debit card, and work on phone and texting skills. Since the early childhood school is connected to the middle school, I suggested she read books to the preschoolers or help in the library. She loves to read and work with younger kids. I plan on including similar goals in her transition plan when she reaches fourteen and a half.

Her seventh-grade science teacher, Ms. Mariam, was amazing! Every day she focused on the big picture of the lesson. Work was modified. She had Talia seated up front so that she could see. She had her help with experiments and engaged in discussion by wording questions so that she could understand and contribute. She made a little box of science puzzles for Talia to use whenever she wanted. I saw the connections at home too. We were driving her to the hospital for surgery very early one morning, and Talia sat in the back seat on commented on the "bright crescent shaped moon." She had recorded moon drawings for a month. One day she was helping me make her brother's lunch and she commented on the sandwich wrap and told me it was "transparent." They studied a unit on light: opaque, transparent and translucent were some of the vocabulary words. Her science lab expanded from her bathroom to her entire bedroom. She recreated some of the experiments for her friends. When Talia had surgery, the students in her science class made her a poster size get-well card for her. Ms. Mariam told me the kids respect her and really don't treat her any differently. Her lab partner truly cared about her and asked to be her partner all year.

Talia has made so many new friends from being included in the general education classes. Her PE teacher, Mr. Tyler, emailed me one day asking about basketball. He said Talia was hesitant to play. I really wanted to take advantage of the teacher reaching out asking for help. We talked on the phone and I assured him that she loves basketball. She shoots hoops almost every day, even in the winter. We talked about different strategies to encourage Talia. I explained that she might be a little afraid because she was going to be playing against a boy team and that she will need a little encouragement. She was capable of participating. She could throw the ball in from the side lines or run along the sidelines with her team. She did not need to be excused from PE or given the option to go to the weight room as an alternative activity. I knew she could participate and she did not have any medical restrictions. He called two days later and told me some of her classmates helped Talia by cheering her on and running along with her. He said she not only played against the other girl team but when it was time to play the boys she played them too. This group of girls became her gym buddies and continues to encourage her. On Talia's birthday in May, they gave her a birthday party at school during lunch, decorated her locker and brought cards and gifts. No one asked them to do it. Some of the girls called her over the summer to "hang out."

One day I looked over Talia's completed work that was sent home. In one pile I saw a science test that was modified with rich challenging content questions. In the other pile I saw some homework from the life skills class. There were social stories on feelings and manners using Picture Exchange Communication System (PEC) pictures that Talia had colored. Talia used PEC pictures in preschool to assist her with communication. The contrast was clear. Side by side I could see that when the work is modified she is more than capable of learning the general education curriculum alongside her peers. And when you place her in a special education class, inappropriate, watered down, low expectation work is given to her. After much thought on how to handle this I called and asked to meet with Ms. D'Angelo to talk about Talia's full day. I wanted an update on all the little things that we talked about during the last IEP.

Everything seemed to be going well: no more weight room options for PE; transitioning to science was good; Talia was carrying her own books and supplies to class (last year she manipulated her aide into thinking she couldn't); class participation was great; she was making new friends; she still loved chorus and wanted to join the lunch bunch group. When I asked about life skills there was no hesitation. Mrs. D'Angelo felt she was not really being challenged either. We talked about other options: history, language arts, two sections of Arts and Tech rotation, or Spanish. We decided seventh grade general education history.

I am so glad the change was made. Talia studied the Civil War and I am so proud of all she learned. She had to keep a journal of a fictional person in the war. She chose to be a soldier for the Union Army. She chose to be from New York, because New York City is one of her favorite cities. She had to create a poster encouraging people to join her side. Her poster read: *Free slaves. Help us. Thank you.* She drew little *peace* signs surrounding the words. She had to write entries about her experiences as a soldier. She wrote to her family and told them about her friends getting shot and hurt, living in a tent, the uniform she had to wear and the food she had to cook on an open fire. She had to collect pictures and include them in her journal. She had to write in code as an example of how messages were sent from different camps.

At the end of the unit, she had to write a reflection. She wrote: *I feel happy the war is over because no slavery and no fighting. No more soldiers get hurt. I got to go home. I got a party with my family. Now we have to fix everything that is broken from the war. I won. No more slavery.* The teacher sent home the power points used in class so that she had a copy to refer to when doing homework. One night when she was working on one of the journal entries, she was confused about the soldiers getting hurt. I explained that during war people hurt and kill each other. Like the rest of us even when war is explained, it doesn't make sense, but she made a few other connections through our discussion. Every night she had been praying for a friend's father who had gone to Afghanistan as a soldier. She asked if that is what could happen to him. She asked again why the man from *Dancing with the Stars* had been injured and his face scarred. I tried so many times to explain the explosion and why he was scarred. Finally, after studying it in class, it made sense to her. After looking at all the war pictures, listening to class discussions, and writing about being soldier she now understood how people were injured and killed and why she was praying. Being in the history class made the concept of war more clear and real to her.

Over the summer, I was flipping through a magazine. In the corner was an advertisement for a Civil War reenactment at a local park. Talia was looking over my shoulder and pointed it out. I was a bit surprised she noticed it and read it. I was curious to see what she remembered. When I asked her, she told me the war was between the Confederates and the Union and it was about no slavery, etc. [...] she learned enough for me! History is supposed to teach us about the past, present and future. I don't want her denied that opportunity because someone makes the assumption she can't learn.

Talia started eighth grade this fall. The last IEP meeting was truly collaborative. Her schedule is more inclusive than when she entered sixth grade. Without any resistance, she is included in general education classes more than fifty percent of her day. Those working with her have a better understanding of why inclusion is so important to us. My hope is that as the year goes on our communication will continue to improve, she will be successful in her classes, the connections from the classroom to the real world continue, her friendships will grow, and she will be encouraged to try new things. I hope she goes to the eighth-grade dance at the end of the year feeling confident, accepted, and secure with who she is. I hope she feels part of the class of 2017. I hope to feel the same kind of sadness I felt leaving Lincoln School; the type of sadness one feels when they leave a place they don't want to leave, because the experience was positive. I hope that on the first day of high school I feel proud of the accomplishments we made toward a more inclusive opportunity not only for my daughter, but also for all the kids that follow in her footsteps. More importantly, I hope Talia has learned and that she is happy.

Probing Questions
- Kathy describes feeling nervous when the phone rings because it might be the school calling. She also feels anxious at the start of the year. What do Kathy's anxieties teach us about the personal experiences of a mother of a child with Down Syndrome in an American public school?
- When Kathy tells Ms. Andress that Talia might change into her clothes slowly at the end of PE and that she may struggle navigating the cafeteria lunch line, the middle school administrator offers solutions that involve changes of location. Why do solutions based on separate locations for Talia make sense to Ms. Andress but not to Kathy? What does this demonstrate about their differing beliefs and attitudes about disability?
- It seems like Talia's inclusion in middle school requires her mother to be incredibly vigilant and assertive. We have to wonder if Talia would simply be excluded if not for the repeated efforts of her mother. Is this what it takes to make inclusion happen in your school and your district? Why or why not?
- What social and academic benefits of inclusive education does Talia experience?
- Kathy tells little about how Talia's presence in general education benefitted the non-disabled students. What do you think the non-disabled students learned by having Talia in their class?

CHAPTER NINETEEN

Respecting and Reaching All Learners in English Language Arts Classes

A Glimpse into a New York City High School

FRAN BITTMAN, SARAH BICKENS, & DAVID J. CONNOR

INTRODUCTION: CONTEXTUALIZING INCLUSION IN NEW YORK CITY

I, David, began my career in the late 1980s in New York City as high school teacher of adolescent students segregated because of labels such as learning disabilities, behavior disorders, and attention deficit disorders. My school was one of the first to pioneer collaborative team teaching to facilitate the integration of students with IEPs. During of the mid 1990s I changed positions to be a professional staff developer based in the Office of the Superintendent of Manhattan High Schools. Much of my work was deliberately focused on inclusive education, and I had the task of engaging faculty from forty schools to transition youth labeled disabled into general education classes. Visiting these schools, I saw firsthand how the movement toward inclusion was being interpreted and responded to educators within each institution. In a word, it was extreme. On one hand, there were schools that genuinely respected all youth as individuals and created intricate, effective support systems that allowed students with disabilities to have the same access to high school content classes, which they were not receiving in segregated environments. On the other hand, some schools used inclusion classes as a dumping ground for large numbers of students with IEPs, "at risk" kids, and chronic absentees. The result was a larger "special ed." class that fooled nobody, least of all those placed within that setting. In between these polarities were lots and lots of mediocre inclusive classes, a result of both legitimate and unfortunate reasons that included little or no resources, faculty resistance, principal distrust, union mobilization, poor organization, inadequate in-service professional development, and a lack of leadership vision. Nonetheless, I took heart in all of the educators I came to know and work with in their schools, teachers and administrators who genuinely wanted the best for all children and youth. I also came to know a good inclusive class when I saw one.

In the mid-2000s, I returned to work in schools for a couple of years as a Literacy Coach. I wanted to go back to actual classrooms and study the dynamics of the interactions within them, and help further build good teaching practices of faculty toward including all students (I also wanted to complete my dissertation, and this job freed up my evenings!). It is during this time that I was assigned to work a number of teachers and schools. Among them were two early-career teachers whose classroom I visited every week. These teachers were Fran and Sara, the co-authors of this chapter. We "clicked" professionally as they were so eager to study their craft, and I was equally eager to engage them in this process. I found both of them to be committed to their students, highly organized, very creative, and willing to be flexible, accommodating of diversity, and mindful of differences among students. When Scot began developing this book, I immediately thought of Fran and Sara's work at Manhattan Village Academy High School as providing a valuable addition.

Manhattan Village Academy is located in the neighborhood of Chelsea, in the middle of a bustling commercial neighborhood. The public school is relatively small by NYC standards, educating between 450 and 500 students that travel from all five boroughs. The student body consists of approximately sixty-two percent Latino, twenty-five percent African-American/Caribbean American, six percent Asian-American, six percent European-American, and one percent Native American/Pacific Islander. Most of the students are from working class backgrounds, many of who live below the poverty level. The school has sustained a good reputation since opening in the mid 1990s, based upon a model created by the noted educator Deborah Meier, who was influential in the "small schools" movement. Strong leadership and a dedicated, highly collaborative faculty have brought recognition to the school from *U.S. News & World Report*, and *America's Best High Schools*, as well as awards for helping to close the achievement gap between White and Black students.

In the following sections, I invited both Fran and Sara to introduce themselves, share some examples of instructional approaches that have succeeded in their classrooms, and spotlight a student with whom they have worked. At the end of this chapter, I offer some further thoughts about the issues they raise.

FRAN AND HER CLASS

I am a much better student now that I have been a teacher. I was always a good enough student. In high school I completed every single assignment on time. I studied for every single test. Usually I did well enough but not always. I often had trouble figuring out exactly what a specific teacher wanted from me. It was frustrating. I can't tell you how many times I have looked back and thought, if I could return to high school I would be an A+ student, because now as a teacher myself I can understand what exactly my teachers were trying to get me to see, comprehend, and learn.

And I know I am not the only one who felt this way. My older sister has an exceptionally high IQ and was a National-Merit Semi-Finalist. However, her GPA for most of high school was below a 3.0. It wasn't that she wasn't working hard enough, but like me, she couldn't always understand what the teacher wanted or convey what she did understand to her teachers. Luckily by the end of high school she was tested by a specialist and found to have ADHD and mild dyslexia. This put her on the path to understand both how she learned and what resources she could get so that she could have the kinds of successes she deserved. Her senior year of high school she earned a 4.3 GPA, and today she is a very successful doctor who runs an entire clinic in the Bronx and holds leadership positions on state and national medical boards.

The problem is that most of the teachers I have had in life taught me in a specific style, their style. Maybe that clicked for me and I did well, but maybe it didn't. If I couldn't grasp how they taught, I had a rough year ahead of me. Obviously I encountered some exceptional teachers who were able to get everyone in the classroom involved, learning, and interested. Those were the teachers who paved my way to become a teacher.

Every year at the start of the school year I get lists of students who have IEPs and who are ESL or former ESL. Usually about twenty percent of my students fall into one or both of these categories. However, I find that about fifty percent of my students each year have unique learning and comprehension styles that wouldn't fit into the regular mold. They could have below average reading levels, never have been taught grammar before, have social or emotional issues, have some difficult home-life issues, or maybe because of some bad teachers in the past they have developed a general disdain for reading, English class, or school in general. Any or all of these things and more can make the "traditional" modes of learning difficult, frustrating, or completely inaccessible to those students. It's our job as educators to make sure that every student in our class is learning. Obviously not everyone is going to learn the exact same thing or achieve mastery level success, but every single student is capable of success as long as we create multiple paths to it. Therefore, unless we practice inclusive teaching methods within our classrooms, we may be leaving up to half our class behind, whether we realize it or not.

TEN EFFECTIVE PRACTICES TO SUPPORT INCLUSION

Not every lesson or unit is going to be perfect. The most important thing when reflecting on your teaching is to be honest with yourself. Take notes on each lesson plan, unit outline, and assignment. Keep tabs on what did and didn't work, what was missing and who wasn't getting it. That way you can go back and with your next unit or in the next year, you can make sure you are restructuring your teaching to help everyone obtain as much as possible from each class you teach. These strategies below are some of the lesson and unit planning formats that have allowed me to get every single student involved and learning.

1. **Literature Circles**: Literature Circles can be a daunting task for any teacher to plan, as they require more than just one lesson and also force you as a teacher to hand the reigns over to the students. However, year after year I find them to be the perfect mode to force students to become involved in learning through themselves and their peers. For example, while teaching a tenth-grade world literature course, I set up a six-week modern literature unit with a focus on human rights issues. Prior to the unit I gave each student a list of the four book options (*The Joy Luck Club, In the Time of Butterflies, Shabanu Daughter of the Wind,* and *The Kite Runner*), which included the difficulty level, and length of each text and a short synopsis of the book. I then had students rank their choices and gave all students their first or second choices. Almost every student always puts him/herself into an appropriate level book, and with the two choice promise, I have a little wiggle room. Occasionally when I have students choose a too difficult book, I discuss the issue individually with him/her, and either I find that the student still wants the "hard" book and really pushes him/herself when given the opportunity or that the student relents and chooses a more appropriate leveled book. I also individually conference with stronger readers who choose the "easy" book to do "less" work. *Throughout the unit I have students complete questions or logs to help keep them on track as they read. Each day in class they have various group assignments: analysis of text, finding and defining difficult vocabulary, character projects, creating missing scenes, literary device discovery, historical connections, etc. Weekly I give either an individual pop quiz or a group pop quiz to keep the students honest in completing their own work and not copying other students' logs or questions. Finally at the end of the unit each group teaches a full lesson to the rest of the class about the completed text.*

2. **Group Work Roles**: Within the above literature circles but also with any type of group work, roles allow each student to self-choose how best to aid his/her group and to show his/her understanding. Roles can include: group leader, spokesperson, artist, literary device detective, vocab finder,

quote analyzer, secretary, editor, etc. At the end of the unit/project, you can grade each student on his/her fulfillment of this role's duties, but it is also beneficial to have students grade each other on how effective each person was in fulfilling his/her tasks.

3. **Multiple Forms of Assessment**: It is easy to become overly reliant on one method of assessment, be it essays, quizzes, projects, etc. However, due to different learning styles, not every student can show his/her understanding completely with each format. For example, I have some students that are very strong readers but due to ESL issues, they may have difficulty earning a high score on an essay because of grammar and clarity issues. Another student may have weak reading abilities but have great oral speaking skills, allowing him/her to excel during the in-class debates, even if he/she struggled with some of the more difficult segments of the novel. *To allow each student to demonstrate the full scope of his/her understanding, each unit should include a variety of assessments: weekly pop quizzes, reading questions, group projects, unit test, closing debate, etc.*

4. **Assessment Options**: Within individual projects I also like to allow some room for student choice. This permits students to take more ownership of their work and to choose the method that best reflects their level of comprehension. Toward the end of my *A Tales of Two Cities*' unit, students complete a creative project. They have the option to: (1) create a sound track for five key scenes in the book with five paragraphs explaining with textual evidence how each song reflects the mood/tone of that scene, (2) illustrate five symbols in the book and write five paragraphs analyzing those symbols using textual evidence, or (3) write five letters between the various characters using a range of letter types (apology, love, revenge, etc.) and using the appropriate characterization for the letter writer and correct textual details from the novel. Before students turn in this project, they must each present one of the five pieces to the class. *Knowing this requirement, students often produce a higher level of work to "show off" to their classmates and feel a higher level of accomplishment by the praise they receive from both teacher and peers.*

5. **(Mandatory) Extra Help**: It is essential to give struggling students extra help. However, forcing the students who fail your test or don't turn work in on time or have low state scores to be "punished" by remaining after school is rarely the best method. When I was teaching eleventh-grade English, students were required to pass the New York State English Regent exam at the end of the year in order to graduate from high school. At the time this test was a two-day, six-hour exam with twenty-six multiple choice questions and four essays. After first semester I would give students a diagnostic exam to gauge their progress so far. I then would analyze each student's results. If a student struggled with multiple choice, he/she would be mandated to stay

the first Monday of each month to work on those skills. If he/she struggled with essay style #1, he/she would be mandated to stay for all Mondays in February; if essay #2, all Mondays in March, etc. This allowed me to focus on just one area with just the students who struggled in that area. This also helped students to understand in what areas they needed support and to not feel unjustly "punished."

6. **Drafts/ Specific, Individual Feedback:** It is easy to skim through a paper and put a letter grade at the top with a comment or two. It's also easy to read through a paper and circle a few boxes on a rubric and tally the score. It is difficult to force students to complete two or more drafts, having them work on content, clarity, and grammar/spelling in each draft. Those first drafts are exhausting for teachers, but they allow for so much more growth in each student from the first to the second. The drafting process also allows teachers to pinpoint who really isn't getting it before the final grades are cast, and it allows you to find out in what areas all students are struggling to address during the revision process and/or with future units.

7. **Connections to Real-Life:** Students like to understand things, but often the ideas seem foreign and antiquated, so whenever I can, I try to connect topics to things that are directly in front of them. Recently I had to teach two lessons on the element of thought "implications" and the critical thinking standard "breadth" in preparation for a portfolio assignment that is a graduation requirement at my school. Since it was just weeks before the presidential election, I found articles on Romney's and Obama's recent actions and we discussed what the implications of these actions would be on the election. The next day students broke up into six groups, each given a different debate topic (taxes, immigration, abortion, etc.). Each group had to read excerpts from the candidates' speeches and present to the class each candidate's stance on the issue. Finally we discussed which issue would be most important in swaying voters and why and how breadth was necessary to analyze each candidate, not just looking at one or two issues. *I could have easily focused on a piece of literature to discuss the importance of implications and depth, but that may have lost some student connectivity. Students were heartily engaged in both lessons, as many had vested interest in both the elections and the specific issues.*

8. **Personal and Peer Modeling:** Often teachers give directions to a project or essay or any assignment and students are immediately stuck by how to start, or a student receives a graded assignment with a low score and doesn't understand why he/she received that score. I try as often as possible to model how I would go through the initial stages of an assignment, giving students my own personal concrete examples. Then when I pass back first drafts of an assignment, I show students peer examples that really achieved the highest expectations, so they know exactly what to shoot for. I often also show medi-

ocre work and discuss how we could make this exceptional work. We discuss where the potential is and where we could go from there. Often kids want to improve, but the pathway isn't always clear unless we make it so.
9. **Frequent Grade Updates/Feedback:** If students know how they are doing, they want to either do better or maintain their grades. Students who are doing poorly may not know why or in what areas they can improve. My school, like many, requires teachers to keep an online grade book so students and parents can always check their status. Even before this was a requirement, I would give monthly progress reports to push students to improve. Now I update the online grade system at least every other week. This also allows me to mini-conference with students and e-mail parents whenever any small problem arises, thus avoiding larger ones in the future.
10. **Planning Your Week Wisely/Fairly:** I had a high school chemistry teacher who read out of the textbook to our class every single day. Whenever she turned around to write an equation on the board, we would all pass calculators to each other so we could read the notes we had been writing to each other during her reading. I learned very little chemistry that year. I still have colleagues who lecture their students every single day and expect students to be heartily engaged and to learn easily from them. It's possible for some students to learn this way but impossible for all. Lectures are necessary sometimes; maybe textbooks too, though I have never used them. When I plan a week's worth of lessons, I like to start heavily, so maybe a lecture about an author and his style and a difficult nonfiction reading about the historical context of the story on Monday; then maybe grammar and part one of a story on Tuesday; then vocabulary and part two of a story on Wednesday. On Thursday we might do a group project on the literary devices within the story. Then on Friday the groups will present their projects and we will end class with a closing debate on the thematic ideas within the story. If you do the same thing every day, students will be bored. If you do the same thing every day, some students will never learn from that style. By mixing up the techniques you use and topics you teach, you will be sure to hit each student at least once or twice throughout the week. *Also, that sense of relief we get Friday afternoon isn't for us alone; students need more engaging and interactive lessons as the week progresses to keep their motors running.*

SPOTLIGHT ON STEVEN

At the end of each year I give the grade above's English teacher a list of students who struggled in my class, especially in writing. That way he/she will know whom immediately to focus on in the coming year. Last year the ninth-grade English teacher gave me a list of fifty students about whom he was concerned (the class had 110 kids), so like I said previously, about fifty percent of students have some kind of learning issue. One of those kids was Steven. He was a student with an IEP whom the ninth-grade teacher said had low writing skills. When the year began, the special education teacher also informed me that Steven had low reading comprehension skills.

When I began working with Steven, I assumed what both these teachers said was true and I labeled him "low-skilled" in my mind. It only took me about a month or two to realize just how much potential Steven had. While these two teachers saw him as low-skilled, I merely saw him as in need of "fine tuning." Steven is a very hard worker, which always makes my job a little easier. He also loves to be successful, but he gets easily frustrated. The first assessment that I collected was character letters based on the students' summer reading book *The Good Earth*. Steven struggled a bit with grammar and clarity, but his letters revealed that he clearly had read the book and understood the protagonist's emotions and motivations throughout the story. *He mentioned in class that the text was difficult to read on his own over the summer but that he did understand most of the basic plot line.*

The first unit we covered together was *Macbeth*. Students then had to choose a theme to analyze in the play with two specific textual examples. Steven struggled with choosing his topic. He voluntarily stayed after school with some other students to receive extra help on structuring his essay. Eventually he decided upon karma and used both Macbeth and Lady Macbeth as examples. While he understood the play well, he had difficulty using the text to thoroughly prove his thesis. In his first draft he mentioned the bad things both characters did in the story, but he failed to make the connection to the "goes around" end of karma. He didn't explain how each character received retribution for his/her actions and what that ultimately teaches us about what happens in life when we choose to undertake evil deeds. Steven again met with me individually after receiving his first draft, and we discussed what aspects of the thesis needed strengthening and how he could better use textual details. His final draft earned him a B-. He was happy over the improvement but wanted to know how he could get a higher grade next time.

The next few months entailed Steven struggling with the *Things Fall Apart* unit because he disliked the book and had trouble deciphering the thematic essay prompt. He thoroughly enjoyed our *Animal Farm* unit and was an active horse member (all students had been put into animal groups and had to represent their animals' concerns throughout the story). *However, with* Animal Farm *students wrote a research essay answering the question: "Was the Russian Revolution a success?" They had to use examples from the story as well as from five nonfiction articles. Steven and most students struggled with Orwell's satire. They had difficulty separating what Orwell was trying to teach the readers from the animal aspect of the story. We also spent time working together on which nonfiction articles best supported his thesis. They were above grade level reading and required Steven to reread and reanalyze, which aggravated him quite a bit.* By March we read *Night*, a book Steven really enjoyed, but he struggled a bit in the in class essay due to time restrictions. While I gave him 1.5 times the regular student's time, as dictated by his IEP, he still was unable to finish his conclusion and felt rushed throughout the essay. Steven spent so much time thinking about which examples to use from the text that he ran out of time for the actual writing. We discussed time management issues in writing and in class we practiced how to quickly analyze a prompt, choose your examples, and write a two-minute outline before beginning the actual writing.

Steven really hit his stride in the last few months of school. He spent six weeks reading *The Kite Runner* in his literature circle group and acting as the group's spokesperson, a perfect role for Steven who loved to share his and his group's insights and opinions. The culminating assessment was for Steven and his group to teach a forty-five-minute lesson to the class centering on one theme in the novel and exposing one or more human rights violations in the story. Steven's group did a phenomenal job with Steven clearly in the lead teaching position. They began the class acting as the Taliban government. Under each desk they placed various infractions each student committed and then went on to "punish" the students accordingly. This immediately allowed students to grasp the severity of this government system. The lesson went on to focus on the theme of redemption, *where his group shared two readings, one where Amir fails to help Hassan during his rape and a second where Amir returns to make up for this failure by attempting to save Hassan's son from the Taliban.* The lesson ended with students writing about instances in their own lives when they have faltered; they then shared aloud if and how they were able to redeem themselves, *like Amir. The class was extremely impressed with Steven and his group's ability to engage the class, organize a well-rounded and deep lesson, and thoroughly connect students to important themes both thematically and historically.* Steven's group ended up earning an A, the highest grade in his section.

The final exam of the year was an in class essay where students had to analyze a thematic prompt and use any two pieces of literature we read over the past year to either prove the prompt true or false. I discussed that this would be used as a diagnostic exam for me to inform the eleventh-grade English teacher of students who would need extra help in the coming year to ensure success on the state English exam. Steven was very nervous to again face the stress of a timed essay. However, he interpreted the prompt correctly and chose *Macbeth* and "Ruined" to prove the quote true. He was able to use very specific textual examples from both stories to adequately convey his thematic understanding of both texts. Steven earned a B+, and he no longer will appear on the "at risk" list. Steven entered eleventh grade this year with much more confidence in his analytical and writing abilities and will, without a doubt, pass the state English exam.

SARAH AND HER CLASS

While I know inclusion often refers to the integration of special education and ELL students, I prefer to think of this term in a broader sense, of ensuring that ALL students feel included in the classroom community as valid contributors to and beneficiaries of the learning that occurs there. If a student is not included, he or she misses out on learning and the future opportunities this provides. This possible failure to educate all students makes inclusion an act of social justice. I became an urban public school teacher eleven years ago with the lofty philosophical goal of enabling all students to access a high quality education, regardless of disability, poverty, or skill level. I was a student who got straight As and thrived in the classes at my middle-class suburban school. However, at my Ivy League college it quickly became clear that my education and skills lagged behind those who attended pricey prep schools. A troubling question began to enter my consciousness: If this gap existed for me, what kind of educational chasm was there for students at impoverished schools, for students who saw the classroom as a place of struggle and alienation? While I couldn't necessarily change the economic inequalities for public education, I could become a teacher who ensured that all of my students left me with the skills to succeed at my alma mater or any college. Of course, having seen my own education's failings, I already knew that I would have to improve upon the traditional trappings of the "chalk and talk," teacher-centered education that I had received.

With this in mind, I embraced (and still do) an American maxim in my philosophy as a classroom teacher: *e pluribus unum*. The United States is a country that promises to embrace diversity, that thrives from approaching problems from multiple and creative perspectives, that defines success through multiple avenues. Counter-intuitively, the American classroom has largely been a place where successful learning remains – especially in the face of increased high-stakes standardized testing – homogenous. "Good students" sit quietly; a "good test" reflects perfectly memorized facts; a "good grade" results from following a specific set of rigid instructions. The real world does not mirror this classroom. A good CEO may lead through quiet pressure or gregarious humor; a good book may be an organized treatise or a free-wheeling stream of consciousness. A more modern, twenty-first-century education should embrace diversity and highlight for students that there are multiple ways of solving problems and looking at the world. When a classroom is inclusive, diverse approaches to learning and teaching must be used, making the environment more reflective of the realities of our diverse world and, ultimately, better preparing *all* students to be successful in college and career.

GOOD PRACTICES

In addition to the lofty goals of social justice and diversity, the practical benefit of inclusionary teaching is that it engages a broader range of students. What might be essential to help a learning disabled child to write an essay will also aid a student who simply struggles with writing. An activity that may engage the kinesthetic learning style of a student with ADHD will also rouse the apathetic teenager who would rather be playing video games. In my eleven years as an English teacher in grades nine through twelve, I have developed a wide variety of techniques to support inclusion. First, in attempting to reach all students and appeal to a wide array of learning styles, I ensure my classroom has a variety of activities. I frequently use acting and skits to engage students. Students may read of Caesar's assassination in *Julius Caesar* and create skits in which they report "live from the scene" as a news team with either Republican or Monarchical bias. Students may bring the characters from *Fences* together in a Maury Povich type confrontation of family dysfunction or show characters at family therapy to try to resolve their problems. These types of activities strive to include students with attention issues, but also engage those with strong social or interpersonal skills and generally make a class more exciting for all students.

Other activities provide students with differentiated choices that fit a variety of learning styles. A group may create a newspaper page about the narrator's speech in *Invisible Man* with options to write an opinion piece, an interview, an editorial cartoon, or a straight reporting piece. The latter two options allow lower skilled writers to find success, while the first two choices may challenge those of higher skill. Moreover, a visual learner may gravitate towards the cartoon while a student with greater interpersonal skills may choose the interview. All of these activities present students with a "break" from the chalk and talk classroom. As a result, students are more engaged in general and learn and remember more content and skills. Students who do not typically experience success in a traditional setting are given authentic ways to be successful contributors to the classroom environment. This success breeds more confidence and general enthusiasm for school, ultimately increasing the quality of students' learning.

However, I do not see an inclusive classroom as a universally fun classroom, as "edutainment" and lessons that consist entirely of skits and drawing pictures. The second key element of a truly inclusive classroom lies in breaking down for students the skills that make a successful English student. This can be tedious or even formulaic work in some cases, but is essential so that all students are able to perform the basic tasks of literacy. Teachers who have found success in their own educations may take for granted the complexity of reading and understanding a text, writing a good essay, or simply being a good student in general. As an inclusion teacher, I look to bring transparency to these often obtuse tasks, breaking each down into a set of discreet skills. One of the first lessons I teach students is how to read actively. Students learn various symbols to notate on pages as they read, including "?" for confusion, "*" for important, "→" for prediction, and "T-S" for text-to-self connection. Students create a "reader response journal," and as they read respond to quotations from the text with a short analysis. This process mirrors what high level readers do naturally: questioning the text, checking understanding, making and revising predictions. Ultimately, all students learn to monitor their understanding as they read, a skill they will use in any high school or college course.

I approach the inclusive teaching of writing much as I do reading. Transforming ideas into logical essay paragraphs can be a mystical process that eludes many students, those with learning disabilities in particular. Ever since I was taught to write a five-paragraph essay in seventh grade, I have been enchanted with the magical utility of this simple breakdown. As a teacher, I decided to take it even further, again making obvious the many smaller steps that go into writing a good academic essay. I developed acronyms for the distinct parts of an essay: OTP (introductory opening, thesis, preview), TELEC (body paragraph topic sentence, example, literary device, explanation, concluding sentence) and RRF (conclusion's restate thesis, restate supporting evidence, make a final comment). With younger students, I break this down even further, creating an essay packet with sentence starters for each part of the essay. While this certainly is a great deal of handholding, I consider the essay packet a type of training wheels. Just as it is difficult to simply start riding a two wheel bike with no experience, so too it is challenging to simply write an amazing essay without working through the foundational steps to do so. That said, I "take away" these training wheels as the year goes on, allowing students to internalize these steps and write their own advanced essays as their confidence increases.

In addition to specifically teaching students the details of good reading and writing, I firmly believe in clear expectations so that how to be a good student and classroom citizen is abundantly obvious. The idea of sitting up, making eye contact, taking notes, and participating can seem like a complicated code to crack for some students. In delineating expectations, students can practice the behaviors that will ensure their learning is of a high quality. Of course, this begins on the first day with a list of rules and guidelines, but I also give students regular and specific feedback about their performance in my class. Every two weeks students receive "citizenship rubrics," an assessment of where they are doing well and what they need to improve. As a teacher it is nearly impossible to have a personal conversation with a student every time he does well or flounders. With this written feedback, a student can see that he missed two homeworks, fell asleep in class, or participated more in a given two-week period. Students then create goals for the next two weeks, thus learning self-reflection and meta-cognition, two skills that come naturally to some students, but seem inscrutable to many, especially those with learning disabilities. While citizenship rubrics could seem like "nit-picking" at students in a way that could lower confidence, the end result is actually the opposite. Students can see distinct steps on the path to success and know exactly what they need to do to reach their end goals. Students notice progress each week and build confidence in the classroom, leading to more success.

SPOTLIGHT ON A STUDENT: MIGUEL

I was able to see the benefits of my inclusionary philosophy and teaching techniques in a ninth-grade student, Miguel, who struggled with dyslexia, processing issues, and ADHD. Miguel reminded me of a rambunctious puppy; he was full of energy and eager to please, but frequently lost focus, had immature interactions with his peers, and gave up in frustration when given a writing task. With Miguel, I knew my first priority was making clear to him how to be a "good" student. He had difficulty determining what was appropriate to do or say in a classroom. Sure, he had been yelled at a lot in middle school to *stop* doing bad things, but he seemed unsure about how to do well instead. The first time I gave Miguel a citizenship rubric, the feedback highlighted many flaws (and suggested how to improve them). Seeing more negative feedback, he angrily crumpled it up and left it in his desk. The next time I handed the rubrics out, I held his and gave it to him after the rest of the students had left the room. Grumbling under his breath, he sat with me while I went over each element of classroom citizenship. He reluctantly set one straightforward goal for next week: to participate two times every class. Over the next week, this did not happen every day, but clearly the small, "doable" goal appealed to Miguel. At the end of every class, he would ask me, "Did I do it?" While he sometimes did not, he liked the extra attention and loved the praise I gave him when he had participated twice or even more.

Miguel's participation had improved, but he was far from a model student. He made silly faces at students sitting across from him or burst out with inappropriate comments. When I raised my voice, he seemed—despite feeling guilty—to like this public attention, and the behavior did not really subside. Inspired by the relative success of the citizenship rubric, I decided to make Miguel's feedback more immediate and specific. After school, I outlined my plan to Miguel. Every day, I would put a post-it on his desk. Every time he acted inappropriately, I would put a line on the paper—no yelling, no public embarrassment, but a distinct warning. If he had three or more lines, he would have detention with me after school. At detention, he would write a reflection about how and why he had acted out and would suggest how he could improve in the future. For the first month of this setup, Miguel had detention almost every day. He became very good at writing his detention reflections (a bonus literacy gain, I suppose). I was close to giving up when one day I forgot to give Miguel his post-it. He begged me to put one on his desk, and I complied, but told him it didn't seem like it was working. He promised he would try harder. While this didn't result in the bad behavior going away, he did not reach three strikes that day. The next day, not only did he "hold" at two strikes, he began to monitor himself. After poking his neighbor in the shoulder, I simply glanced in Miguel's direction and he drew a line on his post-it. This was a turning point. Miguel still earned "slashes" on his post-it and still spent detention with me from time to time. However, he had finally learned the self-awareness to correct his mistakes and behave in a way that would eventually result in greater learning.

Miguel's behavior and focus slowly improved in a whole class setting, but he continued to struggle at other tasks. Diagnostic essay assessments at the beginning of the year revealed that he wrote on a fourth-grade level. While his reading levels were higher at about seventh grade, my informal assessments indicated that he frequently "zoned out" while reading or skipped whole sections of text. When completing a worksheet of questions about a reading, his dyslexia and processing issues made it a challenge to get his ideas onto paper, and he would often stop doing the work and distract others instead. While he participated, his ADHD made it so that he often did not follow the thread of the discussion so said something off topic. Miguel understood most content, but struggled with writing and focus in general, and this struggle manifested itself in inappropriate behavior. Having experienced little academic success in the past, he seemed to have stopped trying to be successful at school and to direct his attentions to socializing, something at which he felt much more competent. The key, of course, was to build his confidence and allow him paths to work through his frustration and complete the task. My organizers, especially for writing, worked well for this. Even when given a "Do Now" Miguel could sit for the entire five minutes, staring at the page or erasing a first sentence over and over. The essay packets allowed him to clearly see the steps he needed to complete and gave him words to start his ideas. When we "graduated" from the packets to writing essays without these training wheels, Miguel adamantly used the essay writing acronyms to remind him of the steps, writing them on the side of his paper when we had an in class essay. After a few months of practice, just this simple series of letters allowed him to know how to start and continue writing, abating his frustration.

Miguel's talent for interpersonal relationships, not to mention comedy and verbal fluency were perfectly suited to the more "active" elements of my class. When in a group performing a skit, he would fight to play the role with the most lines. When asked to pick a role, he would often choose to write an interview with a character, adding funny responses that showed the character's flaws. Miguel still needed reminders in groups to speak less loudly or to refocus, but his enthusiasm for this type of class work was clear. He felt successful, so tried to focus more in class in general. As a result, he remembered and processed more, increasing the quality of his education. Miguel even began taking academic risks, opting to complete an extra credit project in which he memorized a Shakespeare soliloquy and acted it out for the class. Miguel was beginning to see himself as a productive member of the classroom, as a true student, and the effects reverberated throughout all aspects of this learning.

CONCLUDING THOUGHTS

As a teacher educator, I (David) believe it is critical to know *why* inclusive education is a worthwhile goal. Of equal importance is *how* teaching inclusively can be learned. It's never a set recipe, a fixed step-by-step approach, a magic bullet. However, Fran and Sara share some of the approaches they have used across their first decade of teaching that have helped them build units, structure lessons, craft engaging activities, generate formative and summative assessments—all with view to creating a classroom environment in which all students are consciously provided access to learning knowledge and developing skills. Of note is how Manhattan Village Academy is structured to allow weekly meetings among grade-level teachers who use that time productively to identify cross-curricula themes, develop curriculum, reinforce student skills, revisit polices and requirements, examine student work, ask professional questions of one another, and case conference about specific students such as Steven and Miguel. Such a structure shows a commitment by school administration to keep students font and center in all aspects of their work.

In this chapter, by featuring the "real-classroom" skills needed for a teacher to be successful when working with a diverse body of students, we hope you can see how Steven and Miguel benefit—in both specific and holistic ways—from flexible approaches to teaching. A teacher's expectations, words, and actions have great power in either enabling or disabling students in their classrooms. As you can see, an inclusive-centered disposition is a career-long commitment to figuring out how to reach and teach each and every student. As such, teaching inclusively will always be a work in progress, a worthwhile challenge, and the site for continued growth for educators.

Probing Questions

- Fran describes her approach to teaching as a relentless effort to offer a wide range of activities and assessments to meet the needs of students who vary greatly in their styles of thinking and learning. "If you do the same thing every day, students will be bored. If you do the same thing every day, some students will never learn from that style. By mixing up the techniques you use and topics you teach, you will be sure to hit each student at least once or twice throughout the week." Look closely at your own habits and routines of teaching. How you diversify the learning activities and assessments that students experience?
- When Fran looks at Steven, she sees a hard-working student with great potential. How does this philosophy inform and fuel her teaching with Steven?
- Why is Sarah's use of "citizenship rubrics" and "post-it" notes with Miguel ultimately effective in improving his behavior and academic work? How much of this success is due to these techniques and how much is due to Sarah's unyielding belief that Miguel can learn and improve?
- How does Sarah's "training wheels" approach to essay writing demonstrate how instructional scaffolding can be provided and withdrawn as necessary?

CHAPTER TWENTY

What 20+ Years of Secondary Inclusion Has Taught Us

DOUGLAS FISHER AND NANCY FREY

In some ways, it seems so long ago and in other ways, it was just yesterday. Although we have learned a lot about providing inclusive educational experiences for adolescents with disabilities since 1992, it's hard to forget the first student with a significant disability who was included in regular education classes in San Diego, CA. We had wanted to try inclusive education for several months, mainly because we had heard stories told by Ian Pumpian, Jeff Strully, Jan Nisbet, and Rich Villa that challenged our thinking and clearly demonstrated that it was possible to educate children inclusively, at least at the elementary school level. When these experts spoke about students that looked like ours, we realized that we were holding our students back. If Jeff's daughter had attended our school at that time, she would have been segregated. Luckily, she attended a school that understood the range of supports that were necessary to appropriate educate all students.

Today, we recognize that geography is the greatest predictor of inclusive education. Not disability. It's where you live that matters. The high school where we work now educates a wide range of students with very diverse needs. Some of them have disabilities, and some of those students would be identified as having significant disabilities. Other students have histories of drug abuse, or have probation officers, or don't feel loved by their parents. No matter; they're all educated alongside their peers. We also recognize that if the students with disabilities who attend our school enrolled in a school just five blocks away, their lives would be very different. They would be segregated, attending separate classes, organized by their type of disability. At that school, there are classes for students with autism, different classes for students with learning disabilities, different classes for students with significant disabilities, and different classes for students with behavioral support needs, all of which are separate from each other and from students without disabilities. It's what they think is best. They're not bad people. They just don't realize that geography matters; the luck of the draw for students across the United States means that some are educated alongside their peers and others are not. Savvy parents even move (or lie about their address) to gain entrance into schools that will provide the type of educational services they desperately want for their children. We really haven't come that far since 1992 when Jamie enrolled in our school.

Jamie had no history in the local school system because she came from out of state. She was a tenth grader, but had not spent any time in a regular education classroom. She was labeled as having Down Syndrome and "severe mental retardation." She was interested in animals, magazines, and especially clothes. Our principal knew that we wanted to try to provide appropriate supports for a student with a significant disability in regular classes but our director of special education was not supportive. In fact, he said, "I don't want to be on the cutting edge, because it really is the bleeding edge." So we didn't tell him. Jamie's mom conveniently "lost" the transfer paperwork, so we decided that the least restrictive environment was the regular classroom. Actually, it was five regular classrooms because, unlike the stories we heard about elementary school inclusion, we (critical friends who supported the school with student teachers, professional development, and teacher coaching) had to find five different teachers in different content areas who would *allow* a student with a significant disability to enroll. Imagine that. There was a time when professional public school educators were allowed to stand up at a staff meeting and proclaim that they did not want students with disabilities in their classes. It was accepted. Of course, years before this, it was acceptable to declare that you didn't want African-American students in your class (remember *Brown v. Board of Education*?). It had been socially accepted for a teacher to refuse to educate English learners. It was standard practice to counsel girls out of science and into Home Economics (Doug's mom was told that she did not need science and that she should work on her Mrs. Degree instead). We wonder, twenty years later, is it still acceptable for educators to pick and choose the students they want to educate? Are public school teachers, adults that the public entrusts to educate children, allowed to say that they don't want to provide a free and appropriate education for students with disabilities? That's why we didn't tell. And we learned a valuable lesson along the way: It's better to ask for forgiveness than permission.

The five teachers who supported Jamie were awesome, but we were not. We went to every one of her classes and stood by, ready to support her at any time. We got in the way. One example, one of many, illustrates this point. On her fourth day of inclusion, Jamie's biology class was dissecting a squid. This was not the best day for an English major and an elementary school teacher, but we were there for Jamie. With gusto, we participated with the group of students, making sure that they correctly removed each part, appropriately labeled the part, and maintained a clean work area. Students in other groups were flinging squid parts, writing with squid ink, and generally having a lot of fun in their groups. At the end of the class, the teacher asked to see us after school. We were convinced that she was going to ask for help with managing the rest of the class. Instead, when we met with her, she expressed her disappointment in our group's work. She said that students were supposed to have fun with the lab and that none of the students wanted to be in Jamie's group again. In fact, she said that we had interrupted the peer learning that was supposed to take place in this type of experience. We were shocked. We had made sure that they all learned. They made sure that they all took turns. We ensured that they did everything right. In reality, we had removed the need for students to engage in this task. And we remove the opportunities for Jamie to engage in authentic ways with her peers and for her peers to learn to provide natural support.

Over several weeks, we learned a valuable lesson, namely to reduce the reliance on adults and focus on peers. That's not to say that special education teachers and paraprofessionals aren't important; of course they are. It's what we ask them to do that matters. Jamie and her peers taught us that our roles should be to facilitate peer support, to monitor, to provide curriculum support, and then to get out of the way. Today, we practice this in our school. We rely on student support, natural supports, and we intervene only when necessary. We have reduced students' reliance on adults, and keep adults around for the technical aspects that need to be addressed. For example, Brandy (a current student) had a world history test, which needed to be modified. That's an appropriate role for the special educator. Ahmed, another current student, was having difficulty using his speech output device. That's also an appropriate role for the special educator. However, when Justin was having difficulty making friends, the students needed to be involved. Although their planning meeting was facilitated by a special educator, the students helped Justin learn what friends expected. They taught him about eye contact, starting and stopping conversations, and which topics were off-limits for discussion. They even collected some video footage of him interacting with peers and talked with him about times when he was demonstrating good friendship behaviors and when he strayed a bit. We're not suggesting that inclusive education is about abdicating responsibility, but rather that peers have valuable lessons that they can teach.

We noted the role of the special educator in modifying curriculum. Jamie taught us about this as well. Actually, she taught us to make accommodations and modifications only as special as necessary. We had learned from the best, Alice Udvari-Solner and Cheryl Jorgensen, about curriculum accommodations and modifications. We knew that (see Figure 20.1 for examples of accommodations and modifications):

- *Accommodations* increase a student's access to the existing curriculum by altering how the student receives information or demonstrates mastery. Accommodations do not significantly alter what is being learned, only how it is being learned. For example, accommodations might include audio books, enlarged print, or extended time to complete an assignment.
- *Modifications* are more significant changes to the curriculum itself. Most commonly, the student is responsible for mastering specific aspects of the curriculum and the difficulty is reduced. For example, modifications might include fewer choices on a multiple choice test, a different reading selection, or producing an outline of an essay with an associated spoken version, rather than a traditional essay.

Figure 20.1. Comparing and contrasting accommodations and modification.

Accommodation	Example
Size: Size lowers the number of items a student completes, with no change to difficulty.	• Number of assigned multiplication problems is reduced from 20 to 10, but the difficulty of the problems is not altered. • Reducing the chapter review questions from 25 to 15, selecting key questions that assess understanding.
Time: Time you allot for learning, task completion, or testing.	• Extra time to complete a test. • Developing a timeline and checklist for completing an extended project with regular check-ins from an adult.
Input: Input means changing the way instruction is delivered to the learner.	• Listen to a recording of a book after reading the section in a book club. • Student gets note pages in Earth Science.
Output: Adapting how the learner can respond to instruction.	• Create a poster instead of a research paper for World History. • Dictate answers on an addition facts worksheet.
Level of support: Changing the amount of personal assistance to an individual learner.	• Recording a conversation with a teacher for later use in writing using a LiveScribe pen. • A peer aids a student in constructing a diorama of the first Thanksgiving.

Modification	Example
Same only less: The numbers of items are reduced to change the level of difficulty.	• Number of possible answers on a multiple choice quiz is reduced from five to two. • A timed fluency measure is reduced to meet the developmental needs of the learner. • A book at a lower reading level is selected for the student.
Streamline: The assignment is reduced in breadth or focus to emphasize the key points.	• Creates a list of main points in English instead of an essay. • Vocabulary for a social studies unit on of study on explorers is simplified.
Same activity with infused objective: IEP objectives or skills are emphasized.	• Answer yes/no questions using his eyes to locate words on a lap tray. In Music, teacher and classmates remember to phrase questions in this format. • The goal of learning measurements is practice in each science lab. • Sight words are practiced with peers as part of a "read the room" activity.
Curriculum overlapping: The assignment for one class may be completed in another, and is a replacement.	• A student works on a poster for social studies, and receives a grade in Language Arts as well. • A science lab report is used as a report of information to replace a writing assignment.

Source: Fisher, D., & Frey, N. (2012). Accommodations and modifications with learning in mind. *The Special Edge, 25*(2), i–iv.

What Jamie taught us was that we often overcompensated with accommodations and modifications. She needed different levels of support at the outset of a new unit of study than she needed well into the unit. She needed less support over the course of the year, despite the fact that we were still trying to implement the approved accommodations and modifications from her IEP. For example, we remember her English class and the third time she had to present to the class. Previously, we had helped her develop an outline using picture symbols and then recorded her speech for her so that she could play it aloud. We were prepared to do that again when she came to school with an illustration of the book that she had created. She didn't need us to find pictures. She was creating them herself. And she was creating pictures appropriate for the text that the teacher was reading aloud. We still had to address the fact that she had to "present" but we solved that when one of her classmates suggested that she hold up each picture and that he record some of his ideas so that she could play them. He suggested that they work together and that Jamie could approve or not approve the ideas that he recorded based on what he was seeing in her illustrations. Yes, these two students were trying to tell us that accommodations and modifications should only be as special as necessary.

Jamie also taught us about input accommodations. She had a hard time with input in her biology class. The teacher used a lot of animations with sound and Jamie wasn't learning from this approach. The accommodation was fairly simple. We asked a peer to summarize and synthesize the information and meet with Jamie during study times to review the content. We also recorded the teachers' presentations so that Jamie could play the recording over again and again to listen to the information. In her art class, we used a technology innovation to facilitate Jamie's participation. In the past, while she was in a self-contained classroom, Jamie had an objective that required that she push a switch to learn cause and effect. At that time, she pushed a switch to operate a fan that blew in her face. Her team at our school did not see this as relevant, until we connected the switch to the pottery wheel. The wheel would only turn when she depressed the switch, allowing her partner to mold the clay. Jamie received extensive and regular feedback from her peer and learned to maintain her focus and keep the switch pressed.

Having said that, it's important to recognize that not everything from class needs to be studied and learned. It's not like all of us remember all of the content we were exposed to in high school. As Paula Kluth often notes in her presentations, students with disabilities have the same right to forget the content as their peers without disabilities. We are not saying that the content of high school is unimportant; it is important to engage in the thinking of school. It's just that the level of detail of some classes may not be that important in the long run. We need to focus on the big ideas, critical thinking opportunities, and develop learning habits. This was freeing, as we were trying to find ways to force Jamie to learn and remember everything. When we started focusing on developing habits, Jamie was happier and ended up learning more.

When Jamie's mom "found" her IEP a few weeks after Jamie was attending regular classes full-time, it was hard to argue that she should be educated in a special education classroom. We had evidence that she was successful in the regular class. But there were some identified objectives that focused on basic or functional skills. We were faced with a dilemma. Should we remove Jamie from her regular classes to provide these skills or was she better off in the regular education classroom? Thankfully, we met Beverly Rainforth who suggested that supplemental instruction can be provided in the regular classroom. If a skill is worth learning, it's likely that other students are using, or learning, that same skill. Consider the once ubiquitous shoe-tying objective. Despite the fact that there are slip-on shoes and Velcro shoes, many shoes still need to be tied. Students all over high school tie their shoes, but no place more often than in physical education. Jamie needed a PE class so that she could practice her shoe tying, and so we could meet her IEP objective. She also had an objective which related to learning measurements. This was historically seen as a prerequisite skill for learning cooking. Jamie was already in a science class where measuring was frequent. We just needed to make sure that Jamie received instruction in measuring, and practice in the skill, each time the class needed to measure. Simply asking the teacher to alert us to upcoming opportunities to measure allowed us to meet that IEP objective.

Now we know that we need to scour the school to determine the range of skills students learn and practice in different environments so that when we meet a student who needs instruction in a specific skill, we know where that is being practiced. Commonly known as an ecological inventory, this is valuable and worth our time. When Javier's family noted that he needed to learn 200 sight words, we knew that English was the right place for him. There are lots of opportunities to learn words in English and his English teacher was more than happy to add ten or so high frequency words each week to her word wall and invite Javier and his peers to practice them. When Sarah's occupational therapist suggested that she needed more fine motor practice, we knew that three-dimensional art was the right class because students are always touching and moving objects in that class. Yes, as Jamie showed us twenty years ago, skills are functional when they are being learned or used by other people the same age. By extension, she also taught us that when you can't find a place where others are learning or using the skill, it's probably not functional. This was the case for Deborah, who came to us with an objective related to grocery shopping. It's not that other students her age don't do that. It's just that they don't do it during the school day. In talking with Deborah's parents, we noted that she would have to be removed from her classes, away from her peers, to grocery shop when senior citizens and stay-at-home moms were shopping. Instead, we offered to develop picture shopping lists and a task analysis card for her parents to use at night or on the weekends, when others her age might be in the store.

Four years after meeting Jamie, she taught us one last lesson. In her transition planning meeting, Jamie's parents raised the issue of her living situation. They recognized that she was getting older and that she deserved an opportunity to live on her own. They had the means to rent an apartment for her, but were worried about the support she would need to be successful on her own. During the meeting, one of Jamie's peers who had known her for three years, said "I'm going to San Diego State University and wanted to live near campus, but not in the dorm. Maybe Jamie could be my roommate. I mean, I already know her. I know that she likes to walk, but not up or down stairs. Maybe there could be a few us girls who could get a place together [...]."

And there it was. The solution we were all looking for. Jamie moved into her first apartment with three girls from her high school. Of course, her parents were still involved in her life, but so were the parents of the other girls. It was not perfect and they did get themselves into trouble a few times, such as the time when they "forgot" to pay the gas and electric bill and the power was shut off or the time when they were too loud late at night and the police came. But we learned something very important when Jamie's peers advocated for her to live with them. Inclusive education leads to an inclusive life, filled with all of the trials and tribulations that we endure as we create our networks. Segregated education leads to a segregated life. When students are segregated, there's no one to advocate for them, other than family and the people who are paid to be in their lives. When students are segregated, their peers without disabilities fail to develop an understanding of the range of human experience, which includes disability. These peers do not willingly hire people with disabilities or vote to maintain funding for in home support or respite care for individuals in need.

Jamie died a few years ago of a congenital heart condition. Her dad said, "This is the power of inclusion. There are people at her funeral that we don't know. Had she been segregated, it would have just been us." Yes, inclusive education leads to a fuller life; one that you or I would be proud to live.

> **Probing Questions**
> - Douglas and Nancy assert "that geography is the greatest predictor of inclusive education." Is this true? If so, why?
> - Over twenty years after their initial experience with inclusion, the authors ask, (I)s it still acceptable for educators to pick and choose the students they want to educate? Many researchers and experts still recommend doing inclusion only with general educators who volunteer to participate. Does this make sense? Is this right?
> - Notice how arrangements are made for Jamie to complete her IEP objectives in general education classrooms. This acknowledges that, at times, individual IEP objectives do not match neatly with the grade-level curriculum. How can IEP teams and IEP planning work to support students with disabilities in general classrooms?
> - Douglas and Nancy offer a structured approach to modifications and accommodations. How would their approach to differentiation of student tasks apply to the subject matter that you teach?

CHAPTER TWENTY-ONE

"Now, I'm part of the family [...] well, almost!"

Family Matters for Schooling Success

JOHN COLIN AND SRIKALA NARAIAN

Ours is a shared narrative of a high school special education teacher (John Colin) and a university-based researcher (Kala Naraian) inquiring into inclusive practices. We met during a professional development opportunity to strengthen family-school connections offered through a partnership between a university and a large urban school system of more than 1500 schools in the Northeastern part of the United States. The Board of Education in the city had recently announced a special education reform initiative whereby no school could reject a student with disabilities if (s)he was otherwise eligible to be educated within that building. (Typically, thus far, if a school did not feel able to support a student with disabilities, she/he could be simply referred to an alternate site.) All schools participating in the pilot phase of this initiative were eligible to send educators to various professional development (PD) strands that collectively offered an opportunity to develop the skills that could promote inclusive schooling. John was one of several participants in the PD experience, designed and led by Kala, on strengthening family-school connections.

JOHN

I work in a "high need" urban high school that serves students considered "at risk." The label "high need" draws on the fact that over sixty percent of our students' families fall below a certain income level; thus, the students qualify for the city's free breakfast and lunch program. "At risk" means that, statistically, our student population tends to struggle in school, having comparatively low grades, low promotion rates, and poor graduation rates. My school is relatively small with just over 300 students; it is also fairly new—it opened in 2005—and our students are mostly Latino and African American. What is unique about my school, however, is that we have an intensive arts program, offering students the opportunity to major in drama, art, music, or dance. Our students are given the opportunity to perform in multiple shows each year, work with some of the city's most talented artists and producers, and attend many professional artistic performances each year. We require no auditions or pre-testing for student eligibility, giving preference instead to students that reside within the neighborhood in which the school is located. Although a large percentage of our students are from the immediate neighborhood, students from all parts of the city attend my school.

Another unusual characteristic of my school is that about thirty percent of the student population is designated "special education," meaning that these students have been identified as having some sort of disability that entitles them to an individual education program (IEP). Most schools in this city have approximately six percent to ten percent of their students identified as special education; thirty percent is considerably higher. The large population of special education students has presented a unique challenge for the school and my colleagues: how to differentiate instruction so it is accessible to all learners, while at the same time maintaining an appropriate pace of instruction to ensure that students master all the content necessary to pass mandated standardized state assessments—clearly, a very difficult balancing act. This challenge has made us all better teachers, however, forcing us to hone our pedagogy, share best practices, and creatively find effective methods of teaching students of all ability levels.

We offer robust support for our students, both academic and social/emotional. Our very skilled guidance counselor, social workers, and parent coordinator ensure that students are emotionally prepared to learn, and intervene with students and their families when they are not. There is much interaction between student families and the school; formally, through phone calls, letters, emails and conferences, and informally, before and after school performances, during school events and through our rich extra-curricular programs. Each teacher maintains their own website pages and the school utilizes a web-based grading program, so all class content and grades are accessible to parents and students online. We consistently get very high marks from parents on our annual city-sponsored survey regarding how welcomed they feel at the school and how included they feel in their child's education. Still, although my school works hard to keep families involved in the school, despite our many successes, our family school interactions tend to be dictated by the school. I was soon to learn that the very construct within which family involvement is framed can mean the difference between mere family *involvement*, and a more prodigious experience of family *engagement*.

When it was announced that our school would be piloting a new special education reform initiative—specifically, expanding the concept of inclusive classrooms—I knew it would be an exciting and challenging endeavor. Exciting, because my school was already committed to special education students; a school culture, which embraced a philosophy that good "special ed" teaching was in fact just good teaching, had resulted in our "at risk" population beating the odds. Our test results, promotion and graduation rates have been consistently higher for our students compared to other schools in the city with similar student populations. Exciting, because many of the creative things we were already doing in my school were being championed by the current special education reform agenda. Namely, that special education services should be flexible; a student who may need integrated co-teaching services for literacy may not need such services for math, while needing other services for science. This was not a new concept at my school, it was already in practice, and now, by being a pilot school in the reform implementation, we could no longer be considered out of compliance for it.

The challenge, however, was just as significant as the excitement. We were all asking the same questions. Students of all abilities taught in every classroom? How can that possibly work? Having taught for three years in a special education district—in a school composed solely of students with severe emotional disabilities—prior to coming to my current community school, I was very concerned about integrating students across every spectrum of ability into every school, let alone every classroom. Would the city provide the appropriate supports for such a drastic change in education? Was this just a covert way for the city to cut special education funding? My colleagues and I were pressing for answers. Surprisingly some were offered, not directly of course, but in the form of monthly professional development meetings to be held over the course of the school year at a local university. My principal asked me to participate in one of the professional development strands and I was happy to accept. In choosing which one to take up, the words of my deceased Aunt Lorna, an Order of St. Joseph's nun who spent her life as an educator in Brooklyn, came to me, "Education must be about the whole family, not just the student." With this in mind, I enrolled in the "Families" strand.

KALA

My experiences prior to entering academia as a teacher of students labeled blind, visually impaired or significantly disabled, socialized me very early on into the adversarial character of family-school relations common within public schools. All of my colleagues, it seemed, were clearly aware of the lines that demarcated their roles from that of families. I heard many stories of families suing schools, of "troublesome" families and the sheer unreasonableness of families bringing lawyers unannounced to IEP meetings. Senior teachers cautioned their junior colleagues to maintain extensive documentation so that it could serve as crucial evidence to counter imagined family charges against the school. It seemed to me that conflict, rather than collaboration, was the tacit norm when planning for family-school meetings and encounters. I learnt simultaneously to be fully aware of the legal procedures for involving families in the schooling of their children with disabilities. It was not long before it became uncomfortably apparent to me, however, that there could be no regulations on how to both respect their legal rights and simultaneously embrace them as knowledgeable partners.

As I worked with IEP's, progress reports and parent-teacher conferences, I came to see that procedures that carefully structured the relations between schools and families could easily obscure the latter's experience of disability. I often heard educators say, "I can't even imagine what it must be like to raise a child with a disability." Although I understand the good intentions behind this attempt at empathy, I flinch whenever I hear it. Is adversity the only way to frame disability? But with few alternative ways to understand it, teachers, it seems, fall back on typical deficit-based responses to families. *This* family is in denial and "unrealistic" in its expectations or *that* mother is too "pushy" and thinks school professionals should do what she says. I have also heard educators report with frustration that despite their best efforts to encourage their involvement, families do not show up for IEP conferences, fail to return phone calls, or do not carry out the instructions of therapists.

It is much harder to see how the school-based nature of these expectations as well as its stereotypical assumptions of disability can determine whether a parent is described as "involved" or "uninvolved." As both a parent within the public school system and as a researcher, I have been frustrated by the conventional expectation that families should support schools rather than make schools more responsive to families. Along with many other families, I have balked at the cookie-baking, pencil-sharpening, classroom-vacuuming limits of how we are permitted to participate in our children's education. While this may work for some families, the fact remains that schools typically dictate how we can show that we care about our children's education. So, as I designed this strand of professional development for educators grappling with special education reform I wanted to challenge perceptions of families within schools. In privileging the experiences of families of students with disabilities, I simultaneously hoped to bring about a shift in the ways they interpreted disability.

The essential questions of our work together, therefore, were as follows: How does increasing parent involvement differ from strengthening connections between schools and families? What meanings of disability inform the ways we approach families of students with disabilities? How can we use our knowledge of the families in our schools to alter our current practices for families of students with disabilities? What would our work look like if we simply presumed that *all* families cared for their children? We met monthly as a group on the university premises for a period of nine months and grappled with these questions through a variety of inquiry-based exercises. I also required participants to carry out a home visit and interview a family of one of their students with disabilities. While a commonplace practice for many school personnel such as social workers or counselors, I have found that teachers are less likely to consider home visits as generating knowledge that would be useful to them. How would a meeting in a family's home alter the ways a teacher related to a student? How would that influence the type of supports students with disabilities received in the classroom? I had a suspicion that many of my participants would have much to be surprised about.

JOHN

Meeting on a Friday morning once a month from September through June, the Family-School Connections strand provided an intellectual oasis for deep theoretical reflection on my own teaching, and teaching in general; a refreshing and energizing experience for this practitioner. It had been several years since I earned my master's in education, and I welcomed the opportunity to explore current philosophical theories and research regarding education, special education, and the family-school connection. Under the skilled leadership of the university professor that facilitated the group, a language and context was established in which we engaged in genuine inquiry into the issues, questions, benefits, and dilemmas associated with the current level of engagement of families of children with disabilities within the school and ways in which this relationship might be deepened. As the year progressed, it was revealed that each participant would be doing a family interview composed of two parts, an initial interview at the school, followed up by a second interview at the family's home. This interview was an attempt to begin the process of deepening family engagement with the school, an experience framed more by the family and less by the educational institution.

It was at this point that the challenge eclipsed the excitement regarding my association with the citywide special education reform initiative. As a mandated reporter, how could I possibly conduct not one, but two interviews with the family of a student I taught? What if the family told me they practiced corporal punishment, or any of an infinite number of other reportable things? Whether revealed to me, directly by the family members, or through my own observations, I would have to report it, and what would THAT do to the family-school connection, not to mention my relationship with the student? Finally, such personal interactions between the school and families are reserved for the school's family worker, guidance staff or school counselors, not teachers. This was how the school system was structured; what were the consequences of operating outside this protocol? After vetting many of my concerns with the professor, my principal, and several colleagues, I decided I would be able to do the family interview provided I was very clear with the family about my status as a mandated reporter, and all the implications that status carried. Further, I was careful to choose a family with whom I had already developed some relationship for my inaugural interview; albeit a relationship in the most traditional sense of the school-family connection, limited to phone calls home, parent-teacher conferences and special notices.

I worked with my peers in the PD group to develop a list of questions for the interview. This process, in itself, revealed many areas where the bias of the educational institution frames, even dictates, the tone and structure of customary family-school interactions. Serving as the transition coordinator at my school, I decided to use the Vocational I assessment provided in the city's Standard Operating Procedures Manual as a launching point for framing my interview questions. This assessment is in three parts, one to be completed by the student, one by the parent(s), and one by the student's teacher(s). In general, the assessment seeks to find out about the student's current interests and their post-high school goals, that is, post-secondary education and career choices. I was surprised to find that only the teacher version of this assessment asked if the student's goals and expectations were realistic, and whether the parent's expectations of the student were realistic. Couldn't these questions be asked also of the student and their family? Why was questioning the practicality of the student's goals or their families' expectations of them solely the domain of the teacher? After much collaboration, we were able to construct several interview questions framed within the language and goals of the work we were doing within the Families PD group. They were questions that presumed parental and family competence, sought the expertise of the family regarding their child's education, and were open-ended in order to better solicit the families' perspective. Summoning all my courage, I emailed the mother of my student, Talia, asking if she would be interested in participating in the inquiry in which I was involved by allowing me to do this interview. The mom agreed, and we set a date to meet in my office at the school.

KALA

As a researcher who routinely interviews families, I certainly did not anticipate the difficulty many educators would have in developing their questions for families. I realized that the purpose of the interview and home visit was still not fully clear to many of them. I had to help them understand that the goal was not merely to learn more about the student in relation to school. It was to understand the family in deeper ways and then figure out what that would mean for their own practice. In other words, if we are to shift our thinking from families as merely supporting the work of schools, to schools as serving to strengthen families and by extension the entire community, then it must be reflected in the questions we ask of them. This meant that we would need to adopt a posture of "I-want-to-learn-FROM-you" (please tell me your story) rather than "I-am-a-professional-sent-to-learn-ABOUT-you" (I am collecting information about you).

Easier said than done. With a genuine desire to learn about their families, some educators in our group were still tempted to ask: *Does your child respect you? What is the highest level of education that you have completed? Is there an established routine at home once your child is finished with school? Is there someone at home that can help your child with his/her homework? How is it that you do not know pertinent information (for example, grade level, teacher name, class) regarding your child? Do you feel capable of assisting your child at home?* When I asked them to reflect on the assumptions of deficit that underlay such questioning, they struggled to understand what I was asking of them. Did it not make sense to ask families questions that would reveal how much a student was being supported? It took several rounds of discussions before many members of our group realized that such questions suggested that families had little to offer the school besides sharing information about the student's potential for academic success.

So we worked collectively to identify other questions that were open-ended and which could draw out broad areas of family experiences unknown to schools. *Why did you immigrate to the United States? What are some of your cultural rituals and practices? What does your child like about school? What do they often rave about? Complain about? Do you think your child is happy at this school? What are the things that make you uncomfortable at your child's school? What changes would you like to see? What concerns and/or expectations do you have for your child's learning? Do you feel comfortable in asking the school community for assistance or guidance involving your child's education?* Though still rooted in traditional perceptions of family matters as separate from the work of schools, we were nevertheless slowly making the shift from assuming that families needed to change to wondering how *schools* could change from knowing them. This was a difficult process and not everyone in the group accomplished it. John was one of the few who did and who also recognized the limitations of a survey-like questioning method. Adopting the position of "I-want-to-learn-FROM-you" more explicitly he invited his interviewee to speak without limiting her responses. For example, he would say "Talk to me about [...]" or "Would you tell me more about that?" This permitted him to avoid making assumptions about the family and allowed the family member to share what was important to *them* regarding that issue.

Some might argue that we were just trying to get additional data to help us understand why our students performed the ways they did in school—so why all this fuss about types of questions? But such questions can also carry the kernels for changing the culture within school buildings. For instance, asking families different questions (and asking them differently) implied that John was already beginning to think differently about them. As his story illustrates, this meant that he could now begin to pose different questions to his own colleagues regarding the schooling of students with disabilities. In other words, by altering his position toward *this* family he would necessarily have to alter his relations with the *school*. It seems that many educators, regardless of their receptivity to family experiences, are unable to accomplish this. What seemed distinctive about John's inquiry was his readiness to question his own assumptions in the process of developing questions for the family he would interview. That has always remained the most important, and most difficult, aspect of approaching families in non-judgmental ways. What do my questions to this family say about who *I* am and what *I* think?

JOHN

The first interview in my office began as a very typical family-school encounter. Talia's mother was concerned about a recent disciplinary action involving her daughter and wanted to assure me that she supports the school and has addressed the issue with her daughter at home. We talked about the student's progress in her classes and their hopes for the student after graduation. At this point I began asking the questions I had prepared and eventually the interview began to be more focused on the concerns and interests of the student and how they were supported in her family. Having obtained permission, I audiotaped the interview.

Following the interview, I made a transcript of the recording in order to identify what areas I wanted to explore more deeply with the family during the home visit. I was surprised by how much I spoke during the interview. I found myself cringing at how often I jumped in to re-clarify something or comment about a statement the mother made, many times defeating the purpose of asking open-ended questions. The biggest takeaway I obtained from reviewing the transcript was that I needed to remain silent while the family responded to my questions and to allow them to direct the course of their responses without my help.

On the evening of the second interview, while I walked to the family's home situated in a public housing complex a few blocks from my apartment, I realized that I had never been in a public housing building in my life. I had always valued living in the same neighborhood in which I taught. I had a better context from which to relate to my students and teach them. We were affected by a common environment and shared many reference points of daily life. It was common for me to see them on the street, in a store or at a park, sometimes with their friends, sometimes with their families. It was a great opportunity for deepening the teacher-student relationship within an informal context. I wondered how my presence in even closer proximity to their homes, and *in* their homes, might further strengthen my connection with my students and their families.

Conducting the second interview in my student's home allowed me amazing access to her life, her "story," and the story of her family. The house was buzzing with three cousins that the mother cared for after school for another daughter. I was able to see exactly where my student did her homework, and tutored her cousins. I was able to meet and talk with my student's father, which would have been impossible if I were not in their home, as he has a disability that prevents him from leaving the apartment. And I managed to restrain my guiding comments fairly well.

Many insights were gained from my experience in conducting this interview, both tangible and intangible. Holding the interview in the family's home had a profound effect in leveling the power construct of a typical family-school meeting. I found it refreshing to converse with my student and her family without the looming authority of the educational institution physically framing our interaction. Instead, we were in a home with a precocious three-year-old that wanted to crawl on his grandmother and try to play with my recorder. Not only did the home environment alter my perspective, it also allowed the family to interact more freely with me, which was what I had hoped for. I learned a great deal about their history and the resources they provided to their children. I found out that my student's mother served as interpreter for *her* mother who didn't speak any English when they immigrated to this country. As a result, my student's mother knew just about everything there is to know about most institutions in the city, from housing, to hospitals, schools, courts, churches, community organizations, and the list goes on. What a resource I thought for the school and other families in the school! I also learned that my student's sister attended a very highly regarded university in the city, and that the family was very well versed in the process of applying for and getting accepted to colleges, a great asset for my student and another potential resource for other families in my school. More importantly, however, I learned through the family interview process all the other dimensions that made Talia's mother an entire person, as opposed to only being the mother of one of my students. This understanding immediately levels the power construct of the parent-teacher relationship, allowing for more genuine discourse.

After the interview, I was sparking with ideas about how to leverage this family's expertise with other families, while at the same time vetting out the expertise of all the other families that remained hidden, at least to the school and me. Ideas about somehow connecting everyone with each other so that all these resources could be shared, and whereby these families—and, by extension, the school—could be more empowered. I had visions of a whole social media network based on navigating the education system, coordinating daycare, tutoring, extracurricular activities, community events, college preparation, civic actions, etc. To create a web that would foster genuine connections not only between families and schools, but families and other families. The school, acting as the hub of this networking would not only facilitate further empowerment of our families, but benefit from it as well. I was excited to begin this process.

KALA

When I designed the PD sequence in which John participated, I wanted to fold in some compelling concepts that would resonate with educators, but I was also nervous that I would be perceived as too "theoretical" and out of touch with the realities of practice. I was pleasantly surprised at how readily the group participants adopted the notions of *funds of knowledge* (Moll, Amanti, Neff, & Gonzalez, 1992) and *presuming competence* (Biklen & Burke, 2006). I hoped the first would offer a way to learn about and value the knowledges that families develop through their unique sociocultural experiences, while the second might enable group members to avoid evaluative descriptions of family behavior and generate alternate explanations. John was the first to take up the construct of "presuming competence" enthusiastically making it central to his own inquiry process within the PD, after which it became an important organizing logic to our collective work. Clearly, he drew on this when seeking to understand and describe the family he interviewed but also when acknowledging the efforts of his colleagues in understanding the process of inclusion. While eager to work with these concepts, not all group members were able to wield them with such fluency as John. Still, they were able to enter them in partial ways, if not fully. Given the culture of accountability in schools where the priorities of objective measurement of student learning are pre-eminent, the full relevance of these concepts may have been less readily discernible to some of them. As I participated in their struggles, I wondered, too, what competencies teachers needed in order to remain inclusively oriented in the context of these competing goals.

John's inquiry offered a simple example of how this might be accomplished. His first attempt at an inclusive orientation in his practice was to begin by interjecting the family perspective into a process that required documentation of student aptitude. He carried out the activity he was *required* to do by school policies with a simple twist—why not ask the family what they thought about the student's self-reported goals? As his efforts illustrate, strengthening family-school connections does not mean that it is *one more thing for teachers to do*. It means that in the course of routine activities of everyday curricular and instructional planning, teachers come to ask themselves: how can a family perspective make this curricular experience accessible to all my students? Of course, this is not to presume that families are a monolithic group or that they need to be involved in every step of classroom decision-making. Still, as most families know, schooling processes have marginalized the value of their input, relegating it to a cursory signature on faceless forms and/or physical presence during pre-determined meetings held at school. But, intercepting these processes at various points, as John did, to deliberately invite greater family involvement places educators in greater control of their efforts to remain inclusively oriented and stalls the mechanical flow of school practices.

I hesitate to demand that teachers undertake such acts of *intrusion* without paying due consideration to their increasingly beleaguered roles within public schooling. Who can deny that creating respectful communities of learners that embrace diversity must go hand-in-hand with "documentation" of student learning to raise the test scores of students, which are then tracked to evaluate their own applications for professional tenure? Working within such constraints, it can become too easy to presume that families' perspectives on their child's education are "unrealistic" or that they demand too much from schools. On the other hand, it seems that educators who successfully avoid this trap are likely to view families as *resources* for their everyday work, that is, not only for sharpening pencils, making copies or organizing classroom parties, but for implementing curricular practice. For instance, the experiences of family members can serve as the curricular content for guided inquiry in the classroom accomplished through research interviews that support students' extended learning projects (Rogovin, 2011).

I have found few institutionally sanctioned spaces within schools for collective inquiry into conceptions of student achievement. More often than not, questions of "how do we know if the student is learning?" (i.e., the pursuit of test scores) completely mask the issue of what counts as learning in the first place. For example, John's struggle to create inclusionary experiences for his students with disabilities was clearly constrained by the nature of the high school examinations. Yet, he was determined to help his students succeed in them, since an IEP diploma, in his words, was worth "nothing, nothing, nothing." I suspect that this requirement to straddle competing goals may lead to the evolution of forms of practice that may not always be immediately recognizable as "inclusive" in its character. But I also worry about how educators will remain vigilant of the ways in which classroom practices can work both toward and against inclusivity. Exercising such reflexivity may occur best when undertaken collectively with colleagues. While John's school principal supported such "kid-talk" inquiry spaces every week in the school, teachers at other schools may try to create their own "inquiry" groups among their colleagues, meeting periodically to discuss relevant texts that can stimulate reflections on their work.

Perhaps the decoupling of specialized supports from physical location permitted the school system in which John was embedded to take the risk in abandoning segregationist practices and creating more opportunities for the inclusion of students with disabilities. The process of "inclusion," therefore, might have been facilitated because the school district conceptualized special education as a set of services rather than as a place. While I don't want to minimize the significance of this step, I am concerned that such a move still keeps intact the notion of "inclusion" as placement in the general education classroom. So of course, questions like "how can I teach to *all* ability levels?" reflect a rational concern expressed by educators. But retaining the focus on the abilities of different students prohibits creative manipulation of social spaces in the building. The present challenge for inclusively-oriented schools and educators like John, therefore, is decoupling "inclusion" from issues of placement and reconfiguring it as "inclusive education."

JOHN AND KALA

The purpose of the inquiry-based PD series in which John participated was to create a cadre of educators who could stimulate deep changes in their schools. First, educators themselves must be able to bring about shifts in their own thinking, in this case about families, and then, subsequently enlist their colleagues in the same process. While research tells us much about the first process, we know very little about the second. John was one of the few participants who was actually able to make that first shift. We knew that the second process would be much harder to accomplish and even harder to document. Still, deeply connected to his school community, John immediately sought to fold his colleagues into a new perspective on families. He conducted a professional development meeting with them focused on the special education reform and his experience in the Families PD group. They certainly did not all run out afterward to conduct family interviews of their own, but it did introduce a context and language that has become part of the culture in his school and which allows for a more balanced consideration of the family and school connection. Recently, as it considered how to better support the ninth-grade students that were being held back, the question of making the school a more accommodating place for the students and their families was raised, and not by John.

It is also true that the ideas John was so inspired to pursue after the family interview have not come to be. The demands of being a teacher have not allowed him the time necessary to be the community organizer he would have to be in order to realize his vision. But there were other immediate and noticeable effects. Certainly the ease with which Talia's family engages with the school has been greatly enhanced. Her mother and John email frequently about her school work and activities even though he no longer teaches her, and he certainly tracks her down when report cards are distributed to check up on her grades. Of course, she is still a high school student who makes bad decisions from time to time, and still struggles with the demands of high school, but John feels that he has become more of a resource to her because of the experience of the family interview, and the family now sees the school as more of a resource as well.

The many concerns we have regarding implementation of special education reform remain. Besides marshaling public support to undertake bold initiatives, large urban districts have to allocate the necessary resources required for this reform to be successful, namely additional staff in the classrooms, smaller class sizes, professional development around increased integration, etc. In the absence of such supports, we feel that teachers are set up to deliver unrealistic expectations and subsequently, represented as incapable of change. Above all, teachers and schools are still being rated overwhelmingly in a high-stakes environment against standardized test results rather than in consideration of the overall academic improvements made by their students. We have come to understand that teacher practices may, therefore, reflect a fumbling and faltering that do not always resemble our idealized visions of inclusive classrooms. Nevertheless, such efforts reflect and sustain our commitments; John continues to push an agenda for drawing on the experiences of families in many small, not always noticeable, but nevertheless impactful ways, while Kala remains preoccupied with probing the experiences of families in supporting the inclusion of their children with disabilities.

REFERENCES

Biklen, D., & Burke, J. (2006). Presuming competence. *Equity & Excellence in Education, 39*, 2, 166–175.

Moll, L. C., Amanti, C., Neff, D., & Gonzalez, N. (1992). Funds of knowledge for teaching: Using a qualitative approach to connect homes and classrooms. *Theory into Practice, 31*(2), 132–141.

Rogovin, P. (2001). *The research workshop*. Portsmouth, NH: Heinemann.

CHAPTER TWENTY-TWO

On the Ethical Meaning of Human Differences

A Non-Disabled Child in Inclusive Schools

SCOT DANFORTH

One of the most glaring and common misunderstandings about inclusive education is the assumption that inclusion is "for" kids who have disabilities. In the inclusive classrooms of many schools, the students with disabilities are called the "inclusion students," as if the majority of the students who just so happen to not have disabilities are not even present, as if they, too, are not "inclusion students." One publication from the National Institute for Urban School Improvement (Staub, 2005, p. 1) calls the nondisabled students "the other kids." This odd way of referring to nondisabled students is arguably quite accurate. To many educators, inclusion is "for" the disabled kids, and the other students are simply going along for the ride.

In some inclusive preschools, an even stranger term is used to talk about the nondisabled students: "role models" (or "peer models"). The assumption behind this stiff expression is that the nondisabled students are the ones who know how to learn well and know how to behave appropriately. They are present with the disabled kids to serve a specific social function, to "model" all of the behaviors and attitudes and language use that the supposedly deficient disabled students should be imitating.

What this phrasing leaves out is the fact that students interact with one another in reciprocal, two-way fashion. The influence from student to student does not merely go one way, from the nondisabled students who are stereotyped as capable to the disabled youngsters who are stigmatized as needing correction. All students influence each other in their interactions and relationships. What actually occurs in classrooms is a multidirectional dance of influence in many directions, involving all the students and the adults in the activities undertaken at the school. Each child plays the role of teacher and student, leader and follower.

Moreover, the influence is not merely between the people. There is a larger influence of the collective whole, of the entire group, upon the learning and growth of every person in the school. In this way, all persons—regardless of ability, regardless of age—contribute to the social and ethical character of the school, and all effectively are influenced by that dynamic and powerful character.

Researchers and practitioners have given very little attention to how involvement in this kind of rich, diverse learning community can be very beneficial to the moral development of students who do not have disabilities, to the lessons of ethical living that the non-disabled students might enjoy. In this story, I'll explore the opportunities for moral growth that my daughter has experienced as a nondisabled student growing up in inclusive schools.

When my wife MaryEllen and I enrolled our daughter Hope in a Reggio Emilia preschool program in Worthington, Ohio, we were undoubtedly searching for a highly supportive and active social community of learners. We certainly found that. But we found something more that we had not anticipated. To this day, we are thankful that Hope was lucky enough to have Edgar, a boy with Down Syndrome in her preschool class. Being Edgar's friend while simultaneously wondering why her friend seemed a bit different opened the door to important conversations and tremendous moral learning. For our daughter, that experience initiated a development toward one of life's most crucial lessons, how to understand human differences in ways that lead to actions of acceptance, love, and respect and not rejection, disdain, and cruelty.

In 1922, John Dewey (p. 245) said that prejudice likely begins with "an antipathy to what is strange," a defensive posture through which one views a person who seems unusual in relation to one's experience. The uncommon can seem dangerous. People are often afraid of a person who doesn't align with their prior experiences and current expectations. The headlines of the daily news are filled with conflict and violence based on perceived differences between groups of people who view one another as strange. Members of one religious group battle against the adherents of a different faith. Members of one racial group describe people of a different race as ignorant, animalistic, and immoral. Members of the dominant group—regardless of what physical or cultural features make them dominant—view a minority population as aberrant, frightening, and perverse. And so on. These many forms of prejudice involve beliefs and actions that distort reason and judgment.

One might imagine that opportunities abound for children to grow up learning about how human differences—race, culture, nationality, sexuality, language, religion, ability, etc.—need not be a source of antipathy and rejection. Love and friendship can quite comfortably thrive across lines of difference if only we can learn to view the many differences as not strange, as simply ordinary aspects of a rich and complex and wonderful life. Perhaps young children can learn this at an early age so that they don't have to unlearn a variety of ugly prejudices and ingrained enmities later in life. But not all schools intentionally seek such opportunities for their students. Luckily for us, Hope attended a preschool that did.

"Daddy, why doesn't Edgar talk?" a small, spirited voice spouted at me from the back seat. I was driving my daughter Hope home from the Creative Play Center preschool (www.creativeplaycenterworthington.org) in Worthington, Ohio. Hope had just turned five years old, and she had apparently just realized that Edgar wasn't producing words in the way her other classmates were.

"He doesn't talk?" I found my daughter's face in the rearview mirror and probed for more information.

"No, he just goes, 'Bub-bub-bub.'"

"Well, before you learned to talk, you used to make all sorts of sounds that weren't really words," I replied, "I think he is still learning how to say words."

"So he doesn't know the words yet?" Hope asked.

"Good question. When you talk to him, does he know what you are talking about?"

"Yeah," Hope affirmed.

"So he understands a lot more language than he can say. He knows a lot of words and what they mean. But he is still learning how to say the words with his mouth."

"When will he be able to talk?"

"I don't know. I'm sure he will learn. But I don't know when."

Hope had a worried look on her face. "Will it be this year?" She was afraid that the school year would end and she wouldn't get to witness Edgar talking. Like a kid trying to stay awake long enough on Christmas Eve to see Santa Claus come down the chimney, she didn't want to wait a long time only to miss out on the big event.

"I hope he talks before the end of the school year. But if he doesn't, is that OK? I mean, is he still your friend?" I asked.

Hope twisted up her face in a quizzical, Daddy-you're-stupider-than-a-box-a-rocks expression. "Yeah!" she moaned, irritated that I would doubt the obvious.

I had introduced an odd, adult notion, a culturally prominent concept that would confront her later in her development, the idea that differences in ability between persons are sufficient rationale for social rejection. At age four, Hope had not yet thought of this. She didn't know then that she was growing up in a culture where certain differences between people would be called "disabilities" and served as common sense reasoning for social isolation and segregation.

For the rest of the school year, Hope quite naturally lived up to her word. Even though Edgar didn't speak any recognizable words, he was undoubtedly her friend. I don't fully explain this attitude of acceptance as a developmental phenomenon, as Hope not yet reaching the level of cognitive development necessary to make categorical distinctions. She was certainly adept at sorting colors, shapes, and basic concepts into classifications. But social separation based on those classifications was not yet a consideration. All of Hope's classmates accepted Edgar without hesitation or reservation. The great teachers and staff members of the Creative Play Center embraced and enacted a philosophy of acceptance and love in every aspect of their program. The children were taught to deeply value and care for one another as members of a shared community.

After attending Kindergarten at the Creative Play Center in Ohio we moved to San Diego where Hope attended the neighborhood public elementary school for the first three grades. It was a school with high standardized test scores but no comprehensive, intentional sense of ethical mission. It would only be a mild exaggeration to say that the lofty test numbers were the purpose of the school. Unfortunately, the approach to special education was very traditional and uninspired. Some students with so-called "mild disabilities" (i.e., not noticeable in everyday school activities) were taught in the general classrooms. Other disabled students went to special education classrooms. For three years, Hope attended classrooms that chiefly lacked meaningful opportunities to interact with, befriend, learn from, and learn with students with disabilities.

For fourth grade, we again had a stroke of luck. We were allowed to switch Hope to an innovative charter school called the San Diego Cooperative Charter School (www.thecoopschools.org), a very progressive, constructivist school where supporting the diversity of all students and parents was the heart and soul of the school. All students with disabilities, regardless of type or "severity" were fully included in the general classrooms. After a gap of three years without disabled classmates, we should not have been surprised when Hope expressed an opinion about her fourth grade classmate Ellie, a girl with an intellectual disability.

"Daddy, why isn't Ellie in the kindergarten? She can't read," Hope asked one day in late October. As usual, she was in the back seat and I was driving her home from school. All the best father-daughter discussions of life, love, and politics occurred through the visual intimacy of the rear view mirror.

"Even though Ellie is the same age as the other kids in your class, she reads more like the kindergarten kids?" I responded.

"Yeah, she's reading baby books."

"So she's really not a very good reader and maybe she could be in the kindergarten with other kids who read more like she does. Hmmm. Let's think about this. First, how do you think Ellie would feel about moving to the kindergarten?"

"BAAAD!" Hope croaked loudly.

"Why?"

"She wouldn't want to be with all the little kids."

"OK, so she'd feel bad. Now what about this—is there anything that you're not very good at? Ellie isn't a great reader. What are you not-so-good at?"

Hope could see where this conversation was going. She reluctantly responded, "PE."

"OK, so maybe should we send the kids who aren't so good in PE to the kindergarten?"

"No, I'd feel terrible. You know that."

"Yes, I did know that. No big kid wants to be placed in the same classroom with the little kids. But what can be done? Ellie's not a very good reader, and she's in the fourth grade with you."

Hope thought for a moment. Then she had an idea. "I think Ellie should stay in my class so she can still be with all her friends. And Ms. Jessica is a good reading teacher."

"So Ms. Jessica is a good enough reading teacher to teach beginning readers and more advanced readers like you?"

"Yeah, that'll work," Hope concluded with an air of satisfaction. Problem solved. Educational researchers and leaders have debated inclusive education for decades, but this fourth grader solved it to her satisfaction in twenty eight seconds.

Hope's initial assertion that Ellie perhaps belonged in the kindergarten consisted of two linked claims. First, as she pointed out, Ellie's reading level was more similar to kindergarten or first graders than the children in her mixed third and fourth grade classroom. There was a question of the best location for Ellie's reading instruction. Hope claimed that children should learn with other students who are working at a similar academic level even if that disrupted patterns of friendship and community in the school. Conjoined with this concept was the very evident fact that Ellie had an intellectual disability. Hope had noticed this fact, and her suggestion to change Ellie's classroom assignment reflected the common cultural norm that disabled persons require separate spaces, especially spaces that are viewed as lacking value.

The move to the kindergarten would certainly be experienced as a demotion to socially inferior group. In our discussion, we were able to tease apart these two dimensions—the pedagogical and the social—in order to come up with a practical solution that would satisfy Ellie's desire to learn to read while not casting her out of the social and relational community of classmates and friends. Ultimately, Hope and I both believed that preserving the established friendships in her classroom while refusing to demean and harm Ellie were important goals.

The next year, in Hope's fifth grade class, there was a boy named Sal. He had a service dog that stayed with him in class to provide support. He seemed to have autism, but neither Hope nor I had any official diagnostic information available to us. Autism is a disability type that has captured the attention of the American media and the public in recent years. So my daughter certainly knew the word, and had some vague notions about what it might mean. But her interest in such abstractions was dwarfed by her intense focus on the members of the small classroom and school community she belonged to. In that sense, "autism" was a vague and distant concept, and Sal was a very tangible, real boy she interacted with each day in class.

One day, as we drove home from school, I casually asked her how Sal was doing.

"Fine," she replied. She had reached the tween age when her responses to parental questions were often painfully cryptic, primarily telling us that the conversation was not very interesting to her. But this time, after a snappy "fine" came a short pause and then more words.

"Some days he gets really frustrated and makes lots of loud noises," she observed. "Then he runs out of the class."

"Why is he frustrated?" I queried.

"I think he wants his mother. He mostly repeats that over and over."

"What is that like for you?" I asked, zooming in how she felt or what she thought about the incident.

"It's OK," she replied with a little shoulder shrug. Many parents or educators might view this kind of event as a difficult disruption of the educational environment. But Hope wasn't fazed in the least. She seemed to accept that this was simply something Sal did.

"Why does Sal rush out of the class?" I probed, wondering if Hope has some idea what was going on inside this boy.

"He can't talk much. He can't get the words out. His mouth won't make the words. So he gets very frustrated," Hope explained.

Just as I started to ask another question, she cut me off—"But he is smart! He has ideas and words in his head. He just gets upset because he can't get them out of his mouth." With this comment, she attended to the conventional assumption that a child who produces little oral or written language is lacking intellectual competence. She seemed to be putting herself in Sal's shoes for a moment and wondering what it would feel like to have words you want to say but they won't come out of your mouth.

"But how do you know he's smart?" I pressed. As I asked this question, I thought about many years of research by Doug Biklen and his colleagues (Biklen & Burke, 2006; Biklen & Duchan, 1994; Biklen & Kliewer, 2006; Kliewer, Biklen, & Kasa-Hendrickson, 2006) with people with intellectual disabilities and autism. Biklen's research repeatedly demonstrated how people often assume that a person with an intellectual disability or autism is empty of worthwhile, useful cognition. Especially in the case of a disabled person who speaks very little or who engages in unusual behaviors, educators and laypersons frequently presume that the person is intellectually and practically incompetent, incapable of understanding and participating in meaningful social interactions. Unknowingly, Hope's comments about Sal placed her right in the middle of a Professor Biklen seminar on the presumption of competence.

"Oooh, I know he's smart," my daughter in a confident tone. "I can tell that he has ideas he wants to say."

"But how do you *know*?" I pressed, half-expecting that she would not have a substantive response to my question. Perhaps this was just a ten-year-old girl's quixotic wishfulness guiding her view of her classmate. My daughter has a powerful imagination and a strong desire to use it whenever possible. Academic requirements of "evidence" count for little in her world.

But she truly did have an answer based on evidence. She presented her case clearly and succinctly. "Sal knows how to sign. I've seen him do it. If he can use sign language, then he has ideas that he wants to say." In the United States, it is not uncommon to teach American Sign Language to young people with autism who struggle to communicate with oral language. Hope was right. Sal's intelligence could not be fairly appraised on the basis on his lack of oral speech or his frequent outbursts in class. Hope could see Sal's competence. She was curious to know the ideas or feelings that he would like to express to his classmates. Although she did not know what he might say, she knew that he was intelligent.

On another occasion, Hope related a story about working together with Sal and her best pal Rose in a cooperative learning group. "We were working on a project together. At the end, when we were all done, Sal's interpreter (Sal sometimes had an ASL interpreter to facilitate communication with classmates and teachers) asked him, 'What was the best thing about this group lesson?' And Sal answered back, 'The friends are OK.'"

"So what did that mean to you, Hope?" I asked.

"Sal doesn't always want to be with the other kids. He doesn't always like everyone. But he likes me and Rose 'cause we know how to work with him.'" Sal felt some degree of comfort with these two girls, most probably because they interacted with him in ways that facilitated his participation and fostered friendship.

About a month later, Hope told me one more funny and insightful story about her and her friend Rose interacting with Sal.

"We were eating lunch, and I was just holding my apple in my hand. Sal zoomed right by and took the apple away. He took a bite and kept going." Hope started giggling. "Rose looked at me, and I looked at her, and we just laughed."

I didn't understand the story. I certainly didn't see why getting her apple stolen at lunch was the source of humor. As usual, I had to ask questions to get at the underlying context.

"I don't get it. Why was that funny? Weren't you upset that Sal stole your apple?"

"No, I didn't mind."

"But why wasn't it bad for Sal to steal your apple?"

"He didn't mean anything bad by it," Hope corrected me. "That's just Sal. He does stuff like that."

I understood. I didn't know Sal the way Hope and Rose did. They had witnessed him engaging in a number of unusual and possibly perplexing behaviors. But all those behaviors were fine with them because Sal was their friend and classmate. Sometimes he flopped on the floor and screamed. Sometime he snatched an item out of your hand. As far as they were concerned, his actions carried no malevolence, no ill will. Sal was just being Sal, and that was an OK thing to be.

The last little story I'd like to relate shows how Hope and Rose, drawing from their growing awareness of issues of human difference in school, and working together, stood up against an act of exclusion on the playground. As usual, Hope told me about this incident as we drove home from school.

"Dad, today some of the boys were picking on Ricardo. Me and Rose told them to back off."

"Where was this? What happened?" I asked.

"We were on the playground, and some of the guys were giving Ricardo a bad time. We told them to cut it out. They said it was OK to tease him because 'he has problems.'"

"What does that mean? He has problems?" I didn't know Ricardo. I wondered if he had an identified disability. I also knew my daughter probably didn't know who was considered to have a disability in the school system. She lived within the realm of the shared understandings and views of her classmates. Apparently, Ricardo was viewed as a problematic or unusual person.

"Sometimes Ricardo can't control his behavior. But that doesn't mean they can disclude him." Hope had coined that wonderful term 'disclude,' and I liked it so much that I hesitated to correct her. "Those boys didn't even know that Ricardo was equal!"

I chuckled to myself at hearing Hope use John Dewey's concept of moral equality (see Chapter 4) even though I had never taught it to her.

"So did the boys back off when you and Rose stepped in?"

"Yeah, but then they started picking on us [...] because we were girls. Calling us names."

I tried to get Hope to tell me the names the boys were calling them, but she wouldn't. It sounded like an incident of ableism turned into an incident of sexism. I advised her that she should notify her teacher of this experience, and she promised me that she would. To be safe, I sent an email that night to her teacher detailing what Hope had told me. Her teacher told me that she had received this information from a number of sources and would be talking to the boys the next day.

What stands out most about this final vignette is the way that two fifth grade girls put the moral lessons about human differences they had learned into action. They decided to not only think seriously and inquire deeply about complex issues of social diversity but to take a specific action in a moment of conflict. This was a leap forward in moral growth. For Hope, whose development I had followed closely, I noticed that she had moved from wondering, conversing, and inquiring about ethical issues to putting herself on the line, to working for justice in the space of her own social world.

What can I conclude about my daughter's experience as a non-disabled student in two inclusive schools?

First, I think that we have to pay attention to the overall ethos of each of these schools. Both the Creative Play Center and the San Diego Cooperative Charter School are schools that embrace an inclusive approach because it fits with their broader orientation to human diversity and relational community. Both schools view human biological diversity as natural, not a problem to be overcome or corrected. Both schools approach cultural diversity—including race/ethnicity, sexual orientation, religion, and nationality—as part of the richness of living, as opportunities for adults and children alike to learn and grow. From a standpoint of valuing biological and cultural diversity, both of these two schools also placed caring relationships between persons (student to student, student to adult, adult to adult) as the cornerstone of a strong learning community. Within the context of their philosophies of biological and cultural diversity as well as relationship-based community, fully valuing kids with disabilities simply makes sense. Inclusion is not an add-on program, a new fad, a sudden and odd change of course. It is simply a logical enactment of the deep ethical orientation of those two schools.

Second, I think that both of these schools, and the intimate daily presence classmates with significant disabilities, offered my daughter Hope opportunities to learn about herself and the complex, variable, and often uncertain world around her. Rather than providing her with the false comfort that human differences can be precisely classified and uncertainty tamed by the segregation of odd classmates, she has been given the opportunity to experience interactions and friendships with a wide variety of classmates under conditions of strong social support. Those opportunities have allowed Hope to talk to me and to my wife MaryEllen about crucial questions of human difference, relationships, power, and community. We have been fortunate that Hope has been open to learning how to be accepting and supportive to students that might seem unusual. In a world where many adults fear, hate, and persecute people based on religion, race, sexual orientation, and a host of other differences, my daughter has a chance to become a person who feels comfortable with and accepts human differences as part of this wonderful, rich journey we call life.

REFERENCES

Dewey, J. (1922/1976). Racial prejudice and friction. In J. A. Boydston (Ed.), *John Dewey: The middle works, 1899–1924, Vol. 13* (p. 245). Carbondale, IL: Southern Illinois University Press.

Staub, D. (2005). Inclusion and the other kids: Here's what research shows so far about inclusion's effect on nondisabled students. *On Point*, www.niusileadscape.org/docs/FINAL_PRODUCTS/NIUSI/onpoints/inclusion_and_other_kids/Inclusion_and_the_Other_Kids.pdf.

CHAPTER TWENTY-THREE

A Sense of Belonging

Student Perspectives on Inclusive Education

REBECCA BROOKS

As you enter the doors of an adjoining southern California middle school and high school where inclusive educational practices are implemented daily, an immediate sense of belonging and family are clearly evident. This charter high school opened its doors in 2007, followed by the middle school in 2013. All are welcomed here. The middle school consists of approximately 130 students while the high school currently reaches nearly 600 students. Sixteen percent of students at the high school and twelve percent of the students at the middle school receive special education services. It is a diverse campus with approximately twenty percent English Language Learners and seventy-two percent students at a socially economical disadvantage. A range of ethnic backgrounds are represented with the highest being sixty-two percent Hispanic, eighteen percent African American, and ten percent White (non-Hispanic). The school is centrally located in a metropolitan area known for its ethnic diversity.

The school is purposely structured for all students to be taught together in general education classrooms. There are no separate special education classrooms. All students are taught together and are valued as learners who have the right to the same free and appropriate public education. Students are provided an equitable education where everyone learns together, grows together, and socializes together. Students with disabilities, ranging in all ability levels, attend the general education classrooms while any needed supports are provided within the walls of the general education classrooms. Special educators have their desks within the general education classrooms and co-teach with the general educators. There is one special educator assigned to each grade level for ninth to twelfth and one special educator assigned to the sixth to eighth grade middle school.

Paraprofessionals are available in the general education classrooms for any students who need additional personal support. Related service providers, such as speech language pathologists, coordinate with the special and general educators to provide services within the general education classrooms as well. The use of peer support is also used both formally and informally. Informally, general educators use natural peer supports, the students within their classrooms, to provide support to each other through collaboration and cooperative group learning. Peer support is also structured more formally as part of an educational internship program that allows students interested in the field of education to provide peer support to students outside their own classrooms in grade levels other than their own.

In order to develop curriculum that meets the needs of all students, lessons are created during weekly collaboration times with all educators. Special educators are included in all team and grade level meetings in order for curriculum to be created with each student's needs in mind. Universal design is applied and adaptations are made as necessary. Teachers and staff at this school view all students as having a right to be included in all class activities and to have access to the general education curriculum. When something isn't working, they find a solution to make it work. The answer does not lie within removing or separating students, it lies within providing adaptions and support as necessary. The school also embraces restorative practices, which allows students to find solutions and repair any harm done when faced with personal concerns and classroom challenges. This benefits many students who require behavior support.

A truly inclusive school culture is created when schools provide a place for all students to feel accepted and embraced while learning together. The best way to understand the meaning of inclusive education is to listen to students. So, students were asked their perspective on the successful inclusive practices at their school. Middle and high school students from the mentioned adjoining middle and high school were randomly selected to share their understanding and experiences with inclusive education. As students dove into the meaning of inclusive education and their personal educational journeys, their opinions and beliefs were eloquently captured. These students' perspectives are both enlightening and insightful and provide deep meaning to what defines a successful inclusive school and how it benefits students. The foundation of inclusive education rests in meeting all students' needs: emotionally, physically, and educationally. In order for schools to successfully create an inclusive school culture, it is essential that schools understand their students and the components that make a difference. Part of creating an inclusive culture is creating a classroom where students feel they belong, that they matter, and that they can be successful. A place where friendships can flourish and differences are embraced.

HOW TEACHERS MAKE US FEEL

Inclusive teaching impacts everyone. It changes how teachers, staff, and students view themselves and view each other. When asked to share about their experience with inclusive education, many students shared how their teachers made them feel. A twelfth-grader named Dalia shared:

> [Teachers] strongly want to involve you in everything. [They want you to] have opportunities, and nobody is left behind. [I feel] the connections that students and teachers have. I was at some other schools and there was always some kind of barrier between the students and the teachers but when I got here I was very surprised how my teachers can actually become my friends.

Students knowing that they will not be left behind, nor will they leave others behind, has the potential to reduce anxiety for many students and create a sense of comradery, creating a wonderful place for students to be able to focus on learning.

Students are greatly impacted by how teachers make themselves and their peers feel within the classroom. Twelfth-grader Randy explained how teachers make him feel wanted in his classrooms:

> [Inclusion] means that the teachers want you there. They want you to help. They want you to speak. They want to listen to your voice. They want to listen to your opinion. They want to hear what you have to say [...] it matters that you are there.

It is important that all students feel they have a place within their classrooms and that they belong regardless of differences in learning abilities. Eighth grader, Jolai shared her experience with how teachers make her feel in an inclusive classroom:

> They are very accepting of who you are. They take you in. It doesn't matter how many mistakes you make or what you do wrong. They still love you for who you are. I've made my fair share of mistakes for three years and everybody still likes me the way I am.

These students highlighted how much teachers make them feel like they belong, the foundation for growing and learning and the key for successful inclusive classrooms.

As part of creating a sense of inclusiveness, teachers also model for their students how to be accepting of others while building community within their schools. Just as important as teachers being welcoming, so is peers being accepting of each other. Ava, a sixth-grader, stated:

> At my old school, some kids would get annoyed with this one kid with a disability. But at my school now, no one makes fun of kids with disabilities because everyone is nice to each other. I think this is because the teachers show us good examples of how to treat people with disabilities.

Teachers are able to take advantage of natural learning times to model how to interact with and support students that learn differently from each other. They are able to provide opportunities for students with and with disabilities to work together, allowing students to recognize that everyone can be challenged and succeed in their own way. When students observe their teachers embracing the individual and unique qualities of *all* students, it affects how they treat others. Witnessing their teachers celebrate all learning styles also affects how they view themselves and their own vigor for learning impacting their confidence. Hailey was asked to share what inclusion feels like as a tenth-grade student. She responded, "I feel like a student who can actually achieve something, who can be a better person, who can really try hard and get somewhere amazing in life." Twelfth-grader Dalia also shared, "[Teachers] invest their time in us [...] it makes us feel passionate at the same time."

WHERE DO WE BELONG?

Students may not feel as though they truly belong in a general education classroom if they are taught in a separate class or pulled out on a regular basis into a different learning environment. Estrella, a tenth-grader, shared how she would feel if she wasn't currently being taught with her peers in general education classrooms:

> We are all in the same class. We all get the same help. [Teachers] don't make us feel any different than what we are. We don't feel unwanted. We don't feel different. If I was in a separate class, I would feel like [my classmates] would be looking at us [as though] we don't have the same learning abilities and we were less than them. I'm not less than them.

Estrella highlighted how critical it is for students to feel they belong and are wanted within their classrooms with their peers. The impact of not feeling included has the potential to effect students' feeling of self-worth.

Tenth-grader Pricilla explores her perception on the importance of where students are taught. She explains the lack of rigor students may experience when not taught in a general education classrooms:

> I feel like every student in this school has opportunities. [Students] have the right to be in the same classes as any other student rather than being separated just because they have a disability. They can still get the extra attention they need in the same way as everyone else. If I were taught in a separate room every time I needed extra help, I would fall behind my other classmates because I would be missing out on group activities. I would feel like I wasn't being challenged and might even be given easier work—that would make me feel unwanted.

While inclusive classrooms provide differentiated instruction, adaptations, and additional supports, rigor is maintained for each student. Pricilla shared the educational and emotional impact of being pulled out of general education classrooms.

Educators and staff in inclusive classrooms collaborate to find creative solutions so students are included in all activities, feel wanted, and are challenged at their ability level.

Angel, a sixth-grader, shared his view on student rights, where he feels he should be taught, and how where he is taught could affect his friendships:

> I feel all students should be in the same classroom as everyone else. If they weren't, they would feel like they were not as special and important as everyone else. I feel I have the right to be in classes with my peers. I have the same rights as everyone else. I would feel really bad if I was told I couldn't be in general education classes. My friends might make new friends and forget about me if I wasn't in class with them. It's not anyone's fault if they have a disability.

Friendships have the potential to develop when there is proximity to others and opportunities for interactions. A large component of school is making friends and being with friends. Inclusive schools provide these opportunities as Mirian, a twelfth-grader, expressed:

> Students with disabilities should be taught in classes with other kids because they can be friends and have fun with them. I feel happy and excited at school when I go to class with my friends. I used to feel sad when I had to go to other classrooms. I didn't have friends.

A sixth-grader named Bryan also noted the importance of friendship:

> Some people at other schools would make fun of kids with disabilities if they weren't in the same classes. But at my school, people don't do that here. If I had to be in a different class all day due to my disability, I would feel bad and I wouldn't want to come to school that much. I wouldn't be able to spend time with friends.

Providing students with an inclusive education where all students are embraced and taught together allows for students to develop an understanding of each other. It also gives students opportunities to get to know each with the possibility for friendships to develop and be maintained. When students feel they belong, they feel a part of something. When students are in a place where they feel wanted and accepted, friendships develop and being at school becomes something positive. A positive environment is the perfect place for learning to occur.

PEERS EMBRACE INCLUSION

The topic of inclusive education often brings with it the discussion of how needed personal supports will be provided within a general education classroom. A ninth-grader named Edwin often receives his support from peers in his general education classes. He shared, "[My peer tutor] helps me to type, he helps me to ask questions

[...] we do our work together. My teachers help me a lot. They help me to learn: doing English, doing challenges, doing everything!"

Many students without disabilities see tremendous value of having their peers with a variety of needs taught with them in the same classrooms. Tenth-grader Jazmin explained:

> It's good to have all kids taught together even if they have a disability or not. We don't want to make anyone feel different. If kids are separated they aren't going to feel normal. All kids should be taught together. [At my school] we get to know each other and find out that everyone is nice even with their differences. [Students with disabilities] don't think they are different so we shouldn't treat them differently. In my class, where all kids are taught together, everyone is respectful to each other. We try our best to help other kids and make everyone feel the same.

Jazmin's perspective on the value of students with disabilities in general education classes supports the idea that inclusive education provides opportunities for students to support each and get to know each other. This concept lends itself greatly to creating a sense of belonging for students. A seventh-grader named Jennifer shared what she experiences when her peers are not included:

> If kids are treated the same they won't feel left out. I've seen kids left out and that made me feel bad. I used to have to cheer them up. But at the school I'm at now, I don't have to cheer them up because no one feels this way.

Students will not feel as though they belong if they are feeling left out. Feeling as if one belongs is an important part of building a school culture and climate where successful learning takes place. An eighth-grader named Katelyn feels that inclusion does create a sense of family:

> Inclusion makes others feel welcome and not feel left out. When students are included they know they have friends who support [them] rather than being set aside. It makes us feel like we are one big family. You can rely on each other's help. It's like our home away from home. We treat each other like family.

In order to treat each like family, it's important that students feel comfortable around their peers and understand how to talk about differences while avoiding labeling. An eighth-grader named Savannah reflected on her comfortable levels and her opinions on labeling others:

> Inclusion makes students feel not as different. It has taught me how to treat everyone the same. Everyone is just a regular kid like me. Because of this I feel like everyone here trusts each other. This allows us to be more comfortable around each other. It feels like a second home so you participate more and respond more in class.

> If you are labeled something [people will] look at you as different. You forget about the label when people are included and treated the same. At my old school, we would go and visit special education classrooms once a week. I just felt like [these students] were left out. Some of the special education classes were called low classrooms. I felt like this made the kids feel bad for the type of class they were in. They were ashamed if they were in the low class.
>
> At my current school, we all learn as one. Extra help is given, but it is never implied that certain kids have to have help just because they have a disability. Classrooms are not labeled here. This makes all kids feel welcomed. "Welcome" is one of our school pillars. Also, when mistakes are made you try until you get it right and master it. This is our "Never Too Late to Learn" pillar. Everyone has more than one chance to get it right.
>
> We are not pressured like other schools. All kids get the chance to try again, not just kids with disabilities. This makes kids with disabilities feel the same as everyone else. At our inclusive school all kids play sports together, we are not separated. Everyone can participate in all activities. I think this shows we are all in it together.

Savannah spoke of the impact separation can have on students. How can students feel they belong if they are separated from each other? A ninth-grader named Lora strongly supports inclusive classrooms and explains her stance with a personal story of how separation is affecting someone she knows:

> No matter what difficulty you have, you're still able to be a part of the class. Many times kids with disabilities feel left out or feel different, but when you are included it helps you because you feel that you do belong. Just because I have a harder time, doesn't mean I can't do what everyone does. My neighbor has a disability and he is not included in his general education classes. Kids make fun of him and this makes me feel really angry. If he was at my school, that is inclusive, he would be accepted. When people see kids with disabilities being included it teaches them to be a better person.

A seventh-grader name Tatiana also highlights the effects of separation, indicating how it can affect how students' feel about themselves:

> I'm happy we are taught all together because kids with disabilities won't feel like they are different from us. At my old school, I had friends with disabilities who thought they couldn't do things we did because they were treated differently. If they had been treated the same, then they could have done what we did.

These students have shared the impact that inclusive education has had on them, their experiences and opinions based on their previous and current schools, and how it has shaped views towards others. Let's listen to another student who takes us on a journey through his experiences being taught in both special education and general education environments.

ONE STUDENT'S PERSONAL JOURNEY

An eleventh-grader named David shared his personal journey through school being taught in both a resource special education room and later in a general education class. David gives us an in-depth look into how he felt, what he learned, and what he missed out on during his school years.

> My other schools always had a special education classroom. My teachers would take me out of the general education class and into a separate room to do math, English and science. Usually, it was just the two of us. At times, it was okay being taught one-to-one, but this didn't help me with socialization. I didn't get to talk to people. This was hard for me. I didn't know what to do without a teacher next to me.
>
> When I changed schools, I was included in general education classes. I was forced to communicate with others. My peers helped me to learn how to talk with others and how to make friends. Now at my current school, I'm part of the class. I'm learning good communication skills. I'm making friends. I have blossomed because of the whole idea of inclusive education.
>
> I felt I used to be "babied" by all the extra help, which was only given on their time, on their schedule. They chose when to pull me out of my general education class. Different people, whom I didn't even know, would often pull me out of class. I was embarrassed and felt "down" not being taught with my peers. People thought I was stupid. Kids said things because I was pulled out. I felt my peers thought of me as being different.
>
> Being included at my current school feels amazing. I have met so many friends. I have learned so much more not being taught in a separate classroom with only a few kids or by myself. It's a good place. It's a home away from home. I have family-like relationships with everyone. Students are never excluded. They are always in included.
>
> It has also improved my self-esteem. I've greatly improved as a person. I talk more. I feel I can adapt to new environments. I have learned more being inside the general education classes. Everyone helps me, both my peers and teachers. To anyone who as a disability, know you are never different than anyone else. Never doubt yourself.

David's journey is telling of the impact "location" has on a student's emotional and academic school experience. Special education is not a place, it is a service. When services and supports are provided within a general education setting, students may reap all of the benefits school has to offer.

THE POWER OF "LOCATION"

What type of knowledge and understanding do students have regarding individual differences due to where students are taught? Does location really matter? Amina, a seventh-grader, was excited to share her perceptions:

I believe all kids should be taught together because there is nothing wrong with students who have disabilities. They just need a little bit of help. It creates a nice environment. All students are welcome at my school. There is not any discrimination. Kids are not treated differently. I wouldn't want to be treated differently. This would cause kids to have low self-esteem.

In my elementary school, they had a room where all the kids with disabilities went. A lot of kids used to make rude comments about them. At the school I'm at now, you don't hear rude comments because everyone is taught together. No one stands out as different here. We actually banned the "R" word at my school. I feel amazing being a part of this wonderful school, the best one in the universe!

Amina spoke of the "nice environment" her classes create having all students taught together. Her school is modeling for her that having everyone together can create a positive environment. That people different from each do belong together. That location does matter and it does send a message to students. Mona, an eighth-grader, shared how the location of students in inclusive and non-inclusive settings impacts student perceptions of disability:

[Previously at my old school], kids with disabilities would have their own recess. I did not think this was a good idea. I didn't get to know everyone so there wasn't a sense of security. We were told we had to be cautious around kids with disabilities and not to upset them. I felt like they were talking about them as if they were a different species. It was very hurtful to them. Talking about them like this made some of my friends scared of them.

As Mona reveals, word are powerful. The location of different recesses and how students are described leave a long-lasting impression. Separate locations and lack of getting to know each other created fear in students. Mona continued to share that:

They were the nicest kids ever. This confused me and made me wonder what the truth really was. It's not like that at my current school. We don't do that here. Students with disabilities at my school are referred to as just a regular kid. They don't talk about their disability. There is nothing to be afraid of.

Mona points out that when students are taught together the fear of differences is diminished. Imagine a world where the next generation embraces differences rather than creating fear.

Mona continued to share her personal experience of two very different schools:

[At an inclusive school, students] feel comfortable. You can participate more when there is a sense of safety. You're more open. You can be yourself. Inclusion lets us break free from labels. [Students] know they aren't judged so they can be themselves. Everyone is talked to the same.

At my old school, where kids with disabilities were in separate classrooms, [peers] felt they needed to repeat words twice or talk to [students with disabilities] slowly like a small child. I knew some of them personally and knew they didn't need to be talked to like that. Also, if someone made a mistake they were sent to the learning lab. This made kids feel like they weren't good enough. At my current school when people make a mistake, you are not sent away. No one laughs and no one makes fun of you.

When schools value differences and demonstrate this by having all students taught together in one classroom, all students are provided with opportunities to understand, accept, and support each other. Separating students impacts everyone. "Location" plays a huge role in the message we are sending to all students.

BUILDING AN INCLUSIVE FUTURE

Inclusive schools lead to an inclusive community. It is the building block for creating a society in which people understand that differences are a natural part of life. They learn how to ask for help and support each other. Eleventh-grader Isela shared how her experiences in an inclusive school have better prepared her for her future career:

> In an inclusive school, all of our teachers help all students regardless of any disability. They help everyone. This makes kids with disabilities not stand out and feel the same. When you are the only one being pulled out you feel different and not the same, [as if] you can't do it. Sometimes it takes some kids longer to get it and I've learned that this is natural, as well as, the fact that having a disability is natural.
>
> Learning how to wait for others in my class has made me more patient. When I grow up, I will be more understanding if I work with someone with a disability. I want to be a nurse when I grow up. Having students with disabilities in my classes has taught me how to better communicate with people and to slow down when helping others or explaining something to them. I explain things in math to other students and know how to slow down.
>
> This will be good for me when working with different people who need accommodations. It will help me become more well-rounded because everyone is different. I have learned some people need to see things visually or with drawings to understand things.

As students experience what it means to accommodate differences, they are building the skills needed to contribute to the diverse society in which we live. Roland, an eighth-grader, touched on fairness and equality:

> [Inclusion] is a good idea when it comes to a lot of things. It's important to a lot of people because I think it means a lot. It will reduce people being rude and unfair to others. Kids at my school are not treated differently because they are different. Everyone hangs out with everyone. This school is accepting and does so much to help out everyone.

Roland is learning an essential life lesson on fairness that will follow him into his own future, guiding him to make decisions that one can only hope will contribute to a just and fair society.

Tenth-grader Alex's reflection on inclusion embodies the importance of creating inclusive schools:

> Inclusion makes me feel that history is not repeating itself. We are breaking the cycle. We are going to make a difference. Just because I need extra support doesn't mean I should be taught somewhere else away from my classmates in a separate room. I believe all kids should be taught together because we are all one and we are all part of the human race.

LESSONS LEARNED

Listening to students and embracing their opinions allow us to capture a glimpse of their thoughts, beliefs, and experiences. Educators dedicate their careers to teaching others. Successful teachers also dedicate their careers to allowing themselves to be taught by their students. We need to deeply hear our students and value their responses. These students have clearly articulated strong opinions and experiences worth noting as we create a culture for our schools.

This school culture can also be seen and felt by others in the surrounding community. Visitors often come to this school and as they are walking down the halls they are often overheard commenting on the positive impact that they witness, both educationally and socially for all students. Christine, a visiting history teacher from a neighboring middle school, shared her personal insight of this school after spending a day inside the classrooms:

> I was profoundly impressed with the amount of positivity and commitment to the process that I witnessed among everyone at the school. Administration, staff, students, [and] professionals all were aware of their own unique abilities because everyone on the campus supported each other in a positive and accepting way. There was a sense of acknowledgement and praise of each person's story. And I could easily tell that no one on [this] campus was alone. Together [...] as a school [everyone] [...] work[s] toward the best they can be and of course the end goal [is] to reach the students in a way that they [are] empowered to go on and do great things. [Their] influence has extended passed the walls of [the] school into the community.

The reflections heard by visitors of a school speak volumes about the school community. Christine's perspective of this school validates the sense of belonging students describe.

In order to create a successful inclusive school climate, it is critical that all faculty, staff and students feel they belong and are shown that they are appreciated and celebrated for their accomplishments. At the school described, they accomplish this in many ways. "Grit letters" (notes highlighting student acts of perseverance and passion) are written home to students from administration, faculty and staff. Students, staff, and faculty are given "shout outs" during daily staff meetings and then posted throughout the school for all to read. Universal design, curriculum adaptations, and personal supports are put seamlessly into place to ensure all students have access to class content and activities. Educators and staff are provided with trainings on how to co-teach and how to support all students of differing ability levels. It is the entire school community that comes together to create an inclusive culture.

While schools strive to create a sense of belonging, all students are inevitably going to have differences from each other. However, all students have the same desire and need to be embraced and accepted in life. In order for students to thrive in school, they need to have a sense of belonging and importance as supported by Maslow's Hierarchy of Needs. They need to know they are valued and are contributing members of their school community. Inclusive education provides a rich environment filled with opportunities for a sense of belonging to develop. The possibilities for acceptance, friendships and learning flourish. It is our job as a society to create schools that are truly representative of the diverse world in which we live. A world filled with unique individuals who all strive to belong. As heard by these student voices, an inclusive school provides a sense of belonging, ensuring everyone feels welcome in an environment where they can thrive and succeed. When asked to define inclusion, ninth-grader Ryan responded, "[It is] to understand that everyone is different but that's okay. We are not all the same and if we were it would be quiet boring." The importance of sending students into the real world while embracing the concept that it is *okay* that everyone is different is truly immeasurable.

CHAPTER TWENTY-FOUR

Including Students with Developmental Disabilities

Simple, Not Easy

MICHAEL F. GIANGRECO

Hall of Fame football coach Marv Levy was well known for reminding his Buffalo Bills players that, *"What it takes to win is simple, it's not easy."* (Levy, n.d.). This sentiment can also apply to inclusive education for students with developmental disabilities. The elements that combine to create successful inclusive schools and classrooms are seemingly simple, although not always easy to enact and sustain. Inclusive education requires skill, effort, and persistence, along with ongoing evaluation and improvement.

Over forty plus years of working directly with individuals with developmental disabilities (e.g., intellectual disability, autism, multiple disabilities, and deaf blindness), their families, teachers, and other service providers has taught me many important lessons. Here I will focus on just a few and how these relate to advancing inclusive education. At least for me, the points I will share have withstood the test of time in terms of their enduring importance and implications for practice. Consider how these ideas resonate with your own experiences, whether they challenge or support your existing perspectives, and how you might utilize them to support students, families, and colleagues.

SEEING VALUED INDIVIDUALS

Inclusive education is more than an evolving set of increasingly better educational practices, although those are important too. It all starts with how we think about and experience each other as people and the actions that flow from these foundational perspectives. The historical inequities experienced by individuals with developmental disabilities (especially those with the most extensive support needs) have often been rooted in patterns of misguided benevolence (Van der Klift & Kunc, 1994), pity/charity mentalities (Rapp & Arndt, 2012), and being perceived as "less than" others, with the most extreme variation being perceived as not fully human (Bogdan & Taylor, 1989). These antiquated perspectives remain all too commonplace today. Sometimes disguised as forms of helping, they continue to threaten and limit virtually every aspect of education and life experience for individuals with developmental disabilities.

So as teachers and special educators, our ethical responsibilities extend beyond teaching our students, to helping others see and treat them as valued people, and by mere virtue of their humanity provide them with the same range of opportunities available to others along with individually appropriate supports. From this perspective, access to seemingly typical opportunities (e.g., regular class placement and general education curricula) are not determined or restricted by labels or categories, and need not be earned.

Each semester I share online videos with my graduate students, one of which portrays children, teens, and young adults with Down syndrome describing aspects of their lives (e.g., interests, schooling, goals, and dreams). My students' reactions suggest that many of them are seeing vibrant human beings. While they appear tickled at the sheer joy expressed by an adorable toddler in a ballet dress naming and doing her well-practiced arabesque, I am compelled to remind them that there are still too many people who might watch the very same video and react in quite opposite ways (e.g., "Oh, it's so sad that child has Down syndrome." "I don't know how you can work with people who have intellectual disabilities.").

My friend and colleague, Susan Yuan, has pushed back against those who have thought of individuals with developmental disabilities, including her son Andreas (who has Angelman's syndrome), in limiting or "less than" ways. Using the analogy of a bicycle, she challenged characterizations of her son as somehow incomplete, substandard, or broken—a bike in need of fixing. Instead, she preferred to think of him like a beautiful Italian racing bicycle; complete, multifaceted, with lots of gears, and a tandem that she or others would ride with him together (Yuan, 2003). It takes time to learn the intricacies and nuances of such a complex bicycle and skill to balance and coordinate the riding. This family's positive mindset has consistently led to actions that have contributed to Andreas living a full and interesting life, from childhood into adulthood, while continuing to require ongoing supports. How do you see individuals with developmental disabilities (see Figure 24.1., Giangreco, 2007) and how do your actions encourage others to see them?

WHAT DO YOU CHOOSE TO SEE? WEEDS OR WILDFLOWERS?

CHALLENGING EXPECTATION ASSUMPTIONS

A logical and age-old tenet of effective instruction is to use assessment of a student's present level of performance to set learning objectives at a correct level of difficulty—challenging, yet reasonably attainable; not so difficult as to be frustrating. In combination with this sound tenet, it is also vital to continually provide opportunities for students to surprise us with what they are capable of learning. This means continually challenging our own expectation assumptions (and those of others) by not putting limits on what is possible. Some of the simplest ways this can be operationalized are to: (a) include all students in the same range of places and activities with their peers who do not have disabilities, (b) engage with students in chronologically age-appropriate ways regardless of their perceived level of functioning, (c) allow for partial participation if needed (avoiding the too oft used and misguided approach: "If they can't do *all* of it then they won't be given access to *any* of it."), and (d) use contemporary approaches to targeting individually appropriate learning outcomes while simultaneously providing exposure to other learning outcomes within shared activities with peers who do not have disabilities (e.g., multi-level curriculum, curriculum overlapping; Giangreco, Dymond, & Shogren, 2016).

Down syndrome provides a potent example of the combined synergy of changes in attitudes, expectations, and inclusive practices (Vianello & Lanfranchi, 2009). As an early-career special education teacher in the 1970s, most students with Down syndrome were restricted to special education schools or classes and expectations for their achievement were low. Today the educational, social/personal, vocational, and other accomplishments of individuals with Down syndrome exceeds what was considered plausible just a few decades ago (Giangreco, 2009). News flash! The genetic basis of Down syndrome has not changed; our educational expectations and inclusive practices have changed, extending opportunities and yielding valued outcomes (McKenzie, 2008). Challenging expectation assumptions goes hand-in-hand with teaching important skills because people's attitudes may be among the biggest barriers to living a full and self-determined life (see Figure 24.2., Giangreco, 2007).

PETER PONDERS OVER APPAREL TO WEAR TO HIS NEXT IEP MEETING.

TEACHER ENGAGEMENT

As a former special education teacher myself, and someone who currently helps prepare special educators entering the field, I sincerely value the work of special educators. That said, skilled special educators cannot produce quality inclusive opportunities on their own. While collaborative teamwork among educators, families, and other services providers is recognized as a critical element of inclusive schooling, it has been my experience that one of the most essential pieces of this teamwork puzzle is *teacher engagement*, reflected in the level, type, and quality of interactions classroom teachers have with their students who have developmental disabilities. I have yet to encounter a quality example of inclusive schooling where this element is missing or substandard.

Quite to the contrary, every positive, promising, or emerging example of inclusive education I have encountered included at its core, a classroom teacher who thought of their student with developmental disabilities as one of theirs. This sense of ownership is manifested in the teacher being knowledgeable about the student's educational goals, ensuring access and participation to the full range of class experiences, being engaged as co-leader in curricular and instructional planning, and spending time teaching the student, rather than deferring this responsibility exclusively or primarily to special educators, related services providers, or paraprofessionals (Giangreco, Broer, & Edelman, 2001).

Not every teacher starts out by taking ownership for the education of his or her student who has a developmental disability or clearly being headed in that direction. This is not a criticism of these teachers. Some teachers are worried, feel unprepared or inadequately supported, and many have been encouraged to think that they do not have the "special" skills necessary to effectively teach students with developmental disabilities. Not only do they have a great deal to contribute, their engagement is crucial!

It is quite common for the teacher transformation toward becoming successfully engaged to occur over time (Giangreco, Dennis, Cloninger, Edelman, & Schattman, 1993). It often begins with recognition of, and some level of discomfort with, their lack of involvement with a student in their classroom. Most teachers like control over all aspects of their classrooms—so to have a student and another adult (e.g., a paraprofessional) functioning as a substantively separate unit within the classroom is a scenario many teachers eventually find unacceptable (see Figure 3, Giangreco, 2007).

ISLAND IN THE MAINSTREAM
MRS. JONES AND MRS. COOPER ARE STILL TRYING TO FIGURE OUT WHY FRED DOESN'T FEEL LIKE PART OF THE CLASS.

Transformation moves to the next level if and when teachers take actions to get involved with their student who has developmental disabilities in similar ways as they engage with the rest of the class. These engaged teachers serve as powerful models of inclusion to other students in their classroom by demonstrating how diverse learners can be meaningfully involved in virtually any activity and that all students are valued and deserve teacher time. These teachers recognize the importance of their potential contributions and shift their focus from hosting to teaching and from exclusively considering the characteristics of their student with developmental disabilities to reflecting on their own characteristics (see Figure 24.4., Giangreco, 2007).

INCLUDING STUDENTS WITH DEVELOPMENTAL DISABILITIES | 347

> **ERIN IS DOING SO WELL IN YOUR CLASS! HOW HAS IT BEEN TEACHING A STUDENT WITH A DISABILITY?**
>
> **WELL, THE FIRST DAY ERIN WAS IN MY CLASS, I SAW AN INTIMIDATED, SCARED GIRL.**
>
> **THEN I REALIZED I WAS LOOKING IN THE MIRROR!**

INSPIRED BY ERIN MCKENZIE & PEGGY BURNER
© 2005 MICHAEL F. GIANGRECO. ILLUSTRATION BY KEVIN RUELLE

REFLECTIONS OF A HIGH SCHOOL ENGLISH TEACHER

Teachers who successfully navigate the challenges of inclusive education welcome and encourage creative problem solving with colleagues and students (Giangreco, 1993). The cartoon shown in Figure 24.5 (Giangreco, 2007) is not a fictional story. It depicts a real event that happened a number of years ago in an elementary school in upstate New York. The classroom teacher created a classroom community where students felt empowered to offer ideas because they knew the adults would give them serious consideration. In this case, a well-meaning paraprofessional made a seemingly logical suggestion that the teacher initially found reasonable. Yet it was the creativity and advocacy of classmates that led to a quite remarkable solution that not only provided an opportunity for a student with multiple disabilities to be included during recess with his classmates, but also was emblematic of an amazing sense of solidarity among the whole classroom community. Ultimately, building trusting and supportive relationships is the bedrock upon which all good teaching is based.

TYPICAL, RATHER THAN SPECIAL

When I think about the young adults with developmental disabilities I know who have the most interesting and enviable lives, I can often trace their positive outcomes to families who focused on typical life experiences more so than special ones. These are parents who consciously established similar expectations as they would have had if their child did not have a disability. From community preschool to household chores, from youth sports to regular class placement, from high school dances to post-secondary education and employment, they instinctively recognized the power and value of typical experiences and natural supports along with the potential limitations of an over emphasis on all things special. They recognized that many activities labeled as "special" and implemented for "special populations" exclusively often are nearly identical to typically available activities with peers who do not have disabilities (see Figure 24.6., Giangreco, 2007).

DISABILITY LINGO GOES TO CAMP!

These families provide examples of inclusion that can help guide our work in schools. They are continually making simple adjustments that create opportunities for whatever level of participation is possible. Such an approach does not ignore the potential need for individually determined supports, but starts by exhausting typically available natural supports before considering more specialized supports. When specialized supports are warranted, these families lean toward supports that are "only as special as necessary" (Giangreco, 1996, p. 37) to minimize stigma while ensuring what is needed.

CONCLUDING THOUGHTS

The ideas shared in this chapter are meant to facilitate access to: (a) inclusive environments, (b) individualized curriculum, (c) purposeful instruction, and (d) necessary supports (Giangreco, Dymond, & Shogren, 2016). Together, these inclusive educational efforts encourage families and school personnel to recognize that we are all seeking a common goal (see Figure 24.7, Giangreco 2007). Let's work together with a sense of urgency.

FOLLOWING FIERCE FIGURING AND FORMULATING, FERN FINDS THE COMMON DENOMINATOR OF QUALITY EDUCATION.

So as I mentioned at the outset, inclusive education is simple, yet not necessarily easy. Teams that have experienced valued outcomes for their students (and themselves) will likely tell you it was a bumpy ride, with many surprisingly positive experiences along the way, and that persistence is a key. While progressive attitudes and promising of practices can certainly increase the likelihood of success, nothing guarantees positive outcomes. Yet I hope you find encouragement in another of Coach Levy's pearls of wisdom, "If you don't quit, sometimes you get lucky!" (Associated Press, 1990).

REFERENCES

Associated Press. (1990, October 1). Bills make Broncos pay the price, 29–28: AFC: Denver's mistakes enable Buffalo to score three touchdowns in a span of 1:17 during the fourth quarter. Retrieved from: http://articles.latimes.com/1990-10-01/sports/sp-1261_1_denver-broncos.

Bogdan, R., & Taylor, S. J. (1989). Relationships with severely disabled people: The social construction of humanness. *Social Problems, 36*(2), 135–148.

Giangreco, M. F. (1993). Using creative problem solving methods to include students with severe disabilities in general education classroom activities. *Journal of Educational and Psychological Consultation, 4*, 113–135.

Giangreco, M. F. (2007). *Absurdities and realities of special education: The complete digital set [searchable CD]*. Thousand Oaks, CA: Corwin. http://www.corwin.com/booksProdDesc.nav?prodId=Book232648&.

Giangreco, M. F., Broer, S. M., & Edelman, S. W. (2001). Teacher engagement with students with disabilities: Differences between paraprofessional service delivery models. *Journal of the Association for Persons with Severe Handicaps, 26*, 75–86.

Giangreco, M. F., Dennis, R., Cloninger, C., Edelman, S., & Schattman, R. (1993). "I've counted Jon:" Transformational experiences of teachers educating students with disabilities. *Exceptional Children, 59*, 359–372.

Giangreco, M. F., Dymond, S. K., & Shogren, K. A. (2016). Educating students with severe disabilities: Foundational concepts and practices. In F. Brown, J. McDonnell, & M. E. Snell (Eds.), *Instruction of students with severe disabilities* (8th ed., pp. 1–26). Boston, MA: Pearson.

Levy, M. (n.d.). Marv Levy's quotes. Retrieved August 6, 2016, from http://www.marvlevy.net/quotes.html.

McKenzie, B. (2008). *Reflections of Erin: The importance of belonging, relationships and learning with each other*. Seaman, OH: Art of Possibility Press.

Rapp, W. H., & Arndt, K. L. (2012). *Teaching everyone: An introduction to inclusive education*. Baltimore, MD: Paul H. Brookes.

Van der Klift, E., & Kunc, N. (1994). Beyond benevolence: Friendship and the politics of help. In J. S. Thousand, R. A. Villa, & A. I. Nevin (Eds.), *Creativity and collaborative learning: A practical guide to empowering students and teachers* (pp. 391–401). Baltimore, MD: Paul H. Brookes.

Vianello, R., & Lanfranchi, S. (2009). Genetic syndromes causing mental retardation: Deficit surplus in school performance and social adaptability compared to cognitive capacity. *Life Span and Disability, 12*(1), 41–52.

Yuan, S. (2003). Seeing with new eyes: Metaphors of family experience. *Mental Retardation, 41*, 207–211.

CHAPTER TWENTY-FIVE

Conclusion—Old Habits, New Thinking

The great educational philosopher John Dewey (1976c) viewed most human activity as habitual, as routines and social scripts, fairly repetitive ways of doing things that individuals and groups carry out each day with little reflection or investigation. We don't really invent each day's activities anew. We mostly do a slightly revised version of what we have done before. Or when we take on some novel activity—travel to a different place, learn a new skill—we tend to follow in the path worn by those who have gone before, by those who have experience and knowledge in that area of activity. We borrow from someone else's habits.

As long as things go pretty well with our routines, as long as we don't experience extreme discomfort or failure, we continue to reuse the series of practices that have become our individual habits or the social customs of our cultural or social group. Individual habits such as how I take a shower in the morning, eat breakfast, and commute to work recur with little examination or forethought. I seem to be fed well enough, bathed well enough, and my work record involves little tardiness. I don't experience noticeable discomfort or failure while doing those activities. So I haven't seriously reflected about how effective or useful these routine behaviors are. I haven't needed to.

Groups also carry on shared habits or customs that allow multiple persons to cooperate together with little planning, evaluation, or struggle. No one needs to send out a detailed plan to tell all the teachers in a school how to proceed on Monday morning. The general routine of the school day, what people do, how they do it, the timing and location of various activities, is fairly reiterative and predictable.

If we had to make it all up fresh every day, sitting down with a blank slate to plan the actions of each person in the school as if "doing a school day" was a completely original activity, we would be overwhelmed by the uncertainty and chaos of it all. Luckily, we have shared social or cultural habits as well as expectations of one another that allow us to cooperate and coordinate.

Inclusive education begins with the assertion that the traditional schooling routines that isolate disabled students and nondisabled students in different locations are educationally ineffective and ethically questionable, resulting in social configurations that fall far short of the kind of caring and democratic communities that we aspire to have and be. To state things very briefly, segregation is a bad habit that, like many habits, lingers too long in our practices. So our challenge is to think about how to set aside our old educational habits and customs in order to develop new ones that we and our children can be proud of.

Dewey (1981b, p. 165) observed that there are times when communities or groups feel that they need this kind of fresh start:

> There are periods in history when a whole community or a group in a community finds itself in the presence of new issues which its old customs do not adequately meet. The habits and beliefs which were formed in the past do not fit into the opportunities and requirements of contemporary life.

When our communities and our children are failed by the old ways of doing things, especially the habitual and comfortable ways, we are required to truly think. The unconscious routines and trusted habits needed little real thought, just re-enactment of well-worn, habituated scripts. But when we decide to steer away from the inadequate routines of old toward more democratic, caring and valuing ways of being and learning together, the challenge is one of teachers thinking.

What kind of thinking should teachers do? What does Dewey mean by thinking? Specifically, he points to inquiry as the heart of thinking, asking difficult and practical questions about the situation at hand, about where you really are and what you are really doing. "(T)hinking is a process of inquiry, of looking into things, of investigating [...]. It is seeking, a quest, for something that is not at hand" (Dewey, 1976d, p. 155). How can you get from where you are to where you want to be?

For the purposes of inclusive education, this investigative quest often involves individual teachers, pairs and groups of teachers, and entire school faculties working with educational leaders to ask concrete, useful questions about how to create and maintain general education classrooms that provide high quality instruction to all students, that support the emotional and social growth of each individual, and that nurture healthy, caring relationships across the classroom and the larger school community. Although this challenge is very large and is never fully achieved, the useful questions are often small, focused, and immediate. Typically, it is best to start with the right-in-front-of-our-noses sorts of queries that allow teachers to take one hopeful, practical step forward at a time.

This final chapter uses each of the stories in Section Three as a provocation for just this sort of inquisitive thinking, as an ambitious leap into a constructive inquiry to help you and the educators you work with take meaningful steps forward toward classrooms that are more inclusive. From each narrative, I propose a single Bold Experiment, an act of inquiry that is designed to promote teacher learning and growth. I invite the readers to modify these Bold Experiments, to personalize them into forms that are most useful and helpful to educators seeking to become more effective and caring to all students. I also invite readers to invent their own Bold Experiments. Truthfully, in the end, what you contribute to the lives of young people will come down to the experiments that you devise and carry out for yourself.

BOLD EXPERIMENTS

In Carrie Wysocki's story, her presentation of her own research about inclusive education to the faculty of her daughter's elementary school begins a new dialogue of possibility, a discussion of how that one school might craft a path of change that can only be described as daring, hopeful, and courageous. Some schools, when presented with such an opportunity, don't seize the moment. They fall back on a ragged rucksack full of well-known rationales to avoid the new experiment. For there is almost always a good reason not to climb a mountain. Teachers might say that the new inclusive vision is impossible and impractical. Can't be done. Teachers might say that the current way of doing things has been acceptable for years. Why fix what isn't broken? The reasons for not changing, to not set high goals for social justice and school improvement, are numerous.

But some schools—often with the supportive leadership of the administration and a savvy group of key teacher leaders—will embrace such an opportunity. Although the road ahead is uncertain, the work of figuring things out along the way will be not only worthwhile but exciting. Isn't this what we got into this education business for in the first place, to do something great? To change the world, at least our small world in this school?

Bold Experiment: Arrange for a teacher, parent, or university faculty member to present current research in inclusive education to the faculty of your school. What are the most recent developments and challenges? What are the best inclusive schools doing?

* * *

Kimberly Millstead's story describes her repeated efforts to use her interpersonal relationships with general educators to create inclusive opportunities, to plant and cultivate new seeds of inclusion in her school. Her narrative emphasizes the relational and negotiated nature of inclusion in many schools. If the special educator and the general educator can come to an agreement, see one another eye to eye, and develop a little trust, then the social experiment called inclusion gains a toehold. There is an opening and a chance to try something new and innovative.

If the Wysocki story invites teachers into large scale, schoolwide conversations about valuing students and with disabilities and developing more supportive and accepting general education classrooms, then the Millstead story strikes the same theme on a smaller, more intimate scale. She encourages pairs and trios of teachers to ask what is possible if they work together to support all students. One might view her story as applicable primarily to the school where Wysocki's school-wide conversation fails, where the consensus across the school is not to become an inclusive program. Or one can view Millstead's story as the kind of enthusiastic, ground-up work that often precedes the larger, schoolwide discussion. When inclusion "works" in a handful of classrooms because thoughtful and talented general and special educators have achieved the social feat of collaborating effectively, then the moment is ripe and ready for the bigger, whole school conversation.

Bold Experiment: Initiate a new discussion with one of the teachers in your building about how to make one general education classroom more inclusive. If you are a special educator, talk to that approachable, creative general educator. If you are a general educator, chat with the special educator who manages the cases for some disabled students who might be taught in your classroom. The relationship and teaming of one special educator and one general educator can jump start the inclusion and effectiveness of one classroom.

* * *

Meghan Cosier's account demonstrates how a variety of types of data, including the state-required standardized tests, can be employed to show how inclusive classrooms are yielding positive outcomes for both nondisabled and disabled students. Reviewing those data on a regular basis provides the school faculty with the reassurance that the decision to be an inclusive school is indeed correct, that the path chosen is leading to the correct destination.

The danger of this approach, of course, is when the kinds of data available or most esteemed by the school administration—in many cases, standardized test scores—do not show obvious support for inclusive classrooms. If the achievement data are used as a main or most convincing justification for doing inclusion, then when the test scores do not look very good, it is likely that someone will ask, "Well, why are we doing inclusion anyway?" Segregated special education programs are often viewed as the safe default, as the ready-in-waiting standby that can be returned to at any moment when problems arise.

Bold Experiment: If you are teaching in a school where standardized testing data (and the corresponding formative assessments typically employed as midway benchmarks) are often used by the faculty to make curricular and instructional decisions, propose the following agreement: "We will use the data to help us improve our teaching practices, not as a reason to re-segregate students with disabilities in special education classrooms. Our goal is to get better at being inclusive teachers, not to return to segregated schooling that we know is ethically and politically problematic."

* * *

It might be easy to ignore Zachary Rossetti's story of a general educator and a special educator developing a co-teaching relationship that exemplifies relational harmony, effective teamwork, and successful teaching. It might seem to be the rare, superlative example; a bit too perfect to believe. Not how things work in the "real" world.

But positive exemplars can be very useful to those of us who are struggling to even achieve something half that terrific. One way to make use of such outstanding co-teaching examples is to learn from them—why and how do these two teachers work so well together?—while acknowledging quite reasonably that very few pairs of co-teachers will actually do co-teaching that well. It is very helpful to simply admit that not many pairs of teachers will become that fully synchronized, joyful, balanced team. Beginning with that humble admission, taking the perfectionistic pressure off, what specific pieces of useful wisdom about working together can we gather from positive co-teaching exemplars?

Bold Experiment: Identify the one or two best co-teaching pairs in your school (or in another school in the district). Have those pairs of co-teachers give a workshop to the faculty about what they have learned about building a supportive and effective co-teaching relationship. What struggles did they experience? How did they handle those situations and move forward? What advice about co-teaching do they have to give to less experienced or less developed co-teaching pairs?

* * *

One fascinating aspect of the story told by Stacey Hodgins and S. Anthony Thompson might easily escape notice if we do not directly point it out. The faculty of the elementary school is very aware that the children in their care are experiencing strong feelings related to changes that have occurred in the community. The faculty quite wisely know that if the community and the families experience changes or stresses that deeply affect them, the school should consider modifying its standard practices to meet the new challenges and new needs felt by the students and families. Schooling simply cannot march on a usual, doing things along the routines and conventions of prior years, given the profound challenges that the students and the families are confronting. With compassion and creativity, the teachers create a dialogue about how to adapt the school to the new situation and the needs of children and families.

Bold Experiment: Conduct a formal or informal survey of the families of the students who attend your school to discover the challenges that families currently face and the child emotional and social needs that need to be addressed. Armed with this information, form a task force (perhaps teachers and parents together) charged with setting a series of goals and allied new practices to seek those goals.

* * *

Emily Nusbaum's story displays how the freedom to do work that is creative and innovative goes hand in hand with the very human experience of discomfort and uncertainty. Any school faculty that decides to seek new goals or embrace a new set of social arrangements and instructional practices is building a new road with their footsteps. While this experience is exciting and invigorating, it undoubtedly places teachers in uncomfortable, perhaps even anxiety-producing positions where no one has certain, guaranteed knowledge about what to do, what to expect, who to count on, and how it will all turn out. The open-ended nature of the journey is central to the great challenge that the teachers have taken on.

Bold Experiment: Most of life is lived somewhere between absolute certainty and chaos, between "I know what to do now" and "I haven't the foggiest clue where to begin." Set aside portions of faculty meetings to share personal stories about these two kinds of teaching moments, about times when you figured out what you needed to do and times when you were baffled and it all seemed like a house of mirrors set up to overwhelm you. This sharing is likely to be quite humorous (laughter is good!) but also instructive. The overall message is: Everything is in process, under construction, and we are doing this important, uncertain work together.

* * *

Alicia Broderick's story provides a glimpse into the seemingly unending efforts of two parents to arrange and rearrange for the inclusive education of their child. The story illuminates the hard, dedicated work of the family. And it shows how working alliances between parents and educators can make a difference.

The story also raises questions about which parents become the allies of the teachers, which gain the support and favor of teachers, and which do not. It is likely that most schools pay a different kind of attention to parents who carry some sort of cultural privilege—due to race, heritage language, social class, education, gender, sexual orientation, or disability. An honest exploration by school faculty of the parents favored and the parents disfavored, those who gain alliances and support and those who are relatively ignored or perhaps even rejected, is a worthwhile activity.

Bold Experiment: Create a small focus group made up of those specific parents viewed by the school administration and faculty as the "most difficult," the ones who are most critical of the school. Ask the parents frankly what they most like about the school and what they would change if they could. One can simply explain away their critiques as the negative balderdash of people who fail to appreciate the hard work of teachers. Or you can admit that there is something to be learned, opportunities for professional growth, emanating from the most critical voices.

* * *

Kathy Kotel's account of a middle school conference night with signs directing the inhabitants of general education and special education in two different directions offers a chilling demonstration of ableist segregation operating in plain sight. Perhaps most alarming about her story is the idea that any school willing to practice segregation so completely in the light of day, without any attempt to conceal the act, might be doing all sorts of other cruel and demeaning things when no one is really looking.

What stands out in this story is the fact that the many administrators and teachers in this school didn't seem to notice the problem. They apparently thought that channeling so-called "special education parents" one way and "general education parents" the other way was not an ableist and discriminatory way to organize parent-teacher meetings. We have to wonder how that can happen.

As we wonder, we can be assured by a potential solution. If a school involves parents of students with disabilities or if they invite the participation of disabled adults from the community in the planning for an event, that event is far less likely to be filled with ableism and prejudice. The parents and disabled community members often bring a different, very useful set of interpretive eyes and sensibilities to the task that allow them to notice possible problems. When disabled persons and/or the parents of disabled young people serve as advisors to the school, their participation is likely to result in improvements in accessibility and a culture of inclusion.

Bold Experiment: Create opportunities for the parents of disabled children and/or for disabled adults from the community to participate in the planning of events and activities at your school. If you don't know where to find disabled adults, just look up the nearest independent living center on the internet.

* * *

The experienced and insightful advice of Nancy Frey and Doug Fisher, two veterans of many years of inclusive education, directs us to rely less on the adults and more on the students. Their words remind me of what my friend Dianne Ferguson told me many years ago. She had worked with inclusive schools across the country. She told me that a central problem in most schools was, "What do we do with the grown-ups?" Sometimes the adults simply get in the way.

What Nancy, Doug, and Dianne all point to is the tendency of adults to feel comfortable with routines and practices that continue the traditional biases and prejudices they've live with for many years. By contrast, the young people have little or no emotional attachment to the worn out social conventions of yesteryear. Moreover, we should notice the obvious. In any American public school, no matter what the staffing ratios, there are far more students than adults. The young people are mathematically (and socially) a more powerful and pervasive force for social change than the adults.

Bold Experiment: Work together with some supportive colleagues to brainstorm this question: How can we invite and support the students to take roles of greater responsibility in making inclusion successful in our classrooms?

* * *

Sticking with the theme of the vital importance of the students to the success of inclusive classrooms and schools, Rebecca Brooks' narrative delivers morsels of youthful wisdom directly from young people who have gone through many experiences of social and academic learning in an inclusive school. What she provides in her account is unusual because the students speak from rarely heard, highly useful perspectives that allow for a depth of understanding. They are the ultimate insiders, the ones on the ground in the center of the youth social system who have spent many hours in diverse classrooms. They are the ones who know intimately the interactions that encourage and support, that communicate value and solidarity, as well as the social exchanges that discourage and reject. They know what really goes on in their classrooms, and this knowledge makes them experts who can teach the adults the concrete ins and outs of inclusion.

Bold Experiment: Interview students—both nondisabled and disabled—about what makes inclusion work and what makes it fail. Seek out their advice. Consider video-recording the interviews in order to preserve the authenticity and eloquence of the students. How should we teach if we want everyone to learn and feel supported? How should the classroom run if so that no one feels left out? Share these accounts with colleagues as a provocation to improve your school and classrooms.

* * *

Michael Giangreco, drawing from his decades of experience working with inclusive schools, gives us the sage advice that doing inclusion is simple but not easy. The purpose and goal is relatively clear and obvious. But there are many obstacles to achieving this goal. Some of those roadblocks reside in the beliefs and attitudes of the teachers and administrators. In a school where segregating students with disabilities is a routine activity, there are inevitably a host of negative beliefs and attitudes related to disability as well as assumptions about the proper roles of general and special education.

One active and engaging way to challenge segregation-supporting beliefs and attitudes is by visiting an inclusive school and talking to the teachers about their work. In many, perhaps most, communities there is a school that is far more developed and confident about being inclusive than the neighboring schools. That highly advanced or most successful inclusive school can serve as a great learning resource for teachers and school leaders in other schools.

Bold Experiment: It would be ideal if all of the teachers, support professionals, and school leaders in your school could spend a day in a highly inclusive school and then ask frank, open questions of the teachers about how they do what they do. But arranging for everyone to make such a visit is often not possible. So this experiment involves three steps. First, send a small contingent of special educators, general educators, and administrators to visit a nearby inclusive school AND to have a dialogue with the school faculty about their work. Second, follow this up by sponsoring a sharing session where the visiting contingent tells what they learned with the rest of the faculty. Third, create additional opportunities for dialogue—questions, answers, stories, giving advice—between your school and the educators in the inclusive school. This could occur by way of two-way video technology, email, or other communication formats.

* * *

The Colin and Naraian account of one school reaching out to parents leaves us with many questions about how schools and teacher can better communicate with parents, learn from parents, and take seriously the knowledge that parents have to offer about their children. From the standpoint of many schools, parents and families are people who know little about how schools run, what schools do, how classrooms operate, how teachers provide instruction, and what teachers are trying to teach. Inviting them to be more involved with schools seems like asking untrained family members to help a dentist give a child a teeth cleaning and check-up. The dentist is the knowledgeable professional, and the parents would simply get in the way.

Moreover, when students misbehave at school or have difficulty learning the academic content, it is too easy for teachers to think that the important (and very much unknown) responsible adults behind the child are somehow fueling, funding, and even creating the struggles that the child is experiencing in schools. The general metaphor is that students carry problems and weaknesses of the parents and the family into school. Or they learn bad habits at the hands of their parents and then transport those ugly behaviors into the schools. The many familial flaws carried by children to school are planted in the classroom soil where they blossom into issues that teachers have to deal with. Given the metaphor of problems moving in just one direction, from home to school, teachers quite reasonably wonder why the parents aren't solving or preventing these matters at home.

Years ago, a friend recommended that I read Rabbi Michael Lerner's (1979) great book *Surplus Powerlessness*. Lerner studied how the stress of the workplace was carried home by the employees and caused all sorts of struggles and difficulties in their families and home lives outside of the job. The very idea that stress might originate at work and then be translated into family challenges made me wonder why we educators tend to assume that stress moves only in the opposite direction, from home to school. Any parent will tell you that their children come home from school with a bundle of difficult emotions born of the day's experience—frustrations and fears about academic learning, conflicts or worries about friends and peers, feelings of inadequacy or sadness due to experiences of failure, shame and embarrassment due to mistreatment by classmates, and so on. From the standpoint of parents, the stressors and conflicts of school are carried home by their children. Stress travels obviously from school to home and family life.

Truly, problems flow in both directions because students are fully alive and experiencing challenges in both the school and the family, home, and neighborhood. We should think of stress and problems as complex and bidirectional. School issues do effect family life. Family struggles and worries do impact a child in the classroom.

Once we notice that the two primary social spheres of childhood, the family and the school, each generate stress and difficulty that lands in and plays out in the other sphere, we have to again wonder how the two sides can better collaborate and work together. In many cases, the best solutions are created when the adult leaders in both areas of a child's life—the school professionals and the parents or family members—work together in a respectful and mutual way.

Bold Experiment: Propose a schoolwide effort involving teachers in your school conducting an in-home interview of the parents and family members of a student who is struggling academically and/or behaviorally. The idea is for each teacher to select a student whose social, emotional, and educational needs are not being well met and to reach out to that family in an open, receptive way in order to learn about that student and that family. After the teachers conduct the interviews, hold a meeting to share your experiences, what you learned, and how the experience impacted each of you. Consider what about your school might be improved based on what you have learned from the parents and families. Also, how might this one time interview event be expanded into an on-going dialogue between families and educators?

* * *

In my own story of how my nondisabled daughter has grown as a result of her experiences sharing classrooms with disabled peers, one of my goals was to begin to notice what we tend not to look for. If we are optimistic and insightful, we will see how disabled students are learning and growing, the kinds of progress that they are making in our general education classes. We certainly should celebrate those moments of academic and social progress. But we also need to observe carefully to see how the opportunities to learn in school communities marked by high levels of human diversity, where students learn at different rates and in different ways, where human bodies come in varied forms and operate in many ways to accomplish tasks, where communication is achieved through multiple modalities, create avenues of unique social and moral development for nondisabled students. Further, we need to watch carefully for how these underappreciated pathways of learning for nondisabled students also involve growth in academic content and skills.

Bold Experiment: Observe closely the many daily interactions between disabled and nondisabled students. Ask the students questions about their experiences. What are the students learning about the human value, relationships, and community? What are the students learning about the meaning of human differences that in other parts of society would be highly stigmatized? What sorts of friendships and alliances are forming, and what do those friendships mean to the students?

SMALL STEPS OF PROFESSIONAL LEARNING

When educational researchers and school practitioners first began calling for inclusive schools in the 1980s, as Thomas Skrtic (1991) insightfully described in his great book *Behind Special Education*, there were two competing versions of how to improve the education of students with disabilities. The early inclusive educators (at that time called the Regular Education Initiative or REI) proposed wholescale reform of general and special education systems in the United States. Their vision called for unifying the two parallel bureaucratic parts of the school system, bringing general and special education together for the inclusive education of all. While it is obvious that their proposal did not gain widespread acceptance across the United States, in the districts and schools that have embraced inclusion as a schoolwide reform approach, much success has been achieved.

The second competing proposal for how to improve the education of disabled students has been the dominant approach in the field of special education for decades. Faith in "rational technical progress" (Skrtic, 1991, p. 61) involves a belief that a science of special education can, by way of quantitative research, develop diagnostic instruments and interventions that enable school professionals to effectively erase (or reduce) deficits in learning and behavior. Essentially, the idea is that special education researchers will figure out how to decrease the level of impairment in the bodies and minds of individuals viewed as abnormal and therefore problematic. These evidence-based techniques will be taught to special education teachers and the result is that childhood impairments will, in many or most cases, receive effective treatments. In the end, the idea is that biological and cultural diversity itself is a problem located in certain persons and the solution is a scientific pursuit of greater social uniformity. If only science can make us all more alike, the concept of rational technical progress promises. Then we can be together in more homogeneous communities of learning.

This entire book rejects the latter approach as a radical failure to appreciate and accept people for who they are. It fails to understand and embrace this wonderful American democratic experiment of creating thriving and diverse communities across lines of difference. It is also an unfortunate and misleading account of the role of social scientists and university researchers in relation to public school teachers who work with students and families every day. There is no reason to believe that any one group of persons—researchers, teachers, parents, students—alone have access to the knowledge and wisdom that should dictate the actions of all of the other groups. If there is anything that we have learned from many decades of special education research, it is to be very humble about what we know. There is no great puzzle of disability and teaching that is about to be solved by the white-coated sages on the hilltop.

Certainly, whenever possible, the ultimate goal is the first proposal, the development of whole schools or entire school systems that provide a high quality, inclusive education for all students.

Often individual teachers or small groups of teacher do not have the power to convince a school district to effectively blend the general and special education systems into a coherent and caring single system. Often teachers are not able to easily or immediately persuade the other educators in their own building to pursue a commitment to schoolwide inclusion at the building level. The approach to social change must begin with smaller steps that teachers can initiate. Given this reality, I'll suggest a third approach that is perhaps a more immediately practicable way to changing and improving schools.

The third approach to improving the education of disabled (and nondisabled) students is the path this final chapter has charted, working together with colleagues and parents and students to take the practical steps forward that are most achievable, that are readily available within the educational environment where you teach. If the road toward successful inclusion is often a thousand steps (rather than one giant leap), then the most optimistic and useful tactic at the current moment is to imagine, plan, and take the first, second, and third steps on that new road. What can we do right now? What possibilities are available right in front of us? How can we reach one hopeful and hesitant foot out to begin the thousand-step walk?

This form of inquiry really amounts to educators, beginning individually or in supportive pairs and trios, posing bold experiments of the sort that I have presented in this final chapter. The difference between the bold experiments I have outlined and the ones that practicing teachers working every day with a population of students and parents in a community is the way that the latter can grow organically and practically out of the concrete, very real successes and struggles confronted in that specific context. Teachers, students, parents, counselors, school psychologists, and students bump into obstacles and issues every day that, while uncomfortable and perhaps even nerve-wracking, are the invitations to new, bold experiments that can be customized for that school and that learning context. The problems and issues that surround your feet as you walk are the place to begin.

But you wisely ask, how do we know that we are framing these bold experiments, these opportunities for educators to learn and grow, in ways that actually correspond with the goal of inclusive education? How can we be sure, you ask with a nod to John Dewey, that we aren't simply covering bad old habits with a deceptively fresh coat of paint while truly not moving toward more inclusive classrooms? How can educators be sure to pose bold experiments that have *inclusive education potential*?

Let's return to the three central principles of inclusive teaching articulated by Lani Florian (2006) and Kristine Black-Hawkins (Florian and Black-Hawkens, 2011; Black-Hawkins and Florian 2012) in Section Two. If you have ever gone to a bowling alley where they have inflatable rubber bumpers along the sides of the lanes to keep the balls rolled by children (and novice bowlers like me) from going into the gutters, then you appreciate the idea of having a little guidance to keep things on track. Relying on Florian and Black-Hawkins to keep those comforting bumpers in place, we ask that our bold experiments do the following:

1. *Develop classroom communities that notice, welcome, and attend to the needs—emotional, social, relational, intellectual, etc.—of all students.* The overall effort involves not merely the creation of accessible and supportive environments for students with disabilities. The goal is to build caring, supportive, interesting, flexible learning environments and effective supports for all students.
2. *Appreciate the learning capacities, talents, and interests of each and every student.* The goal of schooling is neither to locate nor heal deficits. To the contrary, the goal is to fully appreciate the gifts and contributions that each student brings to the classroom in a way that allows the teachers to then skillfully guide each student forward to great competence and development. The goal is to support each student in becoming the best version of herself.
3. *All challenges are invitations for educators—working with each other, with parents, with students—to learn new knowledge and skills.* Challenges do not exist "in" certain students. They occur in the experiences of educators who are trying to become better educators, who are actively learning how to be more capable, caring, supportive, and masterful in the complex craft of teaching.

Teachers who refer to these three general guidelines will be able to create bold experiments, posing new questions and opening new opportunities that serve as learning experiences to facilitate the improvement of inclusive teaching.

Ultimately, building the path to inclusive education involves losing interest in age-old questions about human flaws—what is wrong with this student?—and gaining interest in opportunities for personal and professional growth. How can we become better teachers? How can we become better persons? How can our school become a better school for all students? These are not questions answered by researchers, scientists, or other experts. These are not questions answered once but over and over again. Educators confront and answer these questions every day. Luckily for you, there is just such a provocative and promising challenge arriving in your classroom and school each day, a fresh invitation to take a mighty step toward becoming a great inclusive educator.

REFERENCES

Black-Hawkins, K., & Florian, L. (2012). Classroom teachers' craft knowledge of their inclusive practice. *Teachers and Teaching, 18*, 5, 567–584.

Dewey, J. (1976c). Human nature and conduct. In J. A. Boydston (Ed.), *John Dewey: The middle works, 1899–1924, Volume 14* (pp. vii–230). Carbondale, IL: Southern Illinois University Press.

Dewey, J. (1976d). Democracy and education. In J. A. Boydston (Ed.), *John Dewey: The middle works, 1899–1924, Volume 9* (p. 155). Carbondale, IL: Southern Illinois University Press.

Dewey, J. (1981b). Ethics. In J. A. Boydston (Ed.), *John Dewey: The later works, 1925–1953, Volume 14*. Carbondale, IL: Southern Illinois University Press.

Florian, L., & Black-Hawkins, K. (2011). Exploring inclusive pedagogy. *British Educational Research Journal, 37*, 5, 813–828.

Florian, L. (2006). Teaching strategies: For some or all? *Kairaranga, 7*, 24–27.

Lerner, M. (1979). *Surplus powerlessness: The psychodynamics of everyday life and the psychology of individual and social transformation*. Atlantic Highlands, NJ: Humanities Press International.

Skrtic, T. M. (1991). *Behind special education: A critical analysis of professional culture and school organization*. Denver, CO: Love.

Disability Studies in Education

GENERAL EDITORS: SUSAN L. GABEL & SCOT DANFORTH

The book series Disability Studies in Education is dedicated to the publication of monographs and edited volumes that integrate the perspectives, methods, and theories of disability studies with the study of issues and problems of education. The series features books that further define, elaborate upon, and extend knowledge in the field of disability studies in education. Special emphasis is given to work that poses solutions to important problems facing contemporary educational theory, policy, and practice.

To order other books in this series, please contact our Customer Service Department:

    (800) 770-LANG (within the U.S.)
    (212) 647-7706 (outside the U.S.)
    (212) 647-7707 FAX

Or browse by series:

    WWW.PETERLANG.COM